Shameless Feminists: World War 3 Il

A word fr

I'm not really a feminist.
Ok. That's fine. So, can I have your car keys, your job, the title to your house, your birth control pills, your voter registration card, all your books and pens and your diplomas, your bank account, your credit card, your trousers, your sports equipment and your comfortable shoes?
BANNERMAN

Isabella Bannerman

Feminism is back, and it's hot.

We have never been so strong, so free, so powerful, and we are under attack. We are breaking glass ceilings, and picking the shards from our eyes. After nearly a century of suffrage, we find ourselves ruled over by the most brazen groper-in-chief in modern history. In response, we assert our rights, our images, our narratives, and we shame our attackers. Survivors are refusing to be shamed for the abuse others have perpetrated upon us. When we tell our stories, we send shame back where it belongs. They may not believe us, but we believe in each other. It's not just about getting women into high places (but we're all for that) it's that respect is a human right that is gender-neutral.

The editors asked artists for their angry, hopeful, untold, and unbelievable stories. We received beauty, guts, truth, and defiance. A slight majority of our contributors are veterans of ***World War 3 Illustrated***. Almost half are new to our pages, and some are having their print debuts. Welcome! We are proud to include a couple of art students, grandmothers, a non-binary artist, and yes, even some guys. We are teachers, nurses, protesters, and activists. We are still mostly from around New York City, but our national reach extends to Baltimore, Chicago, Easton PA, Gainesville FL, Madison WI, Portland OR, and San Francisco. Going global with artists from Indonesia, Italy, Holland, Mexico, and Spain.

WW3 has sought out feminist art ever since one of us was invited to create her first comics for issue #3. Happily, the woman cartoonist is not such a rare beast as she was in the 1980s. We now recognize gender as more fluid, more nuanced than we did when we first published a "women's issue". Now, bigger and madder (is that possible?) than previous female dominated issues: ***Herstories***, from 1992; ***Female Complaints*** in 1999; and ***Bitchcraft*** of 2000, we offer you ***Shameless Feminists***.

- Sabrina Jones, 2019

Issue #50 editors: **Isabella Bannerman, Sandy Jimenez, Sabrina Jones, Rebecca Migdal.**

Contents

Special thanks to
Paula Hewitt Amram,
Susan Simensky Bietila
and Seth Tobocman

Front Cover by
Sabrina Jones,
Isabella Bannerman,
fitri dk
and Sandy Jimenez

Back cover designed
by Sabrina Jones,
photo by
Steve Leialoha

Inside front cover:
Andrea Arroyo

Inside back cover:
fitri dk

Interior design by
Rebecca Migdal

All works in
World War 3 Illustrated
© the Creators

Susan Simensky Bietila

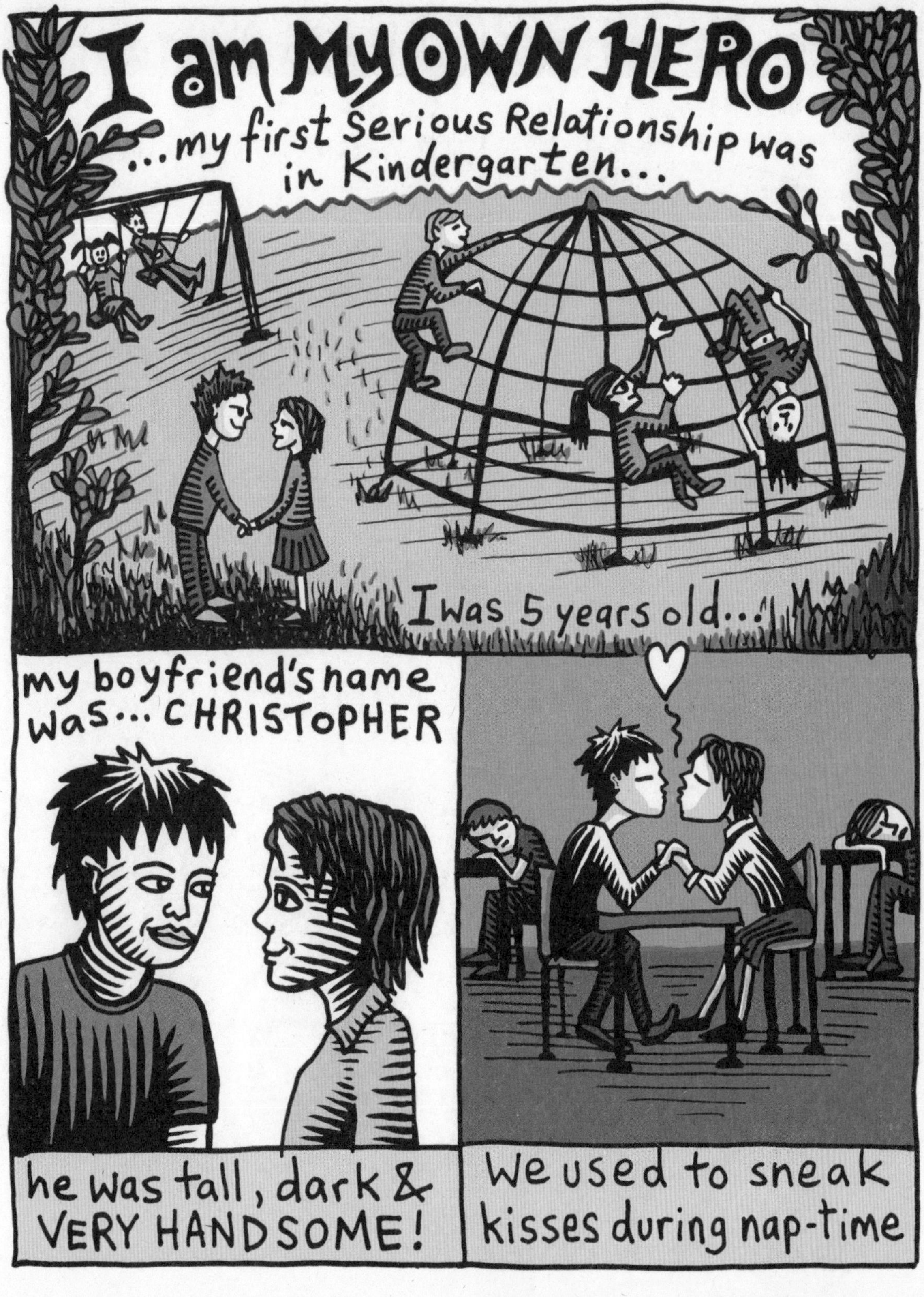
I am MY OWN HERO
...my first serious Relationship was in Kindergarten...
I was 5 years old...
my boyfriend's name was... CHRISTOPHER
he was tall, dark & VERY HANDSOME!
We used to sneak kisses during nap-time

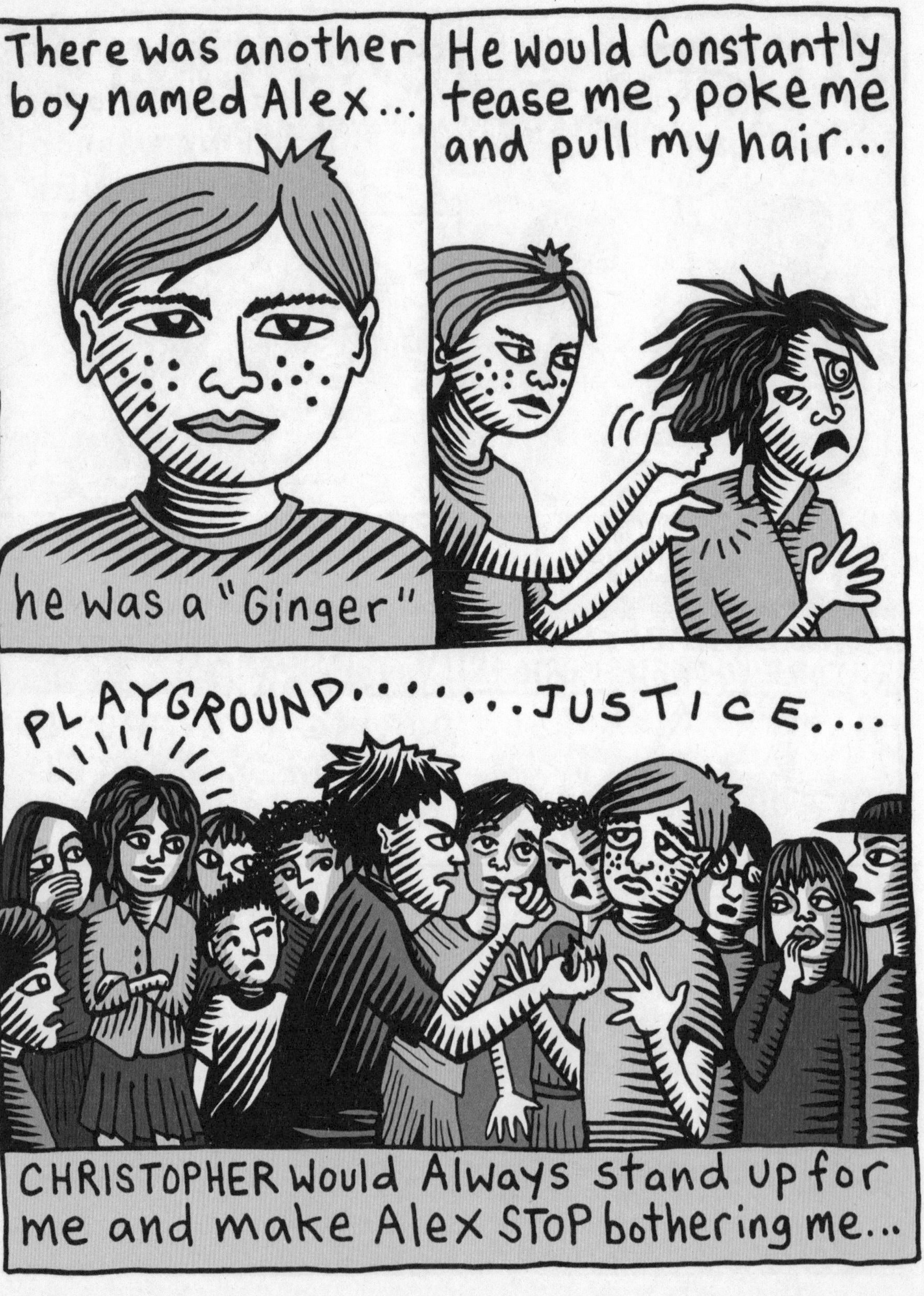
There was another boy named Alex...
he was a "Ginger"
He would Constantly tease me, poke me and pull my hair...
PLAYGROUND.......JUSTICE....
CHRISTOPHER would Always stand up for me and make Alex STOP bothering me...

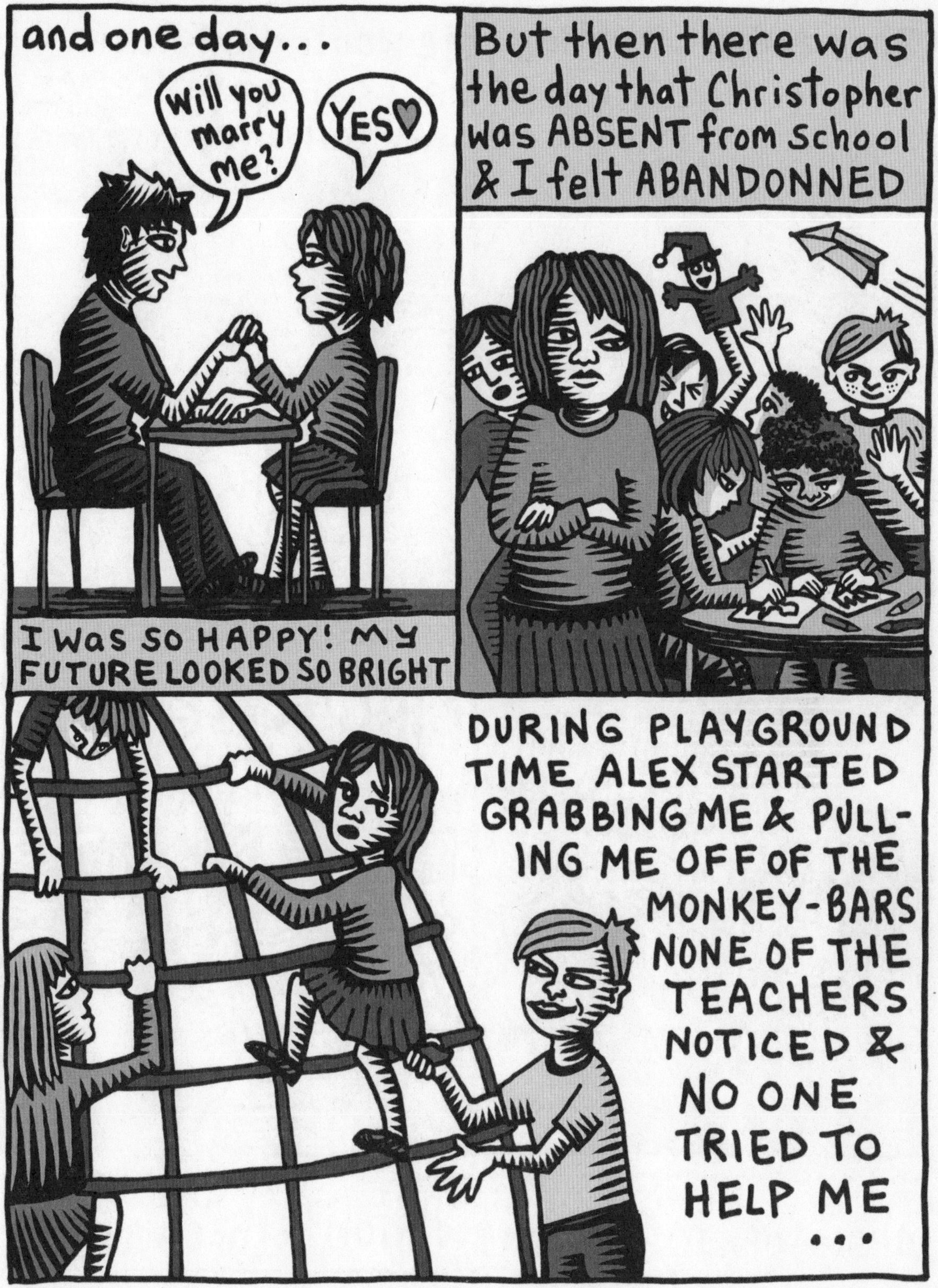

and one day...
Will you marry me?
YES♥
I was SO HAPPY! MY FUTURE LOOKED SO BRIGHT
But then there was the day that Christopher was ABSENT from school & I felt ABANDONNED
DURING PLAYGROUND TIME ALEX STARTED GRABBING ME & PULL-ING ME OFF OF THE MONKEY-BARS
NONE OF THE TEACHERS NOTICED & NO ONE TRIED TO HELP ME ...

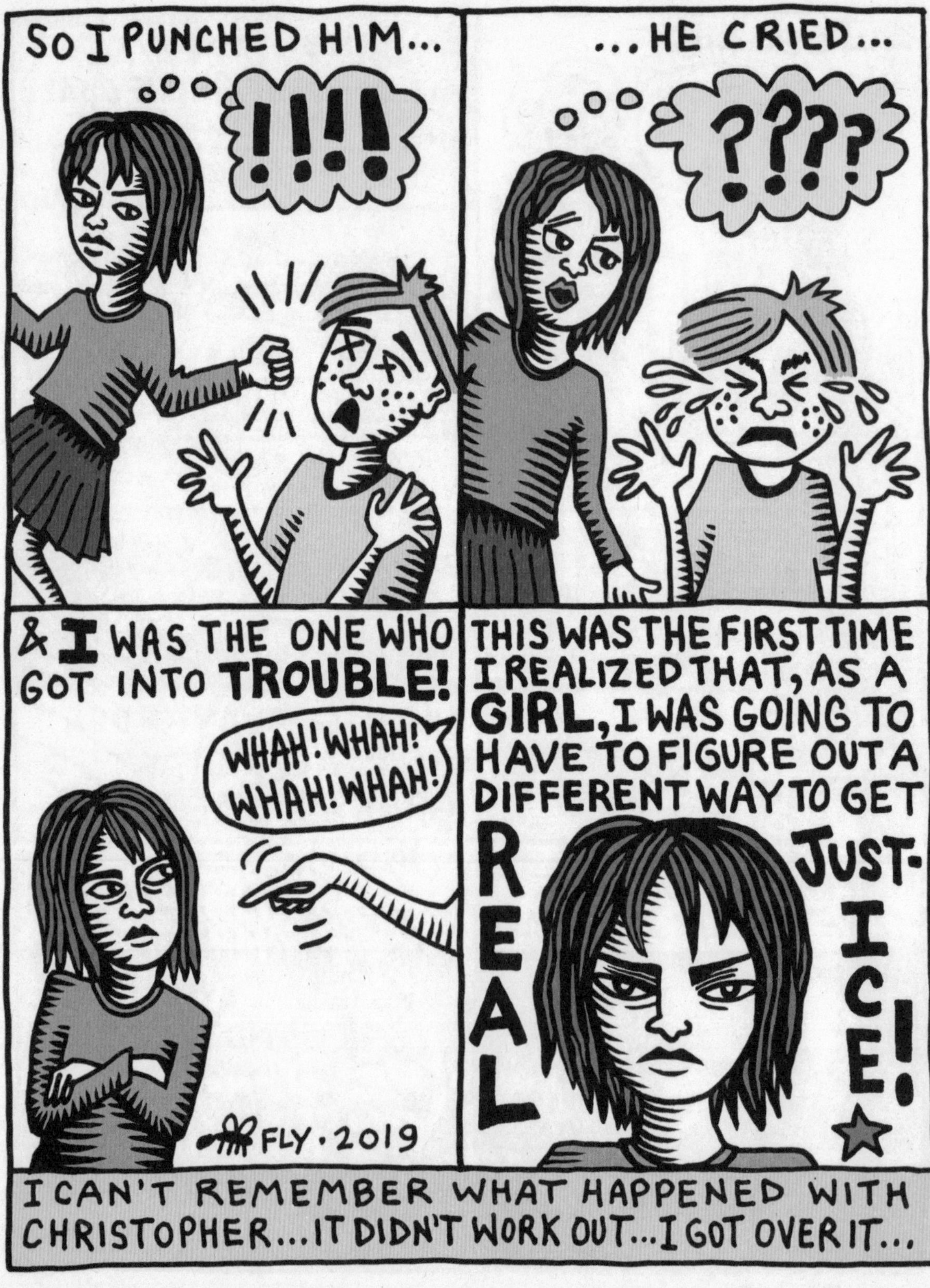
SO I PUNCHED HIM...
!!!!
...HE CRIED...
????
& I WAS THE ONE WHO GOT INTO TROUBLE!
WHAH! WHAH! WHAH! WHAH!
FLY · 2019
THIS WAS THE FIRST TIME I REALIZED THAT, AS A GIRL, I WAS GOING TO HAVE TO FIGURE OUT A DIFFERENT WAY TO GET
REAL JUST-ICE!
I CAN'T REMEMBER WHAT HAPPENED WITH CHRISTOPHER... IT DIDN'T WORK OUT... I GOT OVER IT...

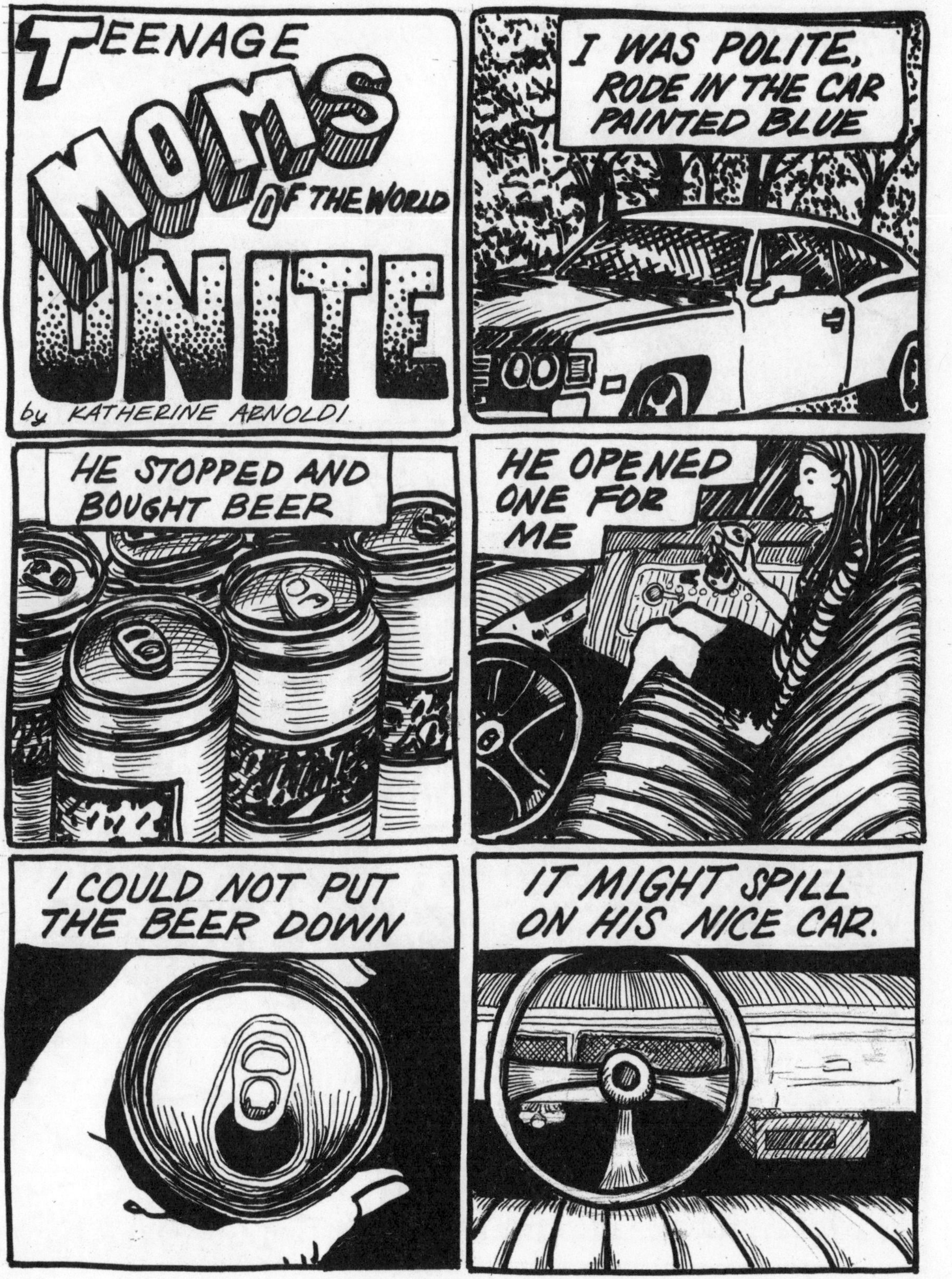
TEENAGE MOMS OF THE WORLD UNITE
by KATHERINE ARNOLDI
I WAS POLITE, RODE IN THE CAR PAINTED BLUE
HE STOPPED AND BOUGHT BEER
HE OPENED ONE FOR ME
I COULD NOT PUT THE BEER DOWN
IT MIGHT SPILL ON HIS NICE CAR.

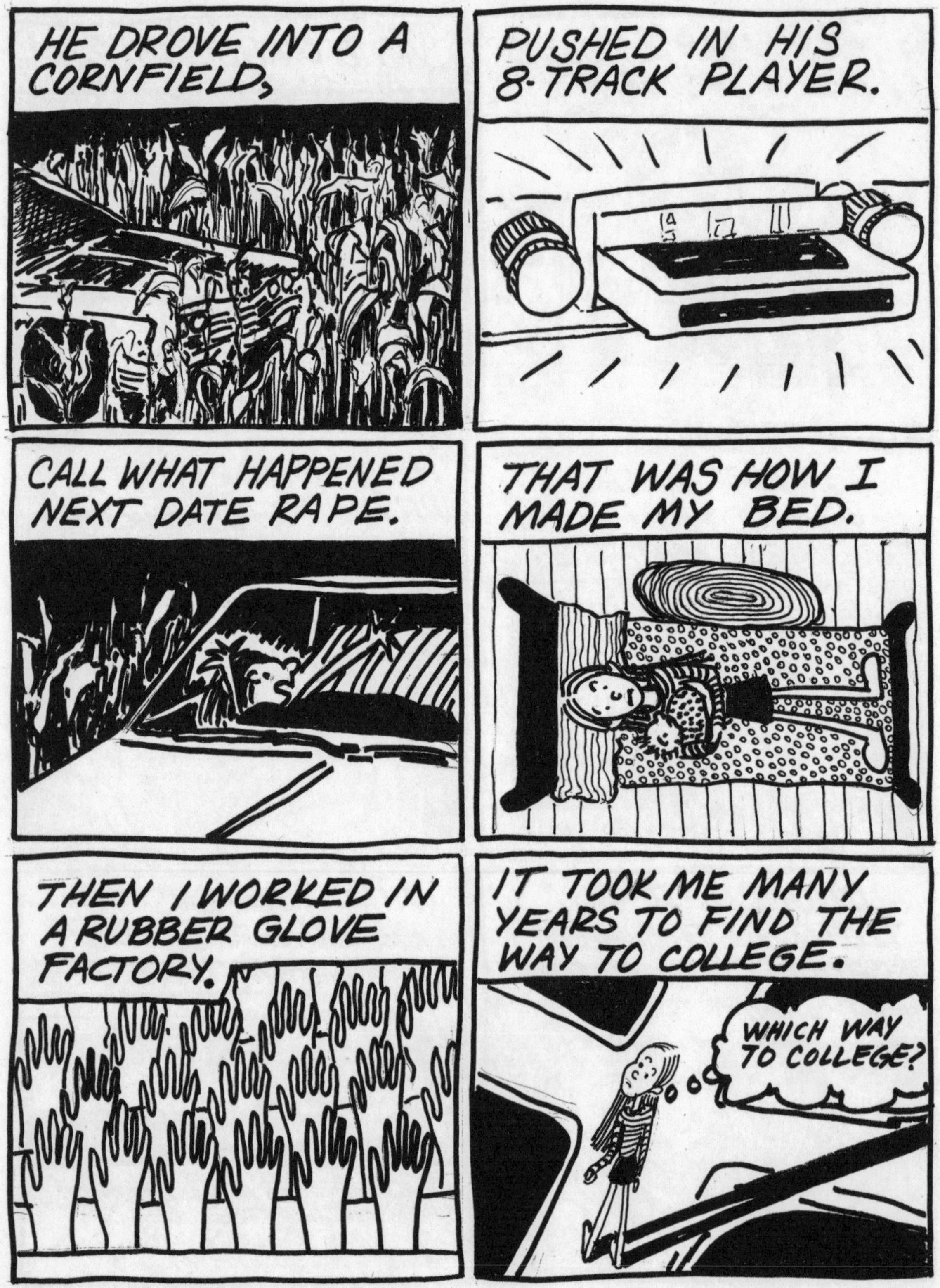
HE DROVE INTO A CORNFIELD,
PUSHED IN HIS 8-TRACK PLAYER.
CALL WHAT HAPPENED NEXT DATE RAPE.
THAT WAS HOW I MADE MY BED.
THEN I WORKED IN A RUBBER GLOVE FACTORY.
IT TOOK ME MANY YEARS TO FIND THE WAY TO COLLEGE.
WHICH WAY TO COLLEGE?

YEARS LATER, I WOULD HAVE A STUDENT

WRITE ON HER PAPER...

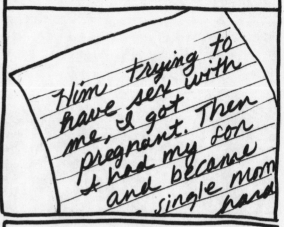

Him trying to have sex with me, I got pregnant. Then I had my son and became a single mom

SHE AND I AND 194,377 OTHER TEENAGE MOTHERS EACH YEAR*

*cdc.gov.

IN NEW YORK CITY WE HAVE 7,488 BIRTHS TO TEENAGERS EACH YEAR.

AND ONLY 600 SLOTS IN THE HIGH SCHOOL CHILD CARE PROGRAM

WHAT HAPPENS TO THE OTHER 6,888 TEEN FAMILIES?

THE HOMELESS POPULATION NOW IS 60% CHILDREN

BY KATHERINE ARNOLDI, AUTHOR THE AMAZING TRUE STORY OF A TEENAGE SINGLE MOM, GRAPHIC NOVEL, (1998/2016)

9

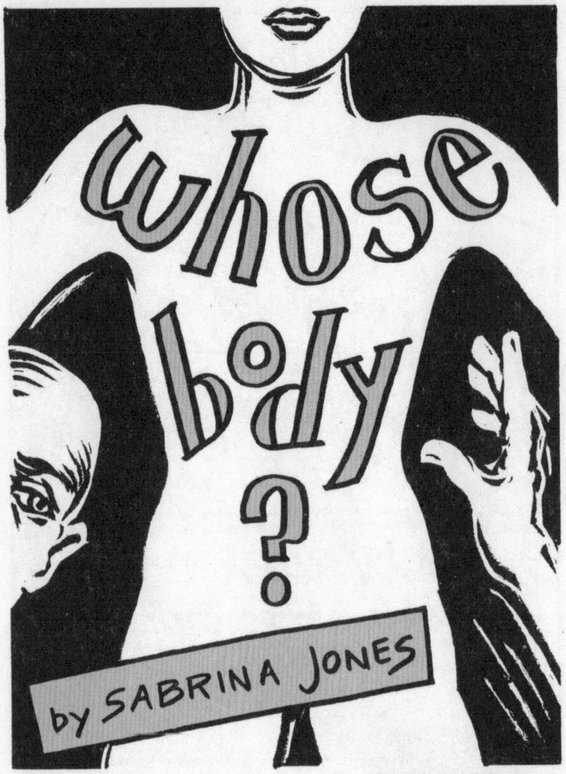
whose body?
by SABRINA JONES

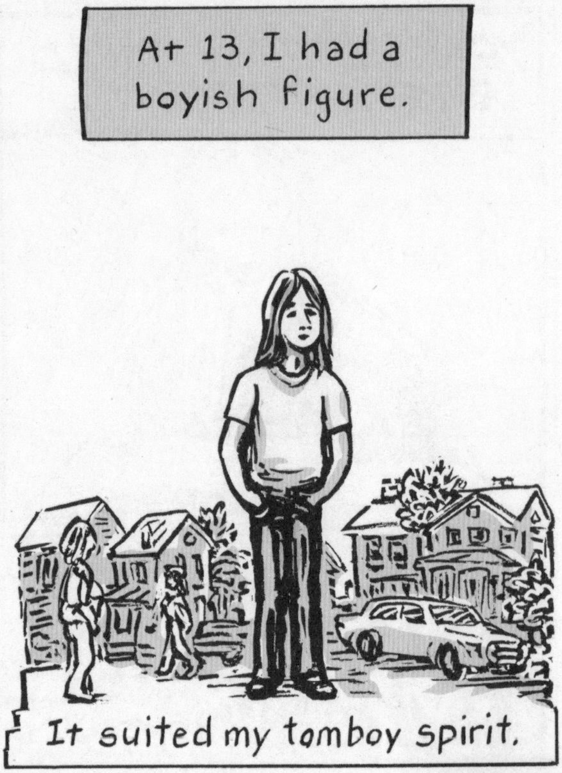
At 13, I had a boyish figure.
It suited my tomboy spirit.

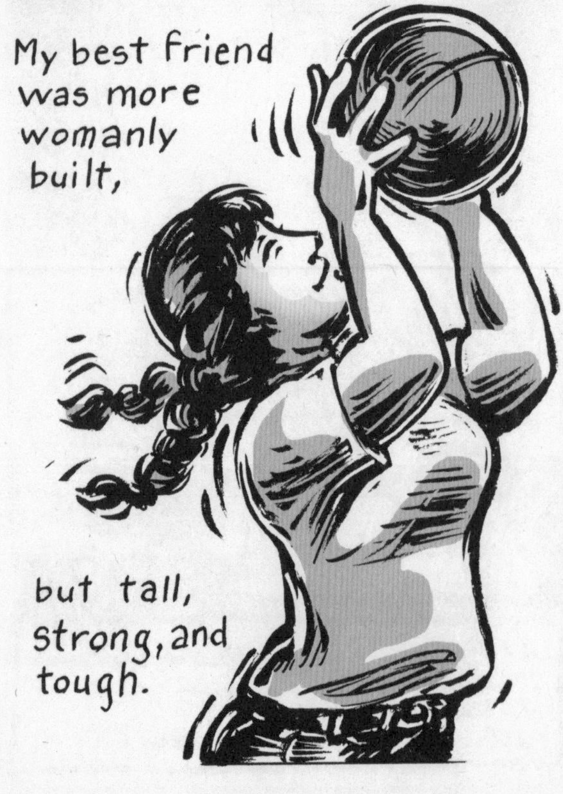
My best friend was more womanly built,
but tall, strong, and tough.

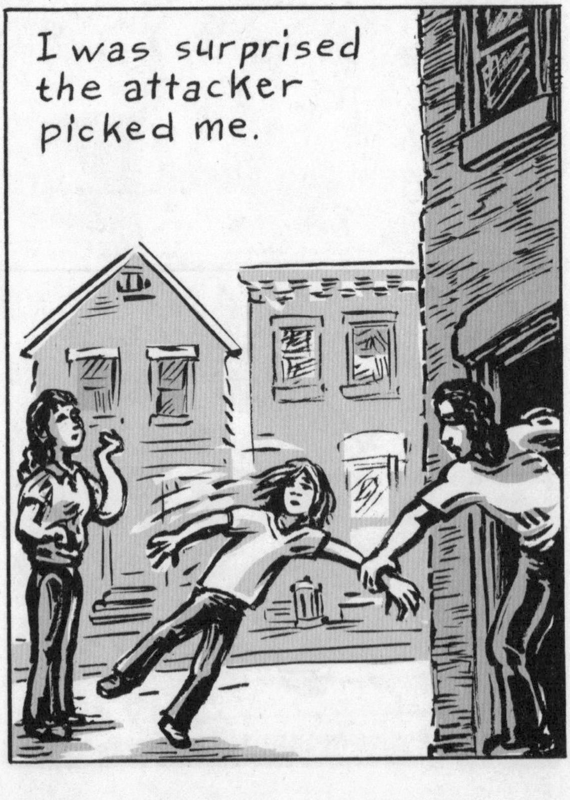
I was surprised the attacker picked me.

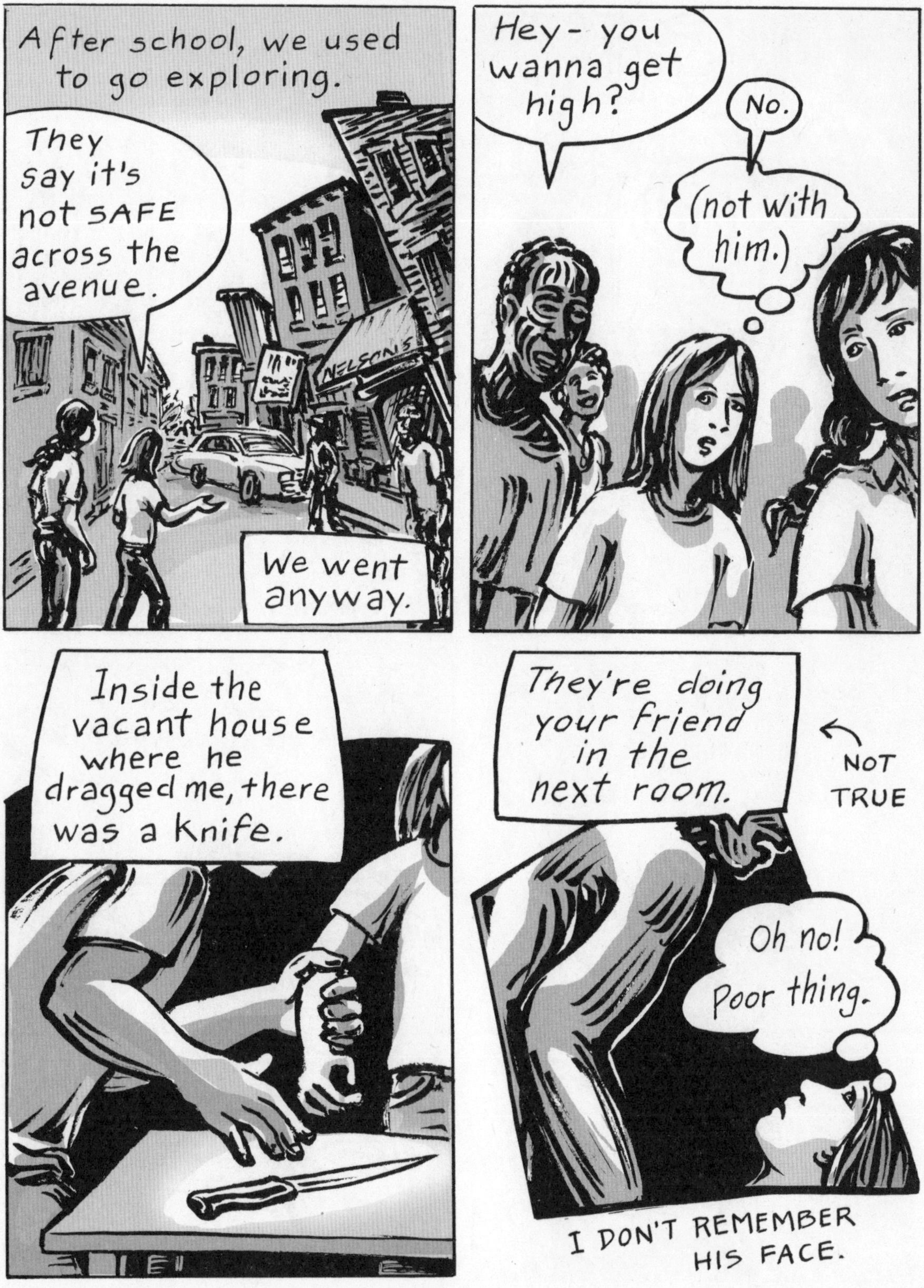
After school, we used to go exploring.
They say it's not SAFE across the avenue.
NELSON'S
We went anyway.
Hey- you wanna get high?
No.
(not with him.)
Inside the vacant house where he dragged me, there was a knife.
They're doing your friend in the next room.
NOT TRUE
Oh no! Poor thing.
I DON'T REMEMBER HIS FACE.

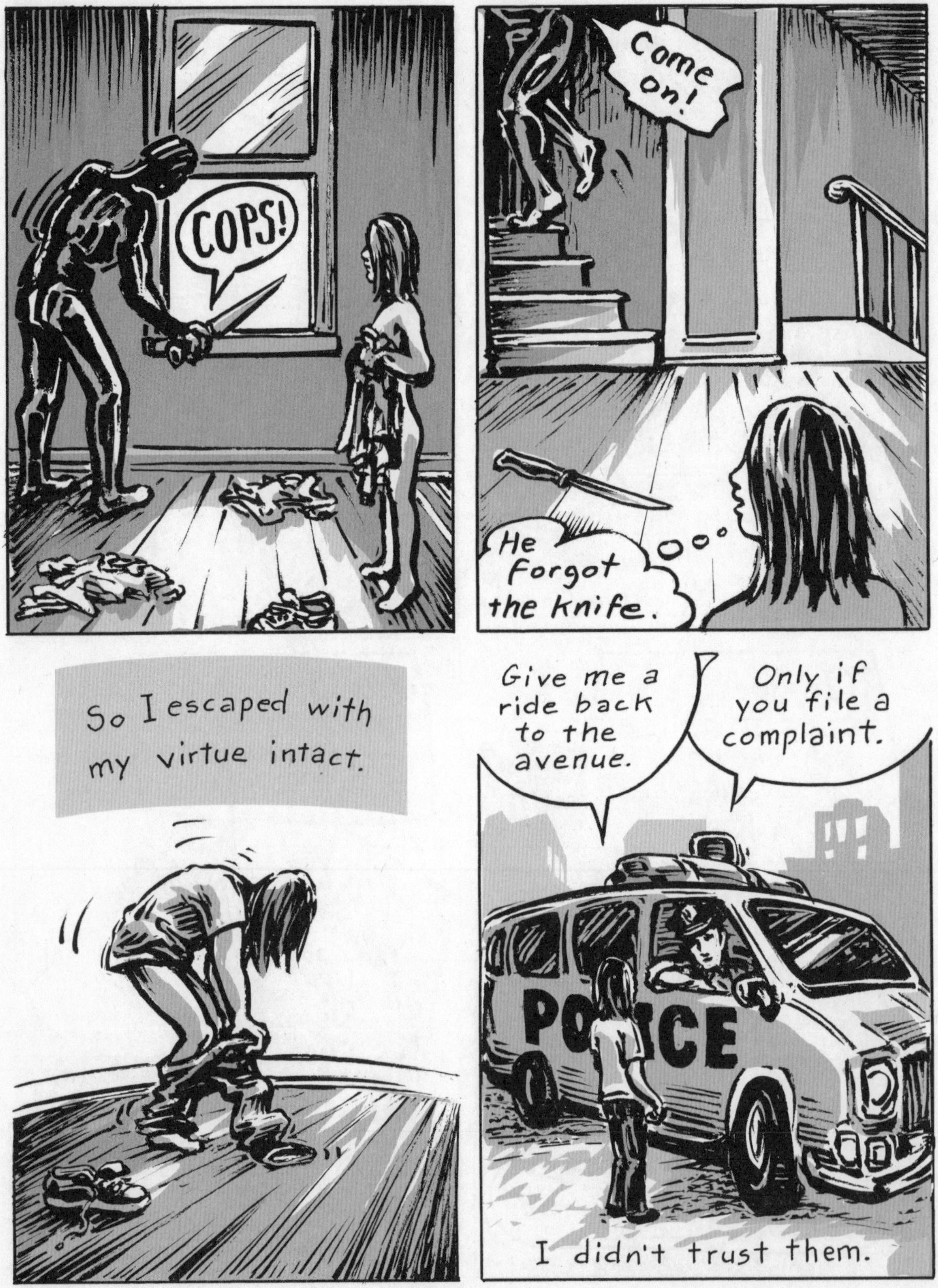
COPS!
Come on!
He forgot the knife.
So I escaped with my virtue intact.
Give me a ride back to the avenue.
Only if you file a complaint.
POLICE
I didn't trust them.

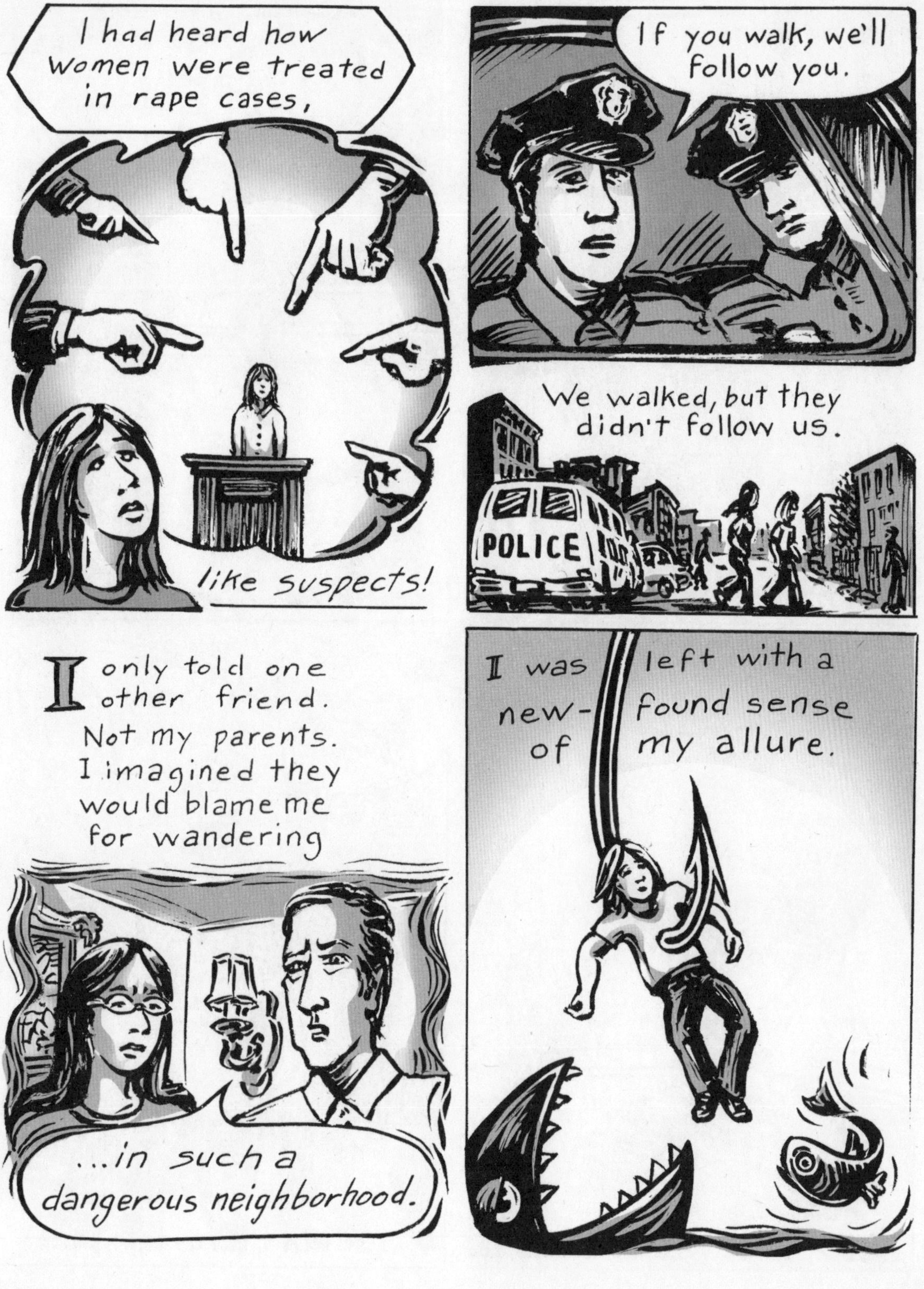
I had heard how women were treated in rape cases,
like suspects!
If you walk, we'll follow you.
We walked, but they didn't follow us.
POLICE
I only told one other friend. Not my parents. I imagined they would blame me for wandering
...in such a dangerous neighborhood.
I was left with a new-found sense of my allure.

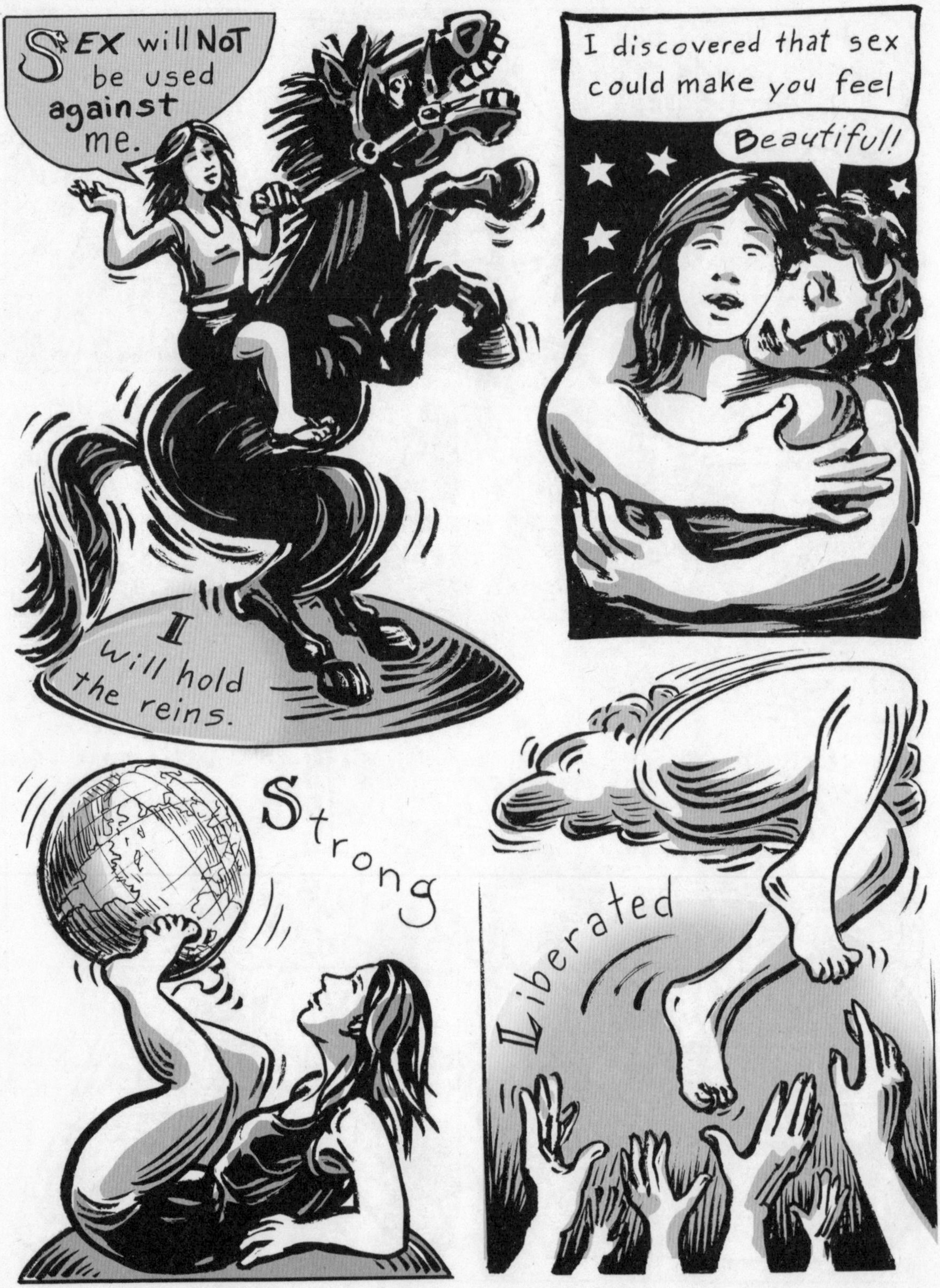
SEX will NOT be used against me.
I will hold the reins.
I discovered that sex could make you feel
Beautiful!
Strong
Liberated

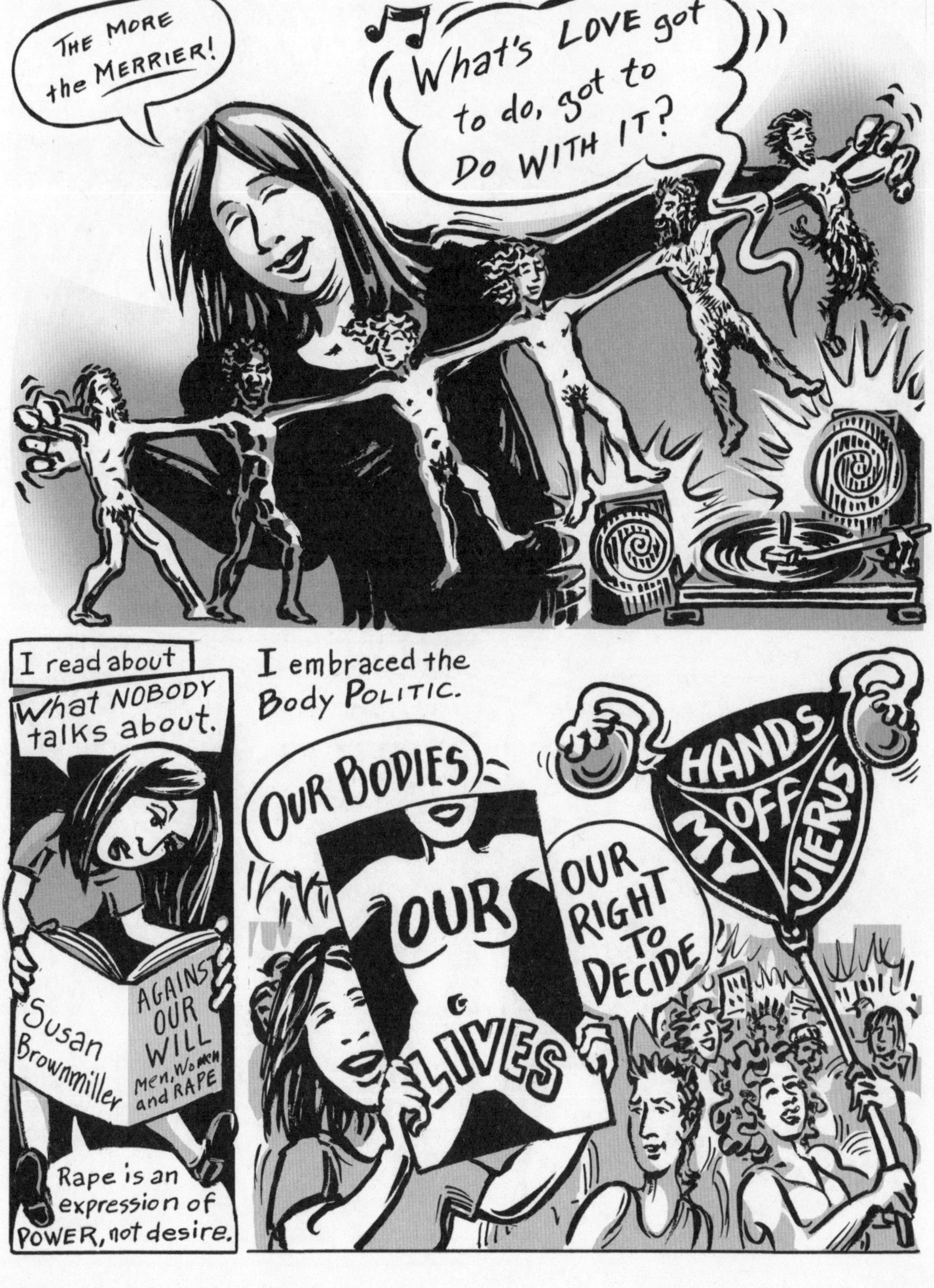

THE MORE the MERRIER!
What's LOVE got to do, got to DO WITH IT?
I read about
What NOBODY talks about.
Susan Brownmiller
AGAINS OUR WILL Men, Women and RAPE
Rape is an expression of POWER, not desire.
I embraced the Body POLITIC.
OUR BODIES
OUR LIVES
OUR RIGHT TO DECIDE
HANDS OFF MY UTERUS

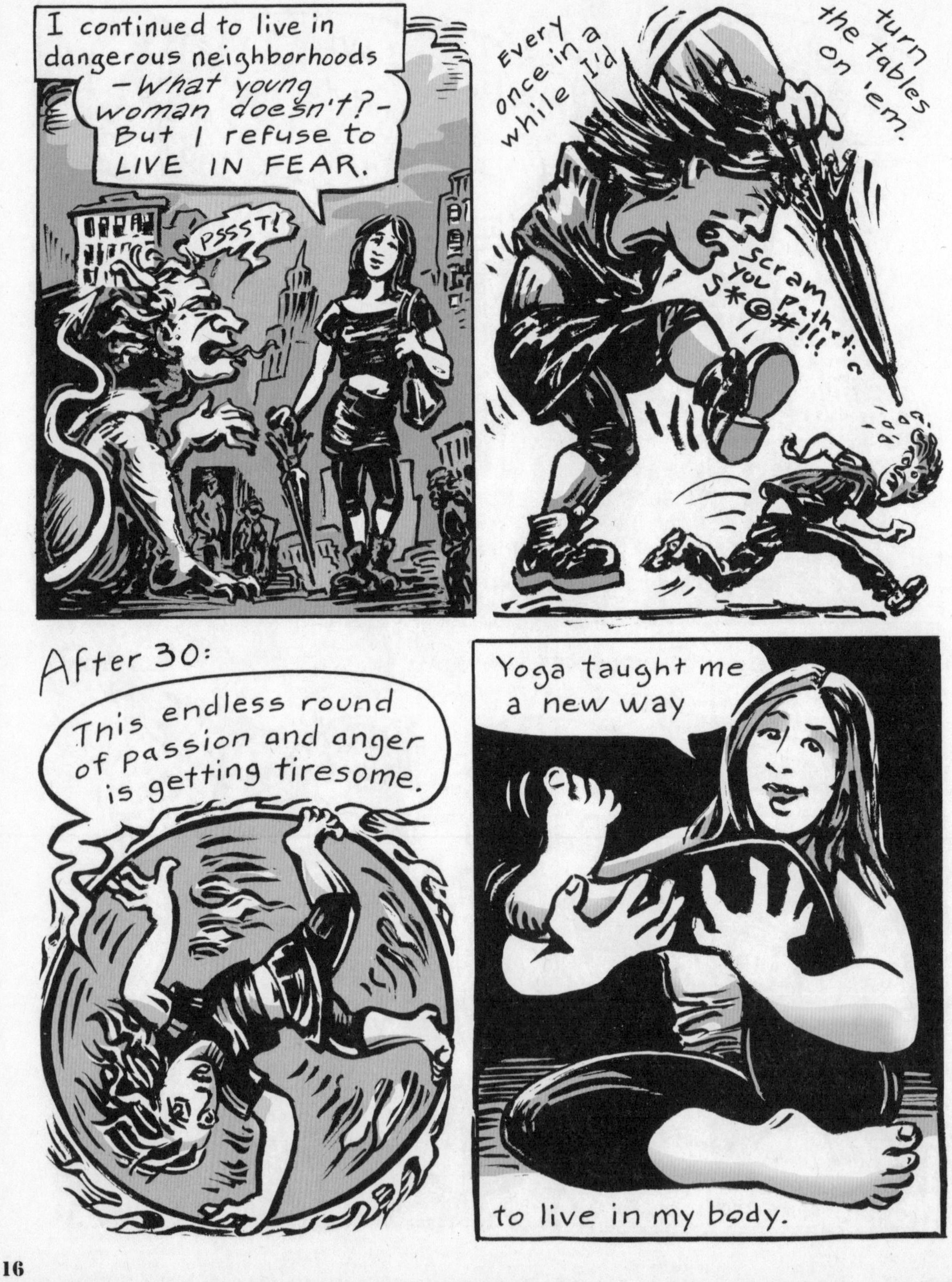
I continued to live in dangerous neighborhoods —What young woman doesn't?— But I refuse to LIVE IN FEAR.
PSSST!
Every once in a while I'd
turn the tables on 'em.
Scram you pathetic S*@#!!!
After 30:
This endless round of passion and anger is getting tiresome.
Yoga taught me a new way
to live in my body.

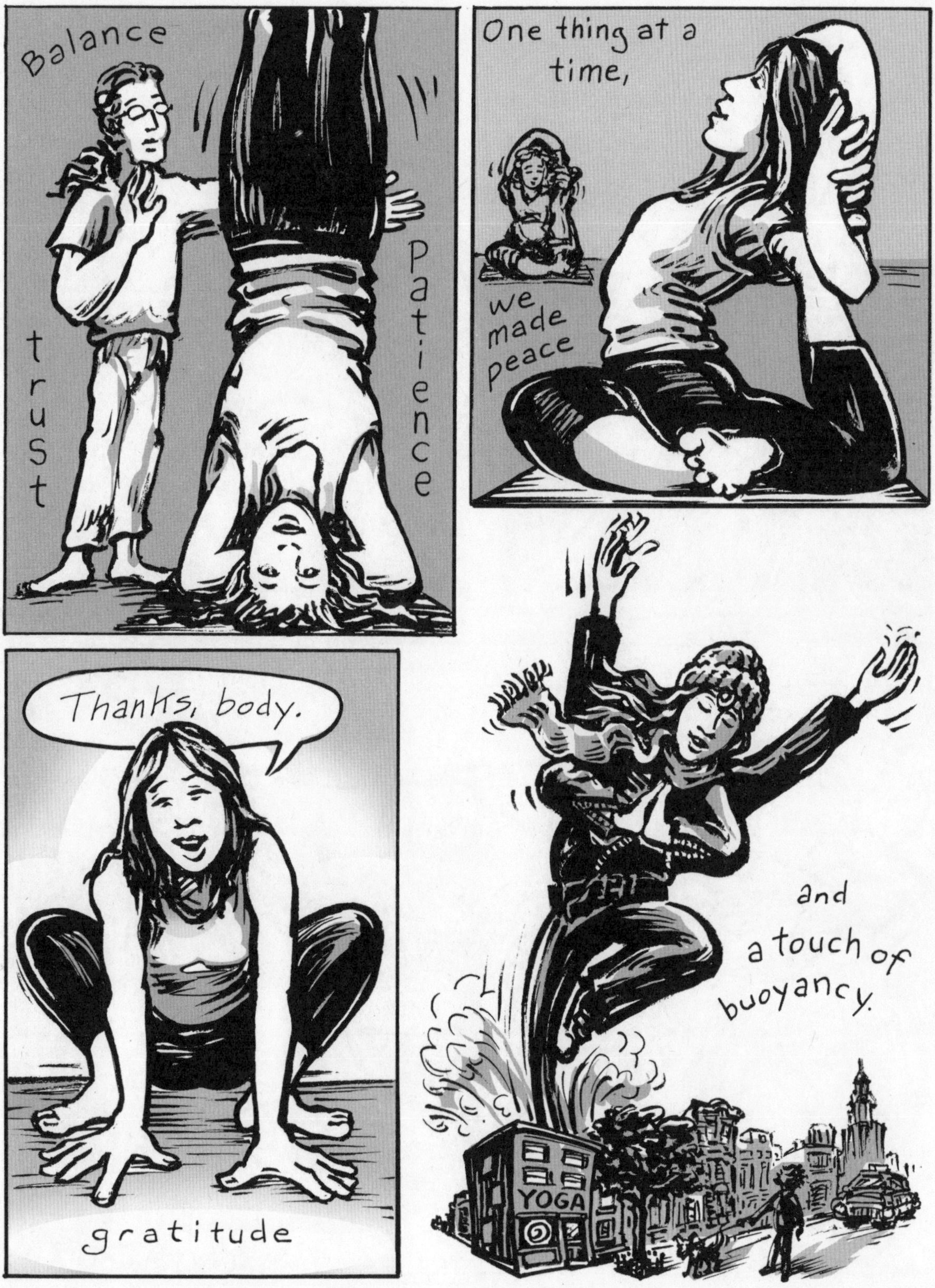

Balance
trust
patience
One thing at a time,
we made peace
Thanks, body.
gratitude
and a touch of buoyancy.
YOGA

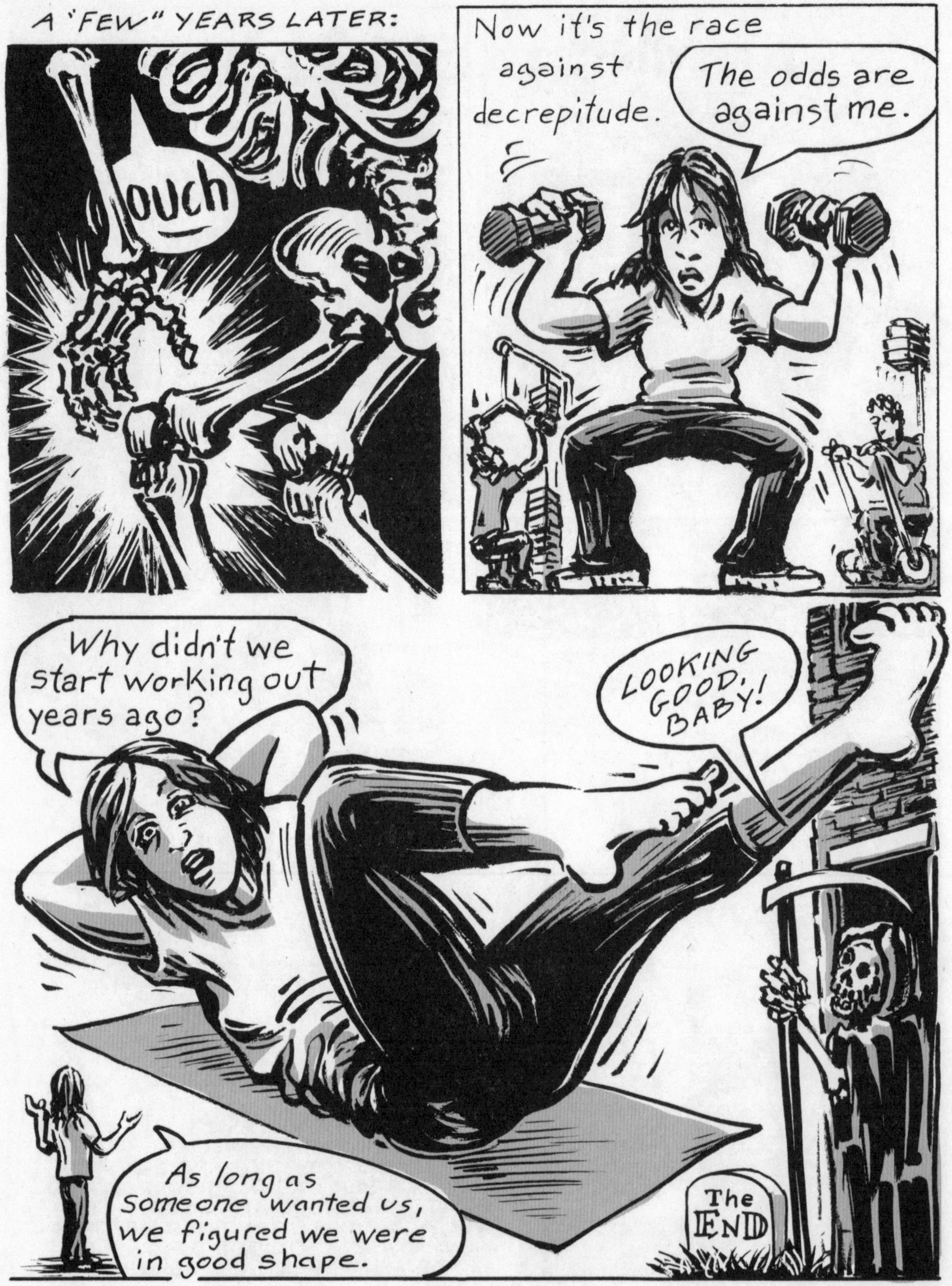

A "FEW" YEARS LATER:
OUCH
Now it's the race against decrepitude.
The odds are against me.
Why didn't we start working out years ago?
LOOKING GOOD, BABY!
As long as someone wanted us, we figured we were in good shape.
The END

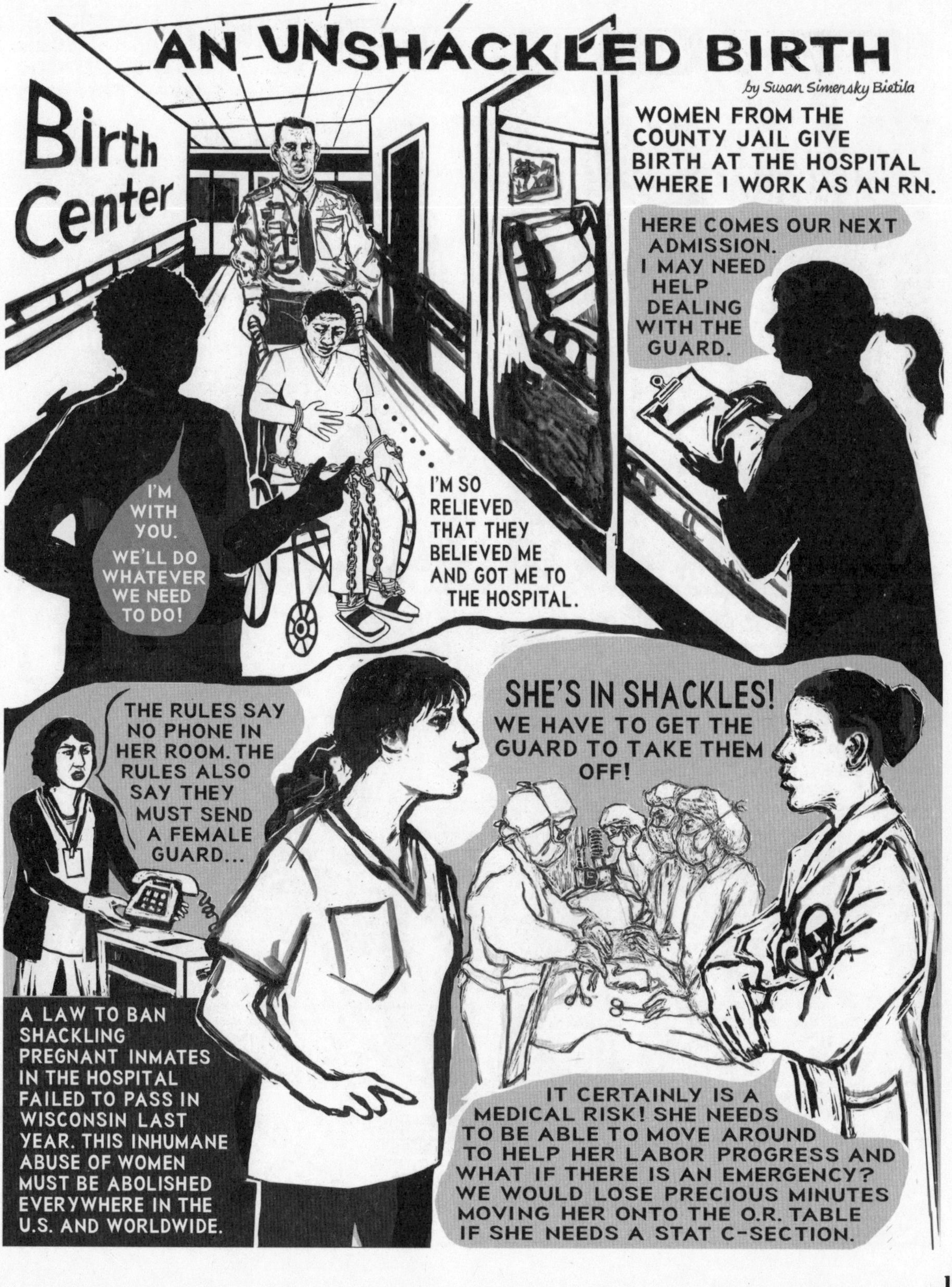

AN UNSHACKLED BIRTH
by Susan Simensky Bietila
Birth Center
WOMEN FROM THE COUNTY JAIL GIVE BIRTH AT THE HOSPITAL WHERE I WORK AS AN RN.
HERE COMES OUR NEXT ADMISSION. I MAY NEED HELP DEALING WITH THE GUARD.
I'M WITH YOU. WE'LL DO WHATEVER WE NEED TO DO!
I'M SO RELIEVED THAT THEY BELIEVED ME AND GOT ME TO THE HOSPITAL.
THE RULES SAY NO PHONE IN HER ROOM. THE RULES ALSO SAY THEY MUST SEND A FEMALE GUARD...
SHE'S IN SHACKLES! WE HAVE TO GET THE GUARD TO TAKE THEM OFF!
A LAW TO BAN SHACKLING PREGNANT INMATES IN THE HOSPITAL FAILED TO PASS IN WISCONSIN LAST YEAR. THIS INHUMANE ABUSE OF WOMEN MUST BE ABOLISHED EVERYWHERE IN THE U.S. AND WORLDWIDE.
IT CERTAINLY IS A MEDICAL RISK! SHE NEEDS TO BE ABLE TO MOVE AROUND TO HELP HER LABOR PROGRESS AND WHAT IF THERE IS AN EMERGENCY? WE WOULD LOSE PRECIOUS MINUTES MOVING HER ONTO THE O.R. TABLE IF SHE NEEDS A STAT C-SECTION.

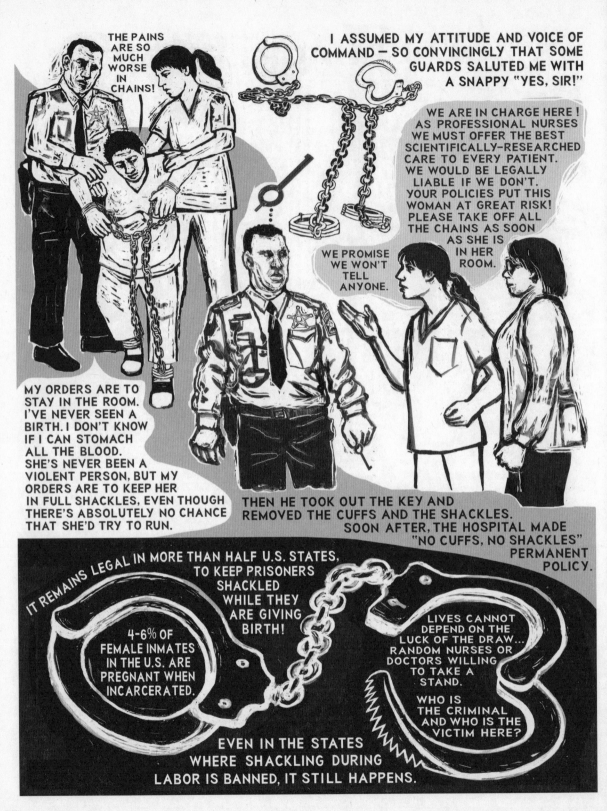

THE PAINS ARE SO MUCH WORSE IN CHAINS!

I ASSUMED MY ATTITUDE AND VOICE OF COMMAND — SO CONVINCINGLY THAT SOME GUARDS SALUTED ME WITH A SNAPPY "YES, SIR!"

WE ARE IN CHARGE HERE! AS PROFESSIONAL NURSES WE MUST OFFER THE BEST SCIENTIFICALLY-RESEARCHED CARE TO EVERY PATIENT. WE WOULD BE LEGALLY LIABLE IF WE DON'T. YOUR POLICIES PUT THIS WOMAN AT GREAT RISK! PLEASE TAKE OFF ALL THE CHAINS AS SOON AS SHE IS IN HER ROOM.

WE PROMISE WE WON'T TELL ANYONE.

MY ORDERS ARE TO STAY IN THE ROOM. I'VE NEVER SEEN A BIRTH. I DON'T KNOW IF I CAN STOMACH ALL THE BLOOD. SHE'S NEVER BEEN A VIOLENT PERSON, BUT MY ORDERS ARE TO KEEP HER IN FULL SHACKLES, EVEN THOUGH THERE'S ABSOLUTELY NO CHANCE THAT SHE'D TRY TO RUN.

THEN HE TOOK OUT THE KEY AND REMOVED THE CUFFS AND THE SHACKLES. SOON AFTER, THE HOSPITAL MADE "NO CUFFS, NO SHACKLES" PERMANENT POLICY.

IT REMAINS LEGAL IN MORE THAN HALF U.S. STATES, TO KEEP PRISONERS SHACKLED WHILE THEY ARE GIVING BIRTH!

4-6% OF FEMALE INMATES IN THE U.S. ARE PREGNANT WHEN INCARCERATED.

LIVES CANNOT DEPEND ON THE LUCK OF THE DRAW... RANDOM NURSES OR DOCTORS WILLING TO TAKE A STAND.

WHO IS THE CRIMINAL AND WHO IS THE VICTIM HERE?

EVEN IN THE STATES WHERE SHACKLING DURING LABOR IS BANNED, IT STILL HAPPENS.

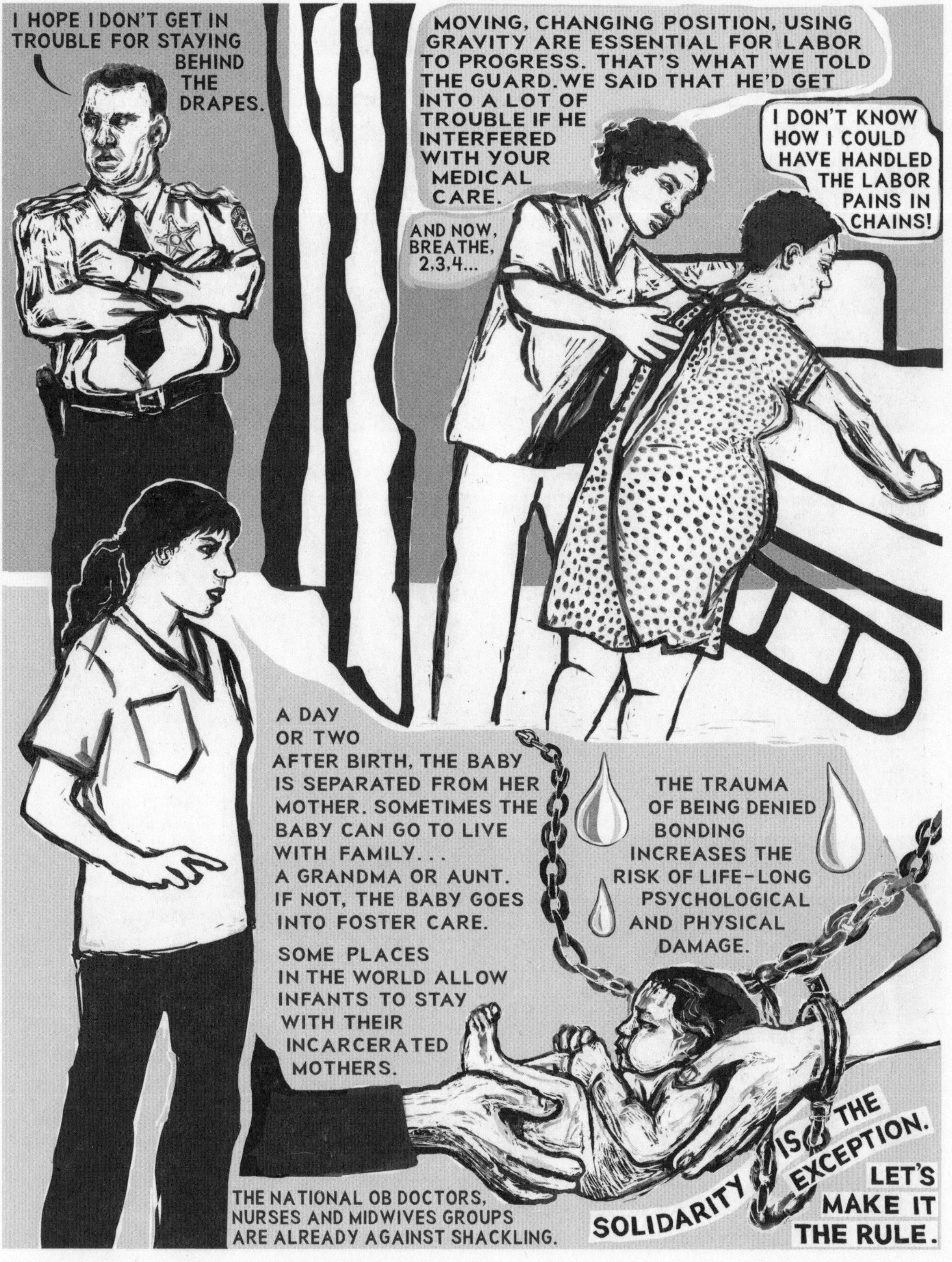
I HOPE I DON'T GET IN TROUBLE FOR STAYING BEHIND THE DRAPES.
MOVING, CHANGING POSITION, USING GRAVITY ARE ESSENTIAL FOR LABOR TO PROGRESS. THAT'S WHAT WE TOLD THE GUARD. WE SAID THAT HE'D GET INTO A LOT OF TROUBLE IF HE INTERFERED WITH YOUR MEDICAL CARE.
I DON'T KNOW HOW I COULD HAVE HANDLED THE LABOR PAINS IN CHAINS!
AND NOW, BREATHE, 2,3,4...
A DAY OR TWO AFTER BIRTH, THE BABY IS SEPARATED FROM HER MOTHER. SOMETIMES THE BABY CAN GO TO LIVE WITH FAMILY... A GRANDMA OR AUNT. IF NOT, THE BABY GOES INTO FOSTER CARE.
THE TRAUMA OF BEING DENIED BONDING INCREASES THE RISK OF LIFE-LONG PSYCHOLOGICAL AND PHYSICAL DAMAGE.
SOME PLACES IN THE WORLD ALLOW INFANTS TO STAY WITH THEIR INCARCERATED MOTHERS.
THE NATIONAL OB DOCTORS, NURSES AND MIDWIVES GROUPS ARE ALREADY AGAINST SHACKLING.
SOLIDARITY IS THE EXCEPTION.
LET'S MAKE IT THE RULE.

INTIMATE PARTNER VIOLENCE
Escape Room

FROM ABUSE TO FREEDOM, SURVIVORS TELL THEIR STORIES

REBECCA M • SADIE ROSE • JENNIE CHI • JASMINE DELUDE • V

DESIGNED, ILLUSTRATED AND EDITED BY REBECCA MIGDAL

A person from any background can become trapped in a pattern of abuse.

Maybe you're disabled, homeless, mentally ill, or have an addiction...

Maybe you're a doctor, college professor, judge or engineer.

Whatever your ethnicity, whatever your gender or sexual orientation...

You're in a troubled relationship. You've tried to make it work, but your partner blames you, bullies, is unreasonably jealous or controlling.

Then something happens, a thing that causes you to realize that the unthinkable is a reality:

I'm in an abusive relationship. I'm in danger.

I HAVE TO ESCAPE, BUT IT WON'T BE EASY. MANY NEVER DO.

15% OF WOMEN AND 4% OF MEN IN THE US HAVE BEEN INJURED AS A RESULT OF PHYSICAL VIOLENCE BY AN INTIMATE PARTNER

1527 WOMEN AND 510 MEN WERE KILLED BY AN INTIMATE PARTNER IN THE US IN 2017

85% OF DOMESTIC VIOLENCE ATTACKS ARE ON WOMEN

HALF OF ALL MURDERS OF WOMEN ARE COMMITTED BY A FORMER OR CURRENT ROMANTIC PARTNER

HOW DID I GET INTO THIS TRAP?

Whatever choices may have led up to your being abused, **remember: it's not your fault.**

The way we have been socialized makes it hard for women to identify abusive behavior as abusive, rather than just an extravagant act of love, and also makes it hard for women to be taken seriously when they are abused. -Nian Hu

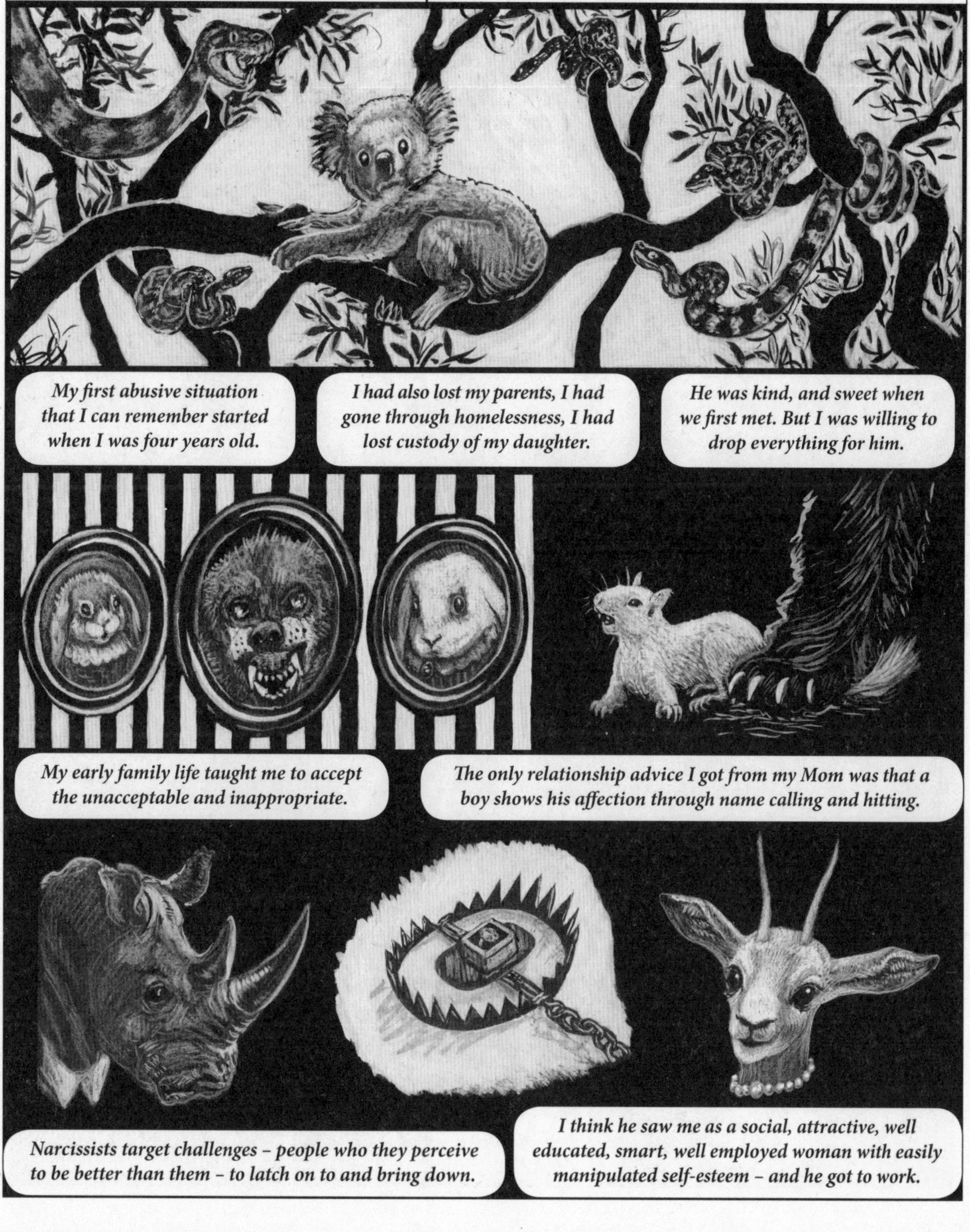

My first abusive situation that I can remember started when I was four years old.
I had also lost my parents, I had gone through homelessness, I had lost custody of my daughter.
He was kind, and sweet when we first met. But I was willing to drop everything for him.
My early family life taught me to accept the unacceptable and inappropriate.
The only relationship advice I got from my Mom was that a boy shows his affection through name calling and hitting.
Narcissists target challenges – people who they perceive to be better than them – to latch on to and bring down.
I think he saw me as a social, attractive, well educated, smart, well employed woman with easily manipulated self-esteem – and he got to work.

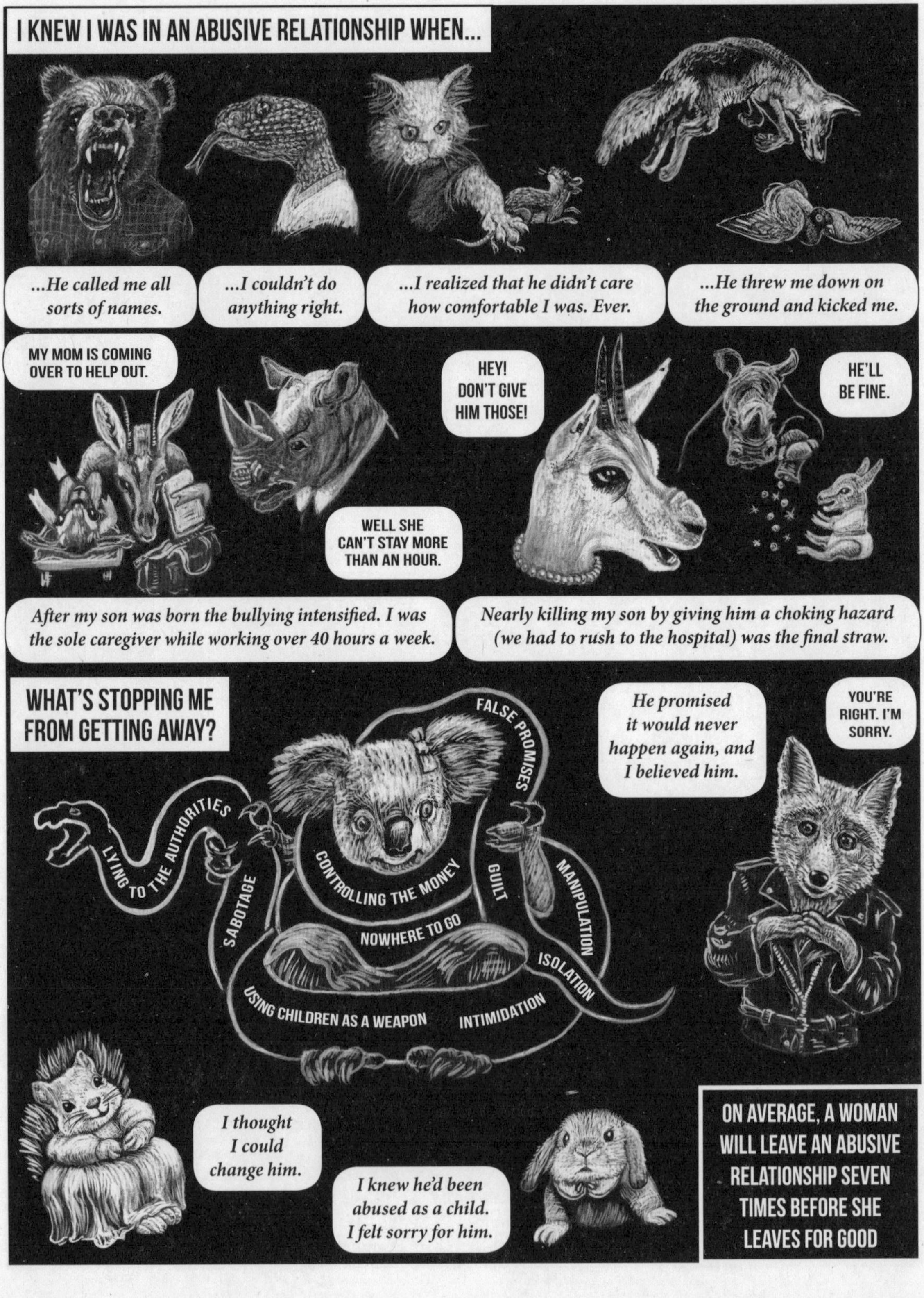
I KNEW I WAS IN AN ABUSIVE RELATIONSHIP WHEN...
...He called me all sorts of names.
...I couldn't do anything right.
...I realized that he didn't care how comfortable I was. Ever.
...He threw me down on the ground and kicked me.
MY MOM IS COMING OVER TO HELP OUT.
WELL SHE CAN'T STAY MORE THAN AN HOUR.
HEY! DON'T GIVE HIM THOSE!
HE'LL BE FINE.
After my son was born the bullying intensified. I was the sole caregiver while working over 40 hours a week.
Nearly killing my son by giving him a choking hazard (we had to rush to the hospital) was the final straw.
WHAT'S STOPPING ME FROM GETTING AWAY?
FALSE PROMISES
LYING TO THE AUTHORITIES
CONTROLLING THE MONEY
GUILT
MANIPULATION
SABOTAGE
NOWHERE TO GO
ISOLATION
USING CHILDREN AS A WEAPON
INTIMIDATION
He promised it would never happen again, and I believed him.
YOU'RE RIGHT. I'M SORRY.
I thought I could change him.
I knew he'd been abused as a child. I felt sorry for him.
ON AVERAGE, A WOMAN WILL LEAVE AN ABUSIVE RELATIONSHIP SEVEN TIMES BEFORE SHE LEAVES FOR GOOD

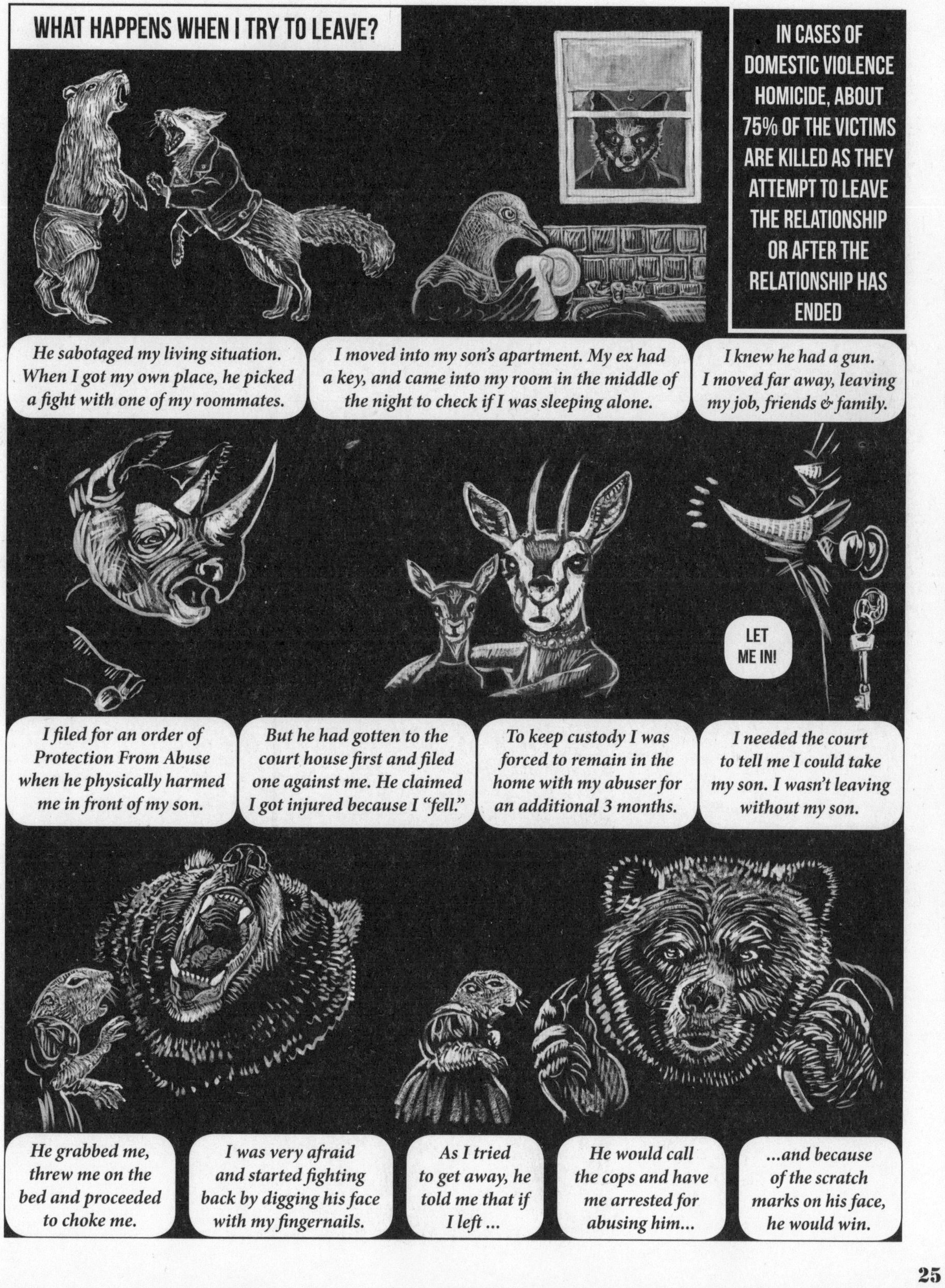
WHAT HAPPENS WHEN I TRY TO LEAVE?
IN CASES OF DOMESTIC VIOLENCE HOMICIDE, ABOUT 75% OF THE VICTIMS ARE KILLED AS THEY ATTEMPT TO LEAVE THE RELATIONSHIP OR AFTER THE RELATIONSHIP HAS ENDED
He sabotaged my living situation. When I got my own place, he picked a fight with one of my roommates.
I moved into my son's apartment. My ex had a key, and came into my room in the middle of the night to check if I was sleeping alone.
I knew he had a gun. I moved far away, leaving my job, friends & family.
LET ME IN!
I filed for an order of Protection From Abuse when he physically harmed me in front of my son.
But he had gotten to the court house first and filed one against me. He claimed I got injured because I "fell."
To keep custody I was forced to remain in the home with my abuser for an additional 3 months.
I needed the court to tell me I could take my son. I wasn't leaving without my son.
He grabbed me, threw me on the bed and proceeded to choke me.
I was very afraid and started fighting back by digging his face with my fingernails.
As I tried to get away, he told me that if I left ...
He would call the cops and have me arrested for abusing him...
...and because of the scratch marks on his face, he would win.

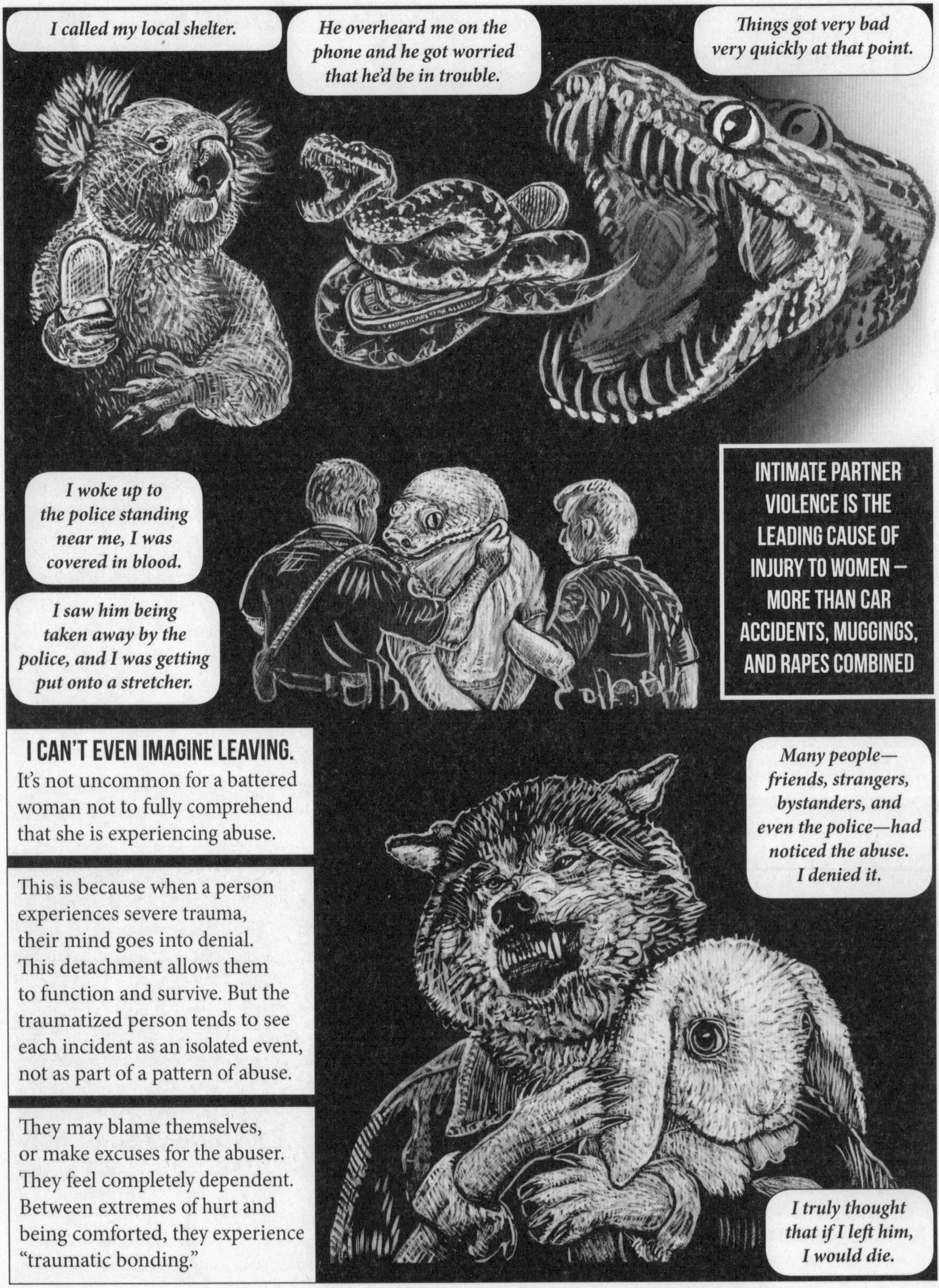
I called my local shelter.
He overheard me on the phone and he got worried that he'd be in trouble.
Things got very bad very quickly at that point.
I woke up to the police standing near me, I was covered in blood.
I saw him being taken away by the police, and I was getting put onto a stretcher.
INTIMATE PARTNER VIOLENCE IS THE LEADING CAUSE OF INJURY TO WOMEN – MORE THAN CAR ACCIDENTS, MUGGINGS, AND RAPES COMBINED
I CAN'T EVEN IMAGINE LEAVING.
It's not uncommon for a battered woman not to fully comprehend that she is experiencing abuse.
This is because when a person experiences severe trauma, their mind goes into denial. This detachment allows them to function and survive. But the traumatized person tends to see each incident as an isolated event, not as part of a pattern of abuse.
They may blame themselves, or make excuses for the abuser. They feel completely dependent. Between extremes of hurt and being comforted, they experience "traumatic bonding."
Many people—friends, strangers, bystanders, and even the police—had noticed the abuse. I denied it.
I truly thought that if I left him, I would die.

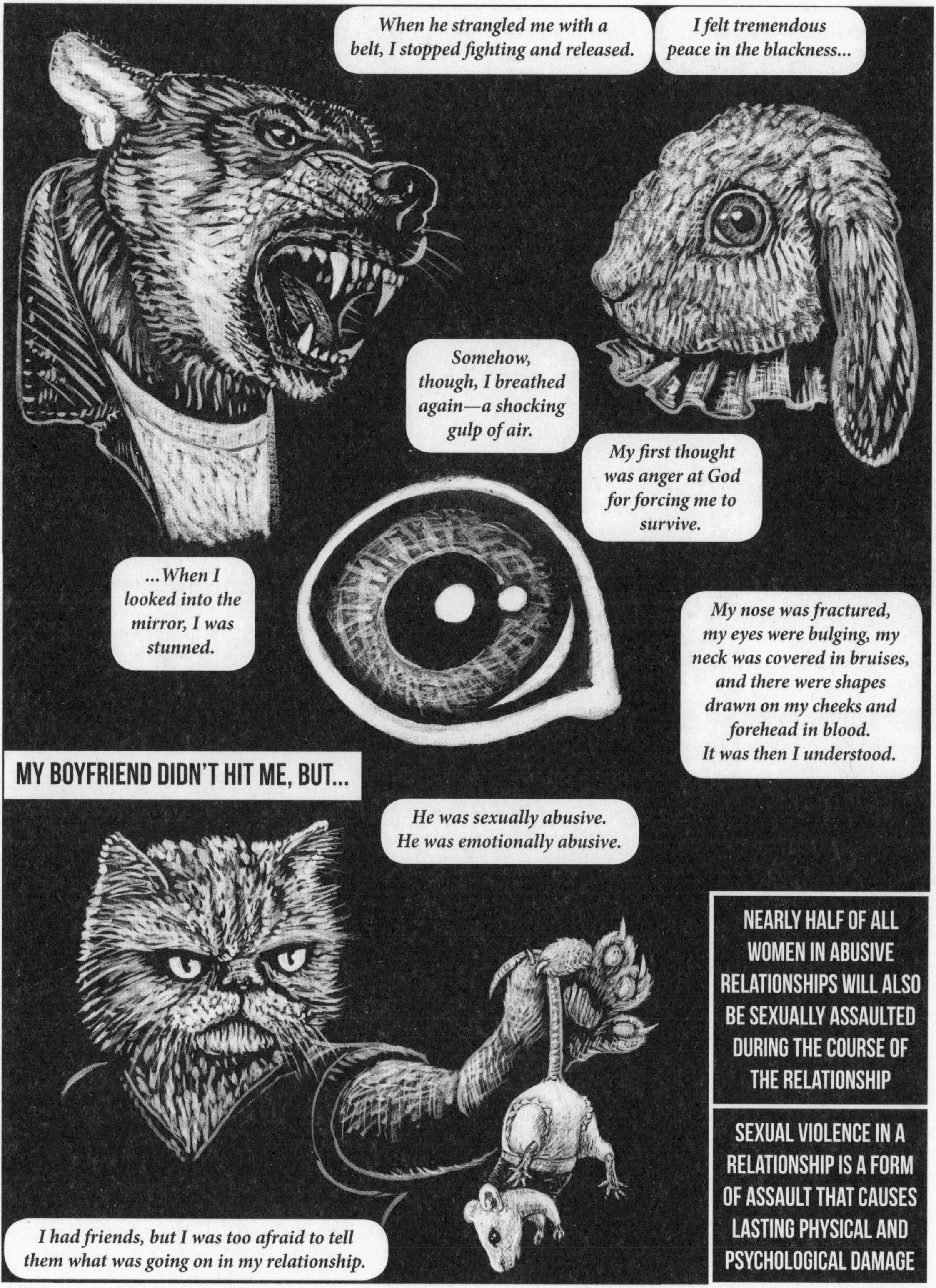
When he strangled me with a belt, I stopped fighting and released.
I felt tremendous peace in the blackness...
Somehow, though, I breathed again—a shocking gulp of air.
My first thought was anger at God for forcing me to survive.
...When I looked into the mirror, I was stunned.
My nose was fractured, my eyes were bulging, my neck was covered in bruises, and there were shapes drawn on my cheeks and forehead in blood. It was then I understood.
MY BOYFRIEND DIDN'T HIT ME, BUT...
He was sexually abusive. He was emotionally abusive.
NEARLY HALF OF ALL WOMEN IN ABUSIVE RELATIONSHIPS WILL ALSO BE SEXUALLY ASSAULTED DURING THE COURSE OF THE RELATIONSHIP
SEXUAL VIOLENCE IN A RELATIONSHIP IS A FORM OF ASSAULT THAT CAUSES LASTING PHYSICAL AND PSYCHOLOGICAL DAMAGE
I had friends, but I was too afraid to tell them what was going on in my relationship.

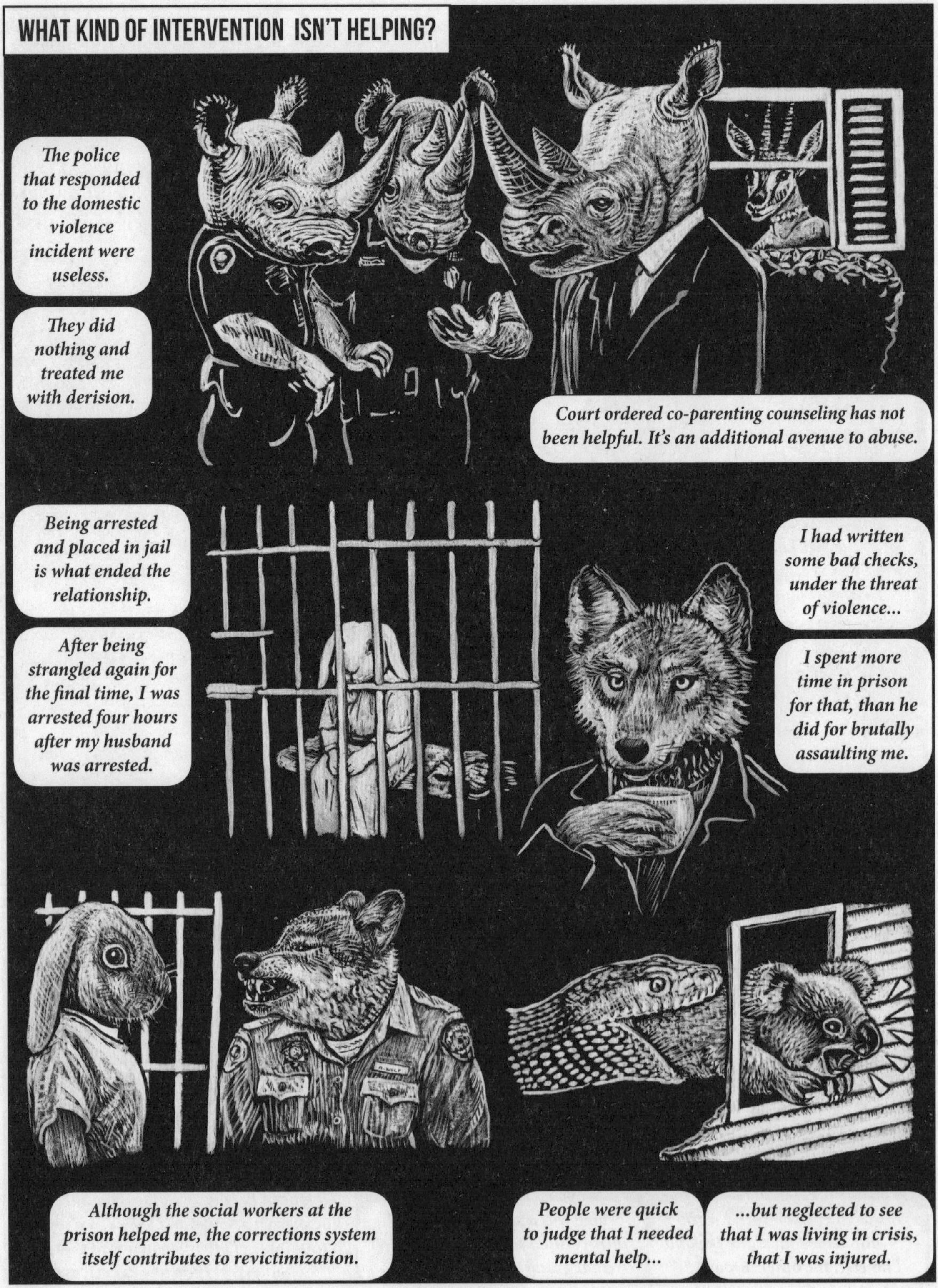
WHAT KIND OF INTERVENTION ISN'T HELPING?
The police that responded to the domestic violence incident were useless.
They did nothing and treated me with derision.
Court ordered co-parenting counseling has not been helpful. It's an additional avenue to abuse.
Being arrested and placed in jail is what ended the relationship.
After being strangled again for the final time, I was arrested four hours after my husband was arrested.
I had written some bad checks, under the threat of violence...
I spent more time in prison for that, than he did for brutally assaulting me.
Although the social workers at the prison helped me, the corrections system itself contributes to revictimization.
People were quick to judge that I needed mental help...
...but neglected to see that I was living in crisis, that I was injured.

I'M AFRAID TO REPORT THE ABUSE BECAUSE I'LL BE ARRESTED/LOSE MY KIDS/BECOME HOMELESS.

ROUGHLY 90% OF WOMEN ARRESTED FOR IPV TOWARD MEN ARE THEMSELVES VICTIMS OF VIOLENT ABUSE	. IN 29 STATES WOMEN ARE PUT IN PRISON IF THEY CAN'T STOP THEIR ABUSER FROM HARMING THEIR CHILDREN	67 % OF WOMEN SENT TO PRISON IN NY IN 2005 FOR KILLING SOMEONE CLOSE TO THEM WERE ABUSED BY THAT PERSON.	79% OF WOMEN IN FEDERAL AND STATE PRISONS HAVE REPORTED PAST PHYSICAL ABUSE	THE INCARCERATION RATE OF WOMEN HAS GROWN BY 834% SINCE 1978, DOUBLE THAT OF MEN

WHERE DID I TURN FOR HELP?

YOU CAN USE MY PHONE. GO AHEAD, CALL!

I didn't have a healthy support system. I had to rely on the shelter services for help, and hotlines.

I reached out to one of my co-workers about what was really going on in my personal life.

With their encouragement, I was able to call the crisis hotline to ask for help. That is not an easy thing for me to do.

It was the prison social workers that helped me...and beyond all else, the other inmates.

There was a support group for incarcerated survivors– For me, that group was everything.

In one of the darkest places on Earth, I experienced love and solidarity with hundreds of other women who shared variations on the same experiences.

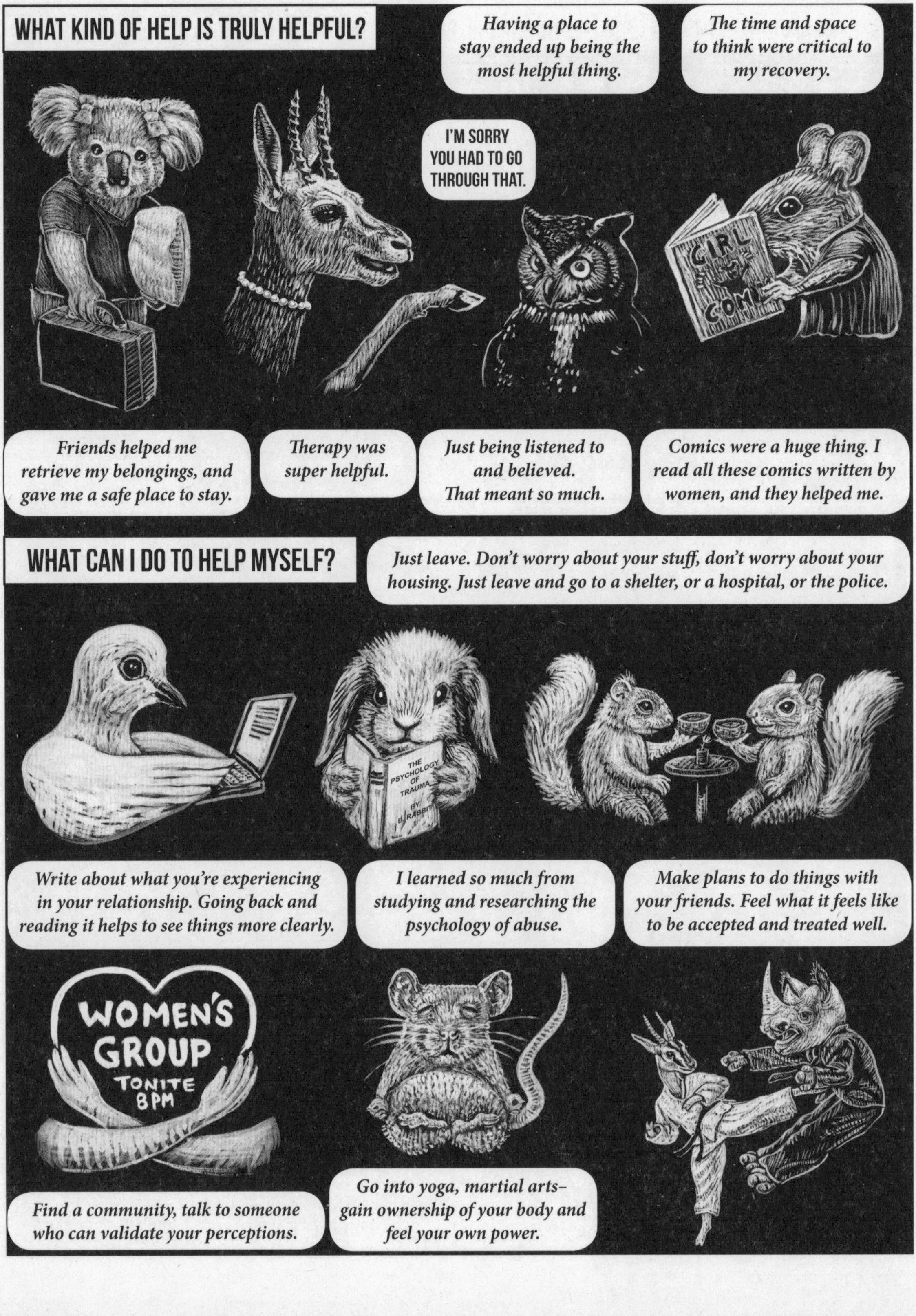
WHAT KIND OF HELP IS TRULY HELPFUL?
Having a place to stay ended up being the most helpful thing.
The time and space to think were critical to my recovery.
I'M SORRY YOU HAD TO GO THROUGH THAT.
Friends helped me retrieve my belongings, and gave me a safe place to stay.
Therapy was super helpful.
Just being listened to and believed. That meant so much.
Comics were a huge thing. I read all these comics written by women, and they helped me.
WHAT CAN I DO TO HELP MYSELF?
Just leave. Don't worry about your stuff, don't worry about your housing. Just leave and go to a shelter, or a hospital, or the police.
THE PSYCHOLOGY OF TRAUMA BY B. RABBIT
Write about what you're experiencing in your relationship. Going back and reading it helps to see things more clearly.
I learned so much from studying and researching the psychology of abuse.
Make plans to do things with your friends. Feel what it feels like to be accepted and treated well.
WOMEN'S GROUP TONITE 8PM
Find a community, talk to someone who can validate your perceptions.
Go into yoga, martial arts– gain ownership of your body and feel your own power.

EVERY YEAR IN THE US INTIMATE PARTNER VIOLENCE:

AFFECTS 12 MILLION PEOPLE

IS WITNESSED BY 5 MILLION CHILDREN

COSTS VICTIMS 6 BILLION IN MEDICAL EXPENSES

✓✓✓✓✓✓✓✓

COSTS VICTIMS 8 MILLION LOST DAYS OF PAID WORK

WHAT CAN COMMUNITIES DO TO HELP?

"I wish there were more follow-ups and more support system building."

- HELP SURVIVORS FIND HOUSING, CHILDCARE AND FINANCIAL ASSISTANCE
- HOST A SURVIVORS SUPPORT GROUP AT YOUR CHURCH OR ORGANIZATION
- BUILD COMMUNITY AWARENESS ABOUT IINTIMATE PARTNER VIOLENCE

"I wish that we had batterer intervention programs that actually work."

- DEMAND LAWS THAT DON'T CRIMINALIZE SURVIVORS, OR PUT THEM OR THEIR CHILDREN AT RISK
- DEMAND BETTER TREATMENT OPTIONS FOR BOTH ABUSERS AND SURVIVORS
- DEMAND BETTER TRAINING FOR LAW ENFORCEMENT IN DEALING WITH DOMESTIC VIOLENCE
- DEMAND LAWS TO REMOVE FIREARMS FROM THE HANDS OF ABUSERS

If you're being abused it doesn't mean that you're stupid, and it doesn't mean that you're incapable of transformation.

It means that you're stuck in a dangerous pattern.

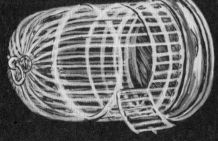

- DEMAND THAT THE US SENATE REAUTHORIZE THE VIOLENCE AGAINST WOMEN ACT

I THINK I'M IN AN ABUSIVE RELATIONSHIP

If your family and friends are trying to help you, let them help you. If they are not supportive, turn to your local Domestic Violence agency, or **call the national DV hotline at (800) 799-7233.** **DO NOT TRY TO GO IT ALONE.**

YOU ARE AT A HIGHER RISK FOR HOMICIDE IF:

YOUR PARTNER MAKES VERBAL THREATS, ESPECIALLY THREATS OF USING A WEAPON

YOUR PARTNER IS UNREASONABLY OR VIOLENTLY JEALOUS

YOU ARE BEING CHOKED OR STRANGLED

YOUR PARTNER FORCES SEX

YOU ARE PREGNANT

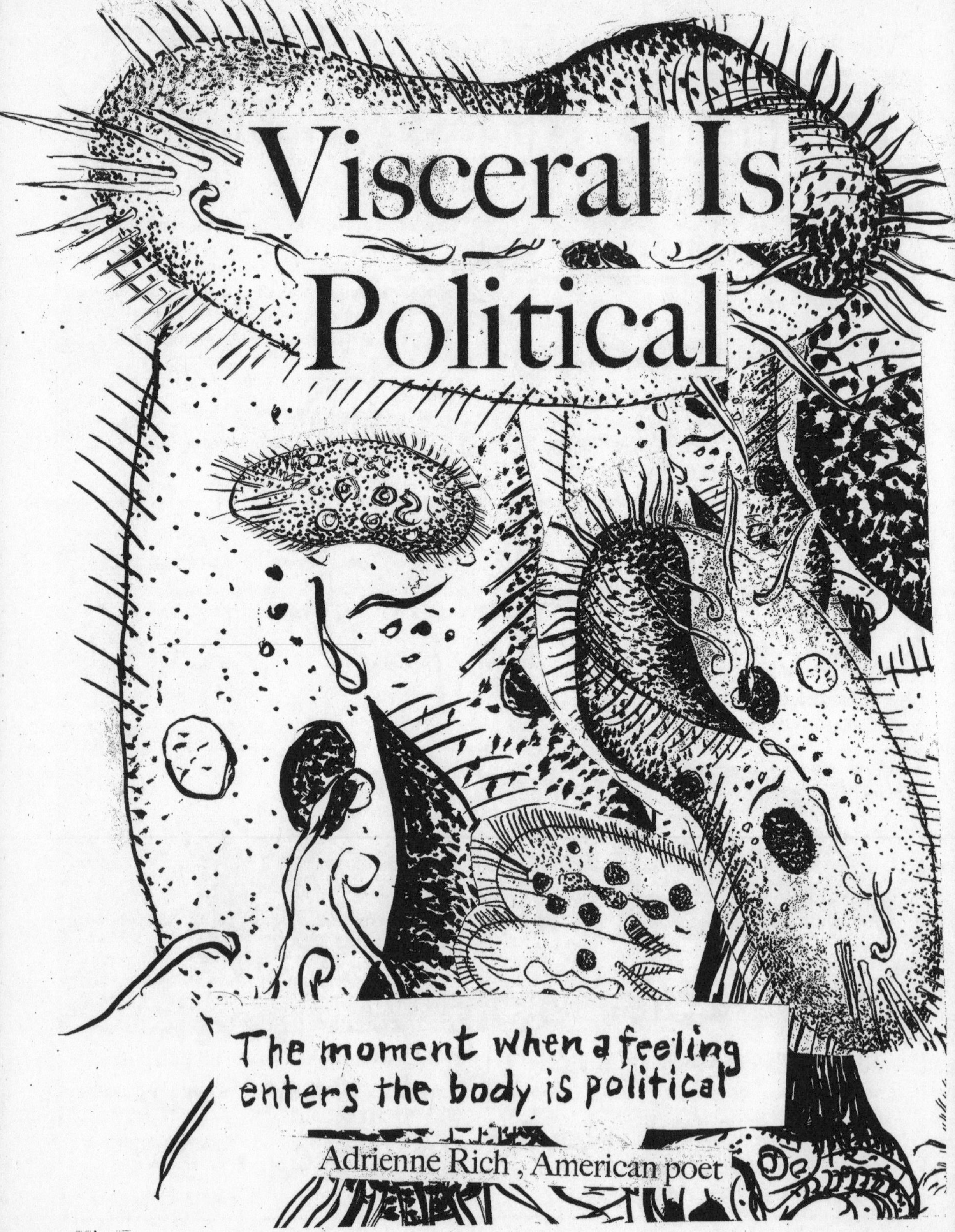
Visceral Is Political
The moment when a feeling enters the body is political
Adrienne Rich , American poet

Some of those moments

your father asks your seven
year old self "if I gave you
an order would you obey it?"

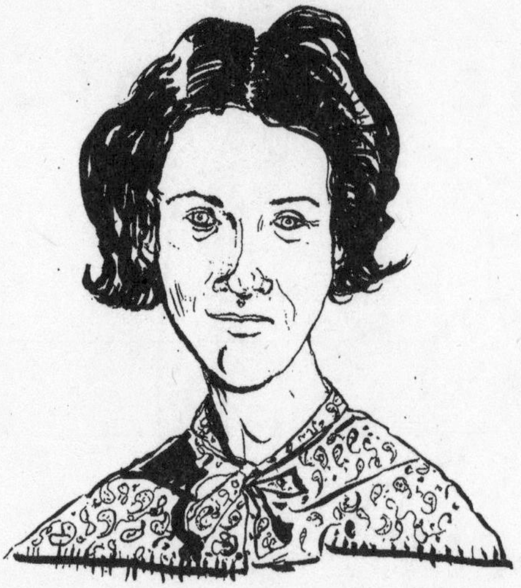

your mother explains because of the war it was not unusual for your father to sleep with a gun under his pillow

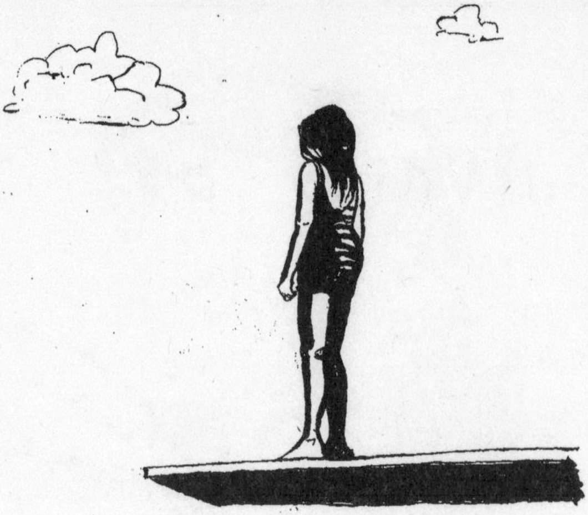

your ride home from school puts his hands around your throat and says "stop moving or I'll have to hurt you"

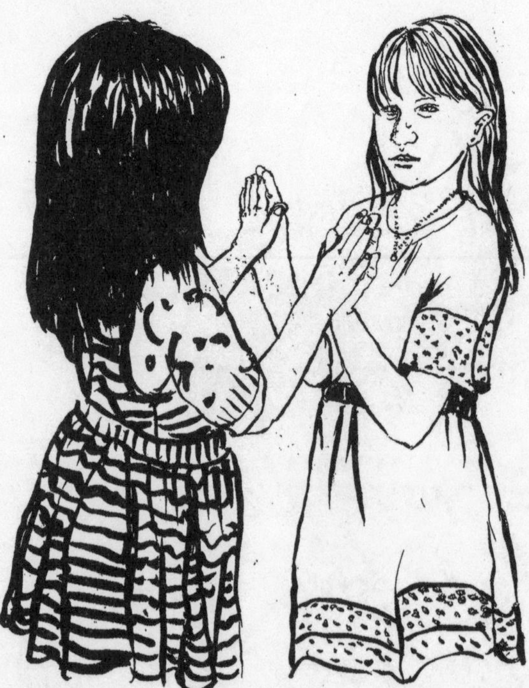

your classmate says you were asking for it

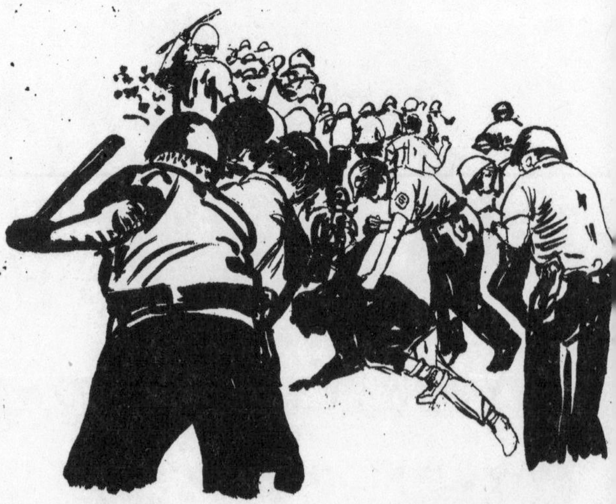

you watch on T.V. armed police beat unarmed war protesters

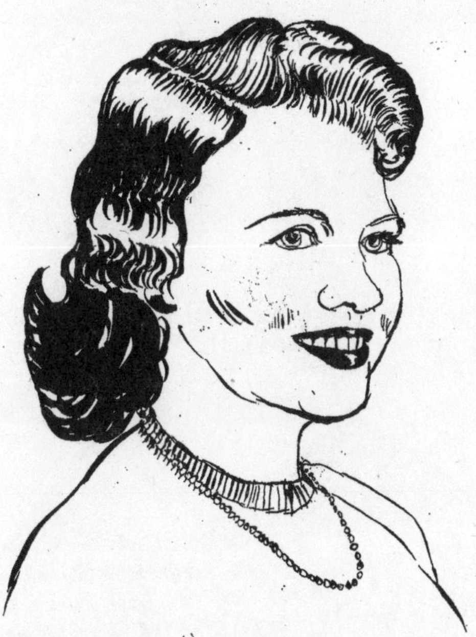

your sister tells you her husband hit her sometimes if she mouthed off

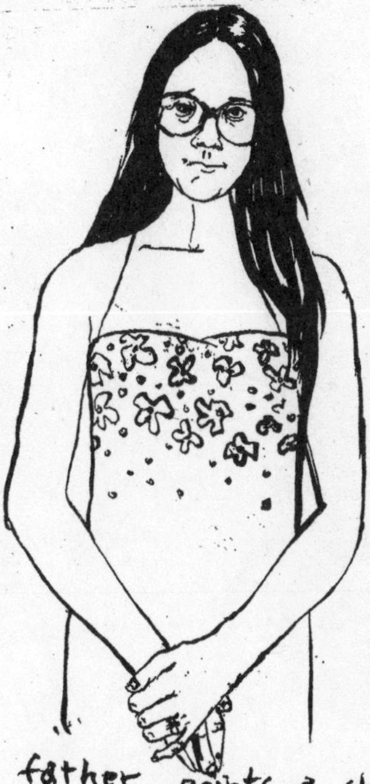

your father points a shotgun at your 15 year old self because you lied about where you went at night

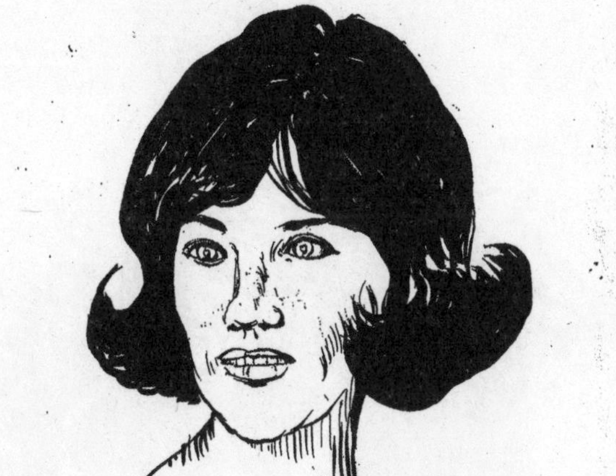

your other sister explains how she sat very quietly in the dark held at knifepoint by her husband

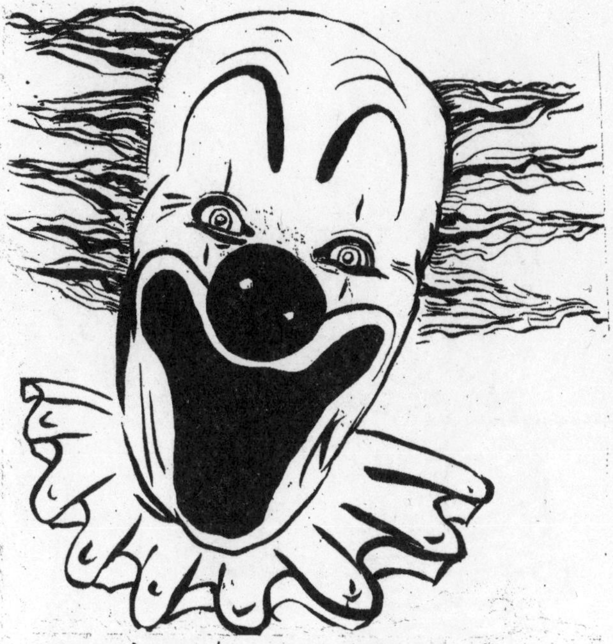

your boss laughs, then yells at you when you ask for equal pay

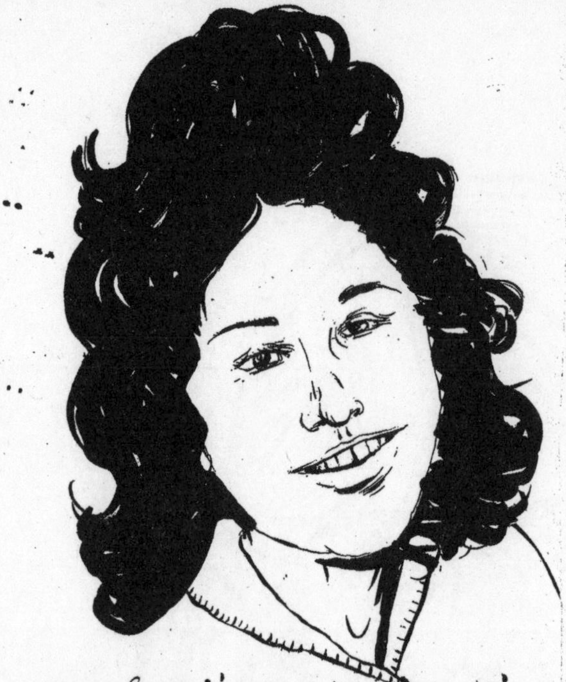

your friend's cousin explains how she pays rent with her body

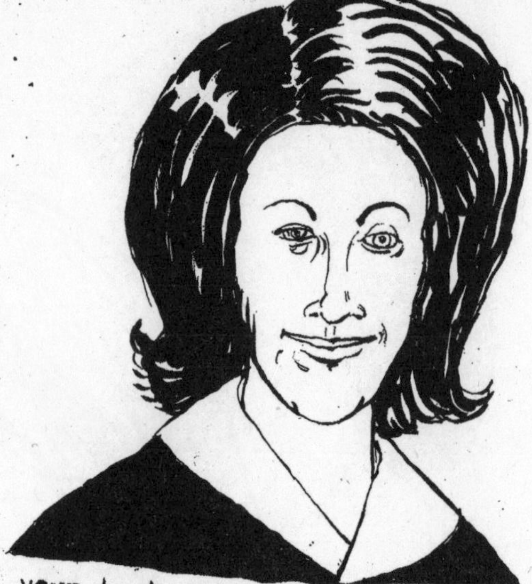

your best friend who works in LOS Alamos says Karen Silkwood's body parts are stored frozen in the rat lab cause they're too radioactive to bury

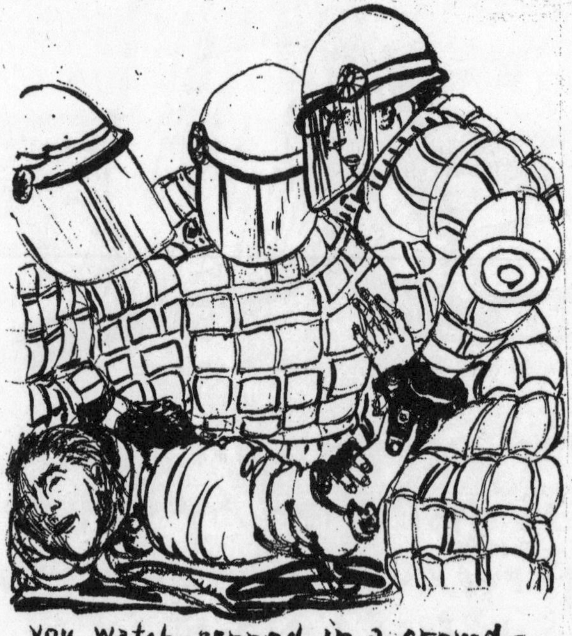

you watch-penned in a crowd-as armed police beat unarmed war protesters

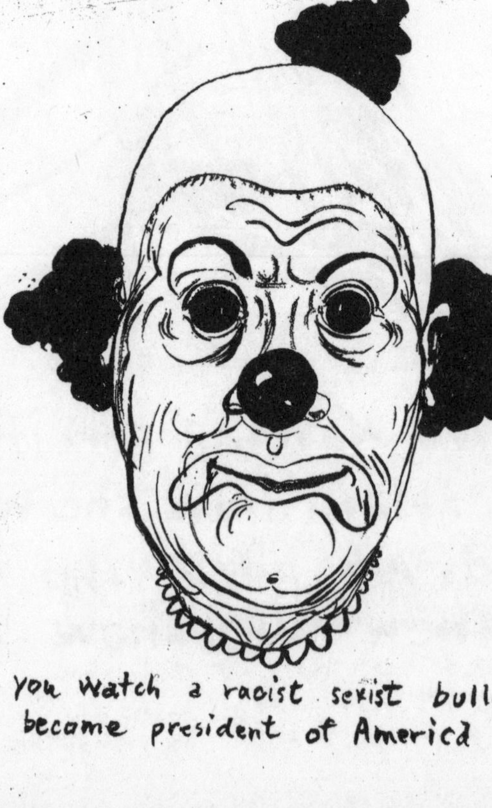

you watch a racist sexist bully become president of America

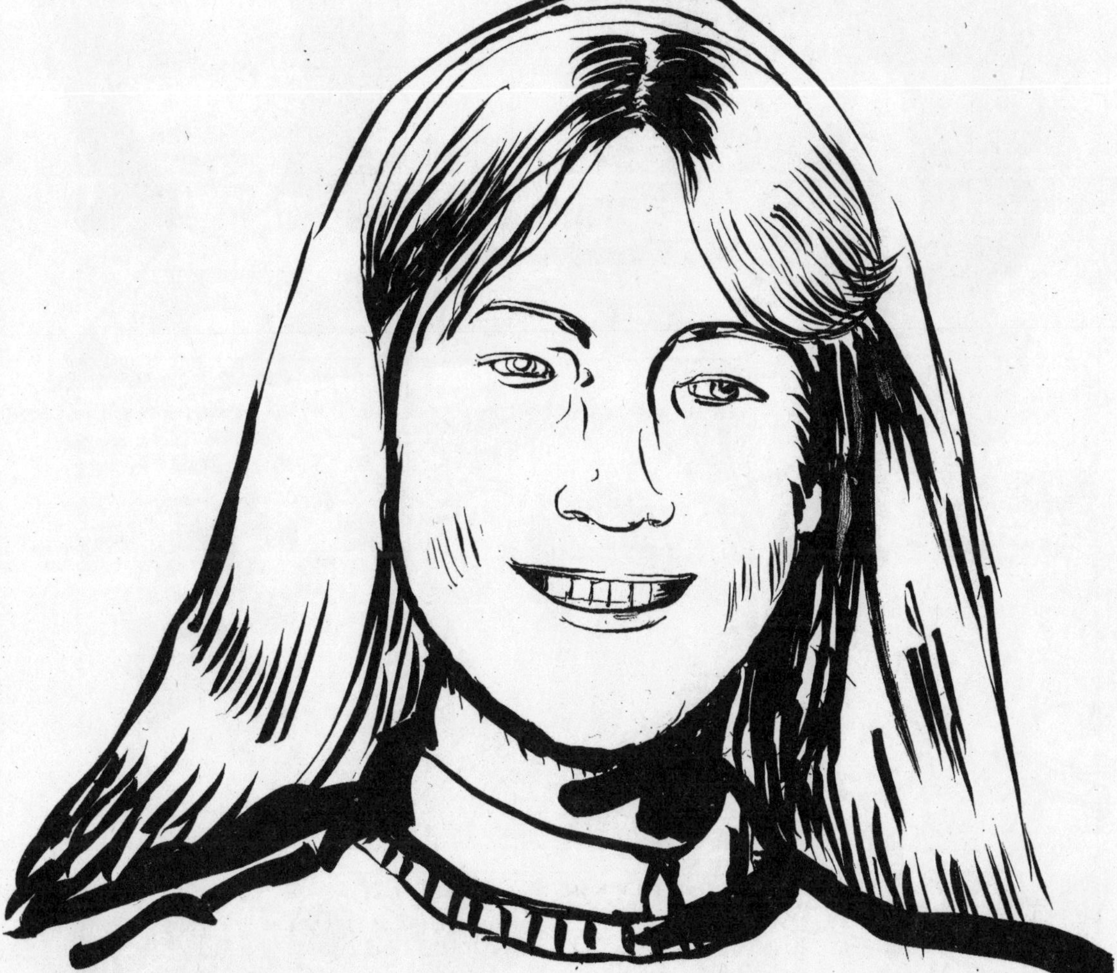

you watch a terrified woman on T. V. Explain how she was assaulted by some drunk boys who grew up to be powerful men who now call her a liar.

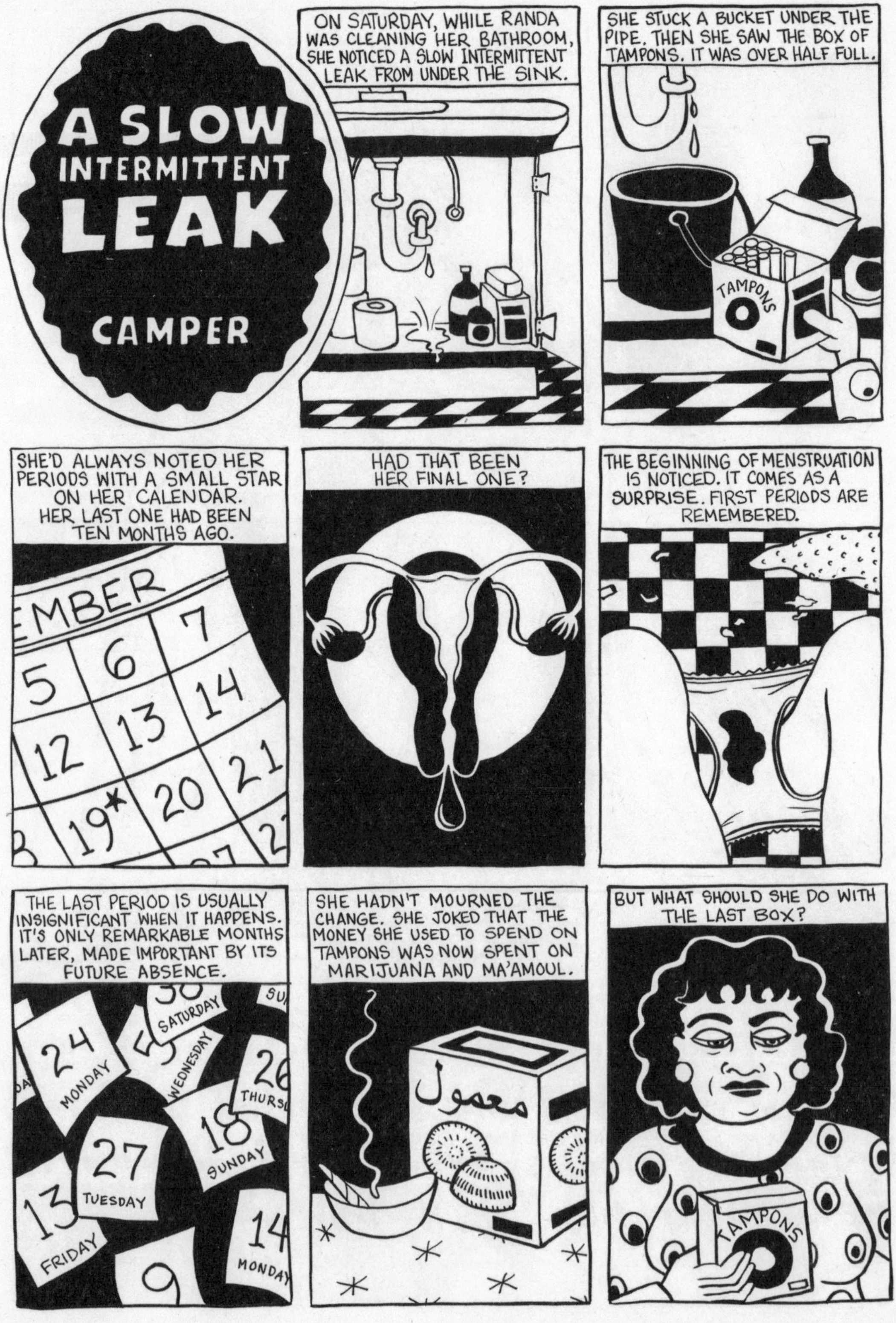
A SLOW INTERMITTENT LEAK
CAMPER
ON SATURDAY, WHILE RANDA WAS CLEANING HER BATHROOM, SHE NOTICED A SLOW INTERMITTENT LEAK FROM UNDER THE SINK.
SHE STUCK A BUCKET UNDER THE PIPE. THEN SHE SAW THE BOX OF TAMPONS. IT WAS OVER HALF FULL.
TAMPONS
SHE'D ALWAYS NOTED HER PERIODS WITH A SMALL STAR ON HER CALENDAR. HER LAST ONE HAD BEEN TEN MONTHS AGO.
EMBER
HAD THAT BEEN HER FINAL ONE?
THE BEGINNING OF MENSTRUATION IS NOTICED. IT COMES AS A SURPRISE. FIRST PERIODS ARE REMEMBERED.
THE LAST PERIOD IS USUALLY INSIGNIFICANT WHEN IT HAPPENS. IT'S ONLY REMARKABLE MONTHS LATER, MADE IMPORTANT BY ITS FUTURE ABSENCE.
24 MONDAY
SATURDAY
WEDNESDAY
27 TUESDAY
18 SUNDAY
13 FRIDAY
14 MONDAY
SHE HADN'T MOURNED THE CHANGE. SHE JOKED THAT THE MONEY SHE USED TO SPEND ON TAMPONS WAS NOW SPENT ON MARIJUANA AND MA'AMOUL.
معمول
BUT WHAT SHOULD SHE DO WITH THE LAST BOX?
TAMPONS

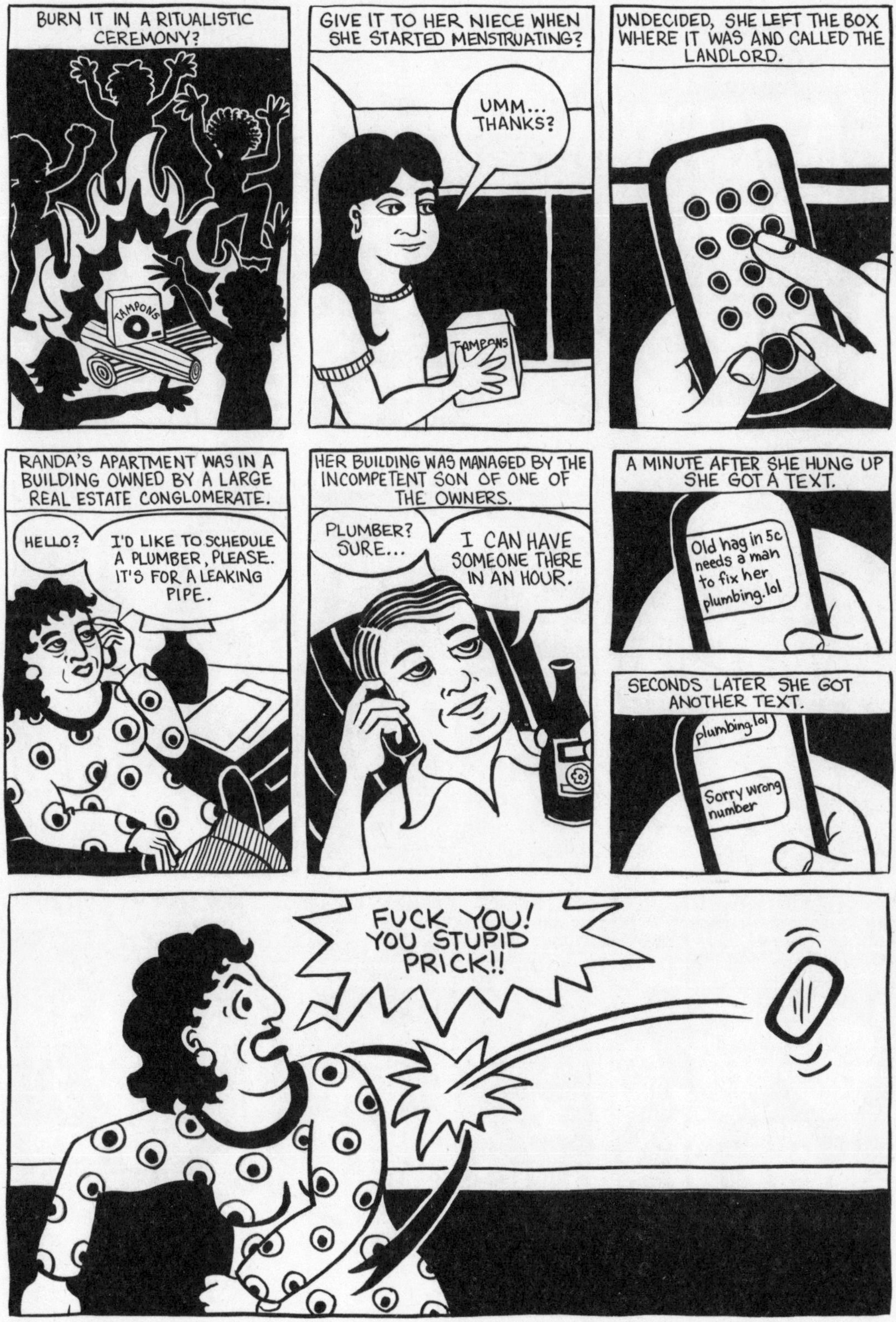
BURN IT IN A RITUALISTIC CEREMONY?
TAMPONS
GIVE IT TO HER NIECE WHEN SHE STARTED MENSTRUATING?
UMM... THANKS?
TAMPONS
UNDECIDED, SHE LEFT THE BOX WHERE IT WAS AND CALLED THE LANDLORD.
RANDA'S APARTMENT WAS IN A BUILDING OWNED BY A LARGE REAL ESTATE CONGLOMERATE.
HELLO?
I'D LIKE TO SCHEDULE A PLUMBER, PLEASE. IT'S FOR A LEAKING PIPE.
HER BUILDING WAS MANAGED BY THE INCOMPETENT SON OF ONE OF THE OWNERS.
PLUMBER? SURE...
I CAN HAVE SOMEONE THERE IN AN HOUR.
A MINUTE AFTER SHE HUNG UP SHE GOT A TEXT.
Old hag in 5c needs a man to fix her plumbing. lol
SECONDS LATER SHE GOT ANOTHER TEXT.
plumbing. lol
Sorry wrong number
FUCK YOU! YOU STUPID PRICK!!

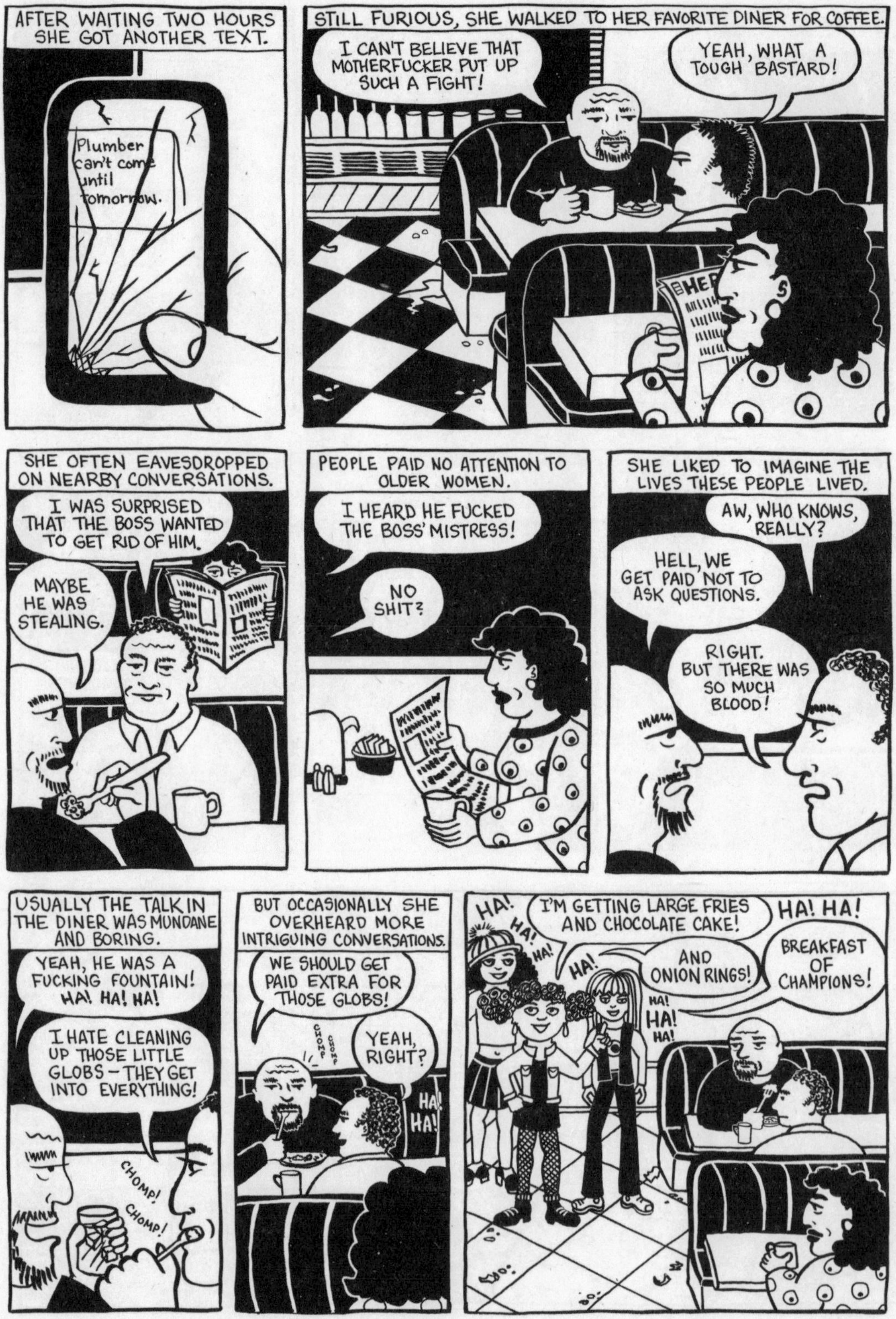

AFTER WAITING TWO HOURS SHE GOT ANOTHER TEXT.
Plumber can't come until tomorrow.
STILL FURIOUS, SHE WALKED TO HER FAVORITE DINER FOR COFFEE.
I CAN'T BELIEVE THAT MOTHERFUCKER PUT UP SUCH A FIGHT!
YEAH, WHAT A TOUGH BASTARD!
SHE OFTEN EAVESDROPPED ON NEARBY CONVERSATIONS.
I WAS SURPRISED THAT THE BOSS WANTED TO GET RID OF HIM.
MAYBE HE WAS STEALING.
PEOPLE PAID NO ATTENTION TO OLDER WOMEN.
I HEARD HE FUCKED THE BOSS' MISTRESS!
NO SHIT?
SHE LIKED TO IMAGINE THE LIVES THESE PEOPLE LIVED.
AW, WHO KNOWS, REALLY?
HELL, WE GET PAID NOT TO ASK QUESTIONS.
RIGHT. BUT THERE WAS SO MUCH BLOOD!
USUALLY THE TALK IN THE DINER WAS MUNDANE AND BORING.
YEAH, HE WAS A FUCKING FOUNTAIN! HA! HA! HA!
I HATE CLEANING UP THOSE LITTLE GLOBS—THEY GET INTO EVERYTHING!
CHOMP!
CHOMP!
BUT OCCASIONALLY SHE OVERHEARD MORE INTRIGUING CONVERSATIONS.
WE SHOULD GET PAID EXTRA FOR THOSE GLOBS!
CHOMP CHOMP
YEAH, RIGHT?
HA! HA!
HA! HA! HA!
I'M GETTING LARGE FRIES AND CHOCOLATE CAKE!
HA!
AND ONION RINGS!
HA! HA!
BREAKFAST OF CHAMPIONS!
HA! HA! HA!

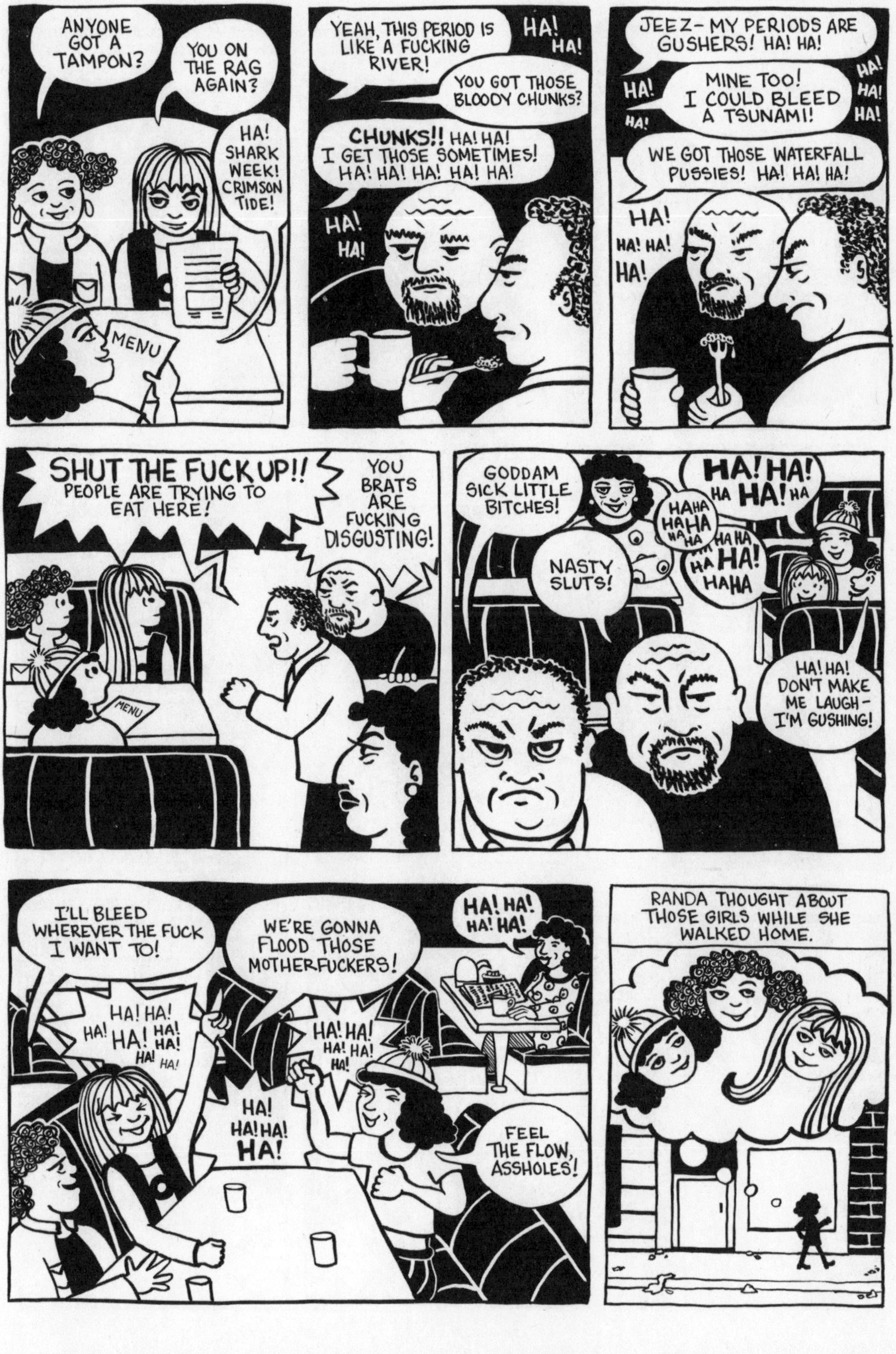
ANYONE GOT A TAMPON?
YOU ON THE RAG AGAIN?
HA! SHARK WEEK! CRIMSON TIDE!
MENU
YEAH, THIS PERIOD IS LIKE A FUCKING RIVER!
HA! HA!
YOU GOT THOSE BLOODY CHUNKS?
CHUNKS!! HA! HA! I GET THOSE SOMETIMES! HA! HA! HA! HA! HA!
HA! HA!
JEEZ- MY PERIODS ARE GUSHERS! HA! HA!
HA! HA!
MINE TOO! I COULD BLEED A TSUNAMI!
HA! HA! HA!
WE GOT THOSE WATERFALL PUSSIES! HA! HA! HA!
HA! HA! HA! HA!
SHUT THE FUCK UP!! PEOPLE ARE TRYING TO EAT HERE!
YOU BRATS ARE FUCKING DISGUSTING!
MENU
GODDAM SICK LITTLE BITCHES!
NASTY SLUTS!
HA! HA! HA HA! HA
HAHA HAHA HAHA
HA HA HA HA! HAHA
HA! HA! DON'T MAKE ME LAUGH- I'M GUSHING!
I'LL BLEED WHEREVER THE FUCK I WANT TO!
WE'RE GONNA FLOOD THOSE MOTHERFUCKERS!
HA! HA! HA! HA!
HA! HA! HA! HA! HA! HA! HA! HA!
HA! HA! HA! HA! HA!
HA! HA! HA! HA!
FEEL THE FLOW, ASSHOLES!
RANDA THOUGHT ABOUT THOSE GIRLS WHILE SHE WALKED HOME.

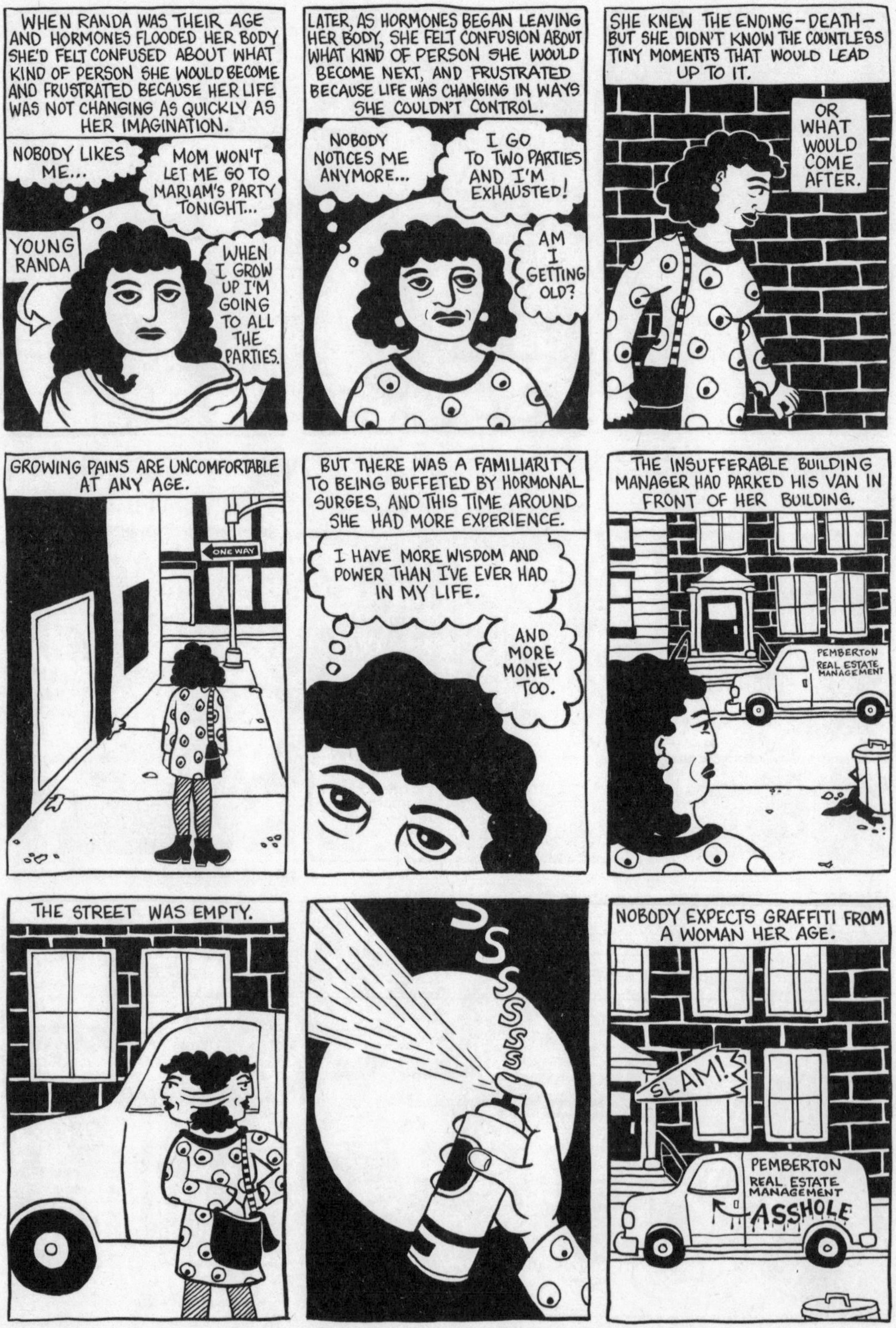
WHEN RANDA WAS THEIR AGE AND HORMONES FLOODED HER BODY SHE'D FELT CONFUSED ABOUT WHAT KIND OF PERSON SHE WOULD BECOME AND FRUSTRATED BECAUSE HER LIFE WAS NOT CHANGING AS QUICKLY AS HER IMAGINATION.
NOBODY LIKES ME...
MOM WON'T LET ME GO TO MARIAM'S PARTY TONIGHT...
YOUNG RANDA
WHEN I GROW UP I'M GOING TO ALL THE PARTIES.
LATER, AS HORMONES BEGAN LEAVING HER BODY, SHE FELT CONFUSION ABOUT WHAT KIND OF PERSON SHE WOULD BECOME NEXT, AND FRUSTRATED BECAUSE LIFE WAS CHANGING IN WAYS SHE COULDN'T CONTROL.
NOBODY NOTICES ME ANYMORE...
I GO TO TWO PARTIES AND I'M EXHAUSTED!
AM I GETTING OLD?
SHE KNEW THE ENDING—DEATH—BUT SHE DIDN'T KNOW THE COUNTLESS TINY MOMENTS THAT WOULD LEAD UP TO IT.
OR WHAT WOULD COME AFTER.
GROWING PAINS ARE UNCOMFORTABLE AT ANY AGE.
ONE WAY
BUT THERE WAS A FAMILIARITY TO BEING BUFFETED BY HORMONAL SURGES, AND THIS TIME AROUND SHE HAD MORE EXPERIENCE.
I HAVE MORE WISDOM AND POWER THAN I'VE EVER HAD IN MY LIFE.
AND MORE MONEY TOO.
THE INSUFFERABLE BUILDING MANAGER HAD PARKED HIS VAN IN FRONT OF HER BUILDING.
PEMBERTON REAL ESTATE MANAGEMENT
THE STREET WAS EMPTY.
SSSSSS
NOBODY EXPECTS GRAFFITI FROM A WOMAN HER AGE.
SLAM!
PEMBERTON REAL ESTATE MANAGEMENT
ASSHOLE

SURE, SHE DIDN'T HAVE THE SAME ENERGY AS BEFORE, BUT SHE ALSO DIDN'T LOSE THREE DAYS EVERY MONTH TO CRAMPS AND LANGOUR.

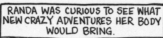

RANDA WAS CURIOUS TO SEE WHAT NEW CRAZY ADVENTURES HER BODY WOULD BRING.

STILL DRIPPING...

BUT WHAT SHOULD SHE DO WITH THAT LAST BOX OF TAMPONS?

TAMPONS

INEVITABLY, SOME VISITING FRIEND WOULD START BLEEDING UNPREPARED.

TAMPONS

SO SHE LEFT THE BOX IN THE BATHROOM FOR GUESTS.

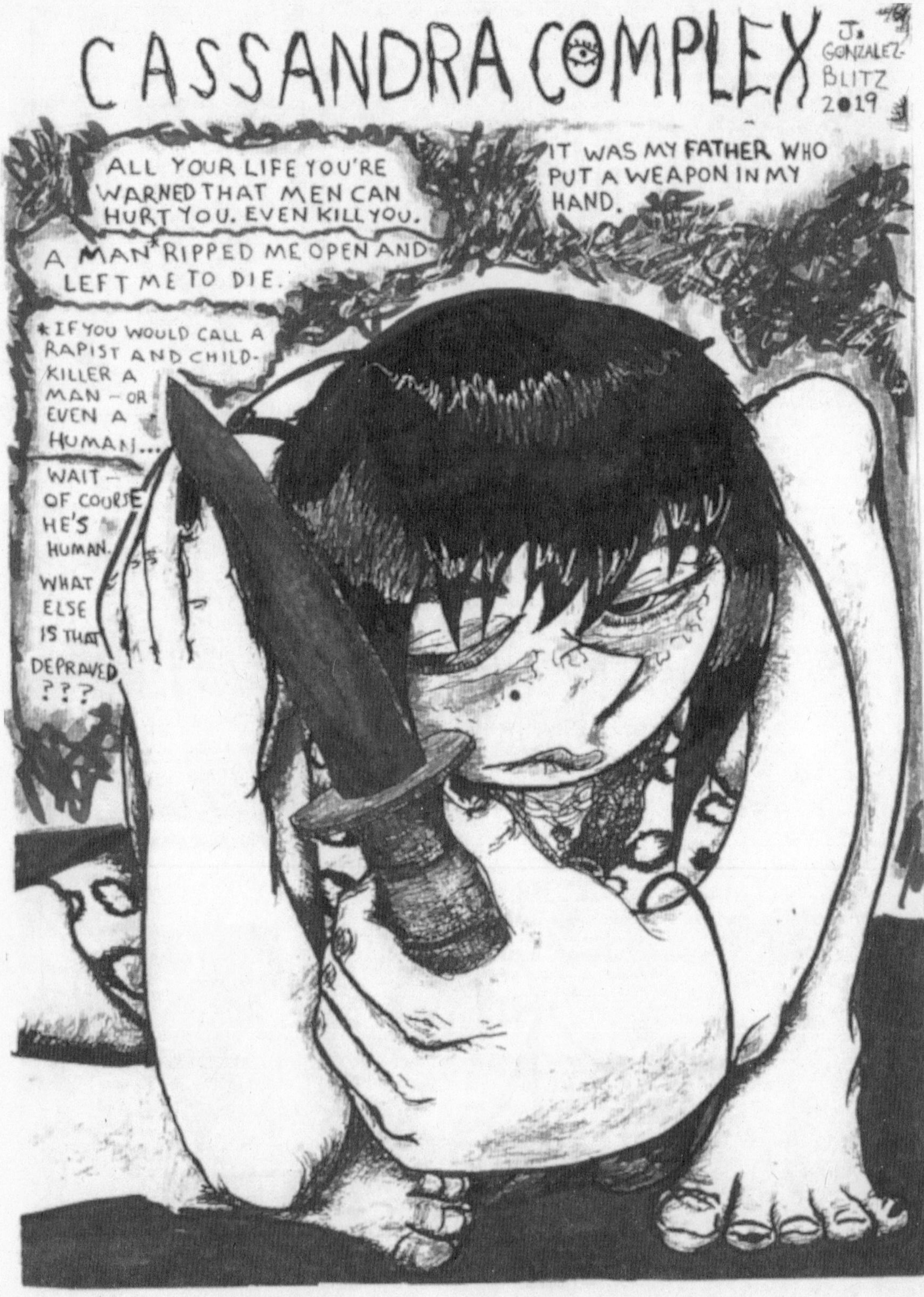
CASSANDRA COMPLEX
J. GONZALEZ-BLITZ 2019
ALL YOUR LIFE YOU'RE WARNED THAT MEN CAN HURT YOU. EVEN KILL YOU.
A MAN* RIPPED ME OPEN AND LEFT ME TO DIE.
*IF YOU WOULD CALL A RAPIST AND CHILD-KILLER A MAN — OR EVEN A HUMAN...
WAIT — OF COURSE HE'S HUMAN.
WHAT ELSE IS THAT DEPRAVED???
IT WAS MY FATHER WHO PUT A WEAPON IN MY HAND.

WHENEVER THEY'VE SAID I'M OVEREACTING I'VE FELT LIKE THEY WERE UNDER-REACTING, WILLFULLY CHOOSING TO IGNORE THAT WHICH HARSHED THEIR BUZZ, MADE THEM UNCOMFORTABLE—

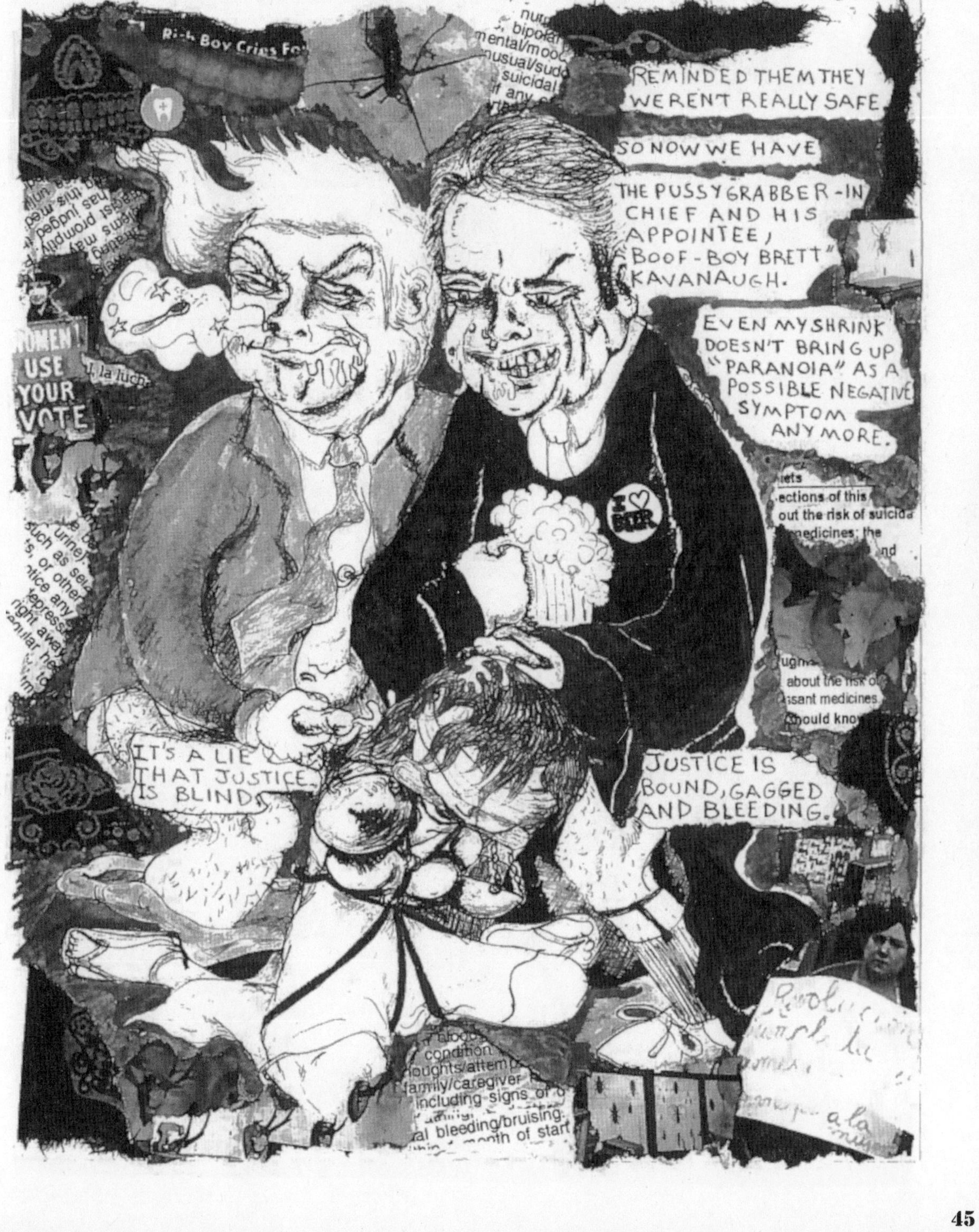
REMINDED THEM THEY WERENT REALLY SAFE.
SO NOW WE HAVE
THE PUSSYGRABBER-IN CHIEF AND HIS APPOINTEE, "BOOF-BOY BRETT" KAVANAUGH.
EVEN MY SHRINK DOESN'T BRING UP "PARANOIA" AS A POSSIBLE NEGATIVE SYMPTOM ANYMORE.
IT'S A LIE THAT JUSTICE IS BLIND.
JUSTICE IS BOUND, GAGGED AND BLEEDING.

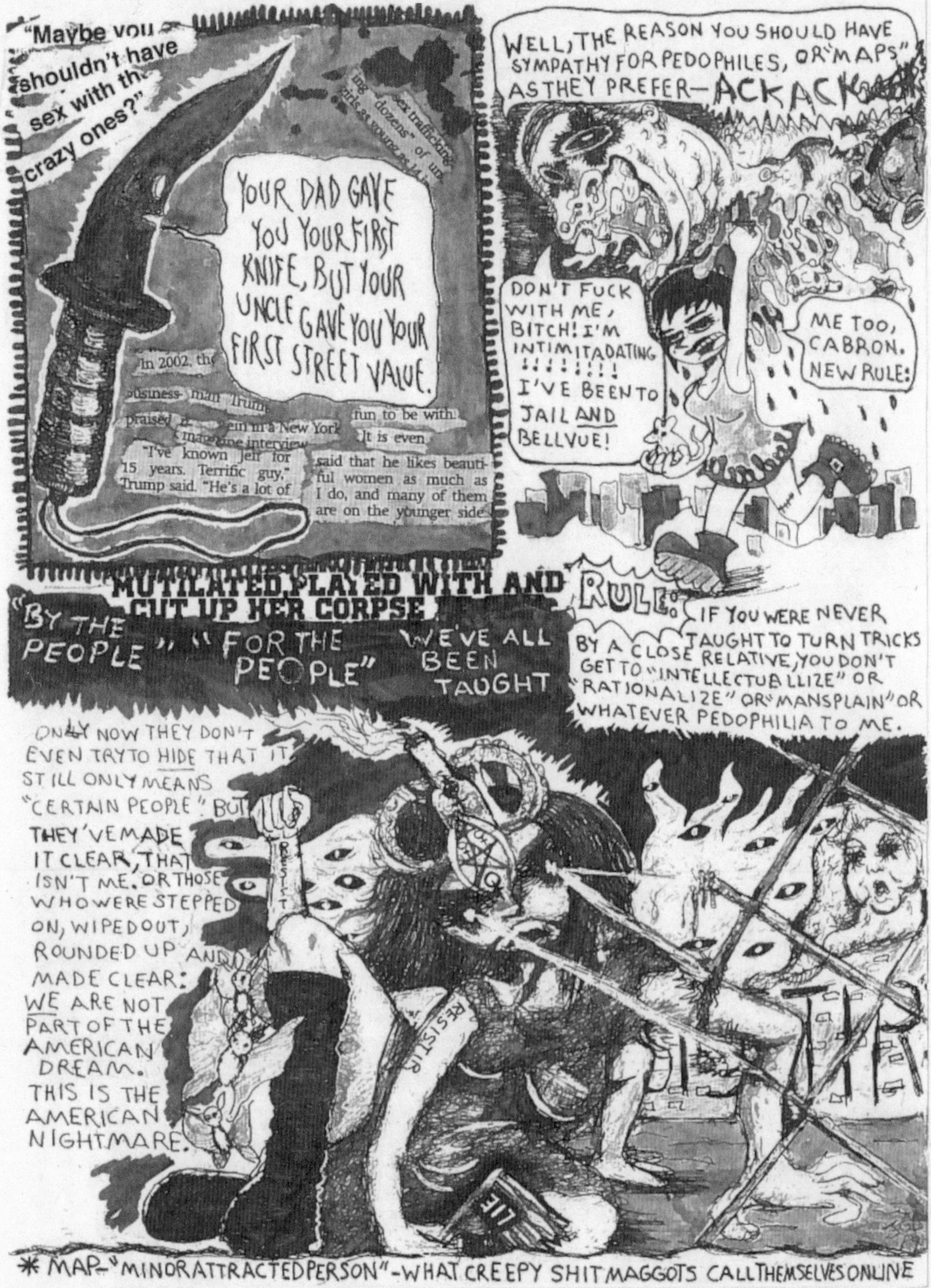
"Maybe you shouldn't have sex with the crazy ones?"
sex trafficking "dozens" of un... girls as young as 14
YOUR DAD GAVE YOU YOUR FIRST KNIFE, BUT YOUR UNCLE GAVE YOU YOUR FIRST STREET VALUE.
In 2002, the
business- man Trump
praised
ein in a New York
magazine interview
"I've known Jeff for 15 years. Terrific guy," Trump said. "He's a lot of
fun to be with. It is even
said that he likes beautiful women as much as I do, and many of them are on the younger side
WELL, THE REASON YOU SHOULD HAVE SYMPATHY FOR PEDOPHILES, OR "MAPS"* AS THEY PREFER—ACKACK
DON'T FUCK WITH ME, BITCH! I'M INTIMITADATING !!!!!!!! I'VE BEEN TO JAIL AND BELLVUE!
ME TOO, CABRON. NEW RULE:
MUTILATED, PLAYED WITH AND CUT UP HER CORPSE
"BY THE PEOPLE" "FOR THE PEOPLE" WE'VE ALL BEEN TAUGHT
RULE: IF YOU WERE NEVER TAUGHT TO TURN TRICKS BY A CLOSE RELATIVE, YOU DON'T GET TO "INTELLECTUALLIZE" OR "RATIONALIZE" OR "MANSPLAIN" OR WHATEVER PEDOPHILIA TO ME.
ONLY NOW THEY DON'T EVEN TRY TO HIDE THAT IT STILL ONLY MEANS "CERTAIN PEOPLE". BUT THEY'VE MADE IT CLEAR, THAT ISN'T ME. OR THOSE WHO WERE STEPPED ON, WIPED OUT, ROUNDED UP AND MADE CLEAR: WE ARE NOT PART OF THE AMERICAN DREAM. THIS IS THE AMERICAN NIGHTMARE.
RESIST
RESISTIR
LIE
* MAP—"MINOR ATTRACTED PERSON"—WHAT CREEPY SHIT MAGGOTS CALL THEMSELVES ONLINE

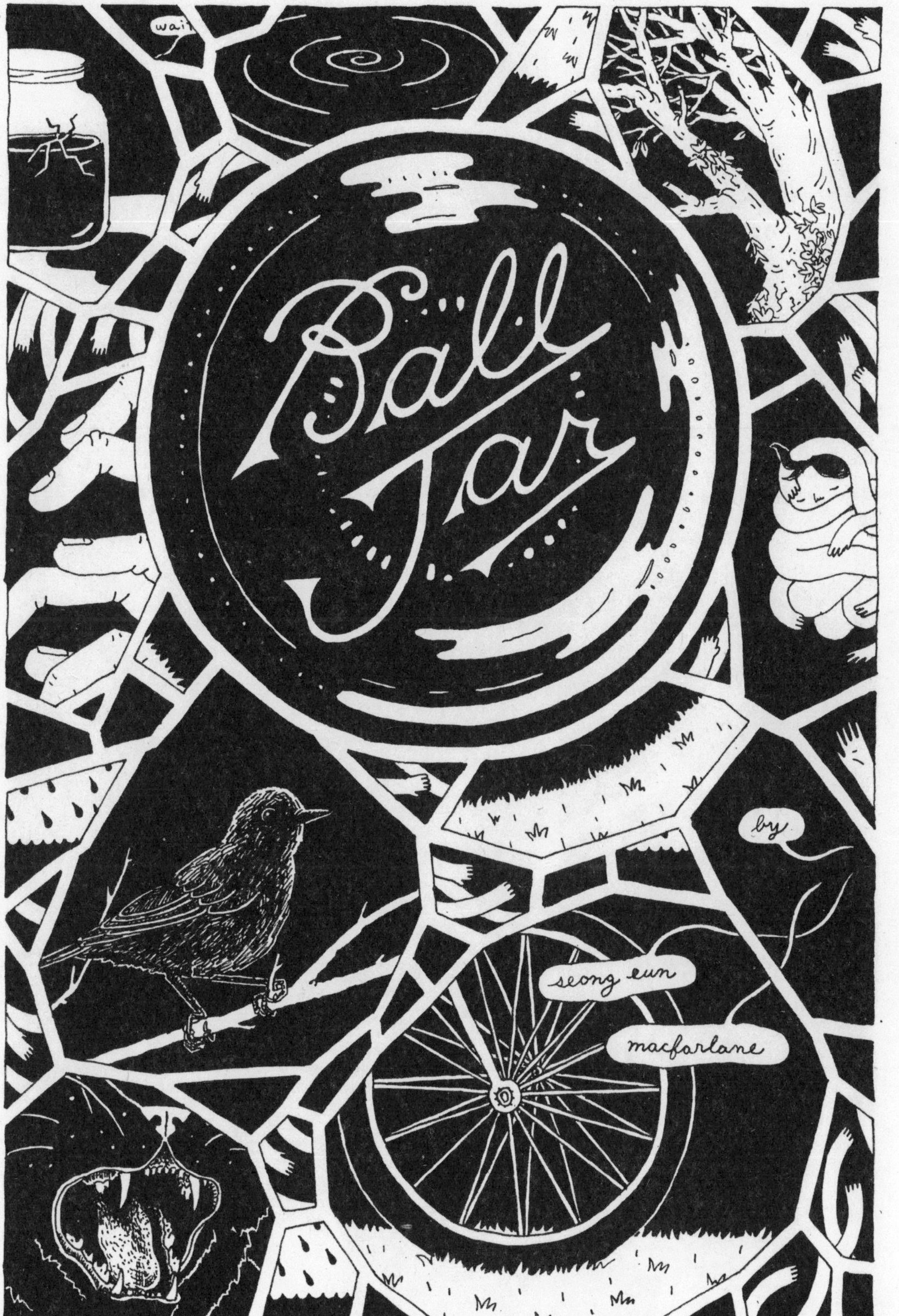
wait
Ball Jar
by
seong eun
macfarlane

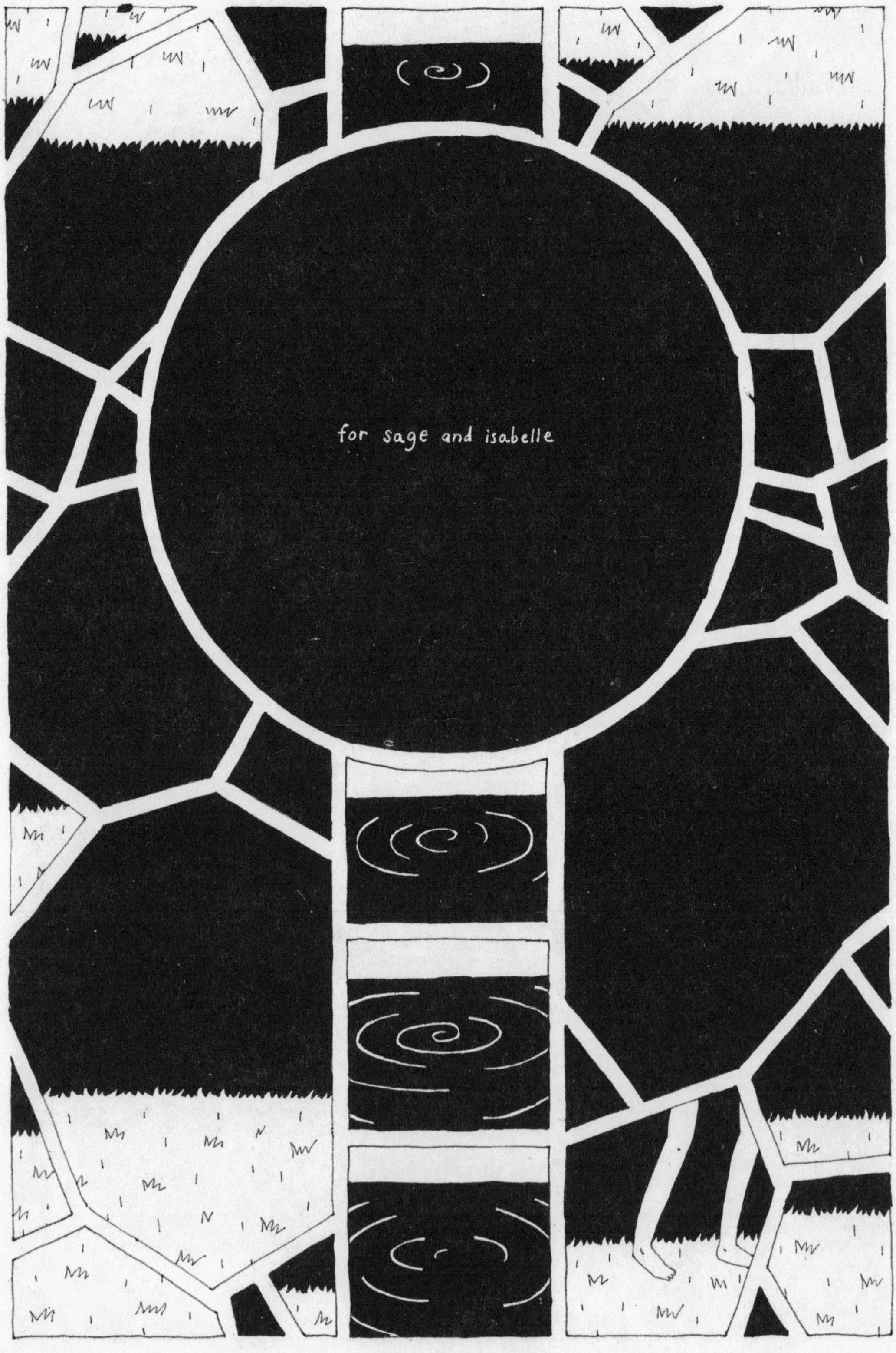
for sage and isabelle

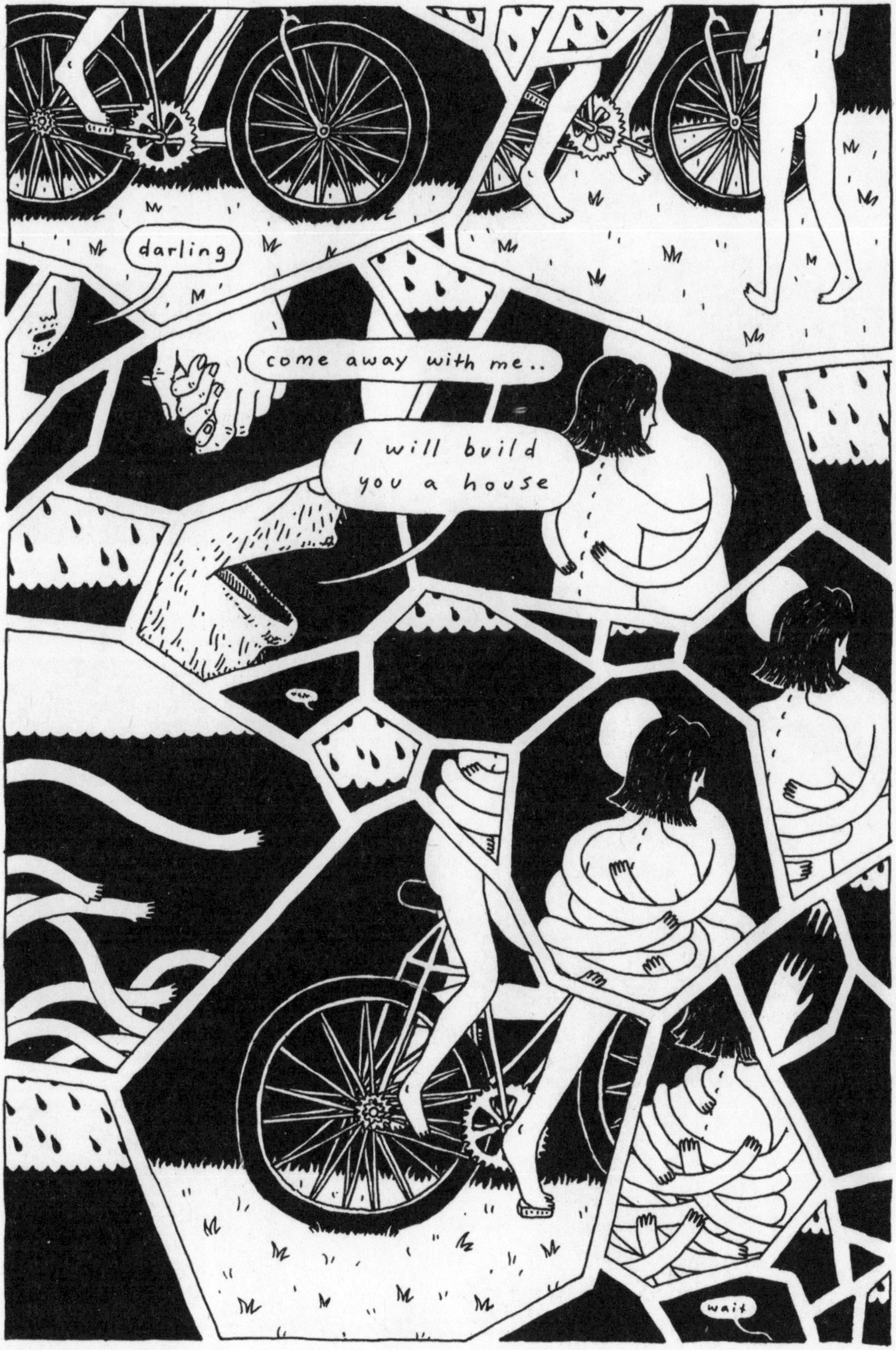
darling
come away with me..
I will build you a house
wait

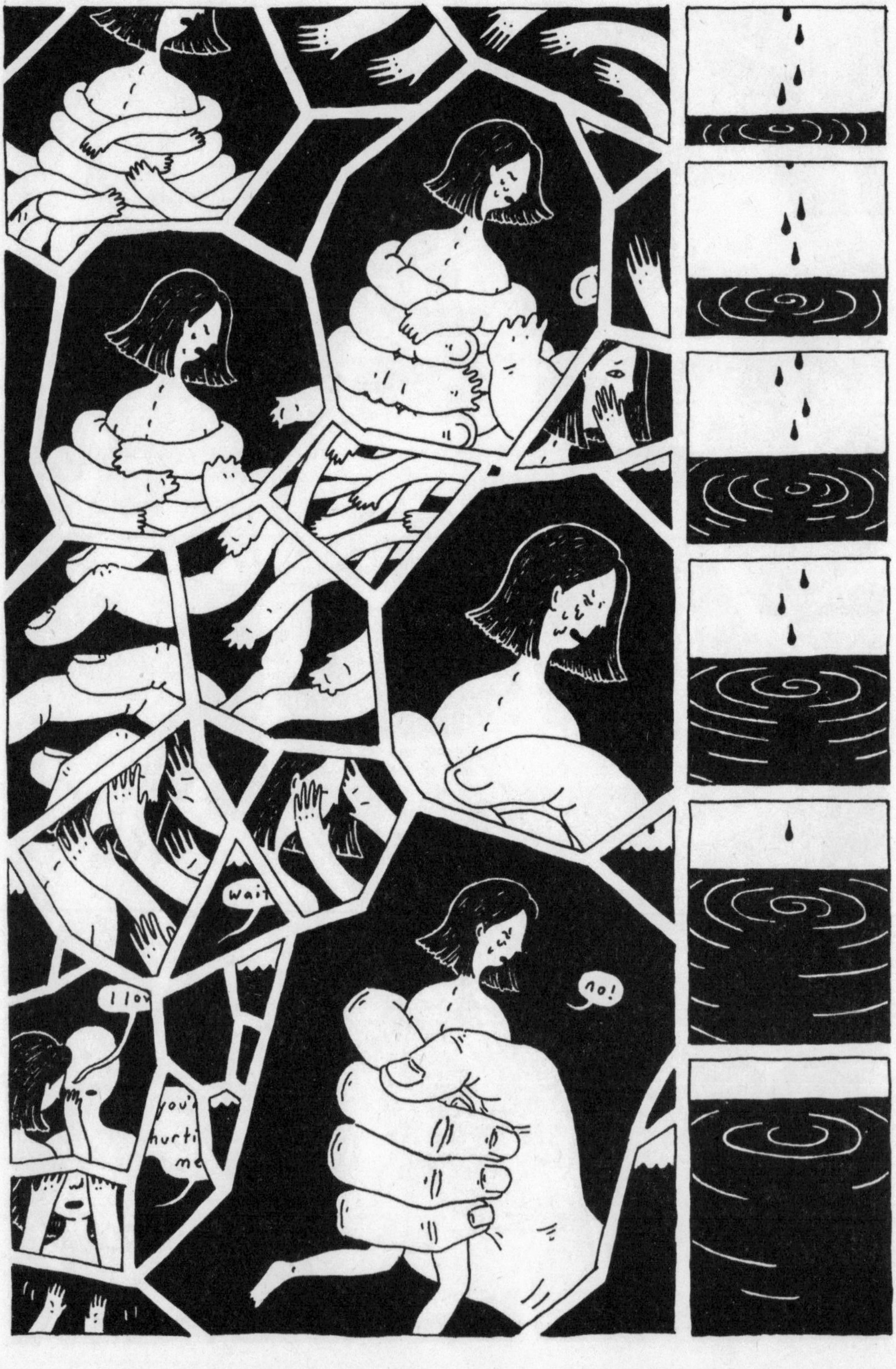
wait
I lov
you'
hurti
me
no!

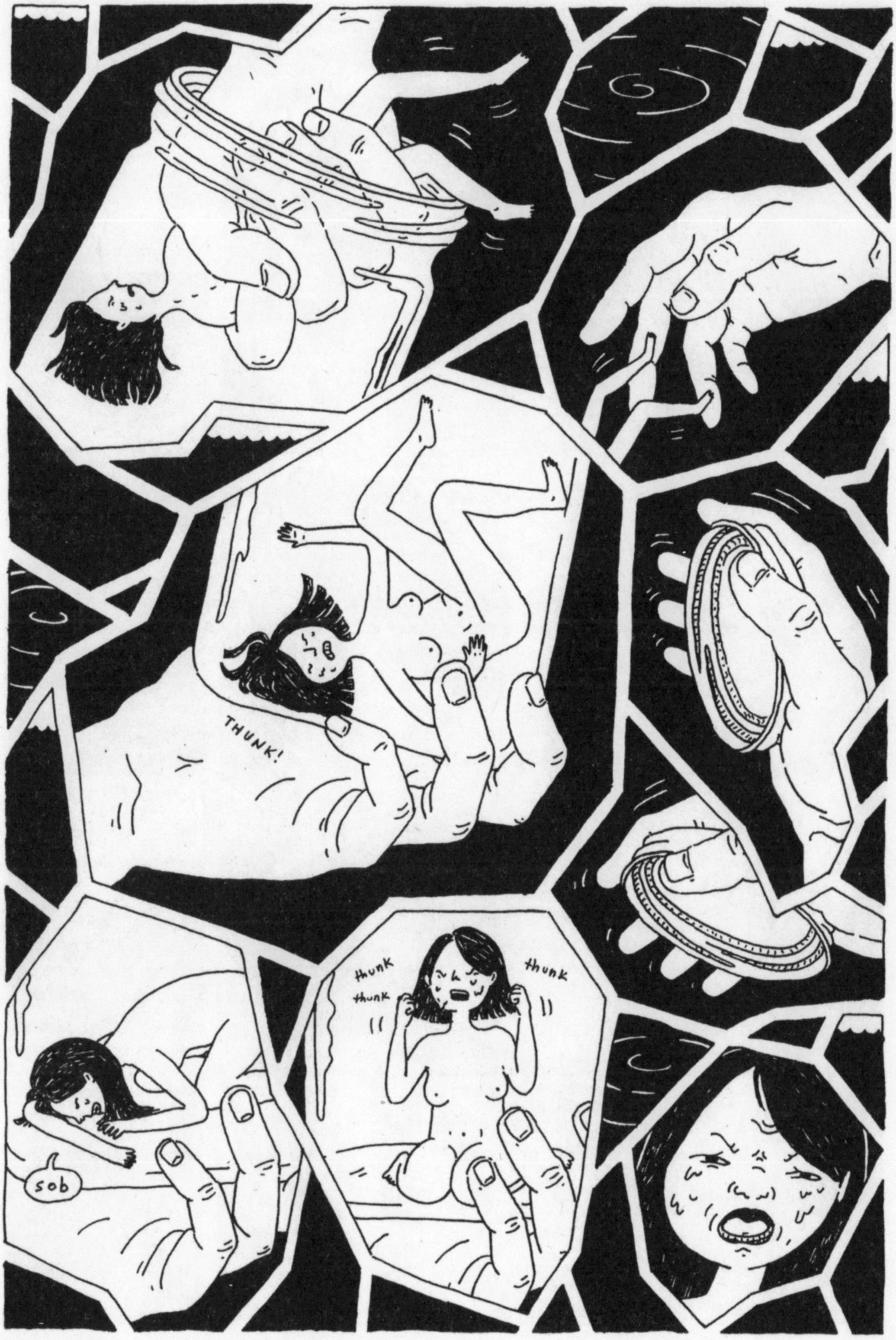
THUNK!
sob
thunk
thunk
thunk

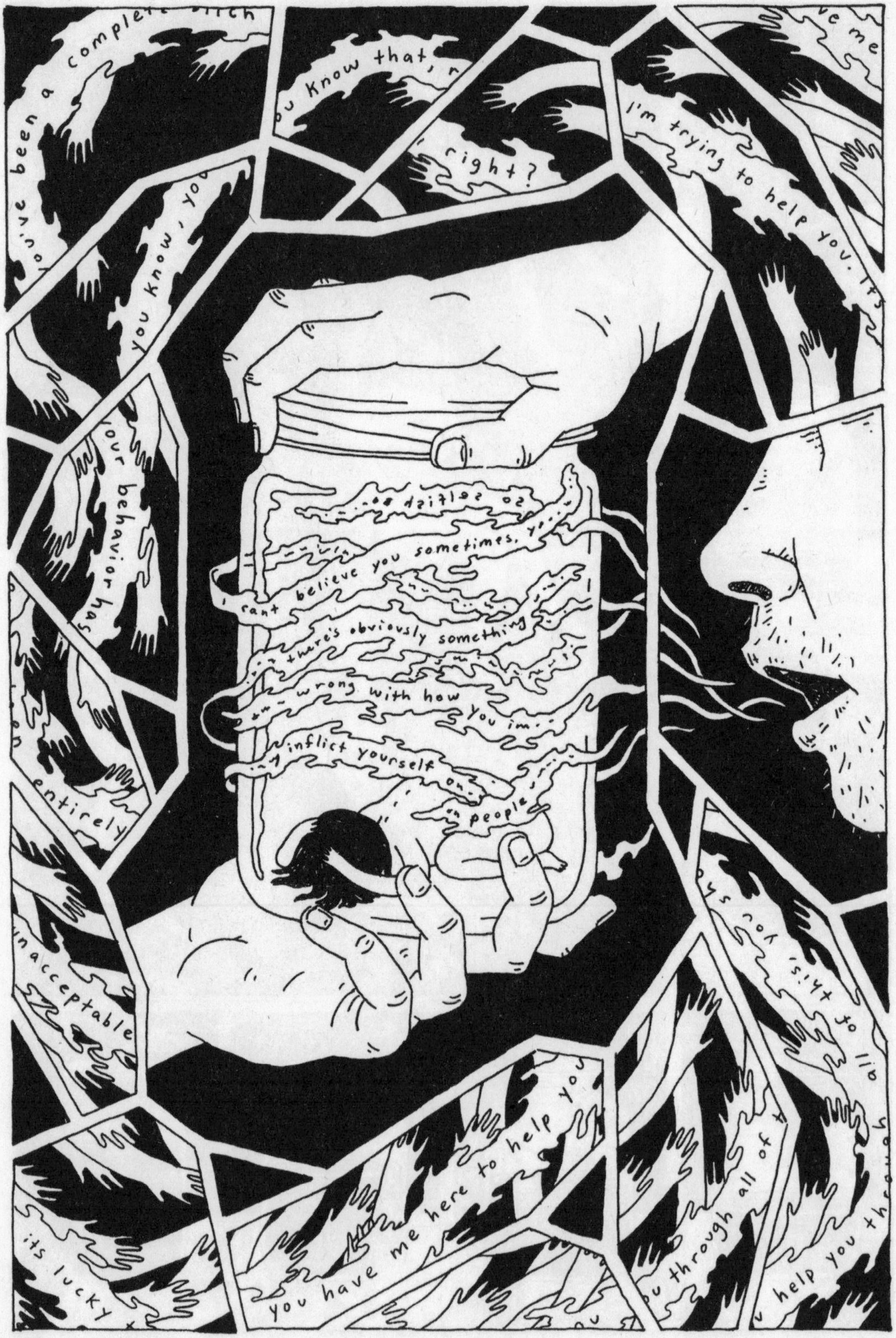
been a complete
you know, you
your behavior has
entirely
acceptable
you know that,
right?
I'm trying to help you. It's
so selfish so
I cant believe you sometimes.
there's obviously something
wrong with how
you im
inflict yourself on
on people
its lucky
you have me here to help you
through all of
help you through
all
of this, you

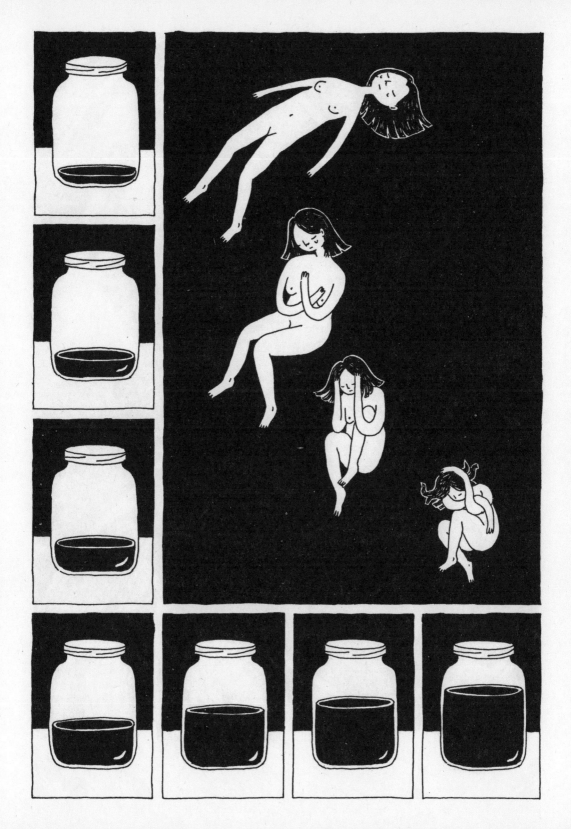

53

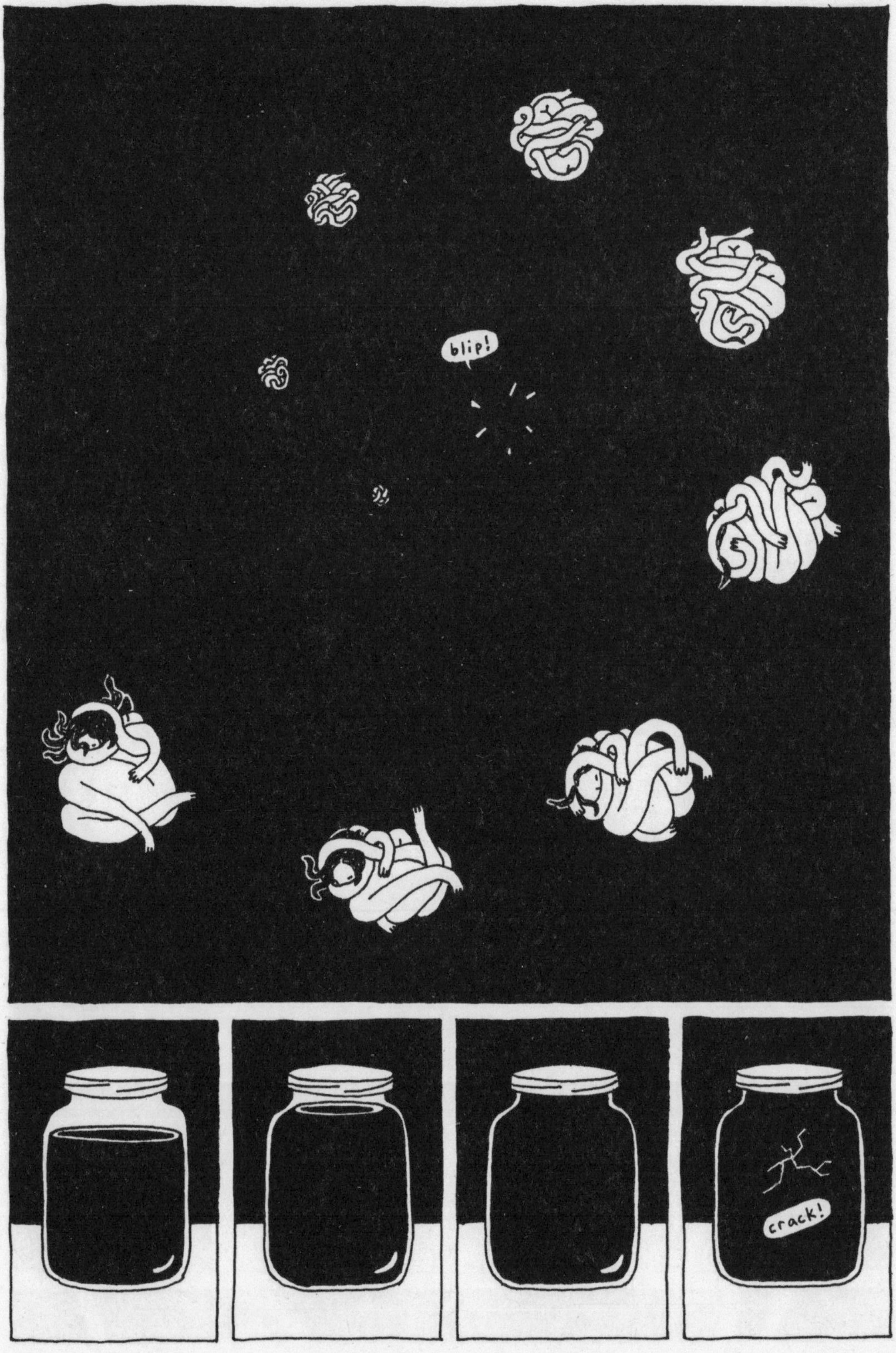
blip!
crack!

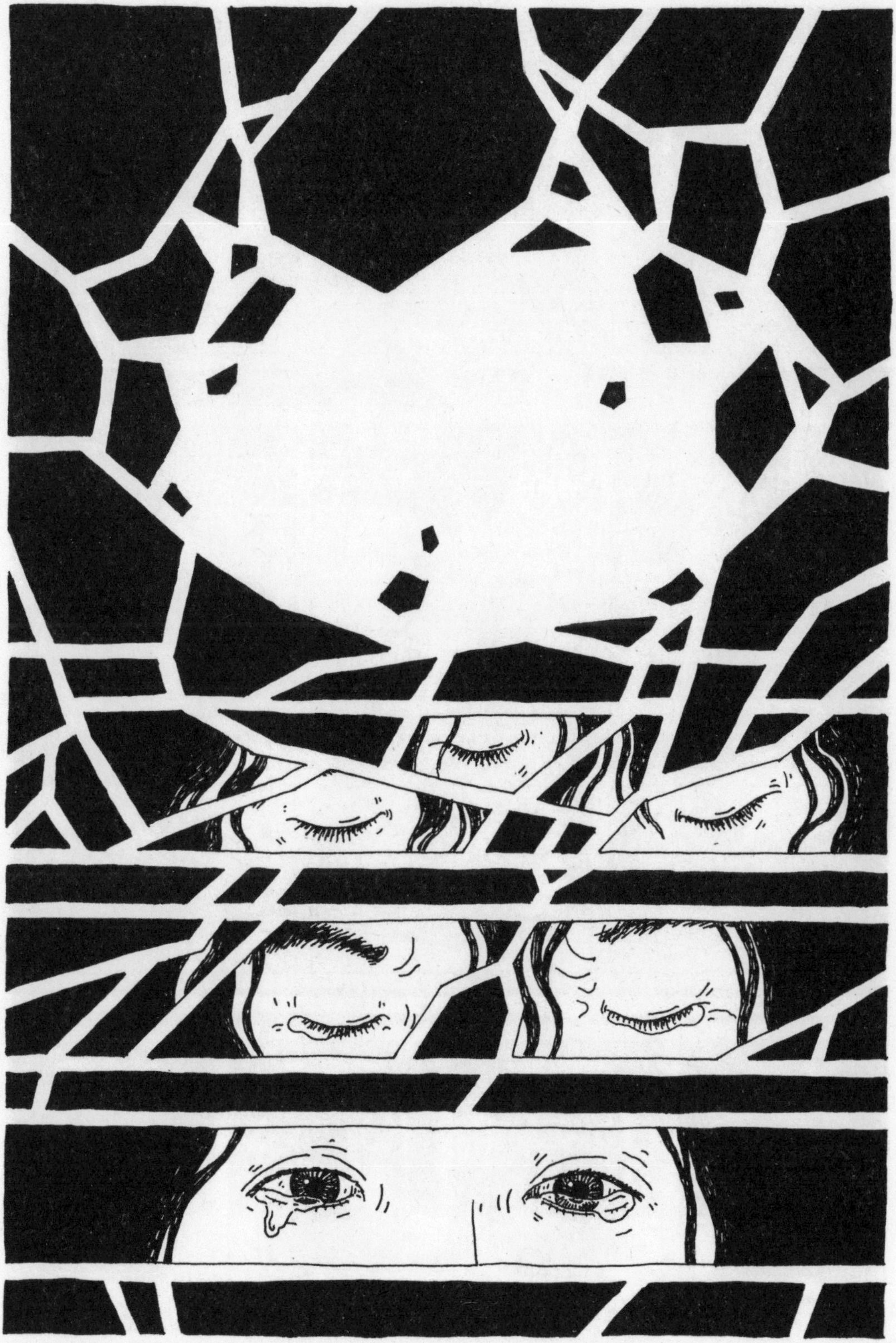

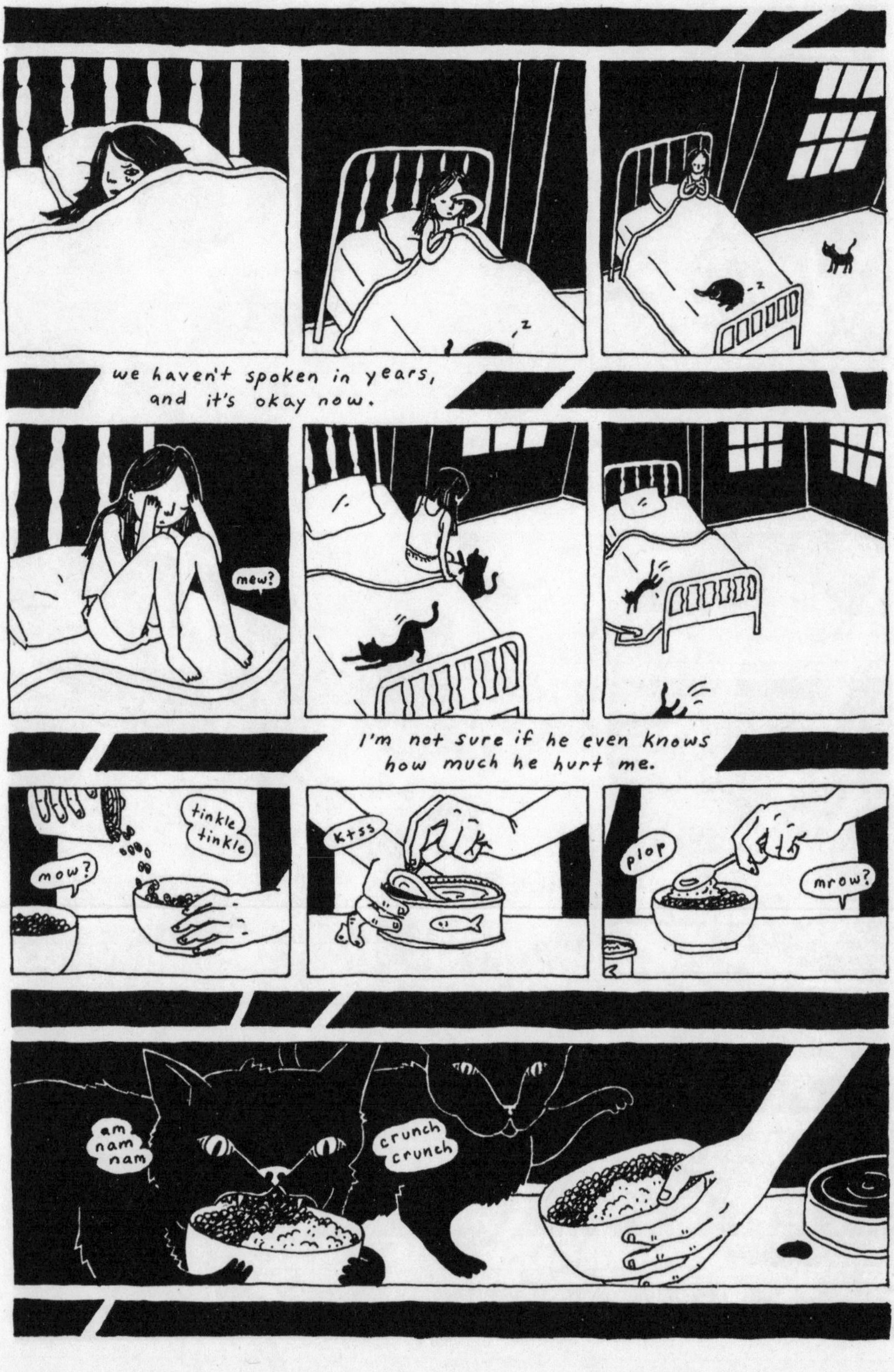
z
z
we haven't spoken in years,
and it's okay now.
mew?
I'm not sure if he even knows
how much he hurt me.
tinkle
tinkle
mow?
ktss
plop
mrow?
am
nam
nam
crunch
crunch

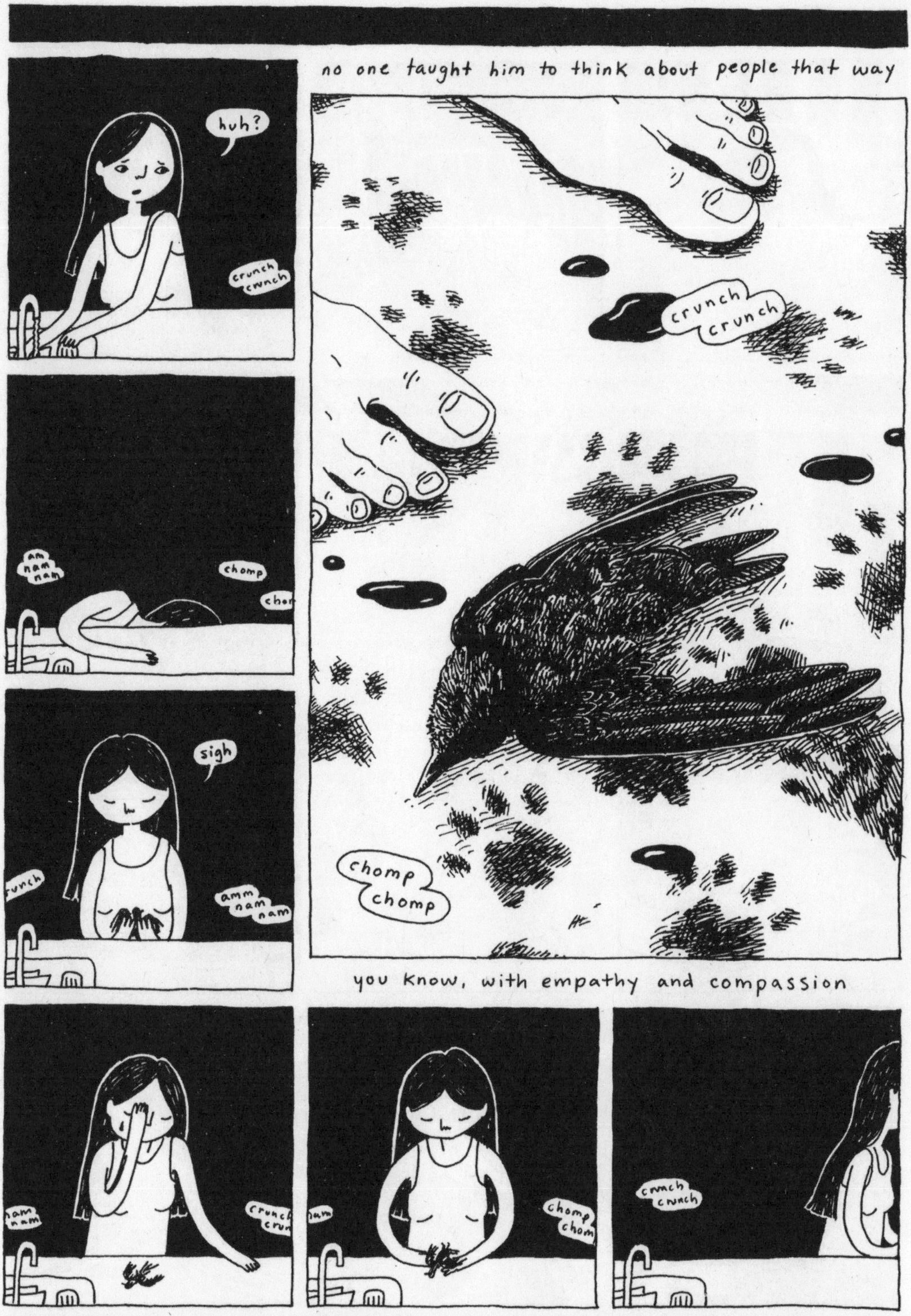

no one taught him to think about people that way
huh?
crunch crunch
crunch crunch
am nam nam
chomp
sigh
amm nam nam
chomp chomp
you know, with empathy and compassion
crunch crunch

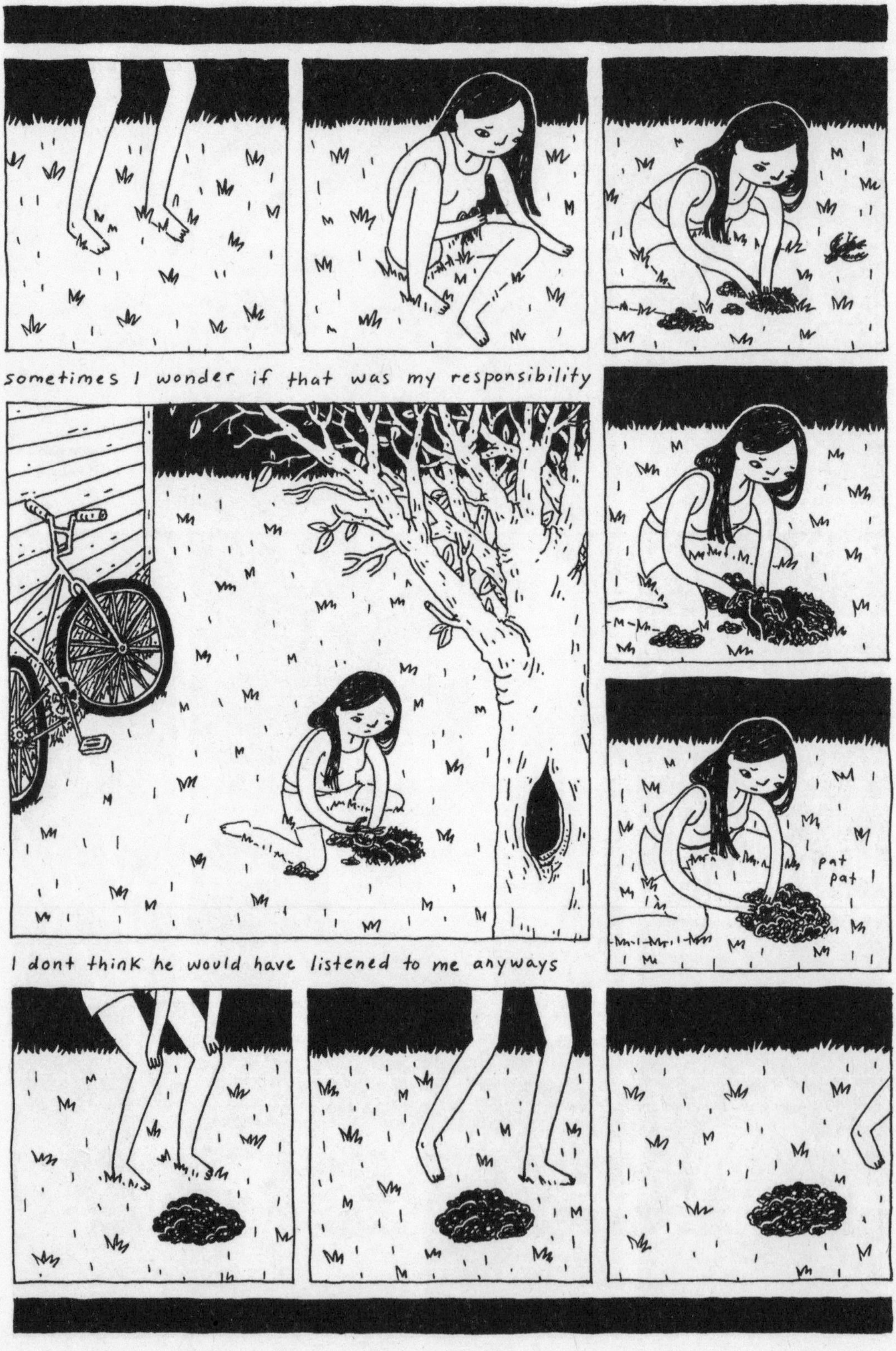
sometimes I wonder if that was my responsibility
pat pat
I dont think he would have listened to me anyways

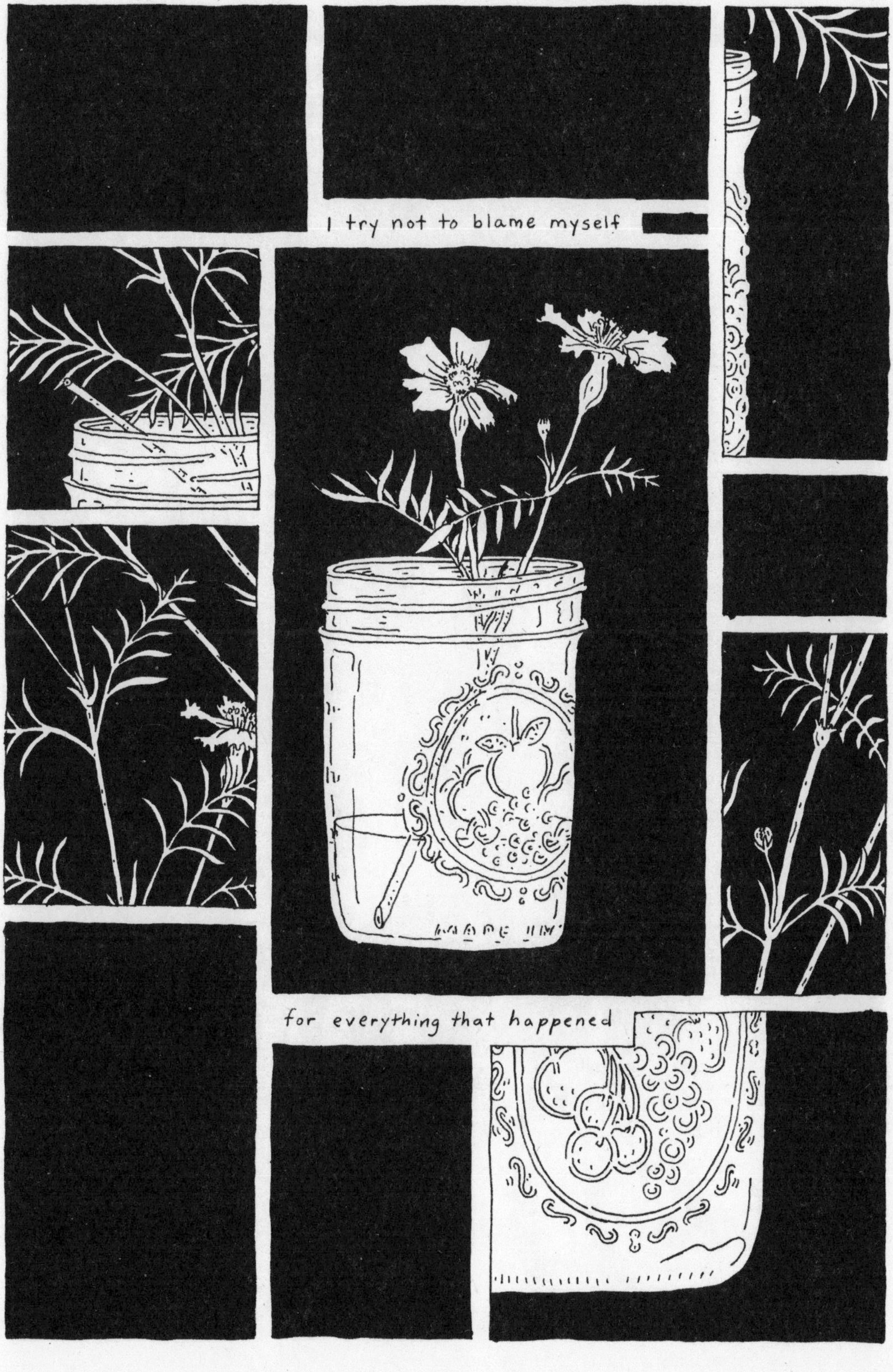
I try not to blame myself
for everything that happened

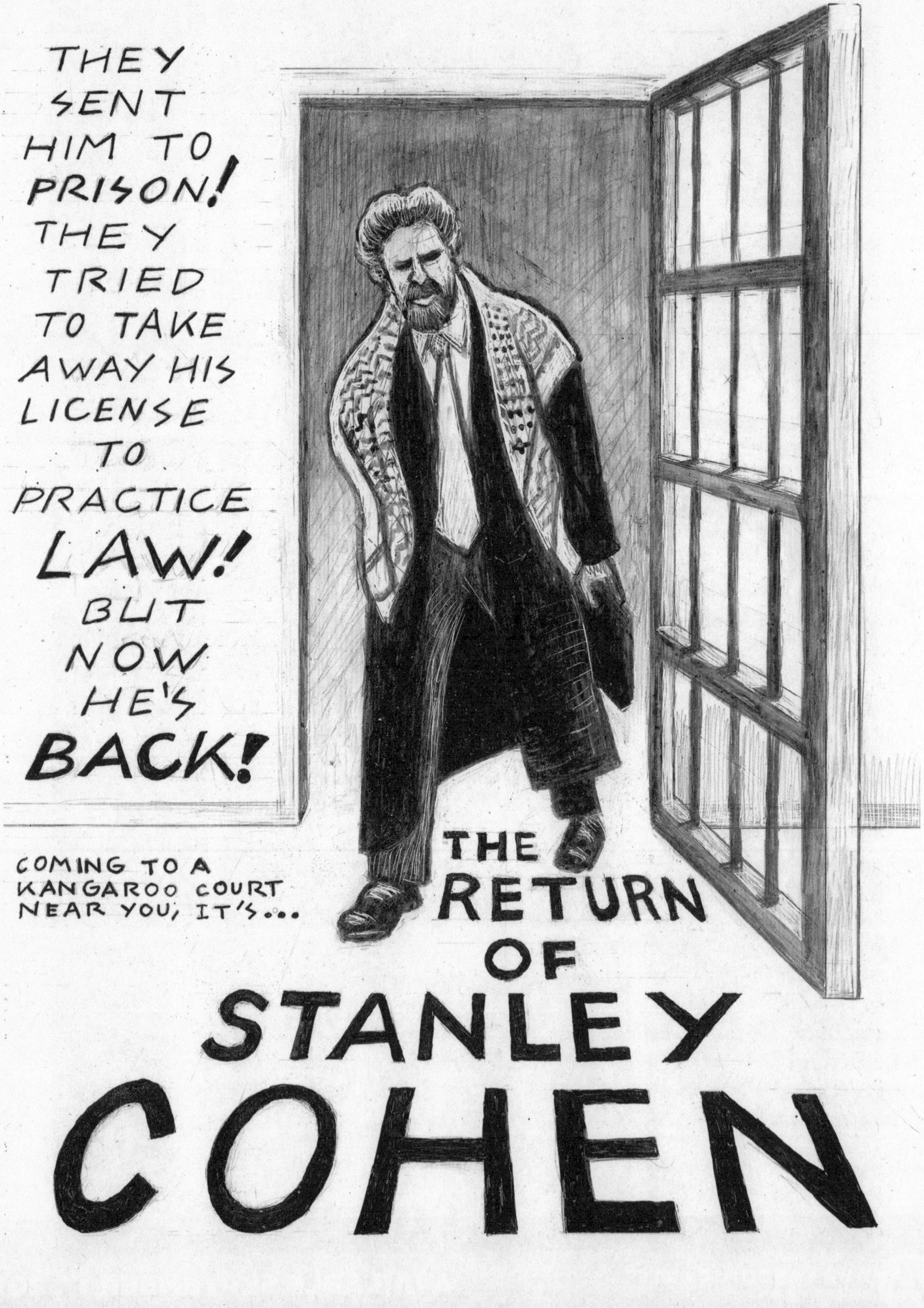
THEY SENT HIM TO PRISON! THEY TRIED TO TAKE AWAY HIS LICENSE TO PRACTICE LAW! BUT NOW HE'S BACK!
COMING TO A KANGAROO COURT NEAR YOU, IT'S...
THE RETURN OF STANLEY COHEN

normel Person

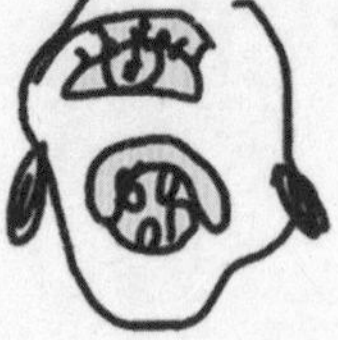

MOTHERS, ARTISTS, CAPITALISM.

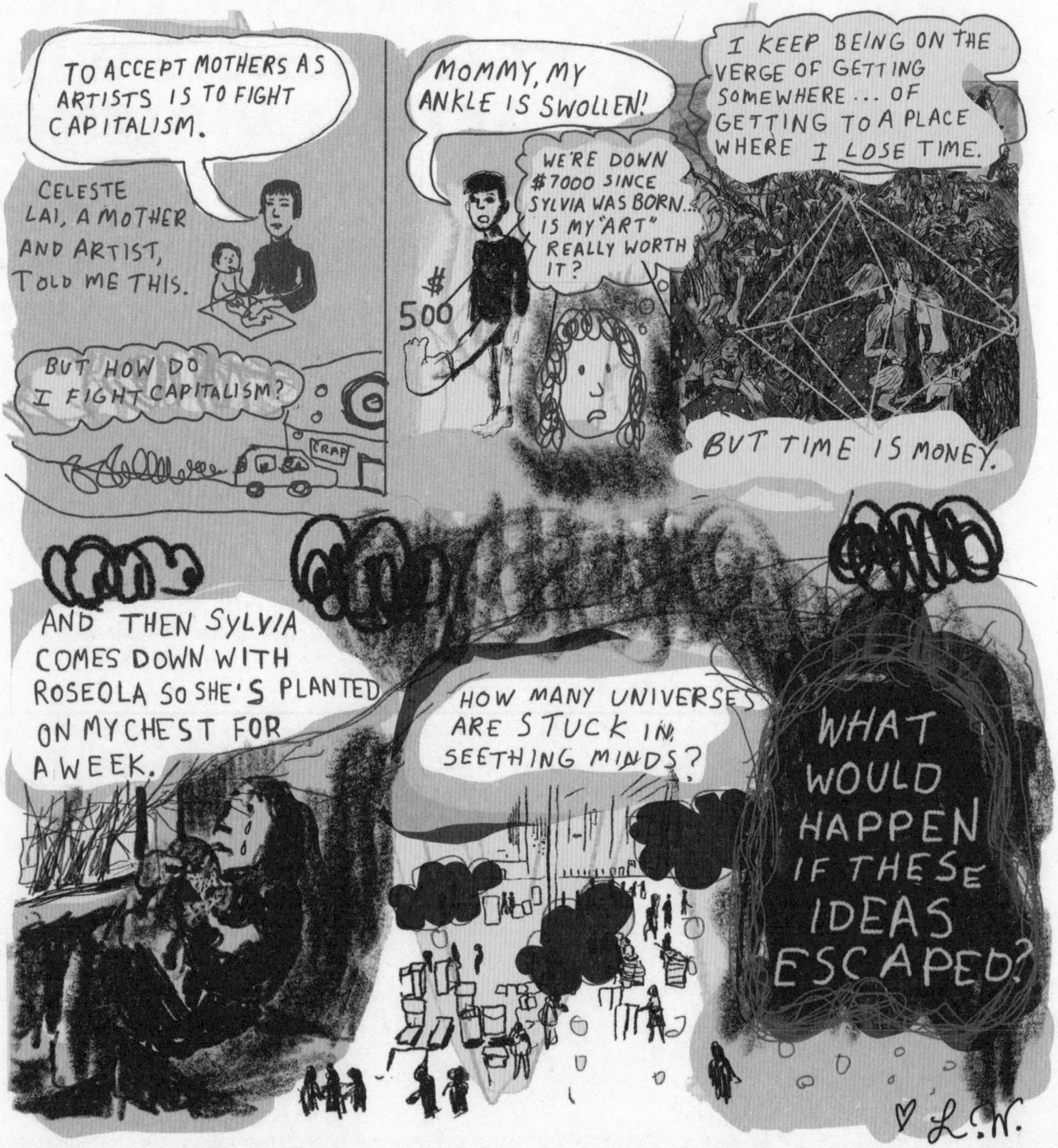

TO ACCEPT MOTHERS AS ARTISTS IS TO FIGHT CAPITALISM.
CELESTE LAI, A MOTHER AND ARTIST, TOLD ME THIS.
BUT HOW DO I FIGHT CAPITALISM?
CRAP
MOMMY, MY ANKLE IS SWOLLEN!
WE'RE DOWN $7000 SINCE SYLVIA WAS BORN... IS MY "ART" REALLY WORTH IT?
$500
I KEEP BEING ON THE VERGE OF GETTING SOMEWHERE... OF GETTING TO A PLACE WHERE I LOSE TIME.
BUT TIME IS MONEY.
AND THEN SYLVIA COMES DOWN WITH ROSEOLA SO SHE'S PLANTED ON MY CHEST FOR A WEEK.
HOW MANY UNIVERSES ARE STUCK IN SEETHING MINDS?
WHAT WOULD HAPPEN IF THESE IDEAS ESCAPED?
♡ L.N.

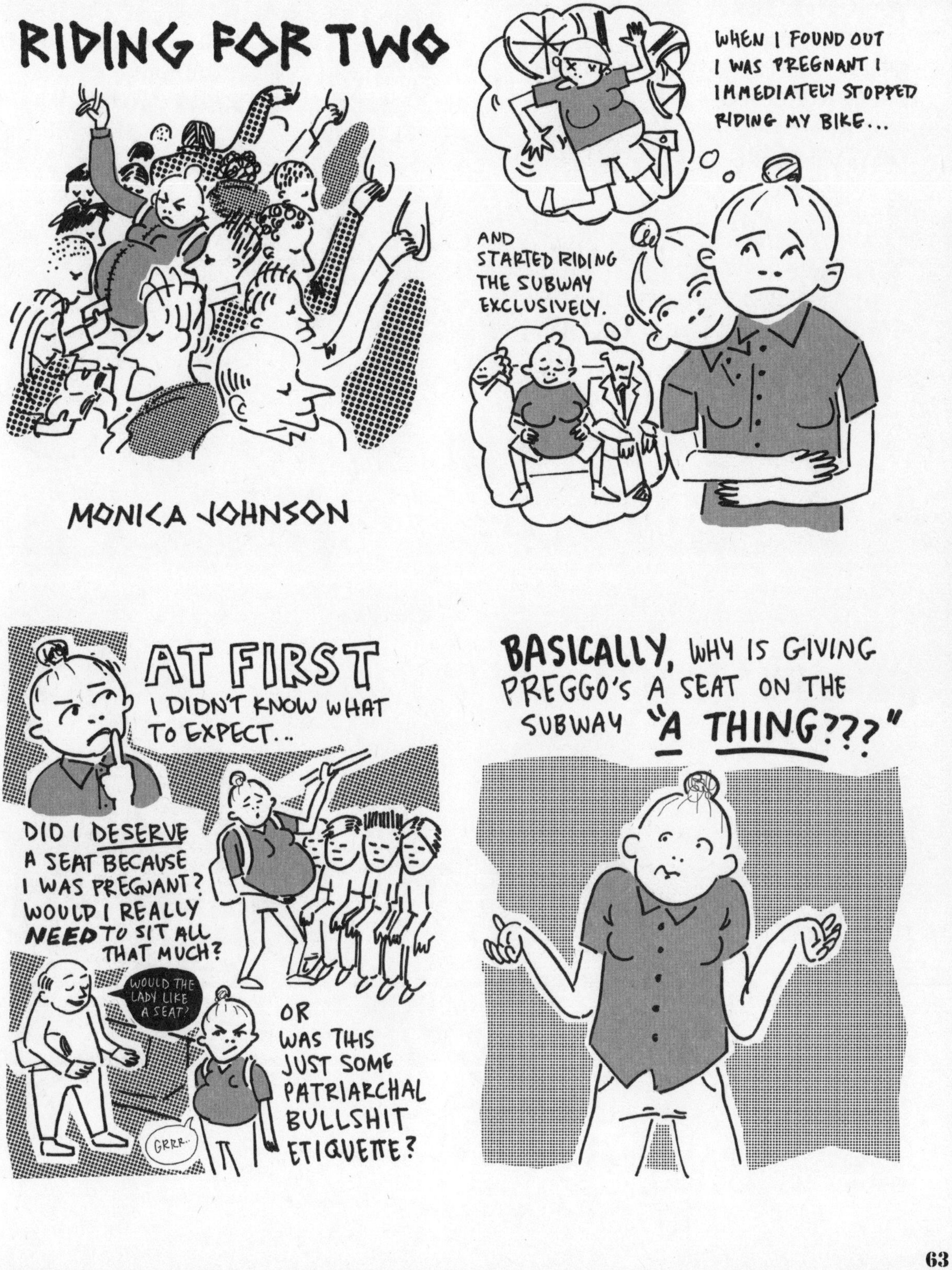
RIDING FOR TWO
MONICA JOHNSON
WHEN I FOUND OUT I WAS PREGNANT I IMMEDIATELY STOPPED RIDING MY BIKE...
AND STARTED RIDING THE SUBWAY EXCLUSIVELY.
AT FIRST I DIDN'T KNOW WHAT TO EXPECT...
DID I DESERVE A SEAT BECAUSE I WAS PREGNANT? WOULD I REALLY NEED TO SIT ALL THAT MUCH?
WOULD THE LADY LIKE A SEAT?
OR WAS THIS JUST SOME PATRIARCHAL BULLSHIT ETIQUETTE?
GRRR..
BASICALLY, WHY IS GIVING PREGGO'S A SEAT ON THE SUBWAY "A THING???"

FOR STARTERS PREGNANT BODIES ARE EXHAUSTED FROM *PRODUCING* AND *PUMPING* **50% MORE BLOOD.** (!!!)

THE BODY ITSELF IS **25-40** LBS. HEAVIER AND BEARING DOWN ON **SWOLLEN FEET** WITH **COLLAPSING ARCHES.**

AND THANKS TO A HORMONE CALLED **"RELAXIN"** (This is real, I am not playing) THOSE EXTRA POUNDS ARE SITTING ON **LOOSE N' SQUISHY JOINTS.**

GOOD FOR PUSHING A BABY OUT OF YER PELVIS

BAD FOR HIPS, KNEES + LOW BACK

DEFINITELY A DESIGN FLAW...

AND THEN THERE'S...

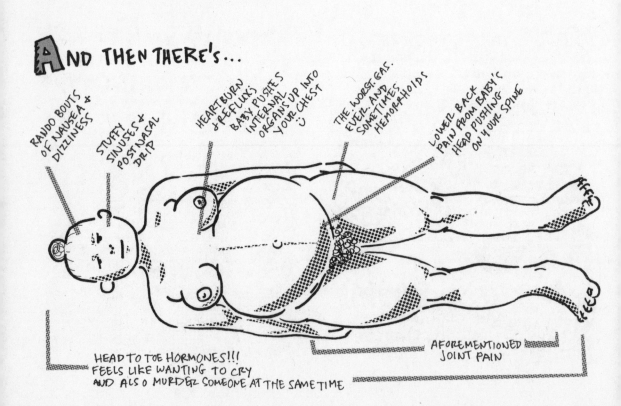

RANDO BOUTS OF NAUSEA + DIZZINESS

STUFFY SINUSES + POST NASAL DRIP

HEARTBURN + REFLUX: BABY PUSHES INTERNAL ORGANS UP INTO YOUR CHEST :(

THE WORST GAS EVER... AND SOMETIMES HEMORRHOIDS

LOWER BACK PAIN FROM BABY'S HEAD PUSHING ON YOUR SPINE

AFOREMENTIONED JOINT PAIN

HEAD TO TOE HORMONES!!! FEELS LIKE WANTING TO CRY AND ALSO MURDER SOMEONE AT THE SAME TIME

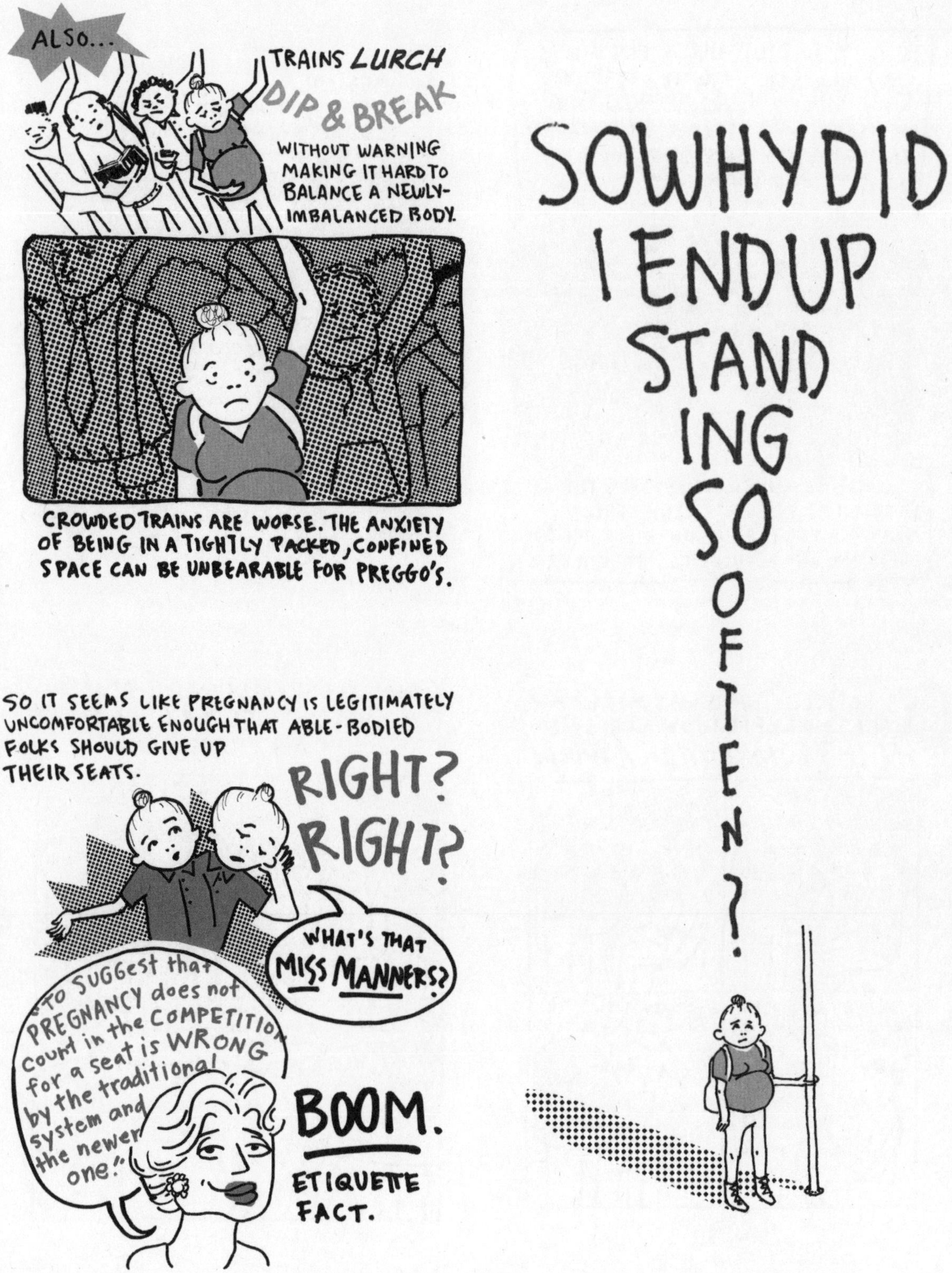
ALSO...
TRAINS LURCH
DIP & BREAK
WITHOUT WARNING MAKING IT HARD TO BALANCE A NEWLY-IMBALANCED BODY.
CROWDED TRAINS ARE WORSE. THE ANXIETY OF BEING IN A TIGHTLY PACKED, CONFINED SPACE CAN BE UNBEARABLE FOR PREGGO'S.
SO IT SEEMS LIKE PREGNANCY IS LEGITIMATELY UNCOMFORTABLE ENOUGH THAT ABLE-BODIED FOLKS SHOULD GIVE UP THEIR SEATS.
RIGHT? RIGHT?
WHAT'S THAT MISS MANNERS?
"TO SUGGEST that PREGNANCY does not count in the COMPETITION for a seat is WRONG by the traditional system and the newer one."
BOOM.
ETIQUETTE FACT.
SOWHYDID I ENDUP STANDING SO OFTEN?

IT GOT SO RIDICULOUS THAT IN MY 3RD TRIMESTER I STARTED KEEPING A *HIGHLY UN-SCIENTIFIC LOG* OF PEOPLE WHO OFFERED ME SEATS AND TAKING SHAME PHOTOS OF THOSE WHO DIDN'T.

I WANTED TO FIGURE OUT WHO THESE PEOPLE WERE. WHAT TYPE OF PERSON OFFERS SEATS TO PREGNANT WOMEN (I.E., THE GOOD ONES) AND WHO REFUSES (I.E., THE SHIT BAGS).

MY NOTES STARTED OUT LIKE THIS:

> Dec 10
> AM, no seat
> PM, black male, 35
>
> Dec 11
> AM, white female, 25
> PM, latino male, 25

AND PROGRESSED TO THIS AS I BECAME MORE VISIBLY PREGGO AND SICK OF STANDING:

> Jan 20
> AM, ignored by couple-black female, white male, 30'ish, when female finally offered seat, male stood up instead.
>
> PM, 50ish white male pretends to sleep while I stand with 2 heavy bags + large drill case.

I NOTICED THAT I WAS MORE LIKELY TO BE OFFERED A SEAT WHEN IN THE COMPANY OF A MAN:

* this happened a lot: dude would look at my belly, then me, then my male companion, and only then would offer me a seat.

I WOULD LITERALLY WATCH PEOPLE GET SUDDENLY VER-R-RY SLE-E-EPY IN MY PRESENCE.

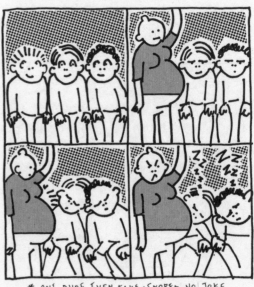

* ONE DUDE EVEN FAKE-SNORED. NO JOKE.

BOOKS BECAME INSTANTLY ENGROSSING. CANDY CRUSH WAS A GAME OF LIFE + DEATH!
AND OF COURSE SOME PEOPLE JUST DIDN'T GIVE A FUCK...
I'm not responsible for your pregnancy.
Your baby, your problem.
No one gave up a seat for me when I was pregnant.
You don't ask, you don't get.

IN SHORT, PEOPLE EITHER

- DID NOT AGREE WITH MISS MANNERS
- WERE SO ABSORBED IN THEIR OWN EXPERIENCE THAT THEY LITERALLY DIDN'T SEE PREGGO'S
- OR ONLY OFFERED A SEAT WHEN THERE WAS A MALE WITNESS

SHITBAGS.

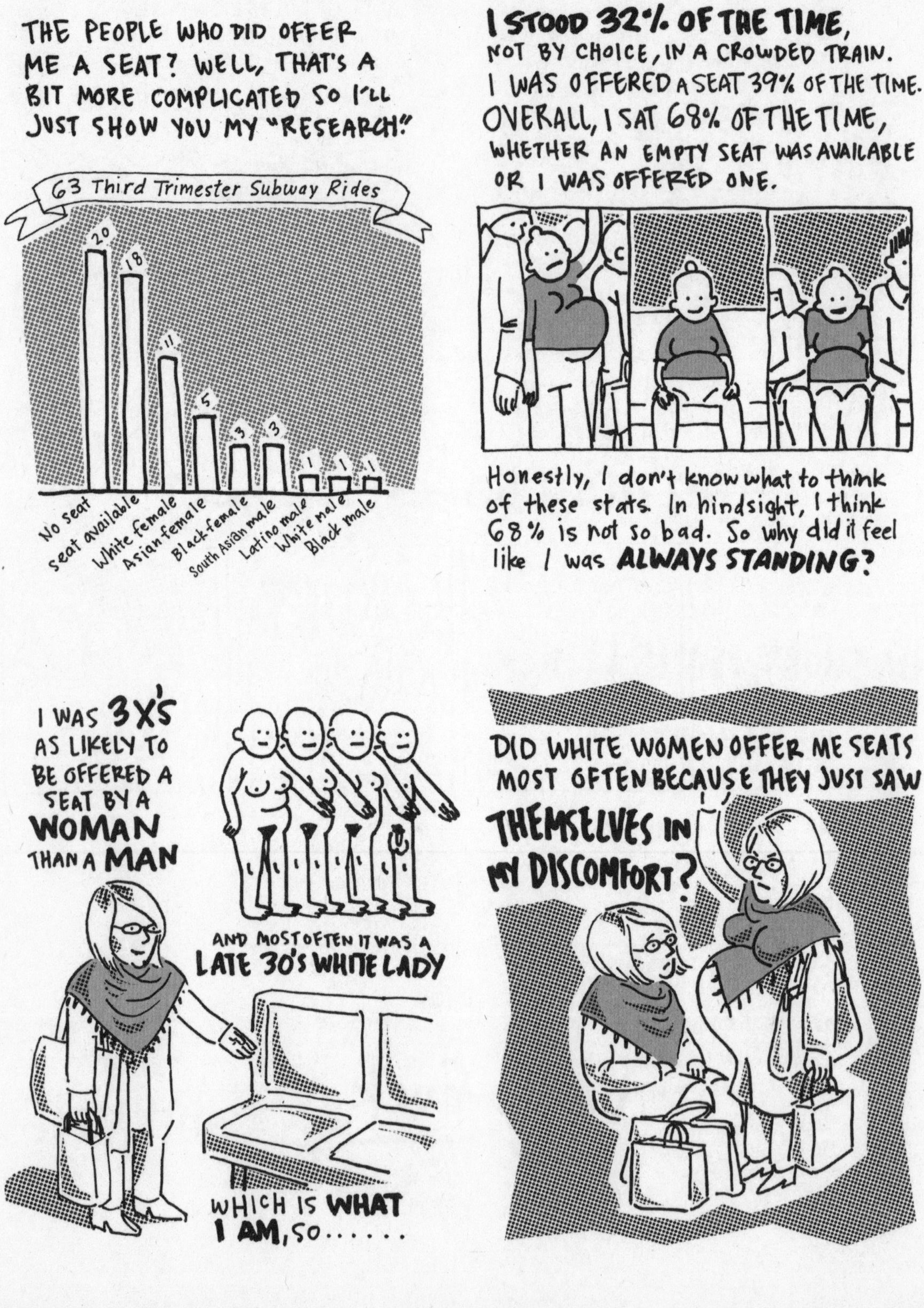
THE PEOPLE WHO DID OFFER ME A SEAT? WELL, THAT'S A BIT MORE COMPLICATED SO I'LL JUST SHOW YOU MY "RESEARCH!"
63 Third Trimester Subway Rides
20
18
11
5
3
3
1
1
1
No seat
seat available
White female
Asian female
Black female
South Asian male
Latino male
White male
Black male
I STOOD 32% OF THE TIME, NOT BY CHOICE, IN A CROWDED TRAIN.
I WAS OFFERED A SEAT 39% OF THE TIME.
OVERALL, I SAT 68% OF THE TIME, WHETHER AN EMPTY SEAT WAS AVAILABLE OR I WAS OFFERED ONE.
Honestly, I don't know what to think of these stats. In hindsight, I think 68% is not so bad. So why did it feel like I was ALWAYS STANDING?
I WAS 3X'S AS LIKELY TO BE OFFERED A SEAT BY A WOMAN THAN A MAN
AND MOST OFTEN IT WAS A LATE 30'S WHITE LADY
WHICH IS WHAT I AM, SO......
DID WHITE WOMEN OFFER ME SEATS MOST OFTEN BECAUSE THEY JUST SAW THEMSELVES IN MY DISCOMFORT?

IS THIS REALLY HOW EMPATHY WORKS?

AND ALSO DOESN'T WORK?

well, <u>fuck</u>.

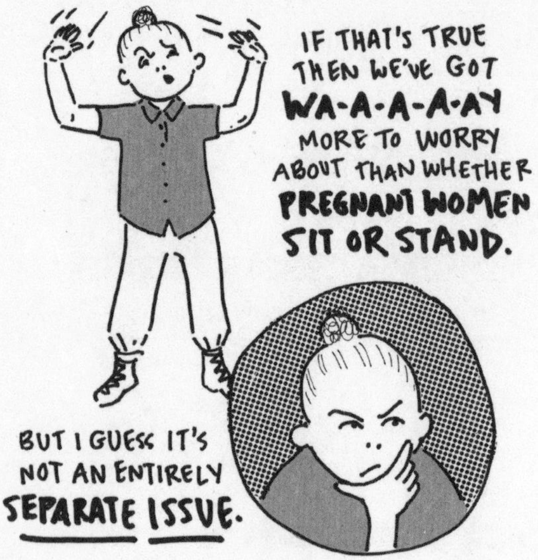
IF THAT'S TRUE THEN WE'VE GOT WA-A-A-A-AY MORE TO WORRY ABOUT THAN WHETHER PREGNANT WOMEN SIT OR STAND.
BUT I GUESS IT'S NOT AN ENTIRELY SEPARATE ISSUE.

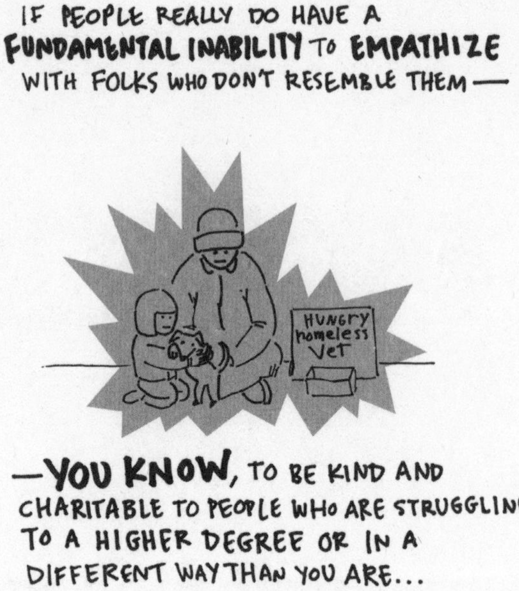
IF PEOPLE REALLY DO HAVE A FUNDAMENTAL INABILITY TO EMPATHIZE WITH FOLKS WHO DON'T RESEMBLE THEM—
HUNGRY homeless Vet
—YOU KNOW, TO BE KIND AND CHARITABLE TO PEOPLE WHO ARE STRUGGLING TO A HIGHER DEGREE OR IN A DIFFERENT WAY THAN YOU ARE...

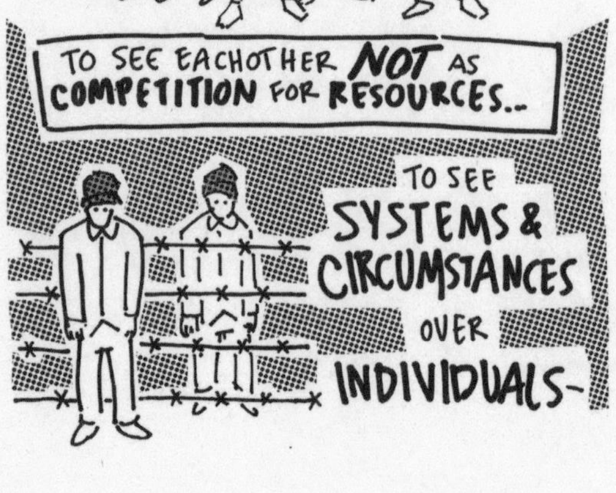
TO SEE EACHOTHER NOT AS COMPETITION FOR RESOURCES...
TO SEE SYSTEMS & CIRCUMSTANCES OVER INDIVIDUALS-

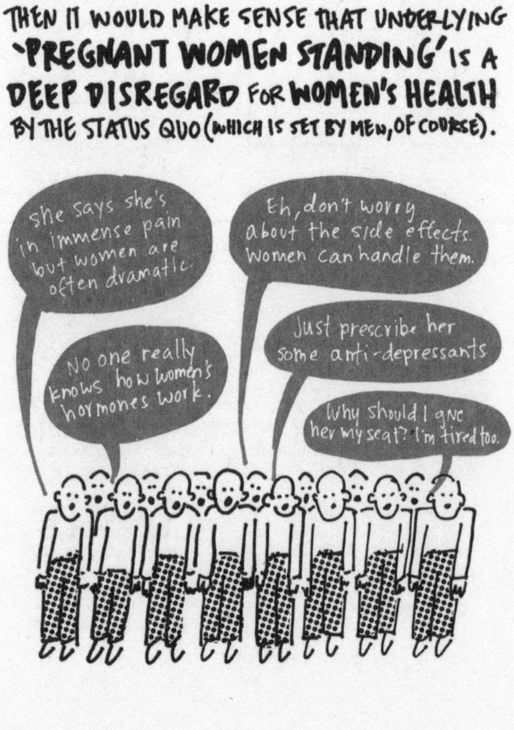
THEN IT WOULD MAKE SENSE THAT UNDERLYING 'PREGNANT WOMEN STANDING' IS A DEEP DISREGARD FOR WOMEN'S HEALTH BY THE STATUS QUO (WHICH IS SET BY MEN, OF COURSE).
She says she's in immense pain but women are often dramatic.
Eh, don't worry about the side effects. Women can handle them.
No one really knows how women's hormones work.
Just prescribe her some anti-depressants
Why should I give her my seat? I'm tired too.

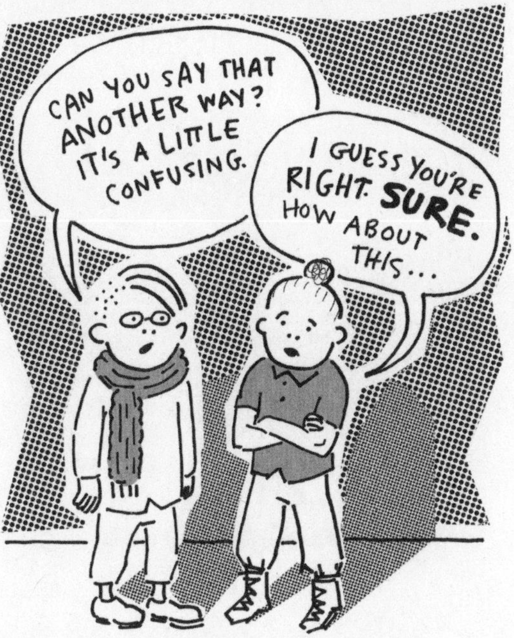
CAN YOU SAY THAT ANOTHER WAY? IT'S A LITTLE CONFUSING.
I GUESS YOU'RE RIGHT. SURE. HOW ABOUT THIS...

THE **MALE EXPERIENCE*** IS THOUGHT TO BE THE **UNIVERSAL** OR **PROTOTYPICAL** HUMAN EXPERIENCE.

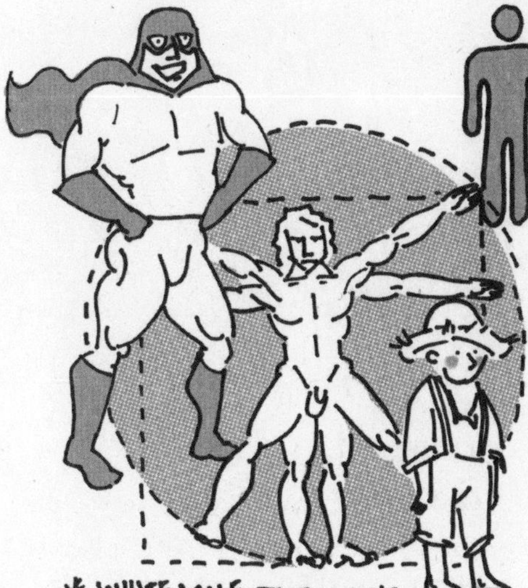

* WHITE MALE, THAT IS. AHEM...

SO-CALLED "**WOMEN'S ISSUES**" ARE THOUGHT OF AS EQUIVALENT TO **SPECIAL TREATMENT**, A.K.A., ***NOT UNIVERSAL ISSUES***.

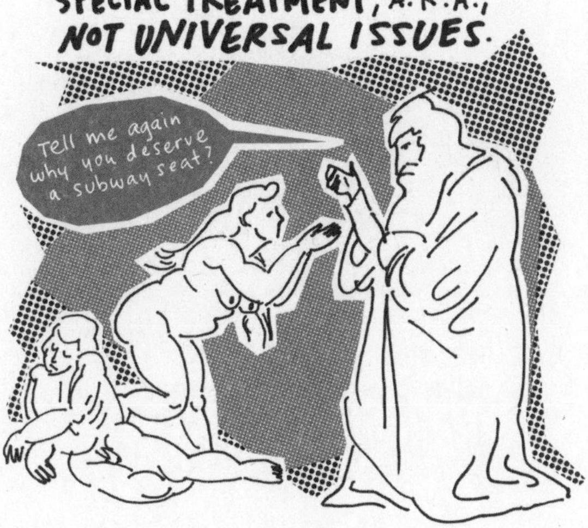
Tell me again why you deserve a subway seat?

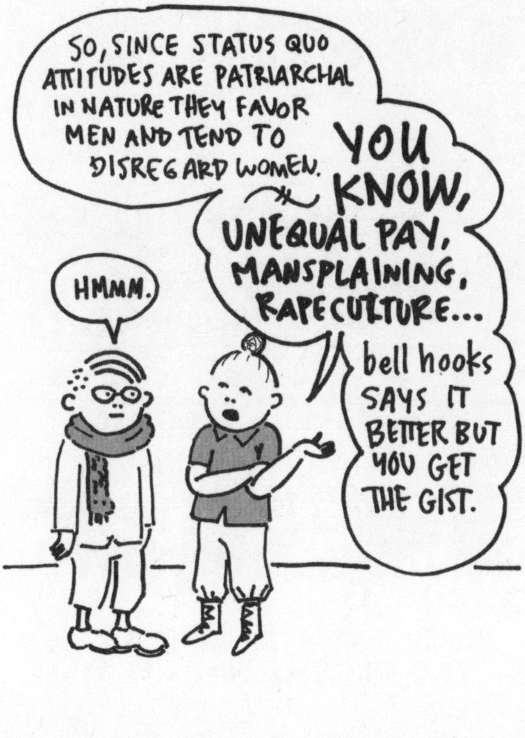
SO, SINCE STATUS QUO ATTITUDES ARE PATRIARCHAL IN NATURE THEY FAVOR MEN AND TEND TO DISREGARD WOMEN.
YOU KNOW, UNEQUAL PAY, MANSPLAINING, RAPE CULTURE...
HMMM.
bell hooks SAYS IT BETTER BUT YOU GET THE GIST.

WHENEVER I STOOD IT WAS ALMOST ALWAYS ON AN OVER-CROWDED TRAIN.

MY BODY WAS HUGE AND OVERHEATED. I WAS SO SWEATY AND MY HEART WOULD RACE WITH ANXIETY AND ANGER. MY HIPS AND FEET HURT LIKE <u>WHOA</u>.

IT WAS WEIRD. PASSENGERS SIMULTANEOUSLY OGLED ME AND PRETENDED NOT TO SEE ME.

tee hee... nothin' to see here, folks...

WHAT THE FUCK ARE YOU LOOKING AT FUCKER?!

AND I FELT SIMULTANEOUSLY SELF-CONSCIOUS AND AGGRESSIVE. I WANTED TO **BE SEEN.** NOT **STARED AT.**

A FRIEND TOLD ME I SHOULD HAVE DEMANDED A SEAT BUT **WHY SHOULD I ?**

Are you seriously gonna make me say it?

Well...

COULD IT BE MORE **OBVIOUS** ?! THAT THIS BODY WANTS TO SIT ?!

YOU'VE MADE YOUR CHOICE BY IGNORING THE OBVIOUS

AND I'M ALLOWED TO MAKE MINE.

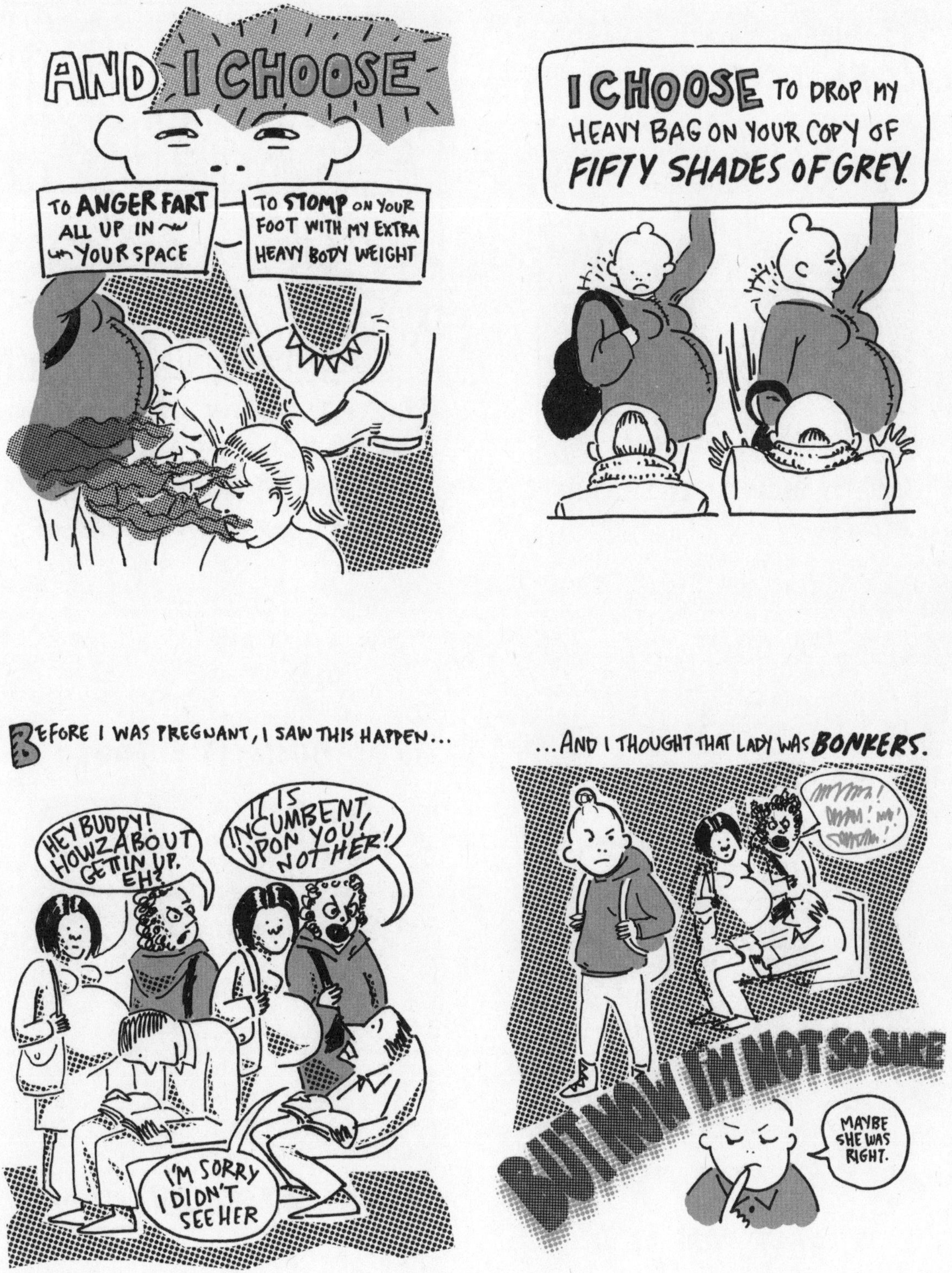
AND I CHOOSE
TO ANGER FART ALL UP IN YOUR SPACE
TO STOMP ON YOUR FOOT WITH MY EXTRA HEAVY BODY WEIGHT
I CHOOSE TO DROP MY HEAVY BAG ON YOUR COPY OF FIFTY SHADES OF GREY.
BEFORE I WAS PREGNANT, I SAW THIS HAPPEN...
HEY BUDDY! HOWZABOUT GETTIN UP, EH?
IT IS INCUMBENT UPON YOU! NOT HER!
I'M SORRY I DIDN'T SEE HER
...AND I THOUGHT THAT LADY WAS BONKERS.
BUT NOW I'M NOT SO SURE
MAYBE SHE WAS RIGHT.

MAYBE WE SHOULD DEMAND A **CULTURE** OF **COURTESY** FROM EACH OTHER?

AND NOT NECESSARILY THE KIND **MTA** PROMOTES EITHER...

THE MTA WANT$ U$ TO BEHAVE $O THEY CAN CONTINUE TO PACK A$ MANY OF U$ INTO TRAIN$ A$ PO$$IBLE WITHOUT INCIDENT.

BUT THE KIND WHERE OFFERING A SEAT TO A PREGGO ON THE SUBWAY...

yasssssss

IS ONLY PART OF IT.

TO BE **SOCIALLY ENGAGED**

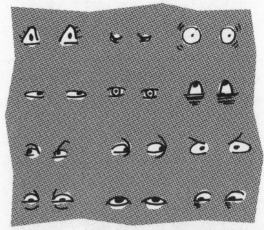

MEANS *PAYING ATTENTION*

DECIDING TO "CHECK OUT" DOESN'T EXCUSE ANYONE FROM **ACCOUNTABILITY**

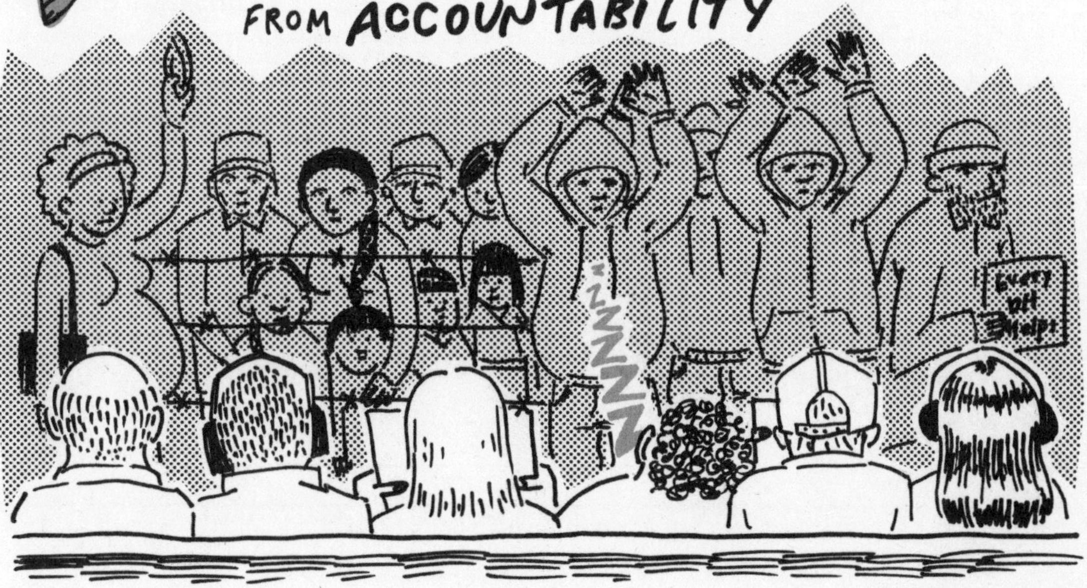
ZZZZZ
Every bit Helps

AS PEOPLE WHO ALL OWE OUR EXISTENCE TO A **PREGNANT WOMAN'S LABOR**

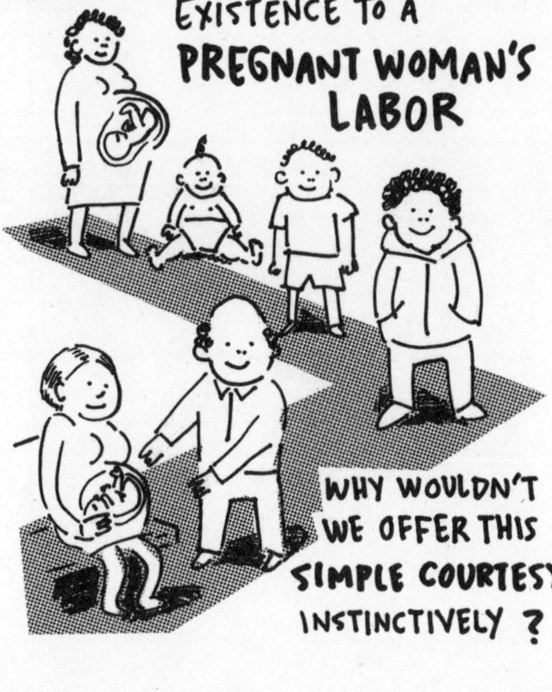

WHY WOULDN'T WE OFFER THIS SIMPLE COURTESY INSTINCTIVELY ?

AND WHY DIDN'T I THINK TO DO THIS BEFORE I WAS PREGNANT MY-SELF ?

PHONE CALL

Story by Jenny Brown
Drawing by Tamara Tornado

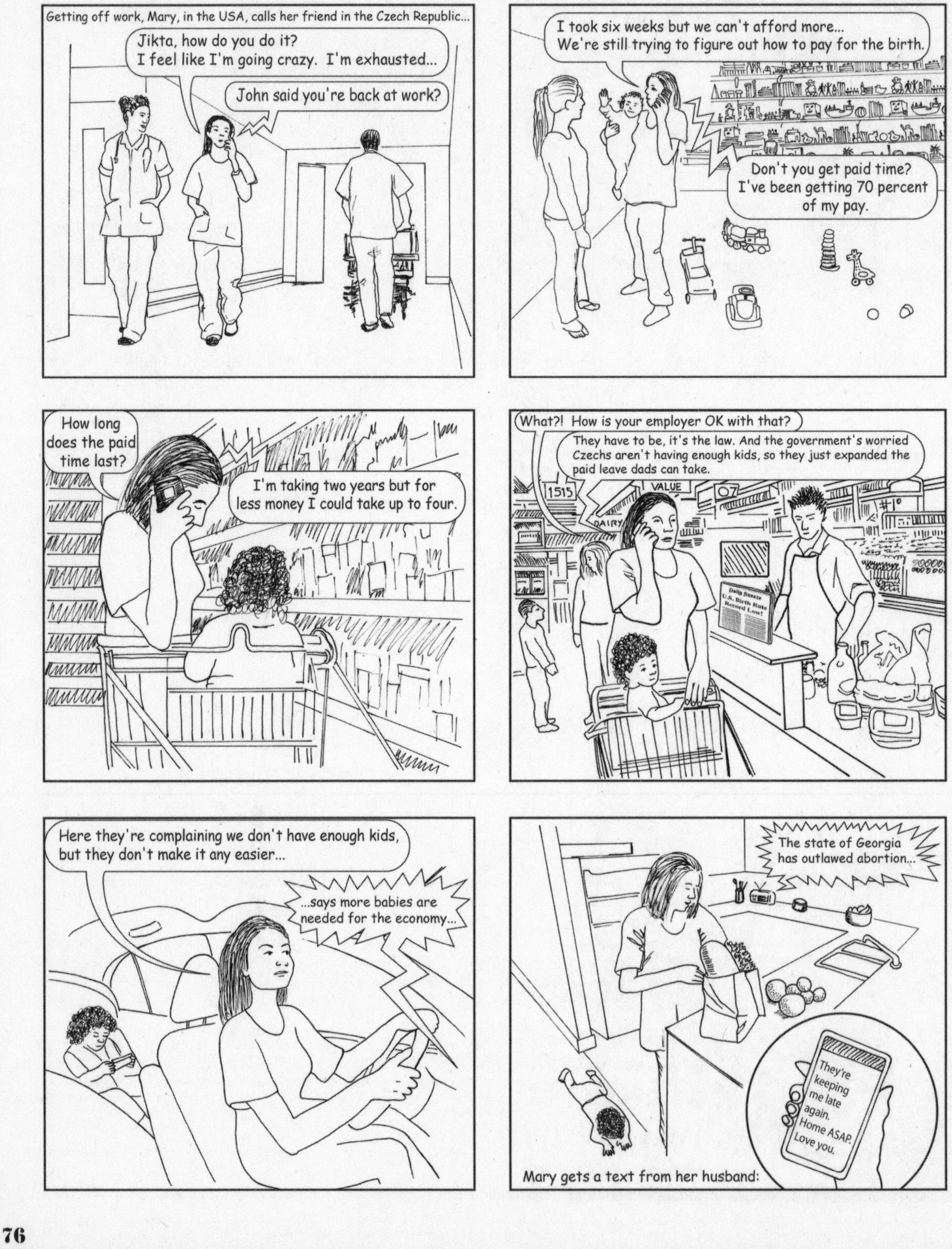

Getting off work, Mary, in the USA, calls her friend in the Czech Republic...
Jikta, how do you do it? I feel like I'm going crazy. I'm exhausted...
John said you're back at work?
I took six weeks but we can't afford more... We're still trying to figure out how to pay for the birth.
Don't you get paid time? I've been getting 70 percent of my pay.
How long does the paid time last?
I'm taking two years but for less money I could take up to four.
What?! How is your employer OK with that?
They have to be, it's the law. And the government's worried Czechs aren't having enough kids, so they just expanded the paid leave dads can take.
1515
VALUE
07
DAIRY
U.S. Birth Rate Record Low!
Here they're complaining we don't have enough kids, but they don't make it any easier...
...says more babies are needed for the economy...
The state of Georgia has outlawed abortion...
They're keeping me late again. Home ASAP. Love you.
Mary gets a text from her husband:

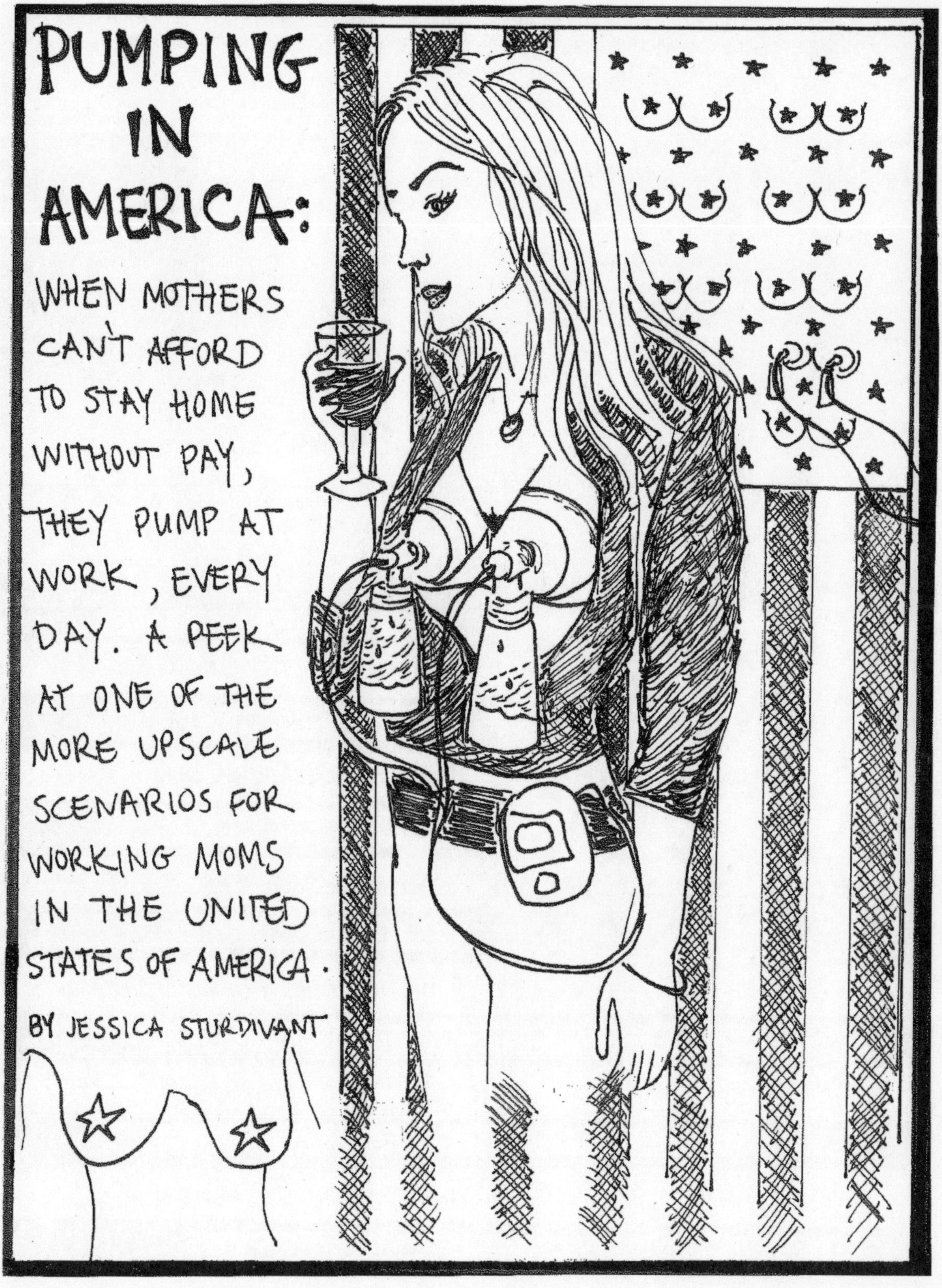
PUMPING IN AMERICA:
WHEN MOTHERS CAN'T AFFORD TO STAY HOME WITHOUT PAY, THEY PUMP AT WORK, EVERY DAY. A PEEK AT ONE OF THE MORE UPSCALE SCENARIOS FOR WORKING MOMS IN THE UNITED STATES OF AMERICA.
BY JESSICA STURDIVANT

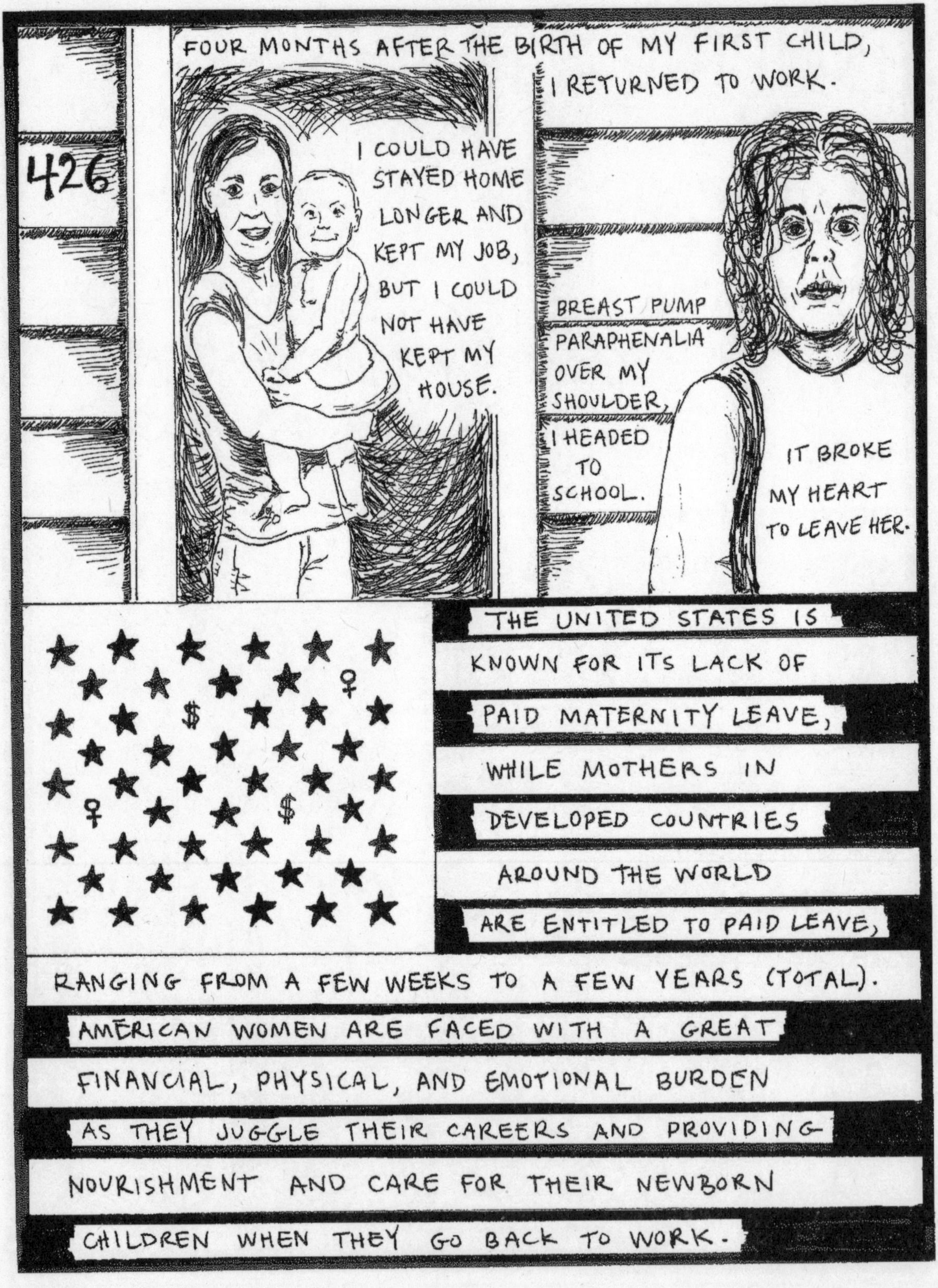
426
FOUR MONTHS AFTER THE BIRTH OF MY FIRST CHILD, I RETURNED TO WORK.
I COULD HAVE STAYED HOME LONGER AND KEPT MY JOB, BUT I COULD NOT HAVE KEPT MY HOUSE.
BREAST PUMP PARAPHENALIA OVER MY SHOULDER, I HEADED TO SCHOOL.
IT BROKE MY HEART TO LEAVE HER.
THE UNITED STATES IS KNOWN FOR ITS LACK OF PAID MATERNITY LEAVE, WHILE MOTHERS IN DEVELOPED COUNTRIES AROUND THE WORLD ARE ENTITLED TO PAID LEAVE, RANGING FROM A FEW WEEKS TO A FEW YEARS (TOTAL).
AMERICAN WOMEN ARE FACED WITH A GREAT FINANCIAL, PHYSICAL, AND EMOTIONAL BURDEN AS THEY JUGGLE THEIR CAREERS AND PROVIDING NOURISHMENT AND CARE FOR THEIR NEWBORN CHILDREN WHEN THEY GO BACK TO WORK.

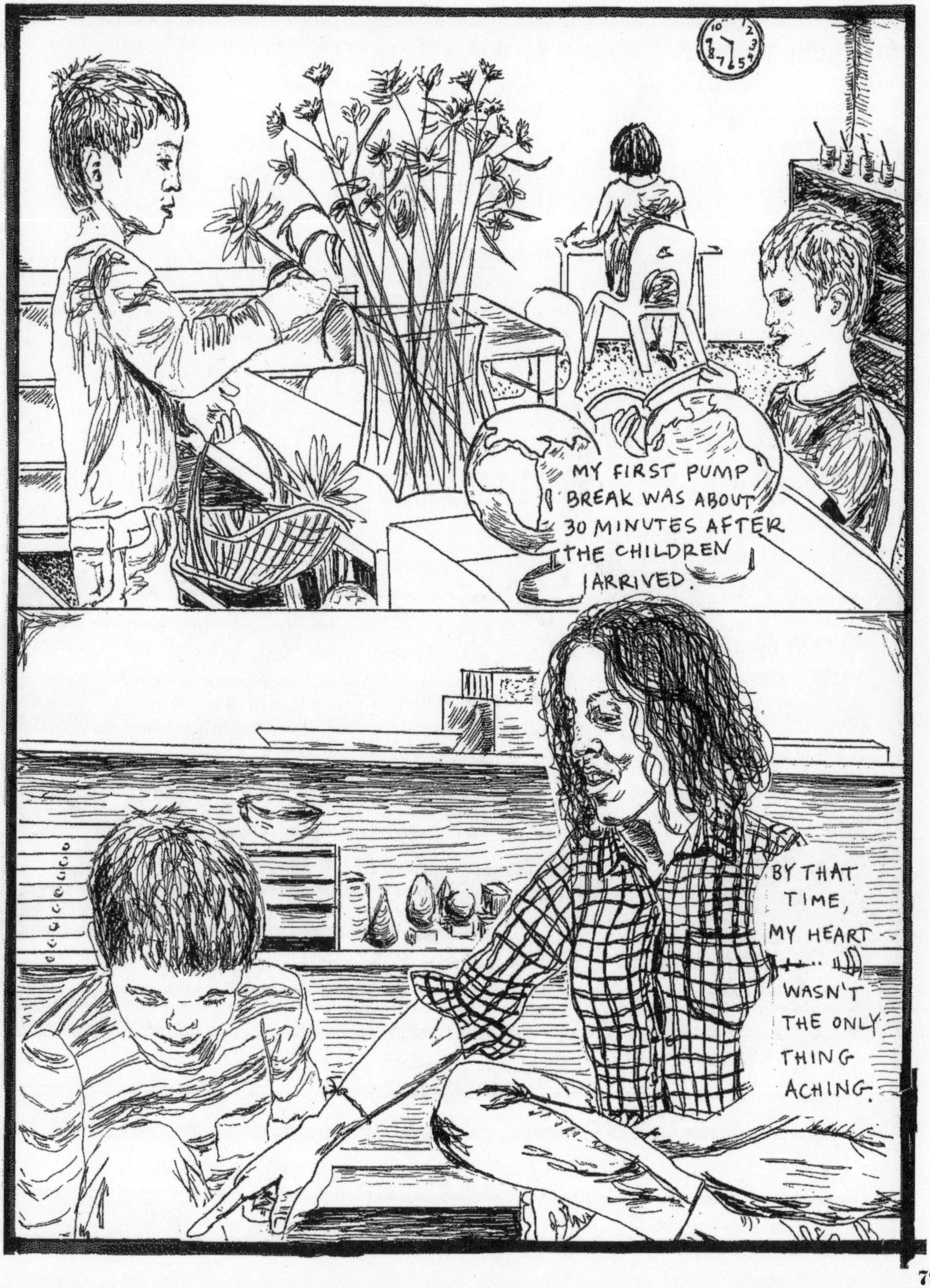
MY FIRST PUMP BREAK WAS ABOUT 30 MINUTES AFTER THE CHILDREN ARRIVED.
BY THAT TIME, MY HEART WASN'T THE ONLY THING ACHING.

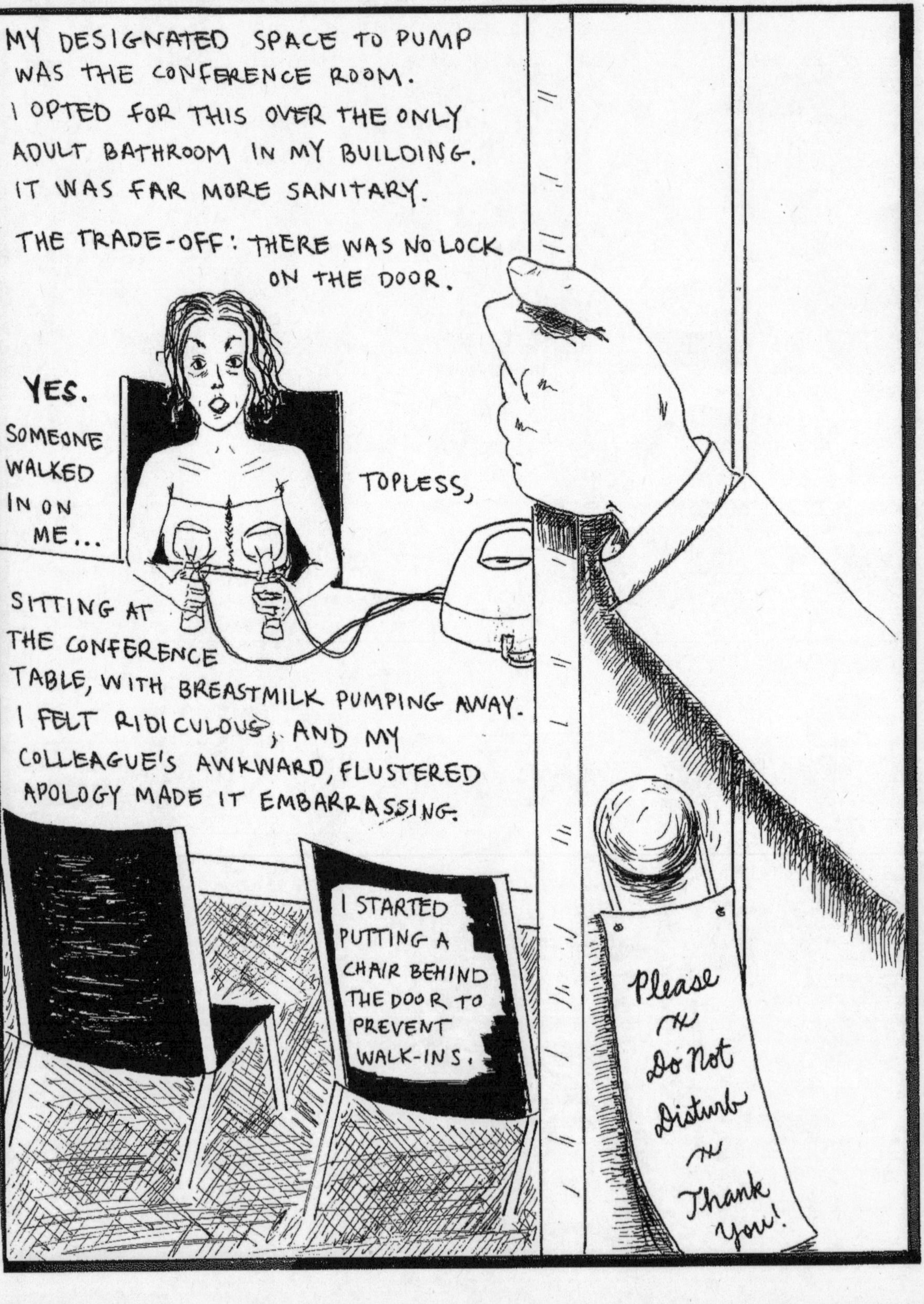
MY DESIGNATED SPACE TO PUMP WAS THE CONFERENCE ROOM.
I OPTED FOR THIS OVER THE ONLY ADULT BATHROOM IN MY BUILDING.
IT WAS FAR MORE SANITARY.
THE TRADE-OFF: THERE WAS NO LOCK ON THE DOOR.
YES.
SOMEONE WALKED IN ON ME...
TOPLESS,
SITTING AT THE CONFERENCE TABLE, WITH BREASTMILK PUMPING AWAY.
I FELT RIDICULOUS, AND MY COLLEAGUE'S AWKWARD, FLUSTERED APOLOGY MADE IT EMBARRASSING.
I STARTED PUTTING A CHAIR BEHIND THE DOOR TO PREVENT WALK-INS.
Please ~ Do Not Disturb ~ Thank You!

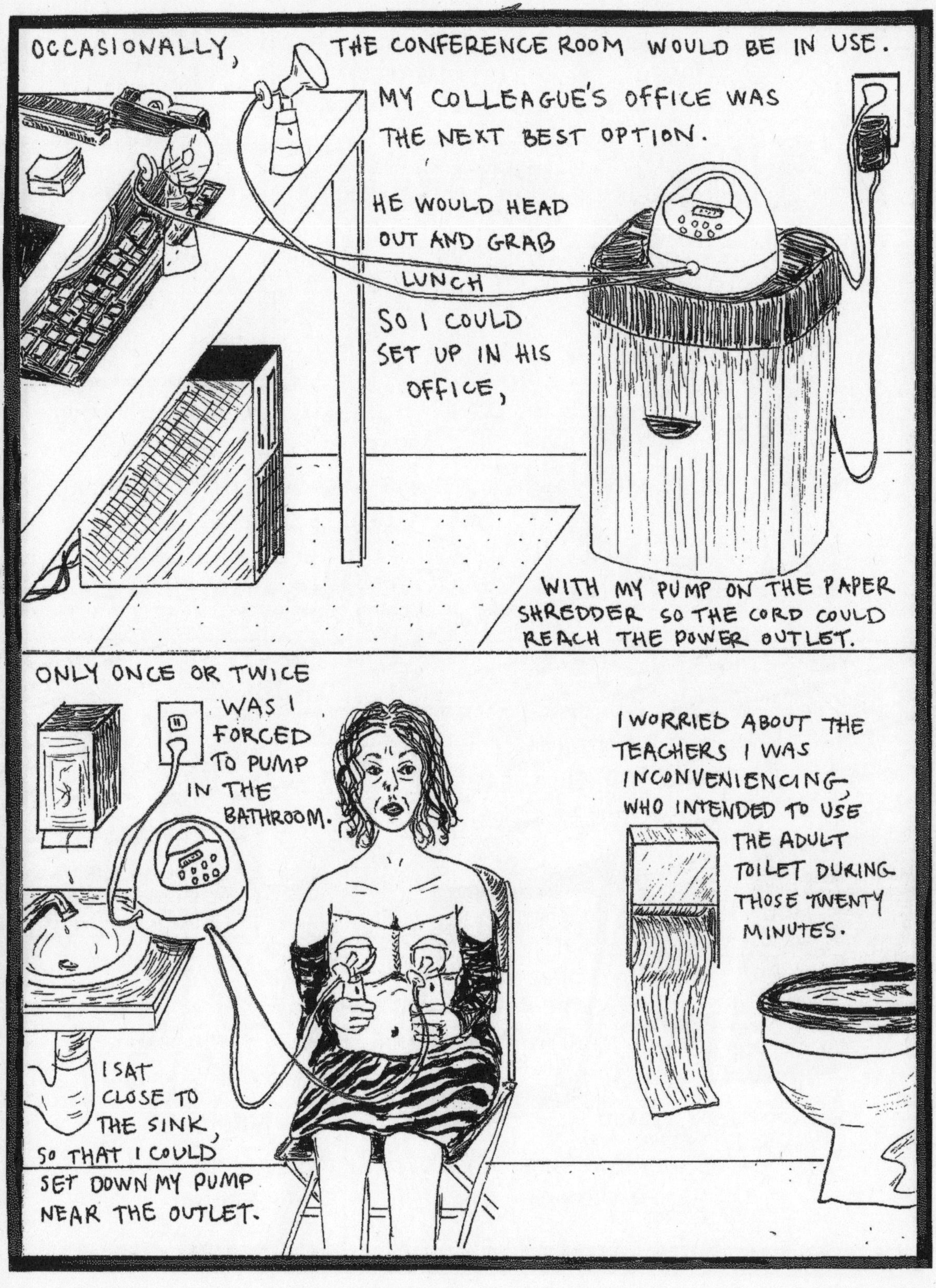
OCCASIONALLY,
THE CONFERENCE ROOM WOULD BE IN USE.
MY COLLEAGUE'S OFFICE WAS THE NEXT BEST OPTION.
HE WOULD HEAD OUT AND GRAB LUNCH
SO I COULD SET UP IN HIS OFFICE,
WITH MY PUMP ON THE PAPER SHREDDER SO THE CORD COULD REACH THE POWER OUTLET.
ONLY ONCE OR TWICE
WAS I FORCED TO PUMP IN THE BATHROOM.
I WORRIED ABOUT THE TEACHERS I WAS INCONVENIENCING, WHO INTENDED TO USE
THE ADULT TOILET DURING THOSE TWENTY MINUTES.
I SAT CLOSE TO THE SINK, SO THAT I COULD
SET DOWN MY PUMP NEAR THE OUTLET.

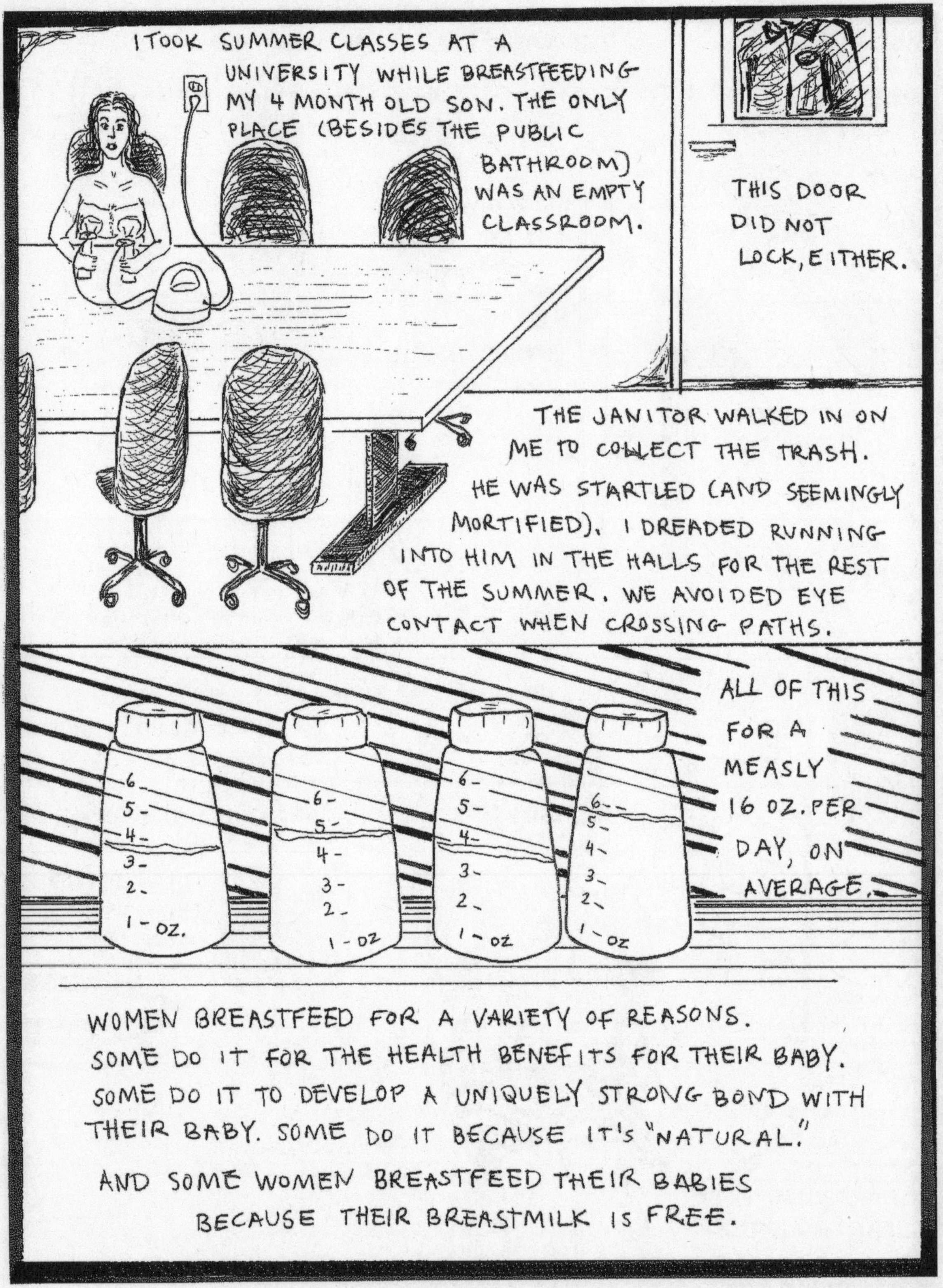
I TOOK SUMMER CLASSES AT A UNIVERSITY WHILE BREASTFEEDING MY 4 MONTH OLD SON. THE ONLY PLACE (BESIDES THE PUBLIC BATHROOM) WAS AN EMPTY CLASSROOM.
THIS DOOR DID NOT LOCK, EITHER.
THE JANITOR WALKED IN ON ME TO COLLECT THE TRASH.
HE WAS STARTLED (AND SEEMINGLY MORTIFIED). I DREADED RUNNING INTO HIM IN THE HALLS FOR THE REST OF THE SUMMER. WE AVOIDED EYE CONTACT WHEN CROSSING PATHS.
ALL OF THIS FOR A MEASLY 16 OZ. PER DAY, ON AVERAGE.
WOMEN BREASTFEED FOR A VARIETY OF REASONS.
SOME DO IT FOR THE HEALTH BENEFITS FOR THEIR BABY.
SOME DO IT TO DEVELOP A UNIQUELY STRONG BOND WITH THEIR BABY. SOME DO IT BECAUSE IT'S "NATURAL."
AND SOME WOMEN BREASTFEED THEIR BABIES BECAUSE THEIR BREASTMILK IS FREE.

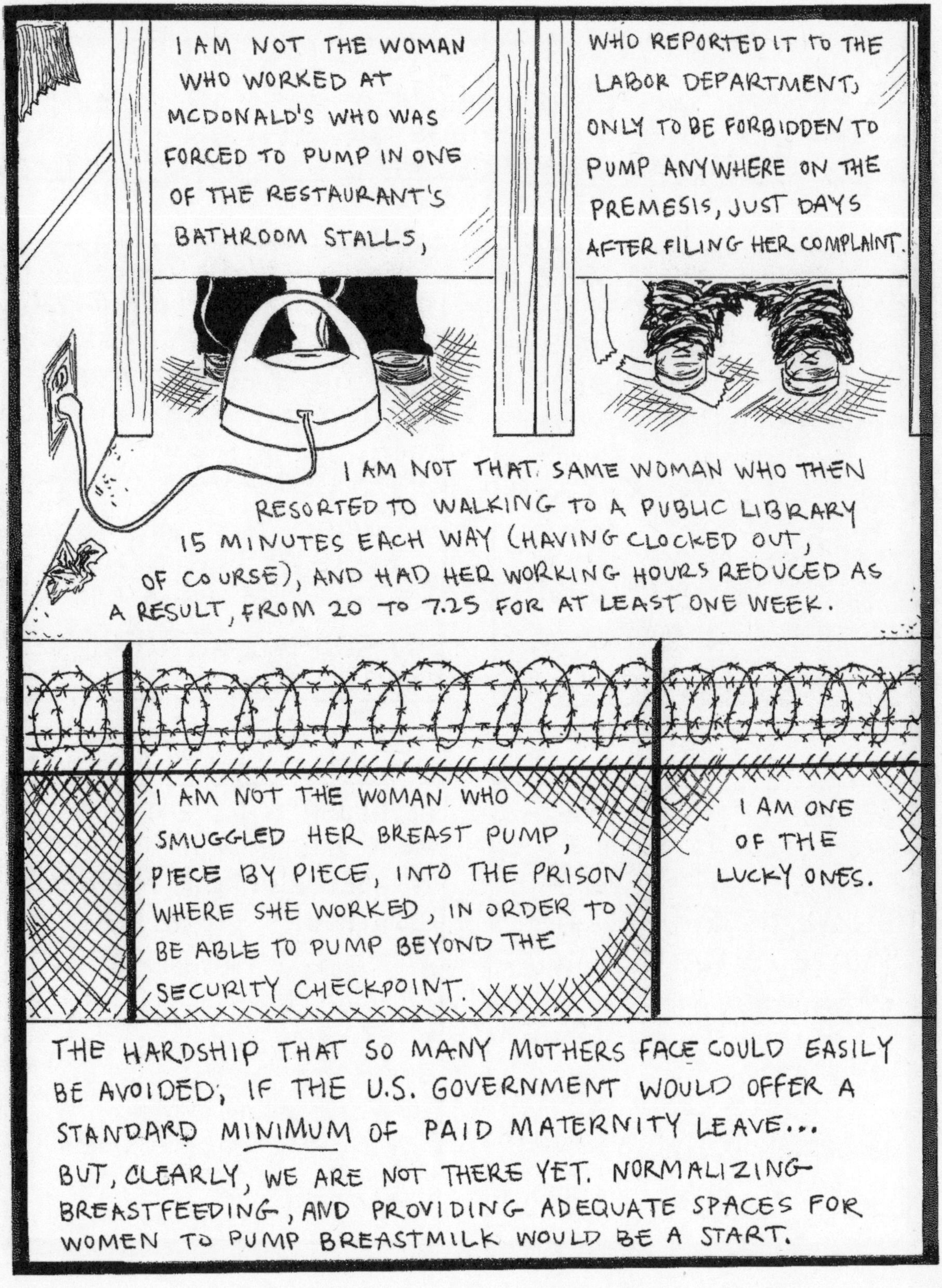
I AM NOT THE WOMAN WHO WORKED AT MCDONALD'S WHO WAS FORCED TO PUMP IN ONE OF THE RESTAURANT'S BATHROOM STALLS,
WHO REPORTED IT TO THE LABOR DEPARTMENT, ONLY TO BE FORBIDDEN TO PUMP ANYWHERE ON THE PREMESIS, JUST DAYS AFTER FILING HER COMPLAINT.
I AM NOT THAT SAME WOMAN WHO THEN RESORTED TO WALKING TO A PUBLIC LIBRARY 15 MINUTES EACH WAY (HAVING CLOCKED OUT, OF COURSE), AND HAD HER WORKING HOURS REDUCED AS A RESULT, FROM 20 TO 7.25 FOR AT LEAST ONE WEEK.
I AM NOT THE WOMAN WHO SMUGGLED HER BREAST PUMP, PIECE BY PIECE, INTO THE PRISON WHERE SHE WORKED, IN ORDER TO BE ABLE TO PUMP BEYOND THE SECURITY CHECKPOINT.
I AM ONE OF THE LUCKY ONES.
THE HARDSHIP THAT SO MANY MOTHERS FACE COULD EASILY BE AVOIDED, IF THE U.S. GOVERNMENT WOULD OFFER A STANDARD MINIMUM OF PAID MATERNITY LEAVE...
BUT, CLEARLY, WE ARE NOT THERE YET. NORMALIZING BREASTFEEDING, AND PROVIDING ADEQUATE SPACES FOR WOMEN TO PUMP BREASTMILK WOULD BE A START.

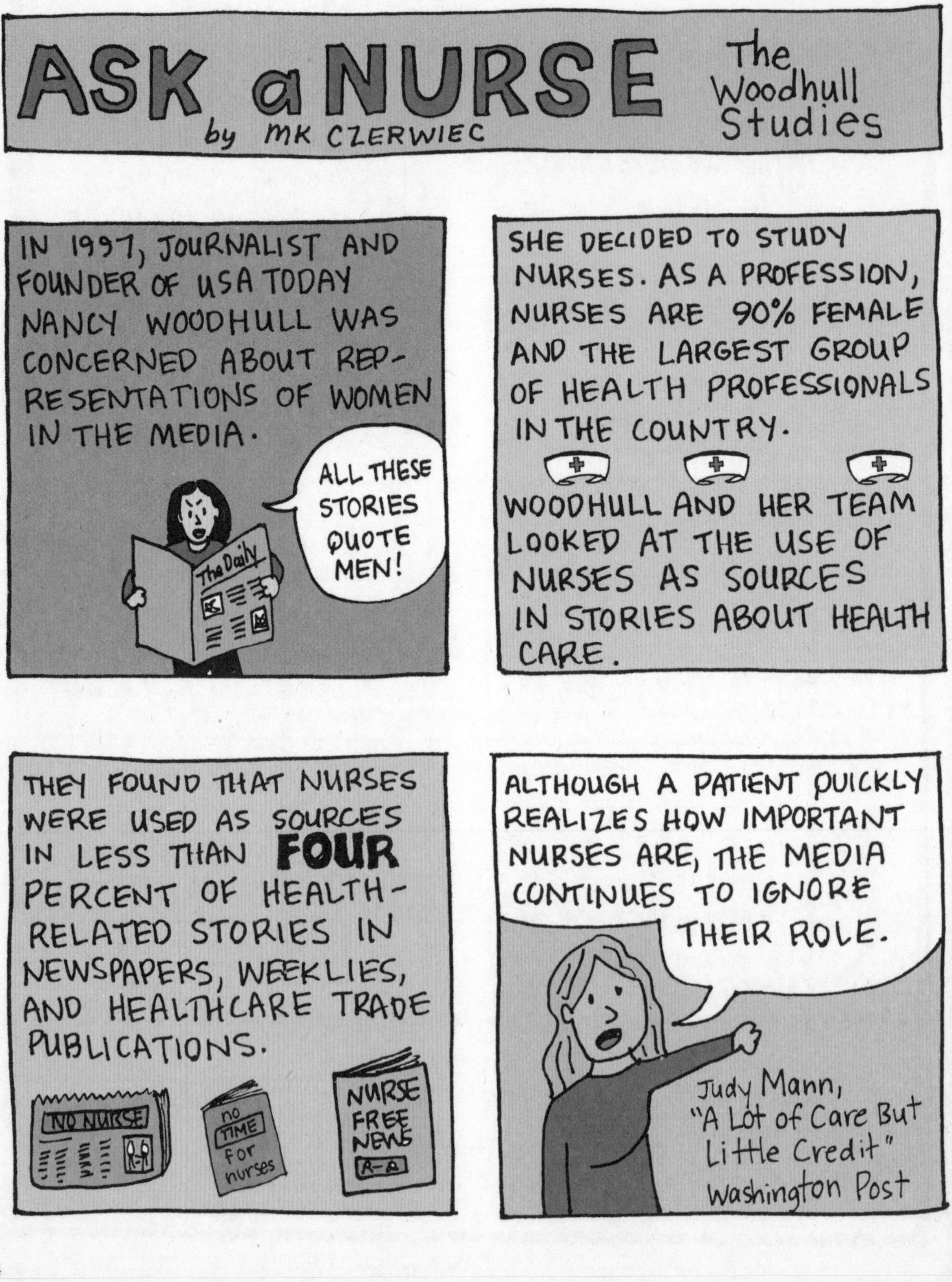
ASK a NURSE
by MK CZERWIEC
The Woodhull Studies
IN 1997, JOURNALIST AND FOUNDER OF USA TODAY NANCY WOODHULL WAS CONCERNED ABOUT REP-RESENTATIONS OF WOMEN IN THE MEDIA.
ALL THESE STORIES QUOTE MEN!
The Daily
SHE DECIDED TO STUDY NURSES. AS A PROFESSION, NURSES ARE 90% FEMALE AND THE LARGEST GROUP OF HEALTH PROFESSIONALS IN THE COUNTRY.
WOODHULL AND HER TEAM LOOKED AT THE USE OF NURSES AS SOURCES IN STORIES ABOUT HEALTH CARE.
THEY FOUND THAT NURSES WERE USED AS SOURCES IN LESS THAN FOUR PERCENT OF HEALTH-RELATED STORIES IN NEWSPAPERS, WEEKLIES, AND HEALTHCARE TRADE PUBLICATIONS.
NO NURSE
no TIME for nurses
NURSE FREE NEWS
ALTHOUGH A PATIENT QUICKLY REALIZES HOW IMPORTANT NURSES ARE, THE MEDIA CONTINUES TO IGNORE THEIR ROLE.
Judy Mann, "A Lot of Care But Little Credit" Washington Post

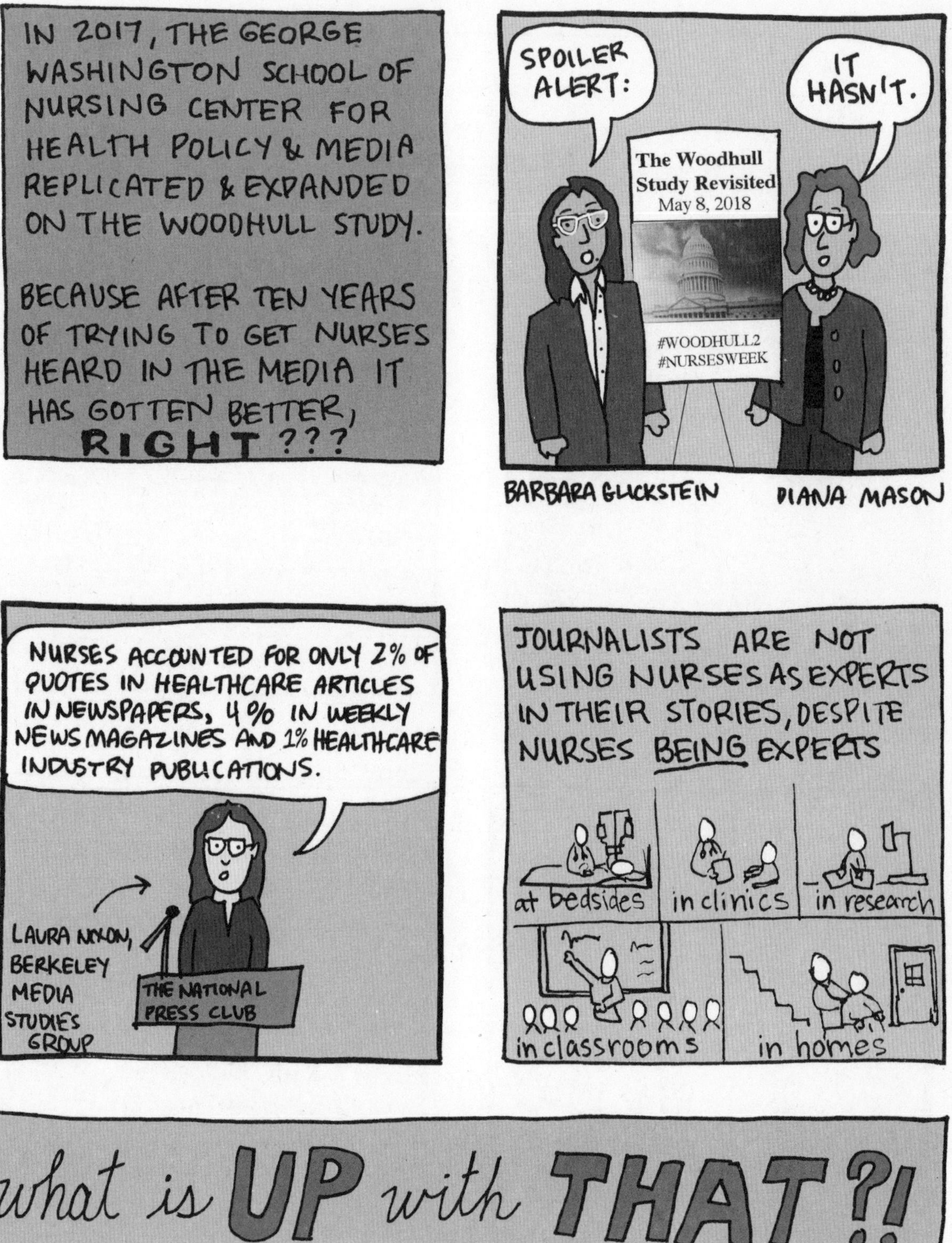
IN 2017, THE GEORGE WASHINGTON SCHOOL OF NURSING CENTER FOR HEALTH POLICY & MEDIA REPLICATED & EXPANDED ON THE WOODHULL STUDY.
BECAUSE AFTER TEN YEARS OF TRYING TO GET NURSES HEARD IN THE MEDIA IT HAS GOTTEN BETTER, RIGHT???
SPOILER ALERT:
IT HASN'T.
The Woodhull Study Revisited
May 8, 2018
#WOODHULL2
#NURSESWEEK
BARBARA GLICKSTEIN
DIANA MASON
NURSES ACCOUNTED FOR ONLY 2% OF QUOTES IN HEALTHCARE ARTICLES IN NEWSPAPERS, 4% IN WEEKLY NEWSMAGAZINES AND 1% HEALTHCARE INDUSTRY PUBLICATIONS.
LAURA NIXON, BERKELEY MEDIA STUDIES GROUP
THE NATIONAL PRESS CLUB
JOURNALISTS ARE NOT USING NURSES AS EXPERTS IN THEIR STORIES, DESPITE NURSES BEING EXPERTS
at bedsides
in clinics
in research
in classrooms
in homes
what is UP with THAT?!

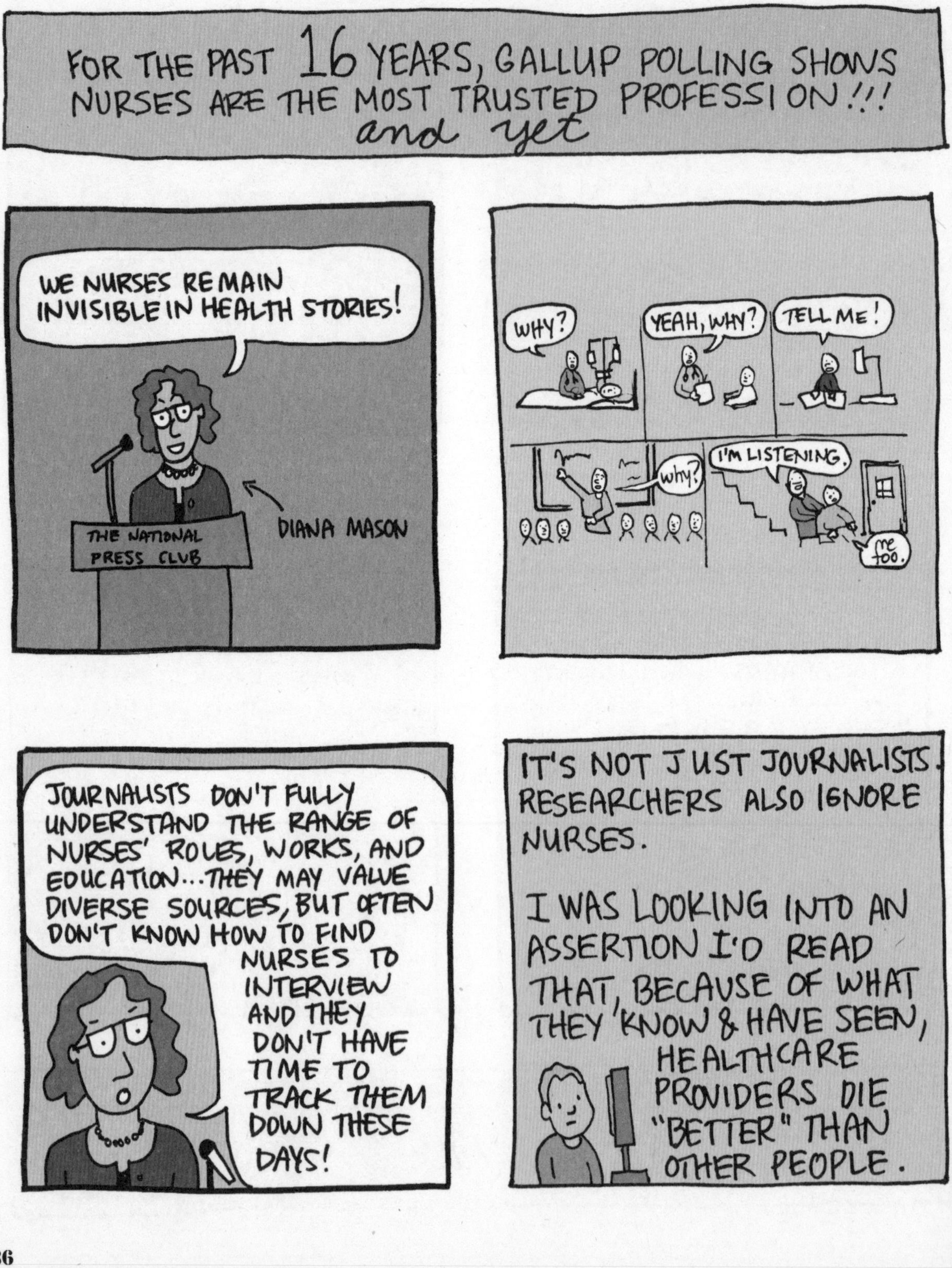
FOR THE PAST 16 YEARS, GALLUP POLLING SHOWS NURSES ARE THE MOST TRUSTED PROFESSION!!!
and yet
WE NURSES REMAIN INVISIBLE IN HEALTH STORIES!
THE NATIONAL PRESS CLUB
DIANA MASON
WHY?
YEAH, WHY?
TELL ME!
why?
I'M LISTENING.
me too.
JOURNALISTS DON'T FULLY UNDERSTAND THE RANGE OF NURSES' ROLES, WORKS, AND EDUCATION...THEY MAY VALUE DIVERSE SOURCES, BUT OFTEN DON'T KNOW HOW TO FIND NURSES TO INTERVIEW AND THEY DON'T HAVE TIME TO TRACK THEM DOWN THESE DAYS!
IT'S NOT JUST JOURNALISTS. RESEARCHERS ALSO IGNORE NURSES.
I WAS LOOKING INTO AN ASSERTION I'D READ THAT, BECAUSE OF WHAT THEY KNOW & HAVE SEEN, HEALTHCARE PROVIDERS DIE "BETTER" THAN OTHER PEOPLE.

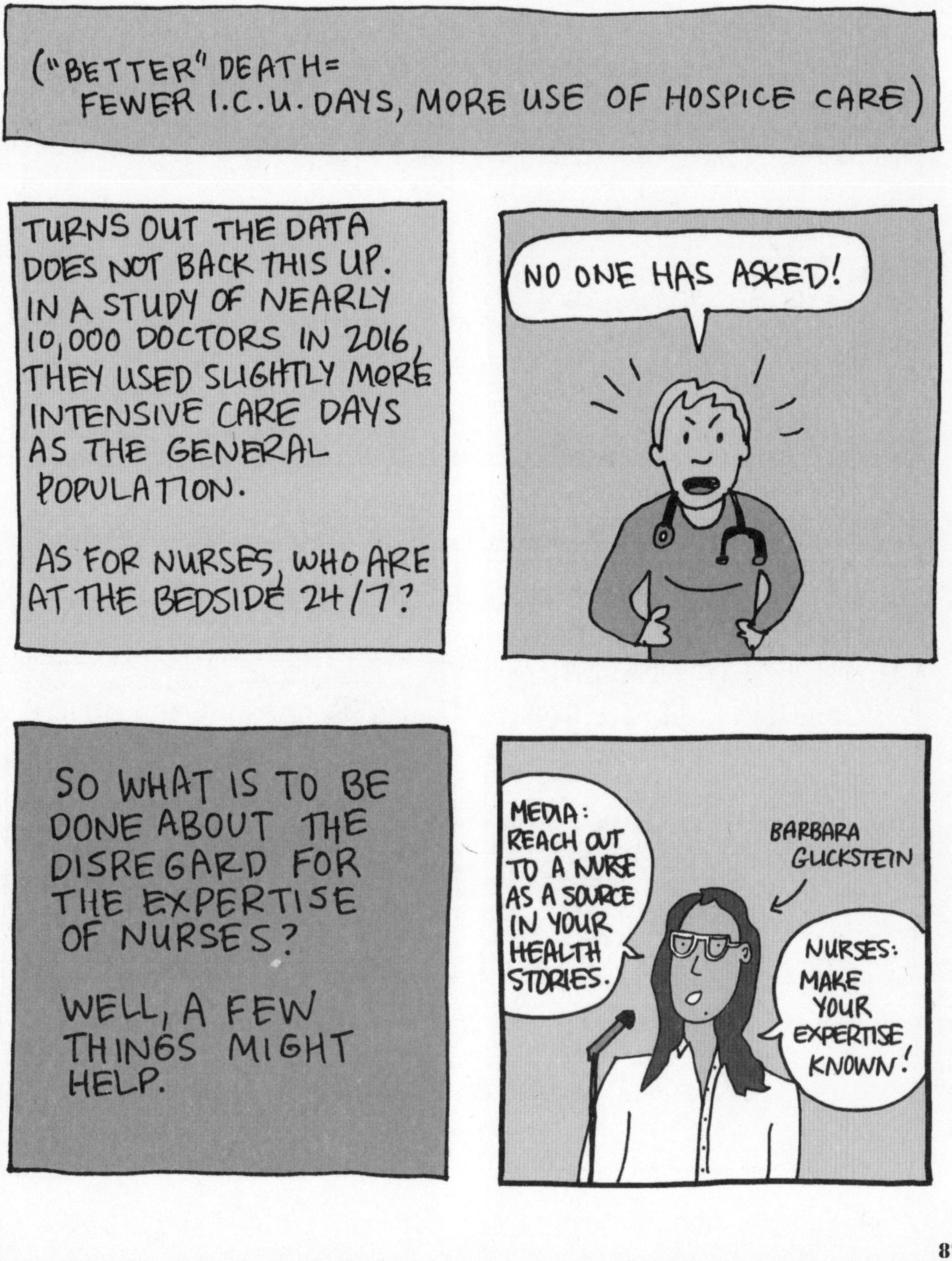
("BETTER" DEATH= FEWER I.C.U. DAYS, MORE USE OF HOSPICE CARE)
TURNS OUT THE DATA DOES NOT BACK THIS UP. IN A STUDY OF NEARLY 10,000 DOCTORS IN 2016, THEY USED SLIGHTLY MORE INTENSIVE CARE DAYS AS THE GENERAL POPULATION.
AS FOR NURSES, WHO ARE AT THE BEDSIDE 24/7?
NO ONE HAS ASKED!
SO WHAT IS TO BE DONE ABOUT THE DISREGARD FOR THE EXPERTISE OF NURSES?
WELL, A FEW THINGS MIGHT HELP.
MEDIA: REACH OUT TO A NURSE AS A SOURCE IN YOUR HEALTH STORIES.
BARBARA GLICKSTEIN
NURSES: MAKE YOUR EXPERTISE KNOWN!

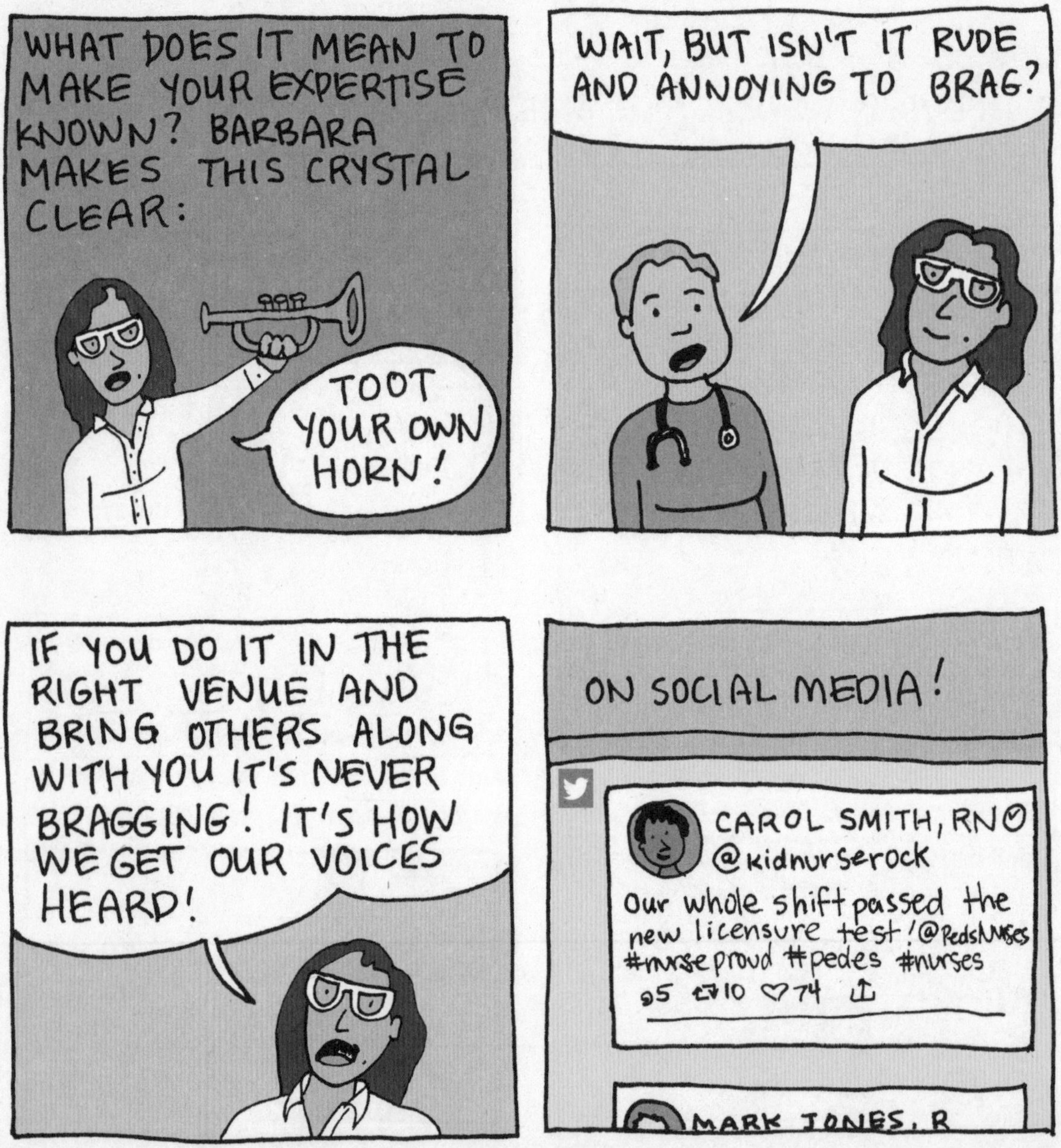
WHAT DOES IT MEAN TO MAKE YOUR EXPERTISE KNOWN? BARBARA MAKES THIS CRYSTAL CLEAR:
TOOT YOUR OWN HORN!
WAIT, BUT ISN'T IT RUDE AND ANNOYING TO BRAG?
IF YOU DO IT IN THE RIGHT VENUE AND BRING OTHERS ALONG WITH YOU IT'S NEVER BRAGGING! IT'S HOW WE GET OUR VOICES HEARD!
ON SOCIAL MEDIA!
CAROL SMITH, RN
@kidnurserock
our whole shift passed the new licensure test! @PedsNurses #nurseproud #pedes #nurses
5 10 74
MARK JONES, R

American Nurses Association Principles for Social Media Networking:

1. Nurses must not transmit or place online individually identifiable patient information.
2. Nurses must observe ethically prescribed professional patient-nurse boundaries.
3. Nurses should understand that patients, colleagues, organizations, and employers may view postings.
4. Nurses should take advantage of privacy settings and seek to separate personal and professional information online
5. Nurses should bring content that could harm a patient's privacy, rights, or welfare to the attention of appropriate authorities.
6. Nurses should participate in developing organizational policies governing online conduct.

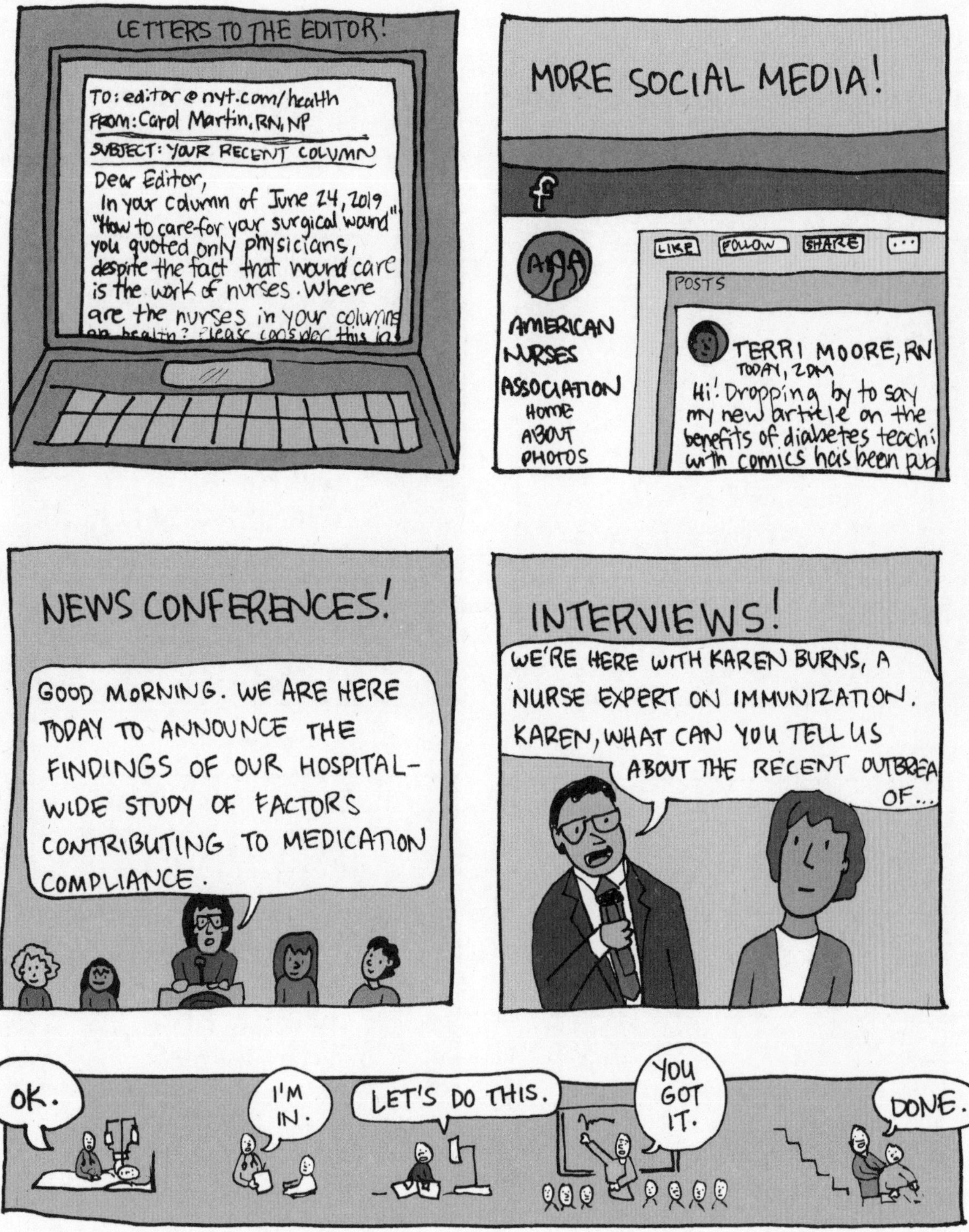

LETTERS TO THE EDITOR!
To: editor@nyt.com/health
FROM: Carol Martin, RN, NP
SUBJECT: YOUR RECENT COLUMN
Dear Editor,
In your column of June 24, 2019 "How to care for your surgical wound" you quoted only physicians, despite the fact that wound care is the work of nurses. Where are the nurses in your columns
MORE SOCIAL MEDIA!
LIKE
FOLLOW
SHARE
ANA
POSTS
AMERICAN NURSES ASSOCIATION
HOME
ABOUT
PHOTOS
TERRI MOORE, RN
TODAY, 2PM
Hi! Dropping by to say my new article on the benefits of diabetes teachi with comics has been pub
NEWS CONFERENCES!
GOOD MORNING. WE ARE HERE TODAY TO ANNOUNCE THE FINDINGS OF OUR HOSPITAL-WIDE STUDY OF FACTORS CONTRIBUTING TO MEDICATION COMPLIANCE.
INTERVIEWS!
WE'RE HERE WITH KAREN BURNS, A NURSE EXPERT ON IMMUNIZATION. KAREN, WHAT CAN YOU TELL US ABOUT THE RECENT OUTBREA OF...
OK.
I'M IN.
LET'S DO THIS.
YOU GOT IT.
DONE.

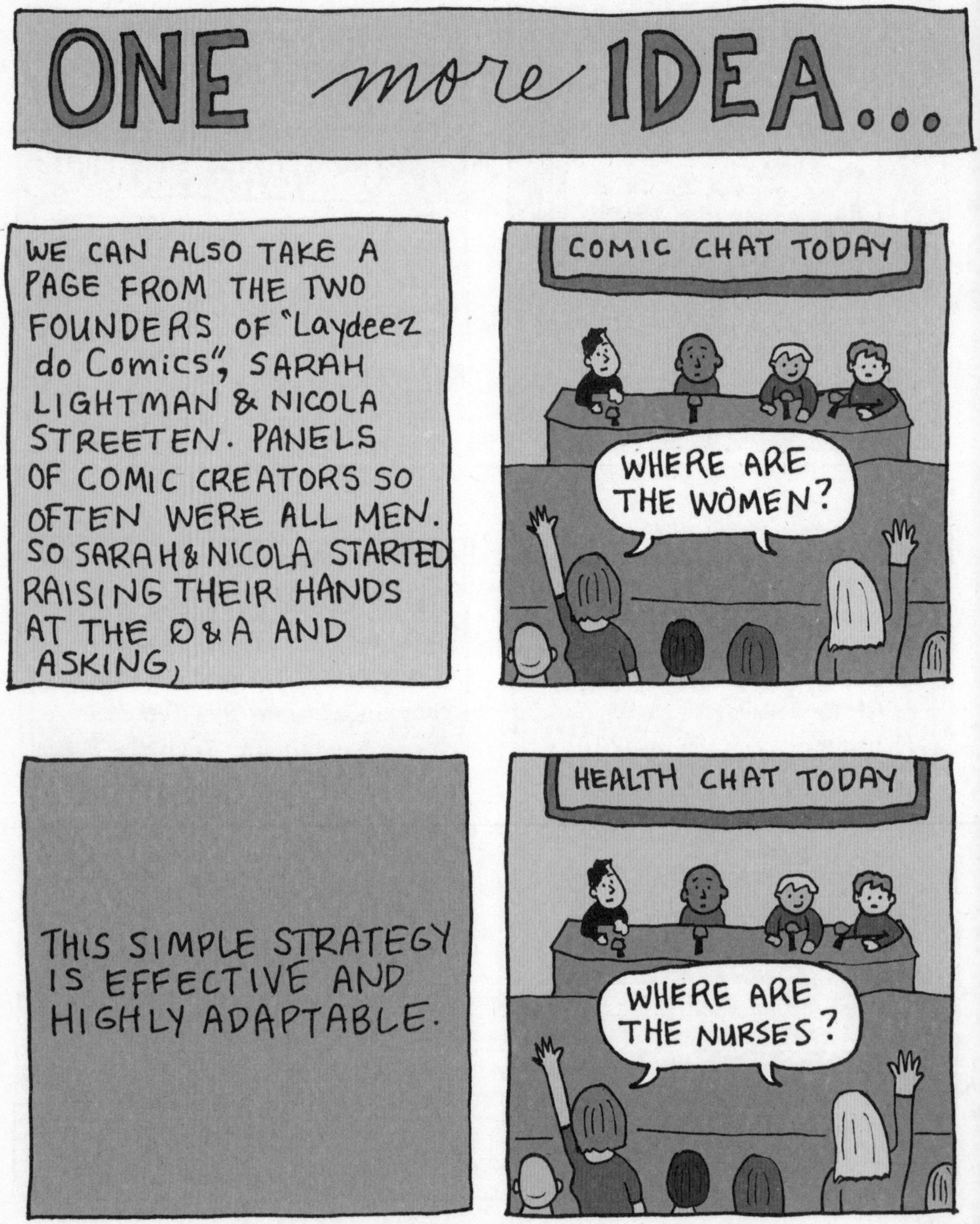
ONE more IDEA...
WE CAN ALSO TAKE A PAGE FROM THE TWO FOUNDERS OF "Laydeez do Comics", SARAH LIGHTMAN & NICOLA STREETEN. PANELS OF COMIC CREATORS SO OFTEN WERE ALL MEN. SO SARAH & NICOLA STARTED RAISING THEIR HANDS AT THE Q & A AND ASKING,
COMIC CHAT TODAY
WHERE ARE THE WOMEN?
THIS SIMPLE STRATEGY IS EFFECTIVE AND HIGHLY ADAPTABLE.
HEALTH CHAT TODAY
WHERE ARE THE NURSES?

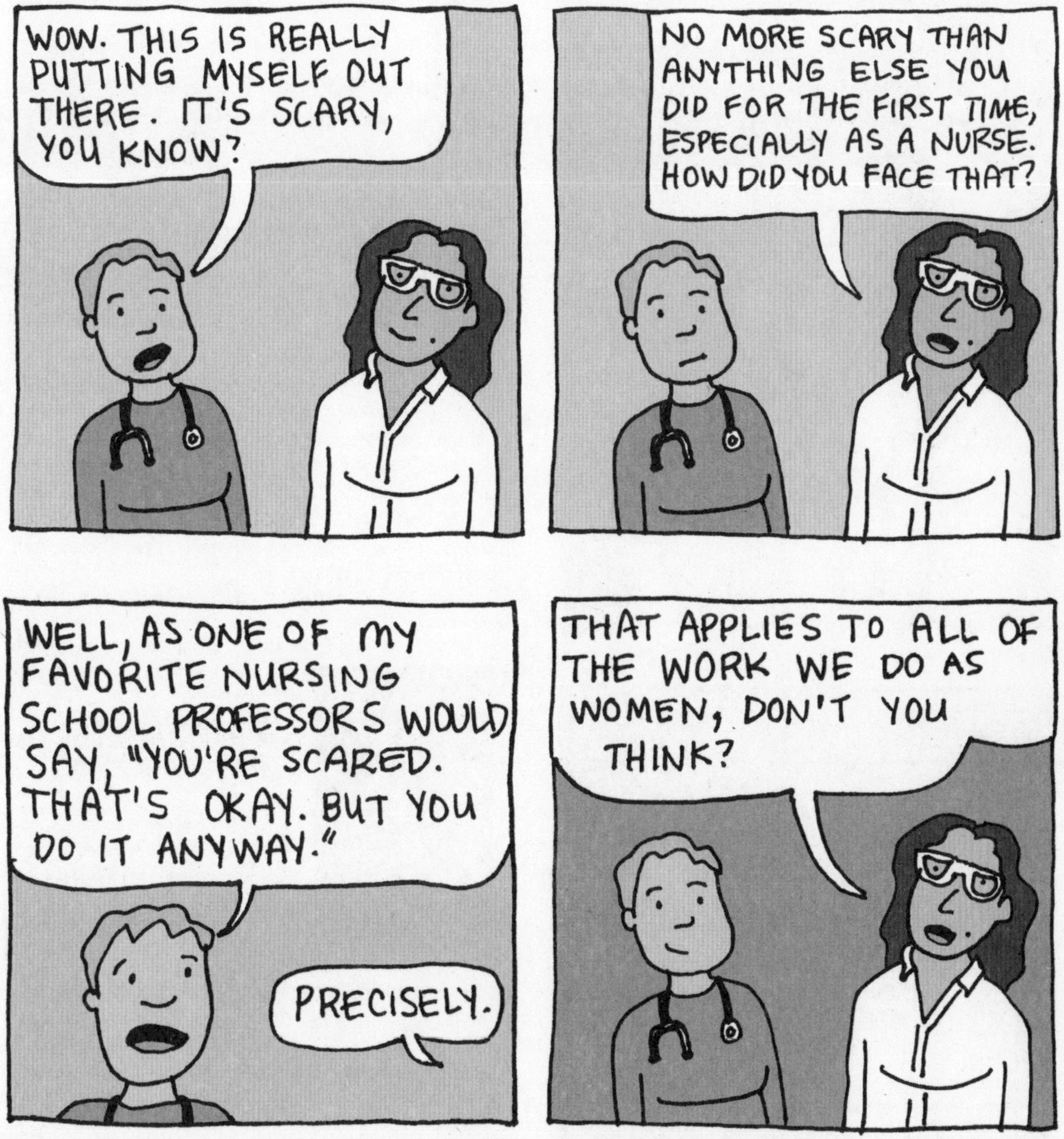
WOW. THIS IS REALLY PUTTING MYSELF OUT THERE. IT'S SCARY, YOU KNOW?
NO MORE SCARY THAN ANYTHING ELSE YOU DID FOR THE FIRST TIME, ESPECIALLY AS A NURSE. HOW DID YOU FACE THAT?
WELL, AS ONE OF MY FAVORITE NURSING SCHOOL PROFESSORS WOULD SAY, "YOU'RE SCARED. THAT'S OKAY. BUT YOU DO IT ANYWAY."
PRECISELY.
THAT APPLIES TO ALL OF THE WORK WE DO AS WOMEN, DON'T YOU THINK?

FOR MORE INFO ON THE WOODHULL STUDIES, GO TO
https://nursing.gwu.edu/woodhull-study-revisited

COMICS AS POLITICAL
EXPRESSION
In 2020 I will be teaching a class in what I do best, making political comics. It will be at May Day Space in Brooklyn. It will be priced affordably. This class is for artists at any skill level who want to produce comic art that makes a difference.
See you there,
Seth Tobocman
For info contact:
josh@mayday
space.org

Salsa for Beginners
Silkscreening
MAYDAY SPACE IS A HOME FOR SOCIAL MOVEMENTS IN BROOKLYN, NY.
WANT TO TEACH A CLASS OR HOST AN EVENT?
Email us:
info@maydayspace.org
Bike classes
Cooking workshops
MAY
DAY

WALK-IN
Draw the figure with
Minerva and friends
91 Canal Street, fourth floor
Chinatown, NYC

NEW SPACE
Just signed the lease
Now a not-for-profit
The Minerva
Foundation for
Figure Drawing

springstudio@earthlink.net

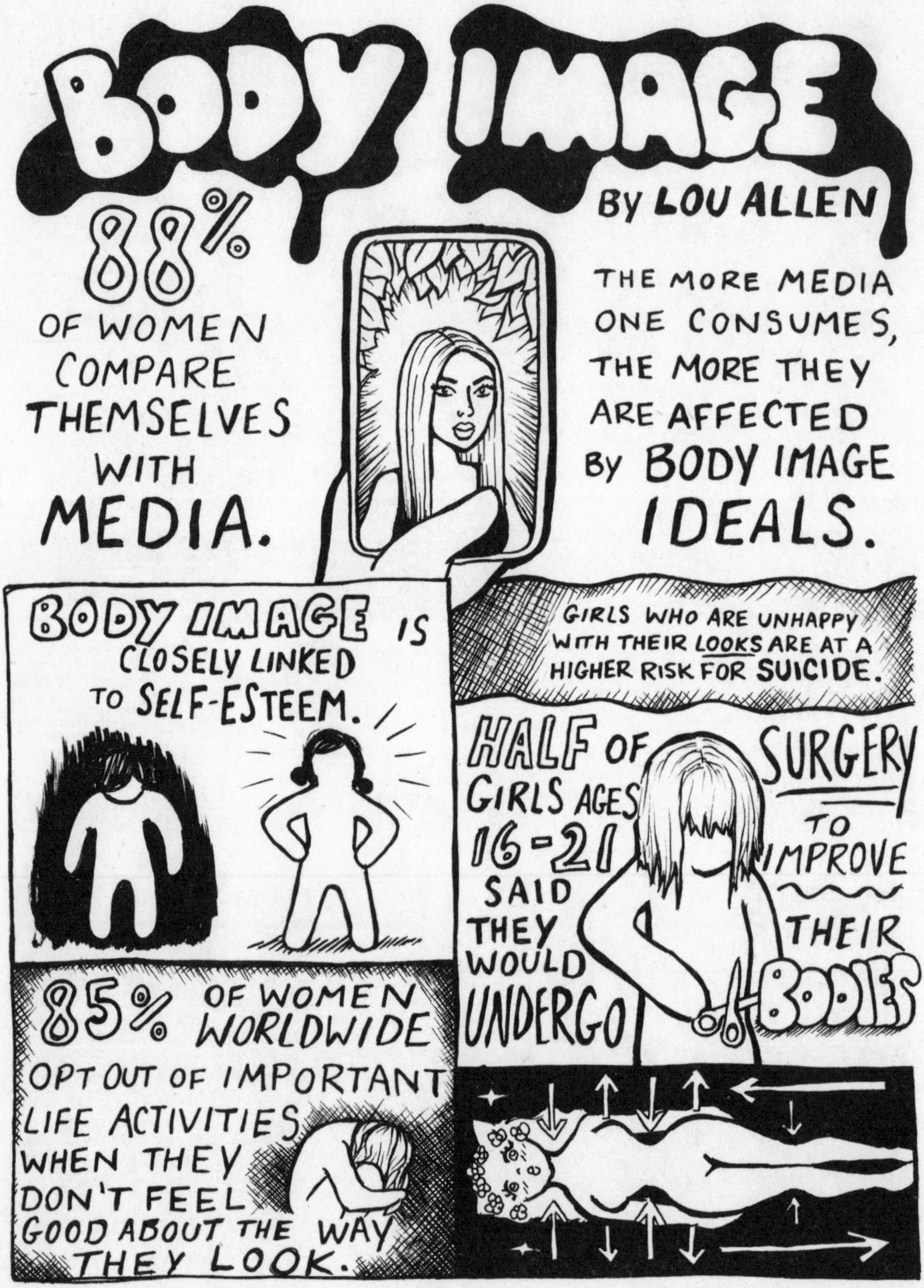
BODY IMAGE
BY LOU ALLEN
88% OF WOMEN COMPARE THEMSELVES WITH MEDIA.
THE MORE MEDIA ONE CONSUMES, THE MORE THEY ARE AFFECTED BY BODY IMAGE IDEALS.
BODY IMAGE IS CLOSELY LINKED TO SELF-ESTEEM.
GIRLS WHO ARE UNHAPPY WITH THEIR LOOKS ARE AT A HIGHER RISK FOR SUICIDE.
HALF OF GIRLS AGES 16-21 SAID THEY WOULD UNDERGO SURGERY TO IMPROVE THEIR BODIES
85% OF WOMEN WORLDWIDE OPT OUT OF IMPORTANT LIFE ACTIVITIES WHEN THEY DON'T FEEL GOOD ABOUT THE WAY THEY LOOK.

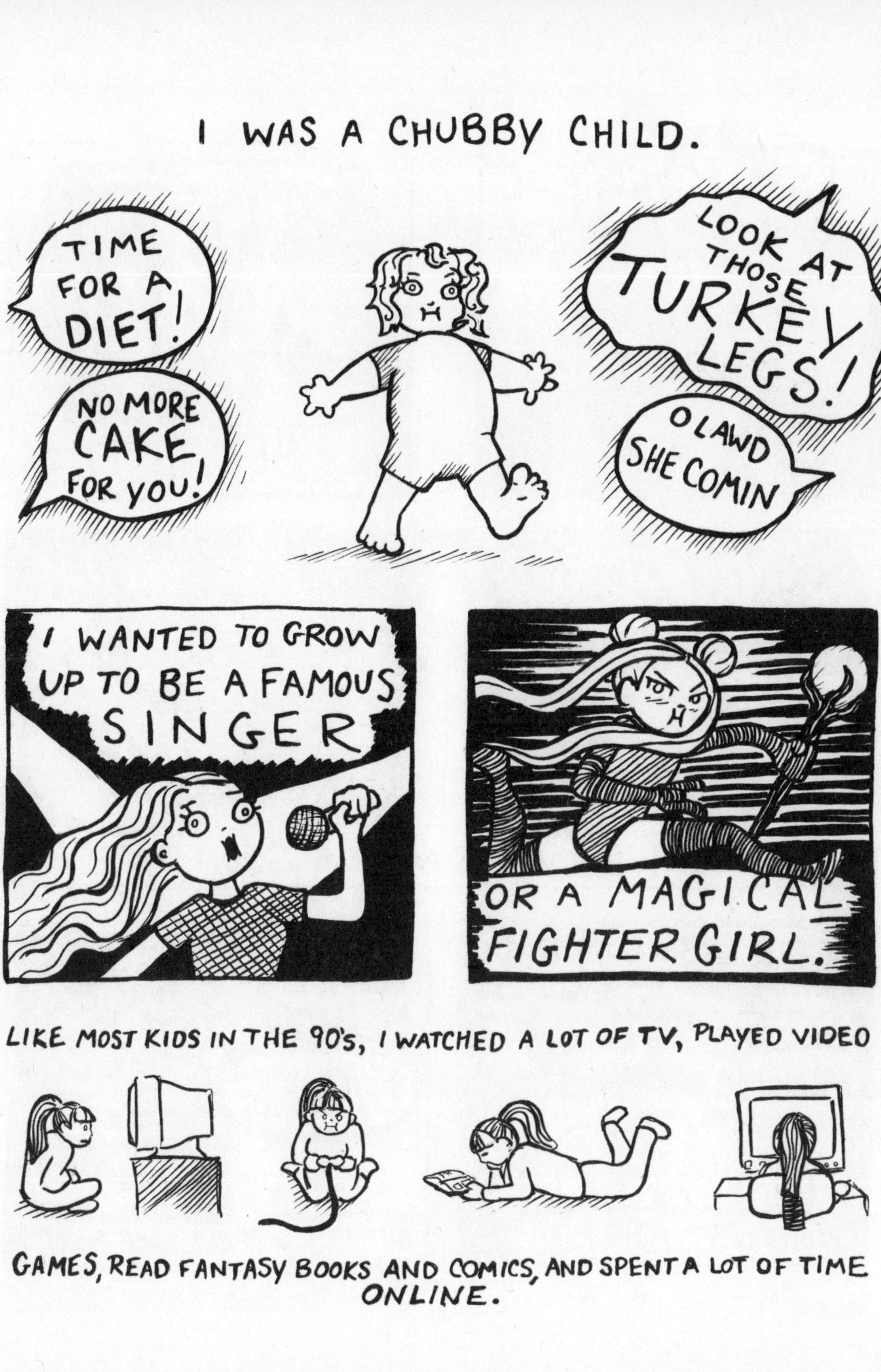
I WAS A CHUBBY CHILD.
TIME FOR A DIET!
NO MORE CAKE FOR YOU!
LOOK AT THOSE TURKEY LEGS!
O LAWD SHE COMIN
I WANTED TO GROW UP TO BE A FAMOUS SINGER
OR A MAGICAL FIGHTER GIRL.
LIKE MOST KIDS IN THE 90's, I WATCHED A LOT OF TV, PLAYED VIDEO
GAMES, READ FANTASY BOOKS AND COMICS, AND SPENT A LOT OF TIME ONLINE.

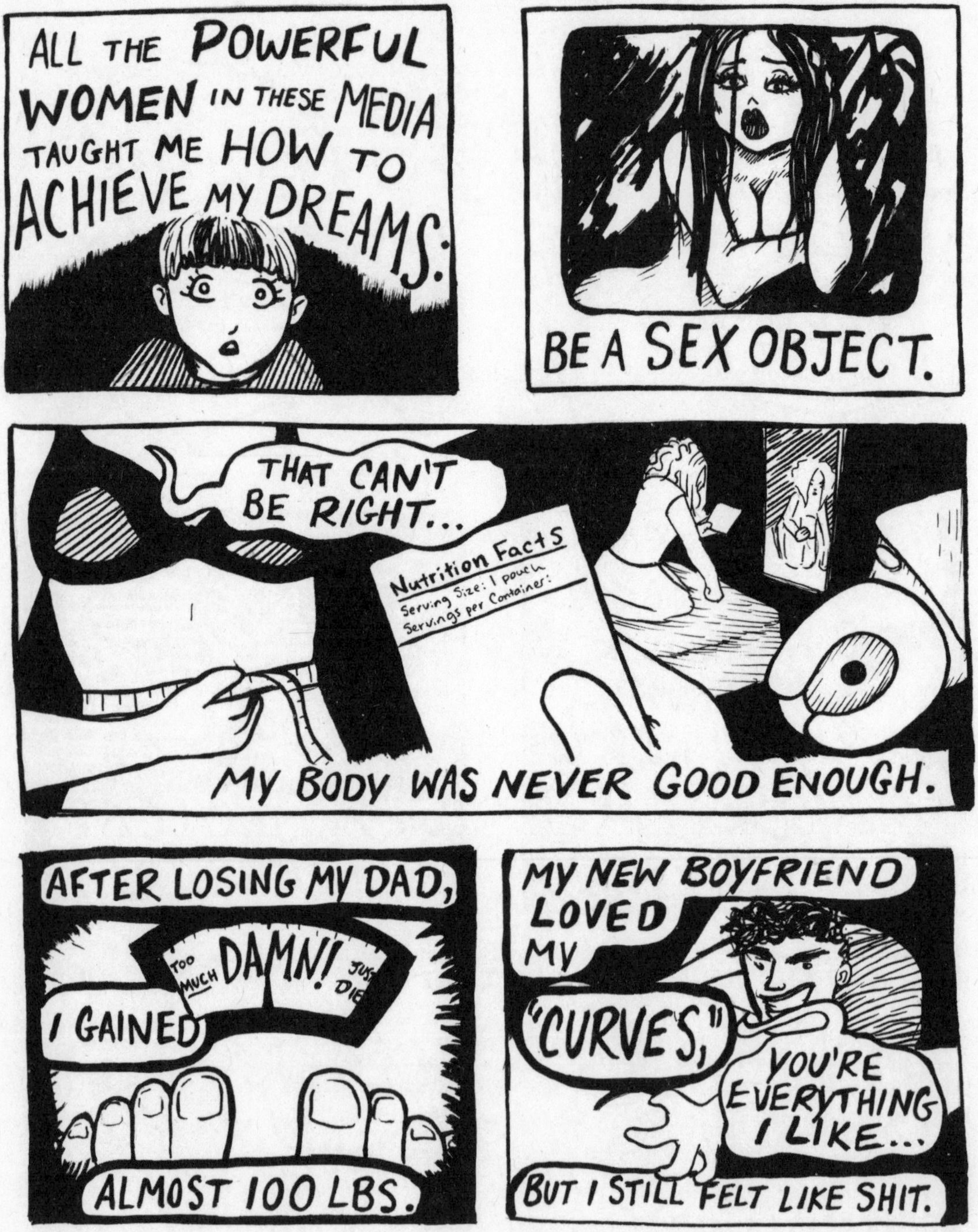

ALL THE POWERFUL WOMEN IN THESE MEDIA TAUGHT ME HOW TO ACHIEVE MY DREAMS:
BE A SEX OBJECT.
THAT CAN'T BE RIGHT...
Nutrition Facts
Serving Size: 1 pouch
Servings per Container:
MY BODY WAS NEVER GOOD ENOUGH.
AFTER LOSING MY DAD,
TOO MUCH
DAMN!
JUST DIE
I GAINED
ALMOST 100 LBS.
MY NEW BOYFRIEND LOVED MY
"CURVES,"
YOU'RE EVERYTHING I LIKE...
BUT I STILL FELT LIKE SHIT.

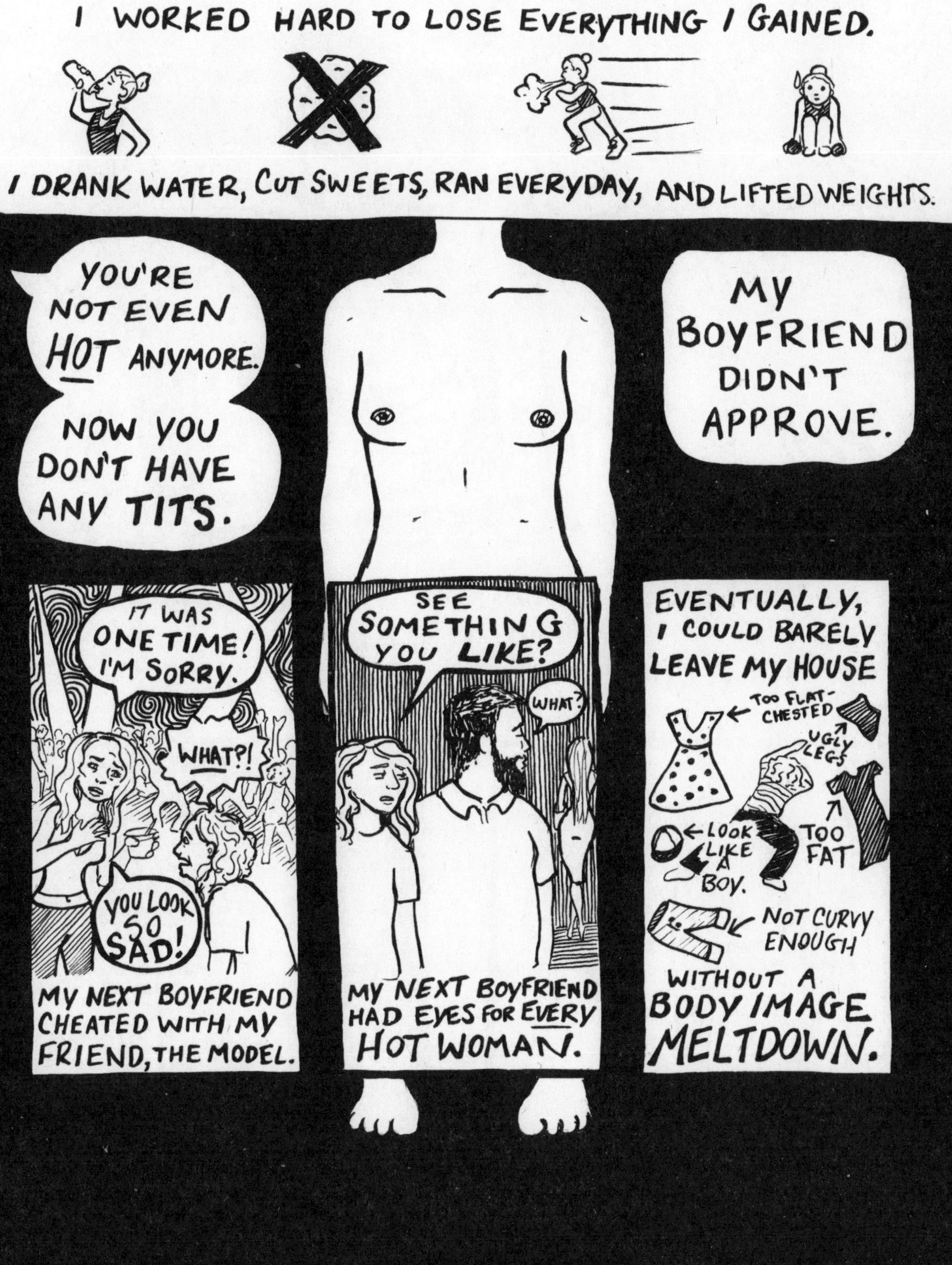
I WORKED HARD TO LOSE EVERYTHING I GAINED.
I DRANK WATER, CUT SWEETS, RAN EVERYDAY, AND LIFTED WEIGHTS.
YOU'RE NOT EVEN HOT ANYMORE.
NOW YOU DON'T HAVE ANY TITS.
MY BOYFRIEND DIDN'T APPROVE.
IT WAS ONE TIME! I'M SORRY.
WHAT?!
YOU LOOK SO SAD!
MY NEXT BOYFRIEND CHEATED WITH MY FRIEND, THE MODEL.
SEE SOMETHING YOU LIKE?
WHAT?
MY NEXT BOYFRIEND HAD EYES FOR EVERY HOT WOMAN.
EVENTUALLY, I COULD BARELY LEAVE MY HOUSE
TOO FLAT-CHESTED
UGLY LEGS
TOO FAT
LOOK LIKE A BOY.
NOT CURVY ENOUGH
WITHOUT A BODY IMAGE MELTDOWN.

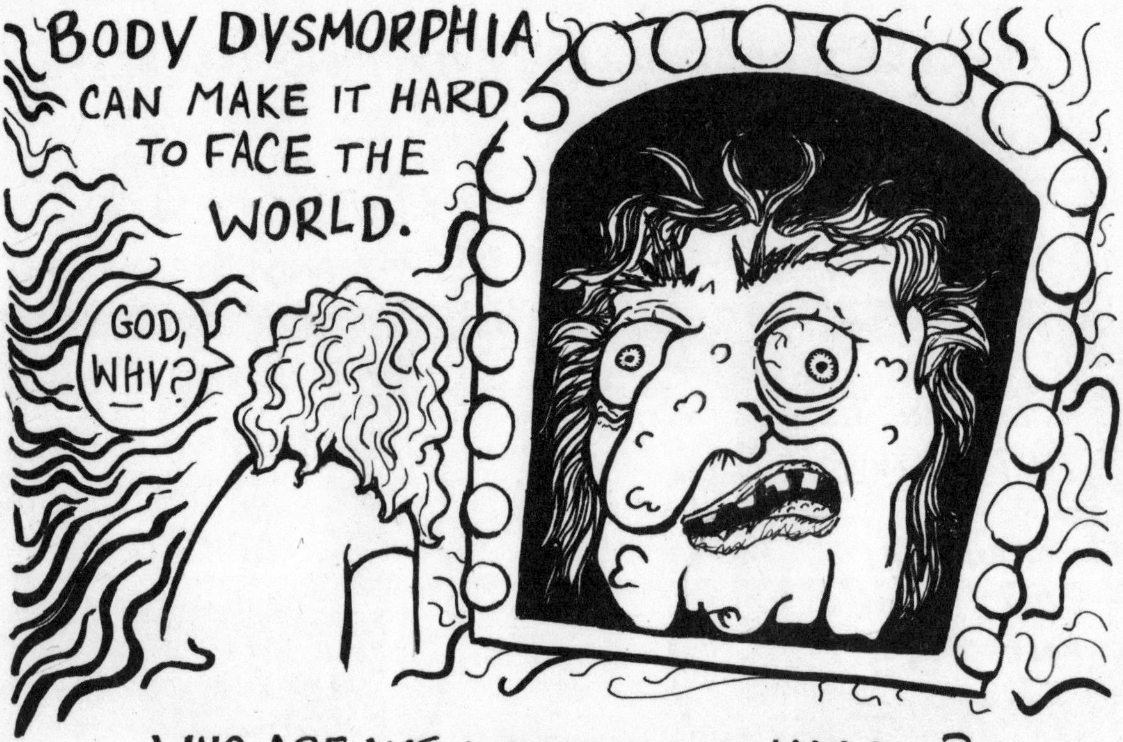
BODY DYSMORPHIA CAN MAKE IT HARD TO FACE THE WORLD.
GOD, WHY?

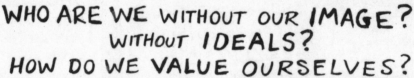

WHO ARE WE WITHOUT OUR IMAGE?
WITHOUT IDEALS?
HOW DO WE VALUE OURSELVES?

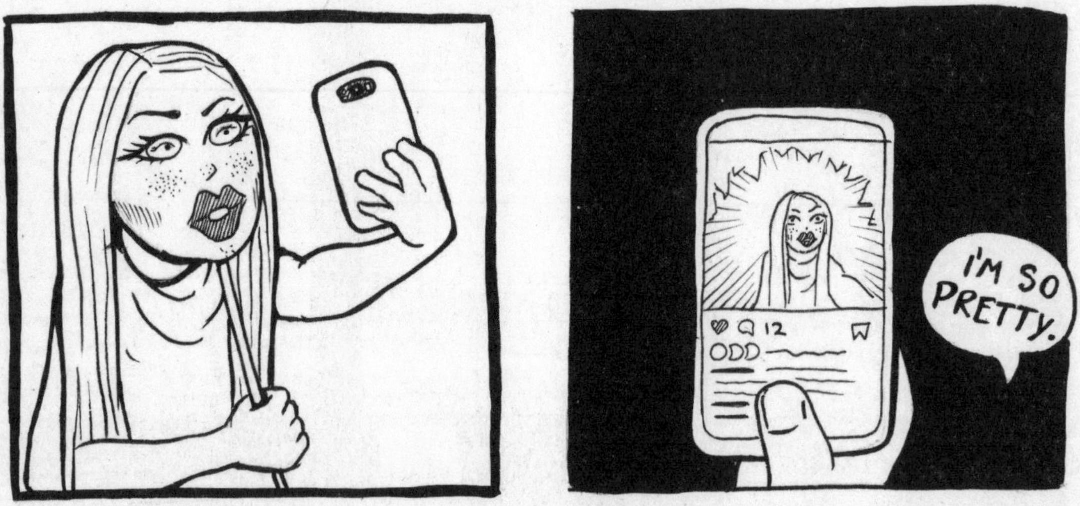
12
ODD
I'M SO PRETTY.

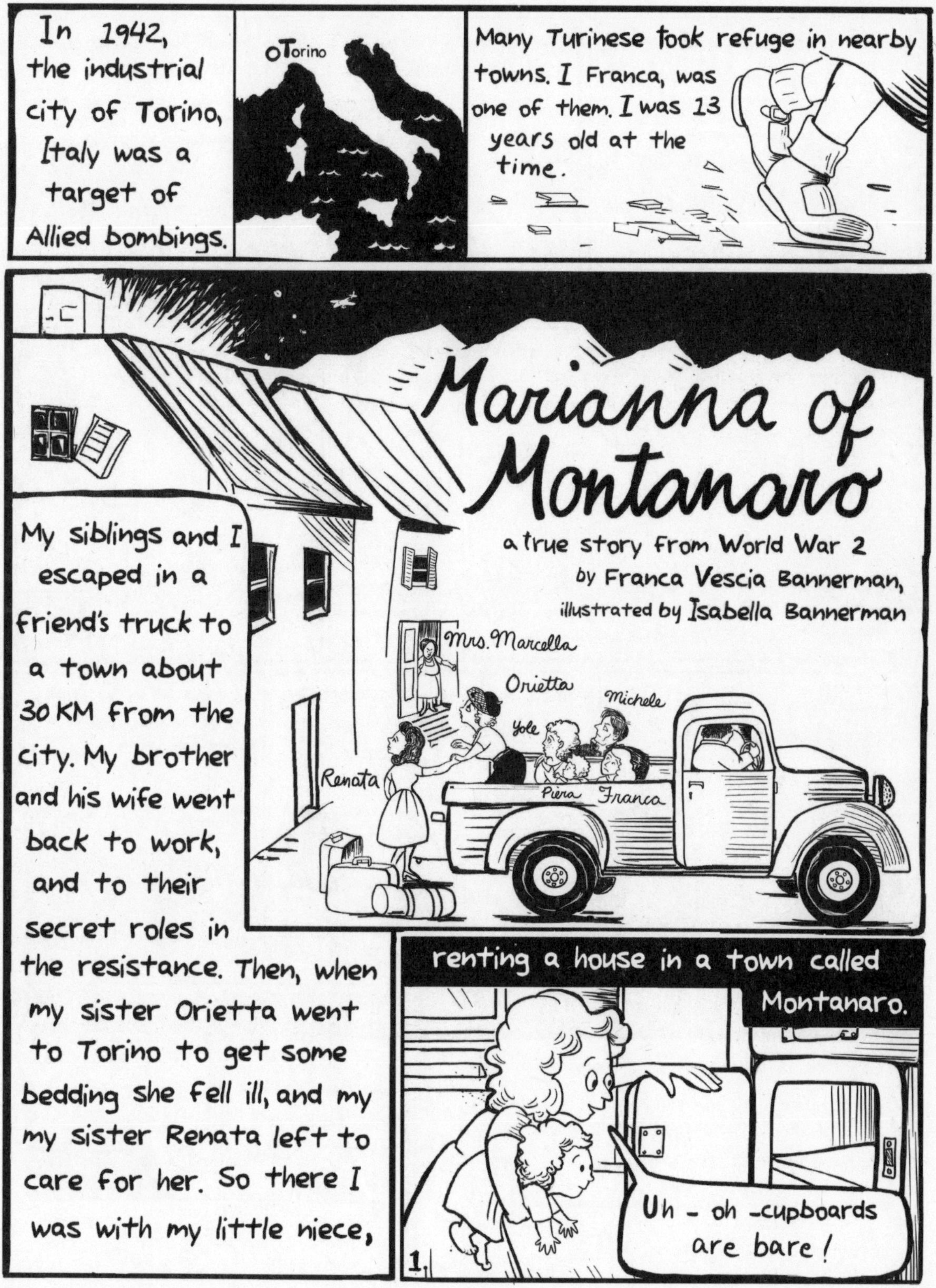
In 1942, the industrial city of Torino, Italy was a target of Allied bombings.
Torino
Many Turinese took refuge in nearby towns. I Franca, was one of them. I was 13 years old at the time.
Marianna of Montanaro
a true story from World War 2
by Franca Vescia Bannerman,
illustrated by Isabella Bannerman
My siblings and I escaped in a friend's truck to a town about 30 KM from the city. My brother and his wife went back to work, and to their secret roles in the resistance. Then, when my sister Orietta went to Torino to get some bedding she fell ill, and my my sister Renata left to care for her. So there I was with my little niece,
Mrs. Marcella
Orietta
Michele
Yole
Renata
Piera
Franca
renting a house in a town called Montanaro.
Uh - oh -cupboards are bare!
1

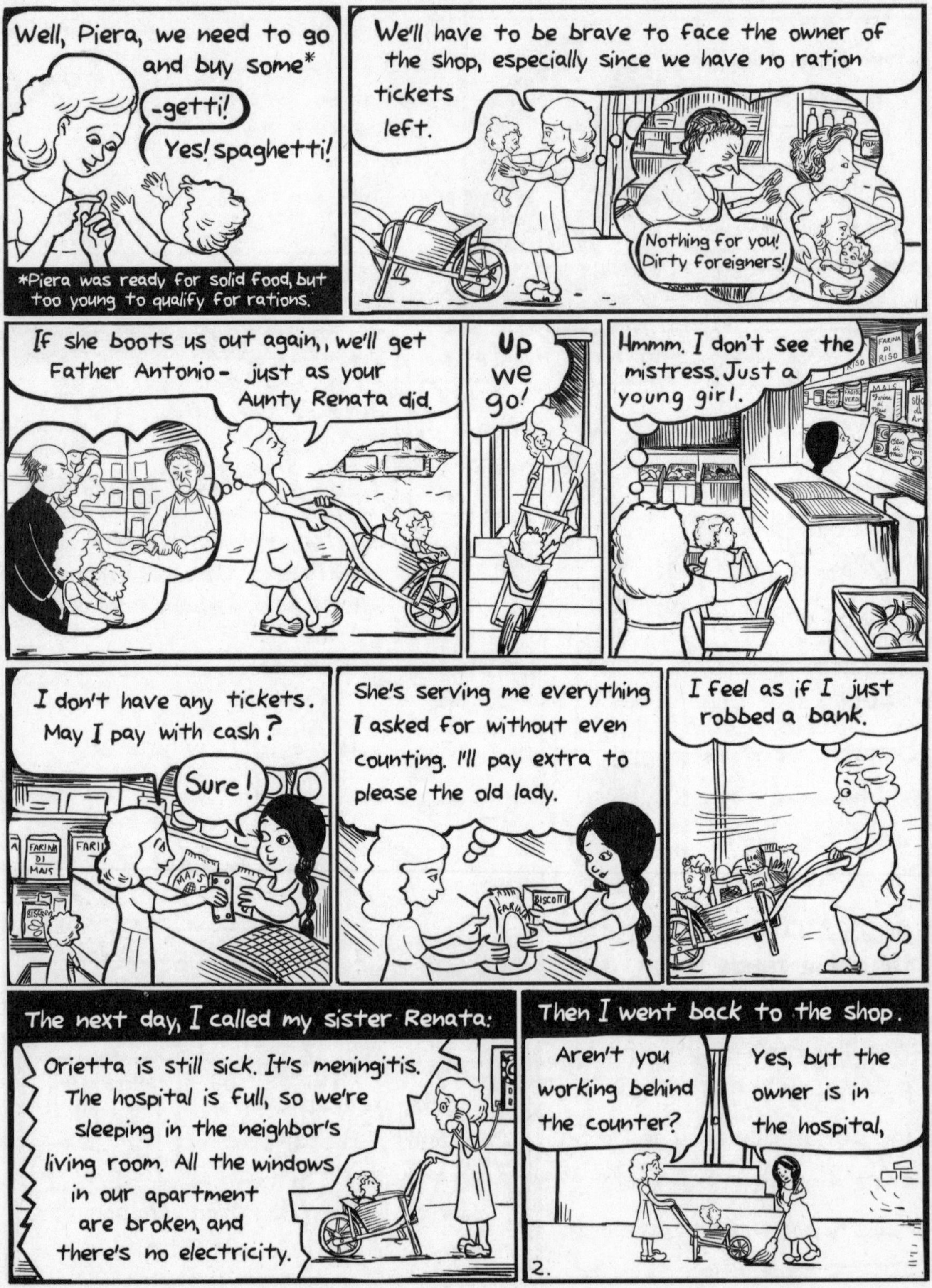
Well, Piera, we need to go and buy some*
-getti!
Yes! spaghetti!
*Piera was ready for solid food, but too young to qualify for rations.
We'll have to be brave to face the owner of the shop, especially since we have no ration tickets left.
Nothing for you! Dirty foreigners!
POMO
If she boots us out again,, we'll get Father Antonio- just as your Aunty Renata did.
Up we go!
Hmmm. I don't see the mistress. Just a young girl.
FARINA DI RISO
RISO
MAIS
I don't have any tickets. May I pay with cash?
Sure!
FARINA DI MAIS
MAIS
She's serving me everything I asked for without even counting. I'll pay extra to please the old lady.
FARINA
BISCOTTI
I feel as if I just robbed a bank.
The next day, I called my sister Renata:
Orietta is still sick. It's meningitis. The hospital is full, so we're sleeping in the neighbor's living room. All the windows in our apartment are broken, and there's no electricity.
Then I went back to the shop.
Aren't you working behind the counter?
Yes, but the owner is in the hospital,
2.

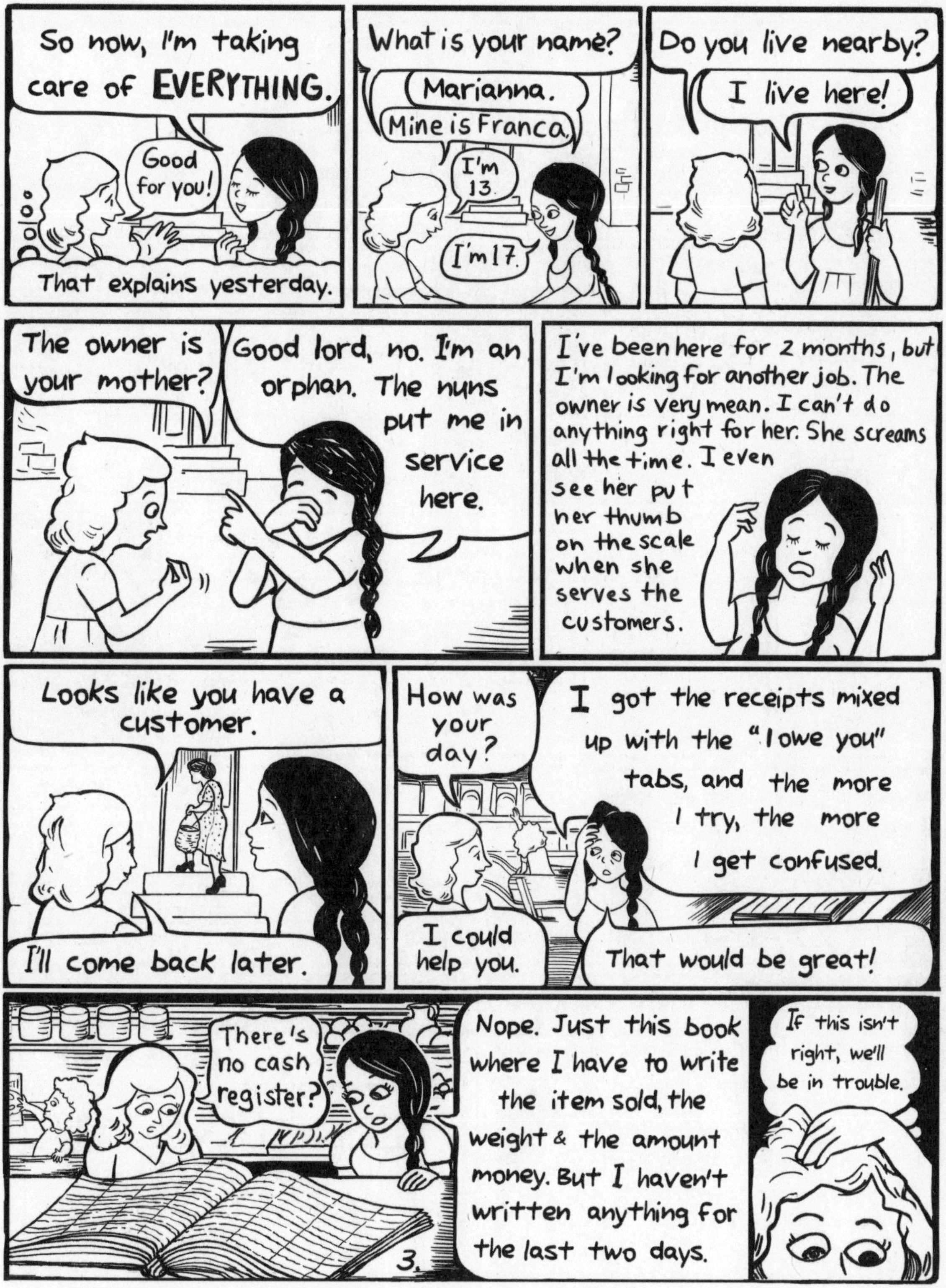
So now, I'm taking care of EVERYTHING.
Good for you!
That explains yesterday.
What is your name?
Marianna.
Mine is Franca.
I'm 13.
I'm 17.
Do you live nearby?
I live here!
The owner is your mother?
Good lord, no. I'm an orphan. The nuns put me in service here.
I've been here for 2 months, but I'm looking for another job. The owner is very mean. I can't do anything right for her. She screams all the time. I even see her put her thumb on the scale when she serves the customers.
Looks like you have a customer.
I'll come back later.
How was your day?
I got the receipts mixed up with the "I owe you" tabs, and the more I try, the more I get confused.
I could help you.
That would be great!
There's no cash register?
Nope. Just this book where I have to write the item sold, the weight & the amount money. But I haven't written anything for the last two days.
3.
If this isn't right, we'll be in trouble.

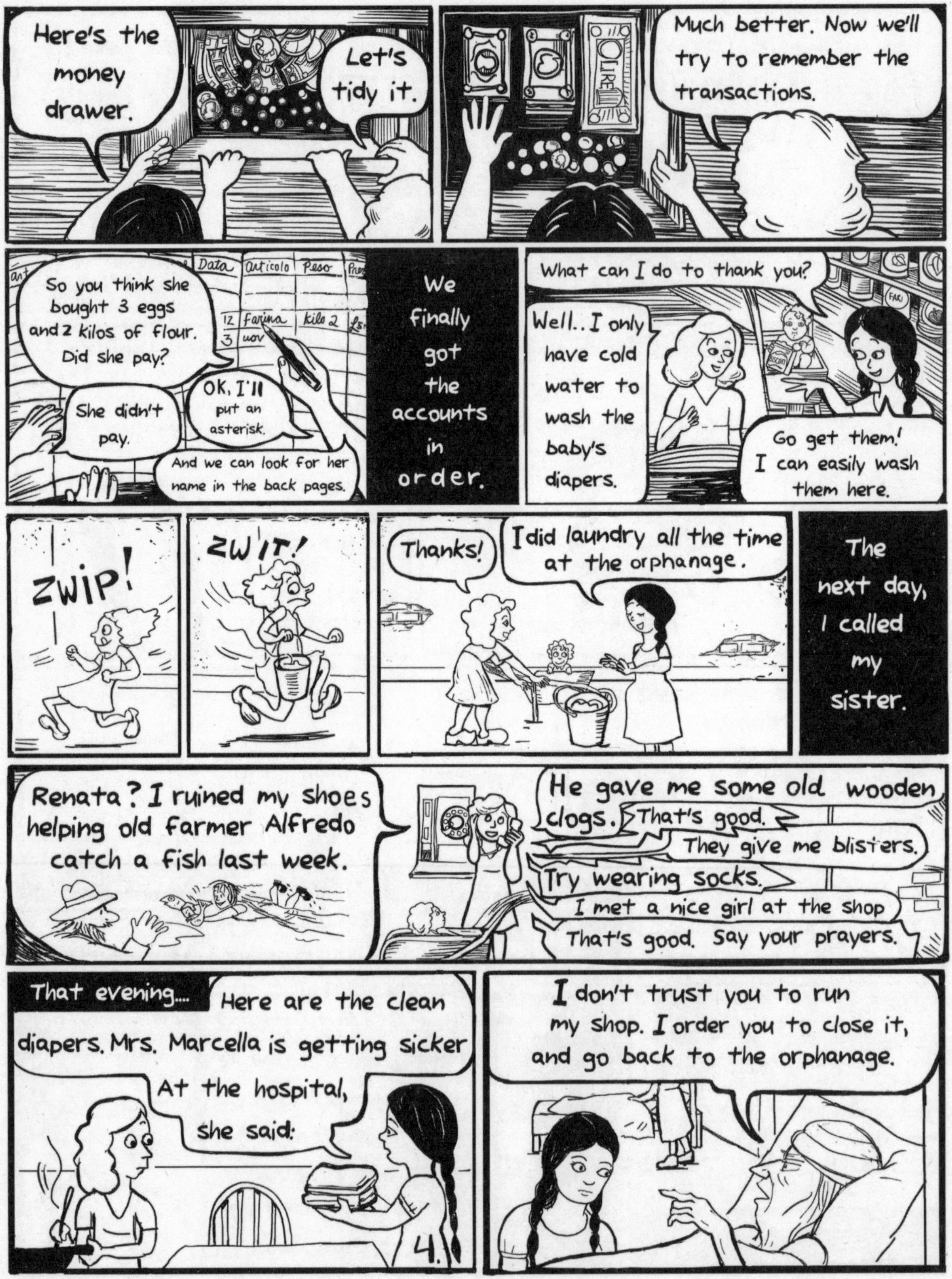

Here's the money drawer.
Let's tidy it.
Much better. Now we'll try to remember the transactions.
So you think she bought 3 eggs and 2 kilos of flour. Did she pay?
She didn't pay.
OK, I'll put an asterisk.
And we can look for her name in the back pages.
We finally got the accounts in order.
What can I do to thank you?
Well.. I only have cold water to wash the baby's diapers.
Go get them! I can easily wash them here.
ZWIP!
ZWIT!
Thanks!
I did laundry all the time at the orphanage.
The next day, I called my sister.
Renata? I ruined my shoes helping old farmer Alfredo catch a fish last week.
He gave me some old wooden clogs.
That's good.
They give me blisters.
Try wearing socks.
I met a nice girl at the shop
That's good. Say your prayers.
That evening....
Here are the clean diapers. Mrs. Marcella is getting sicker
At the hospital, she said:
I don't trust you to run my shop. I order you to close it, and go back to the orphanage.

I don't want to go back. The nuns make me work non-stop and I am always hungry.
You can live here.
I'll pay you to help me with the baby. Let's go close the shop.
MMWA!
I should be thanking you!
And I'll buy more food for us.
Agreed!
Ok, now the registry is tidy, and we have 2 inventories: one for the police, and one for Mrs. Marcella.
We brought the food back to our house, and
Marianna gave the papers to
the policeman, and he locked up.
Got all your things? In the morning, we'll go to the hospital, and see what Mrs. Marcella wants to do with the keys, register book and money.
By Order of the Town of Montanaro Province of Turin Carabinieri
Closed until further notice
M.G. Vergnano
Registro
You did a good job.
Did it go all right?
Yes, and the policeman said he would let me in if I needed to do laundry.
A few days passed peacefully.
But at night, I worried:
I know it wasn't right to buy food without ration tickets, but I had none. Will the police arrest me? Did I do the right thing to have Marianna move in here?
5.
Sometimes, there was "good" news.
THE BOMBINGS OF TORINO HAVE ENDED!
They say it as though it's a victory-when, in fact, there's nothing left to bomb.

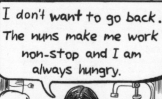

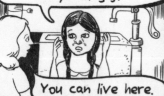

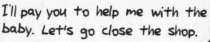

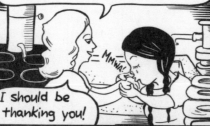

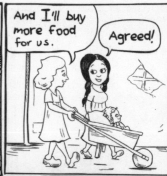

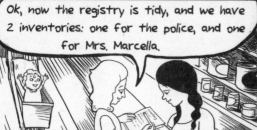

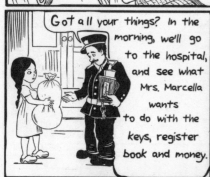

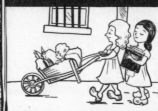

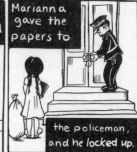

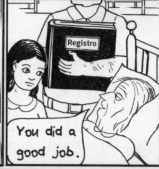

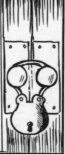

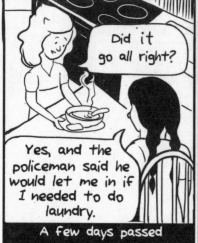

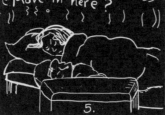

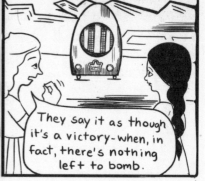

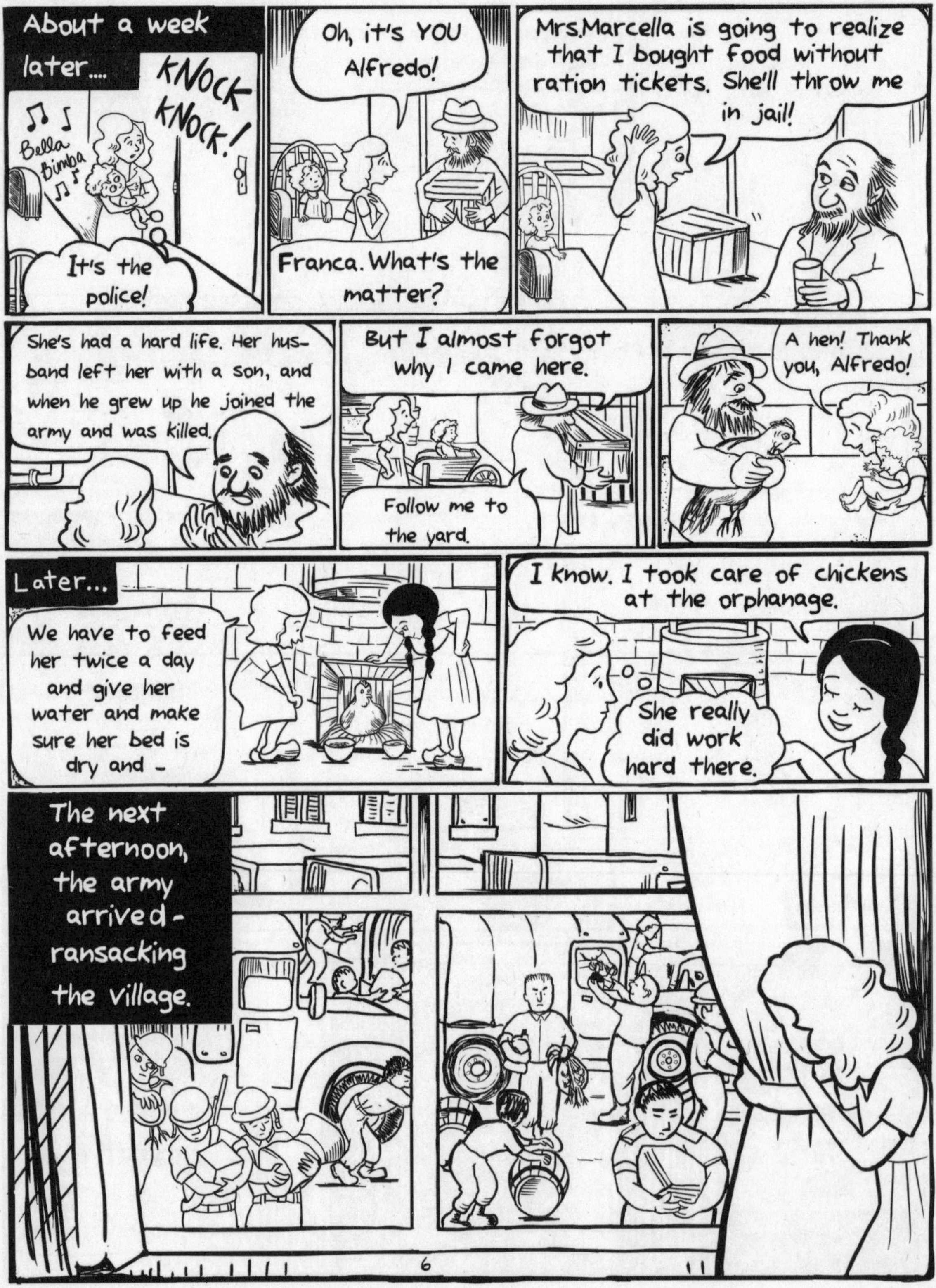
About a week later....
♫ Bella Bimba ♫
KNOCK KNOCK!
It's the police!
Oh, it's YOU Alfredo!
Franca. What's the matter?
Mrs.Marcella is going to realize that I bought food without ration tickets. She'll throw me in jail!
She's had a hard life. Her husband left her with a son, and when he grew up he joined the army and was killed.
But I almost forgot why I came here.
Follow me to the yard.
A hen! Thank you, Alfredo!
Later...
We have to feed her twice a day and give her water and make sure her bed is dry and –
I know. I took care of chickens at the orphanage.
She really did work hard there.
The next afternoon, the army arrived – ransacking the village.
6

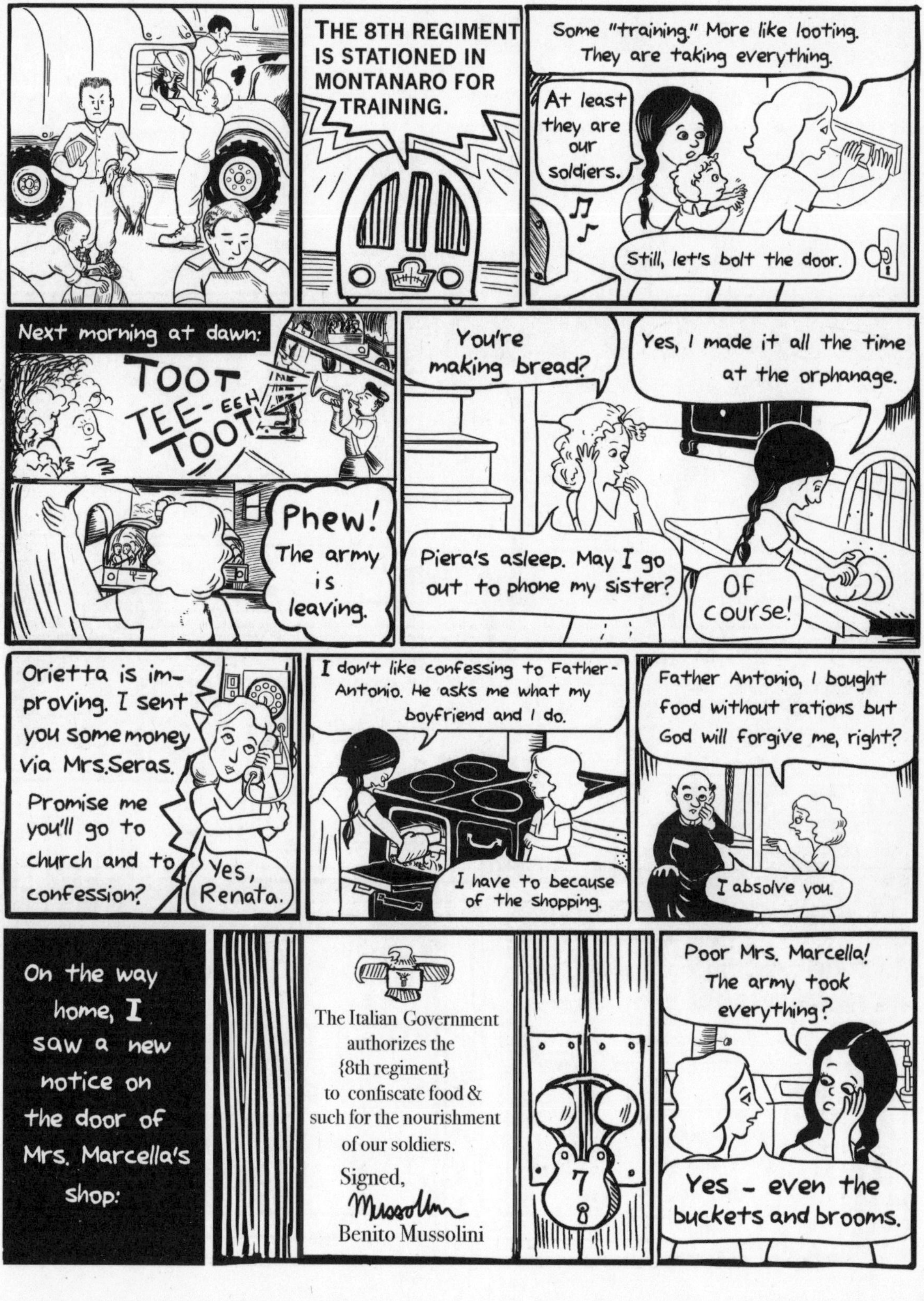
THE 8TH REGIMENT IS STATIONED IN MONTANARO FOR TRAINING.
Some "training." More like looting. They are taking everything.
At least they are our soldiers.
Still, let's bolt the door.
Next morning at dawn:
TOOT TEE-EEH TOOT!
Phew! The army is leaving.
You're making bread?
Yes, I made it all the time at the orphanage.
Piera's asleep. May I go out to phone my sister?
Of course!
Orietta is improving. I sent you some money via Mrs.Seras.
Promise me you'll go to church and to confession?
Yes, Renata.
I don't like confessing to Father Antonio. He asks me what my boyfriend and I do.
I have to because of the shopping.
Father Antonio, I bought food without rations but God will forgive me, right?
I absolve you.
On the way home, I saw a new notice on the door of Mrs. Marcella's shop:
The Italian Government authorizes the {8th regiment} to confiscate food & such for the nourishment of our soldiers.
Signed,
Mussolini
Benito Mussolini
7
8
Poor Mrs. Marcella! The army took everything?
Yes - even the buckets and brooms.

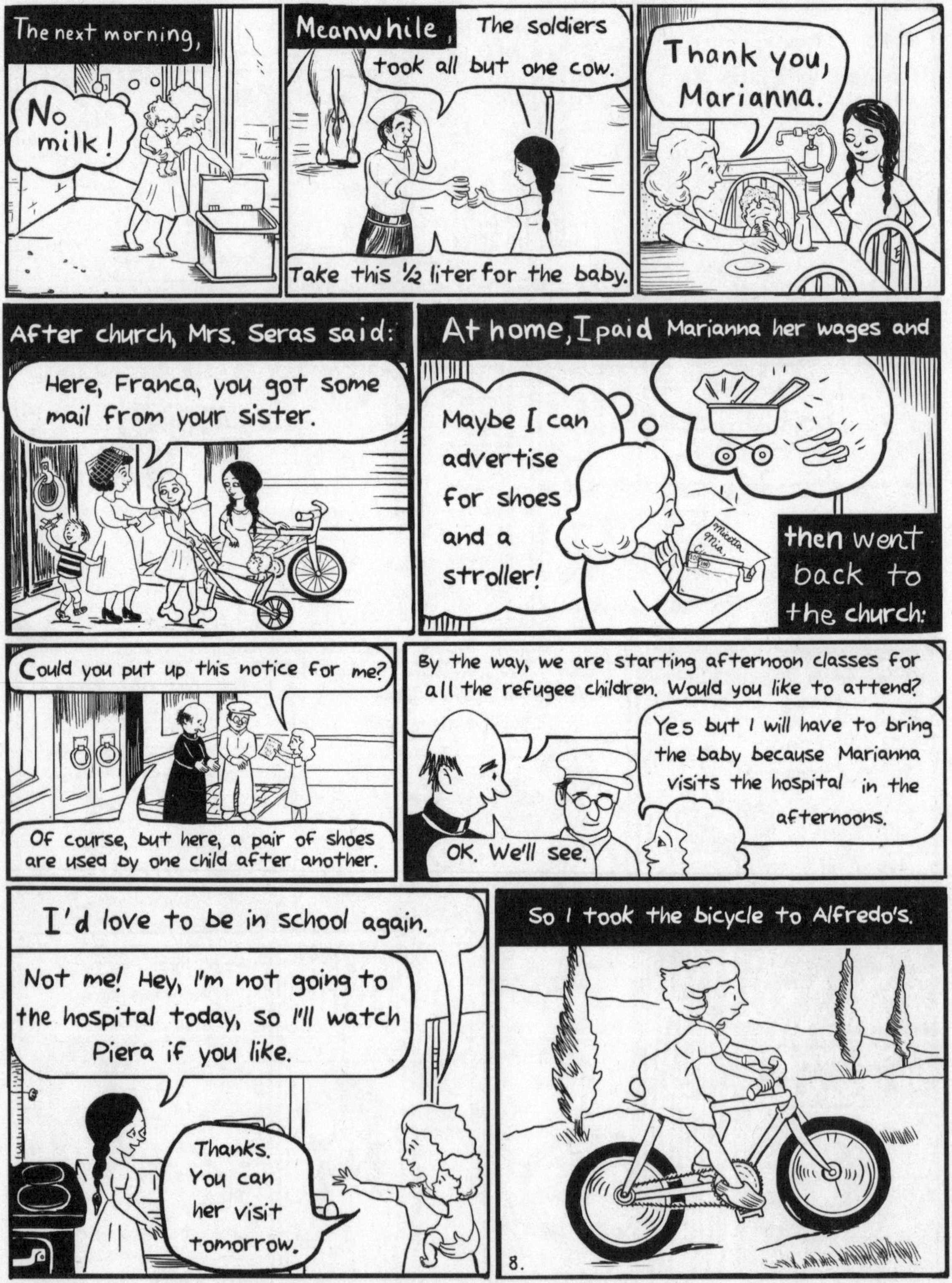
The next morning,
No milk!
Meanwhile,
The soldiers took all but one cow.
Take this ½ liter for the baby.
Thank you, Marianna.
After church, Mrs. Seras said:
Here, Franca, you got some mail from your sister.
At home, I paid Marianna her wages and
Maybe I can advertise for shoes and a stroller!
Micetta Mia, Cia
then went back to the church:
Could you put up this notice for me?
Of course, but here, a pair of shoes are used by one child after another.
By the way, we are starting afternoon classes for all the refugee children. Would you like to attend?
Yes but I will have to bring the baby because Marianna visits the hospital in the afternoons.
OK. We'll see.
I'd love to be in school again.
Not me! Hey, I'm not going to the hospital today, so I'll watch Piera if you like.
Thanks. You can her visit tomorrow.
So I took the bicycle to Alfredo's.
8.

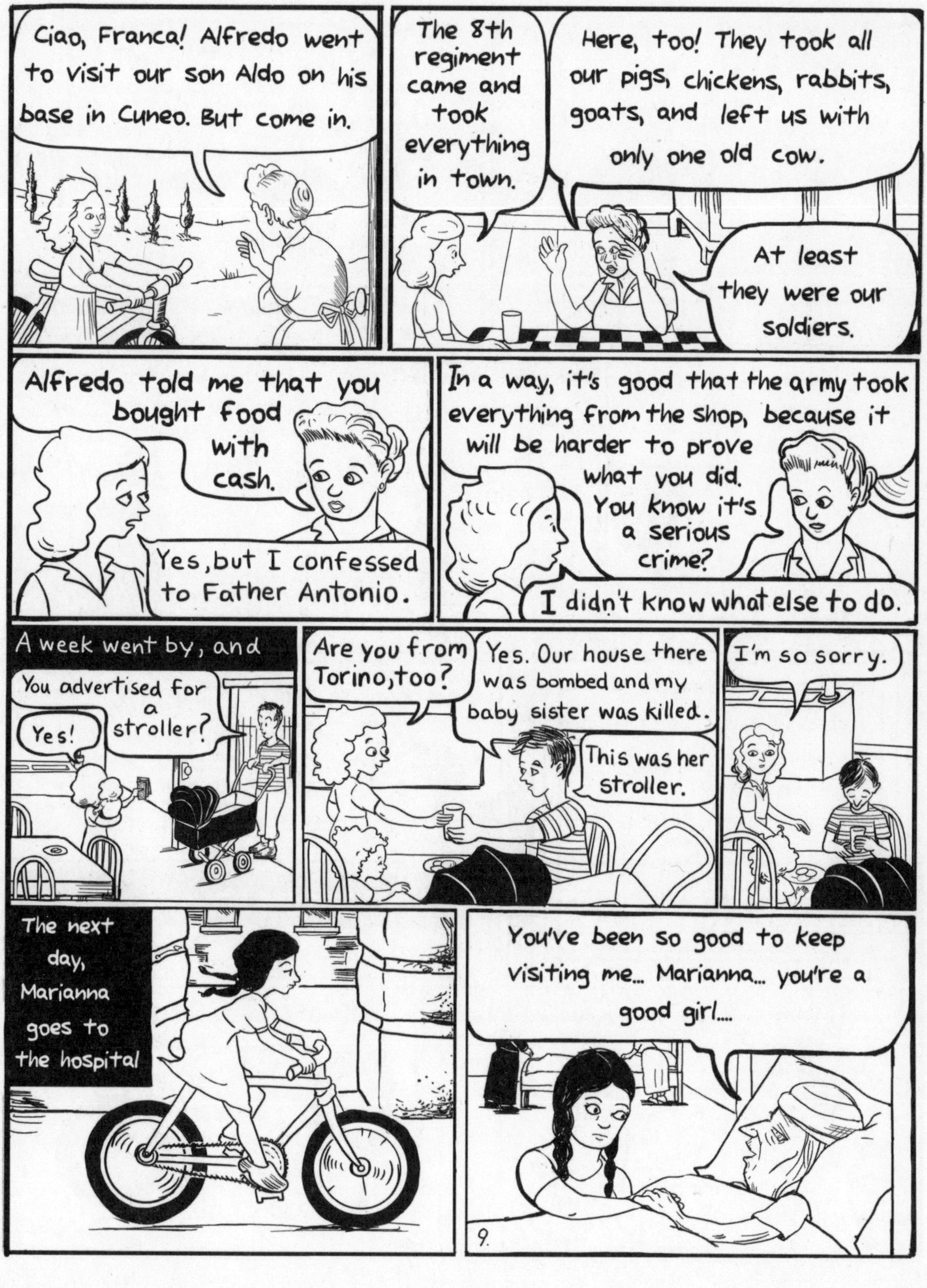

Ciao, Franca! Alfredo went to visit our son Aldo on his base in Cuneo. But come in.
The 8th regiment came and took everything in town.
Here, too! They took all our pigs, chickens, rabbits, goats, and left us with only one old cow.
At least they were our soldiers.
Alfredo told me that you bought food with cash.
Yes, but I confessed to Father Antonio.
In a way, it's good that the army took everything from the shop, because it will be harder to prove what you did.
You know it's a serious crime?
I didn't know what else to do.
A week went by, and
You advertised for a stroller?
Yes!
Are you from Torino, too?
Yes. Our house there was bombed and my baby sister was killed.
This was her stroller.
I'm so sorry.
The next day, Marianna goes to the hospital
You've been so good to keep visiting me... Marianna... you're a good girl....
9.

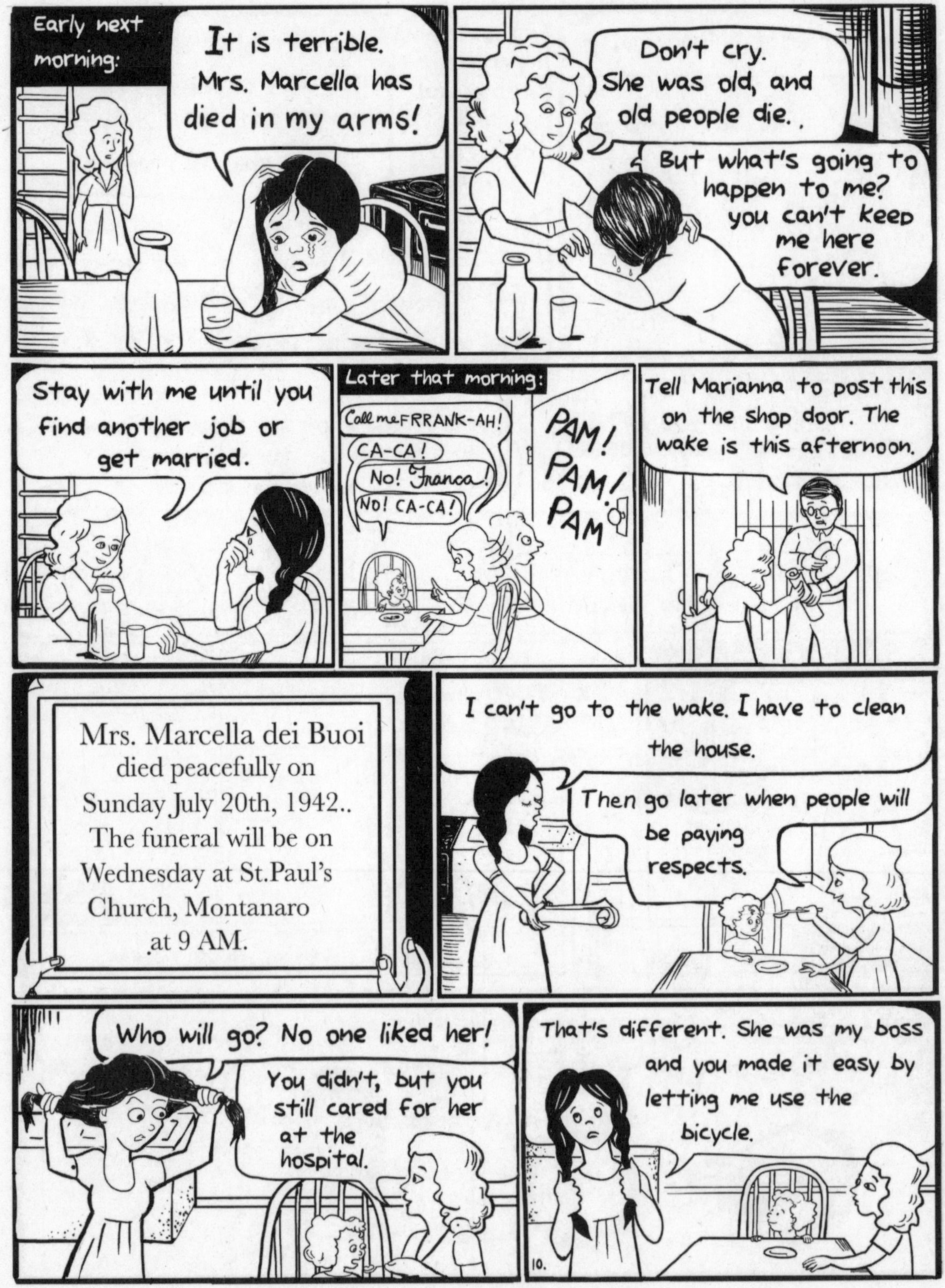

Early next morning:
It is terrible. Mrs. Marcella has died in my arms!
Don't cry. She was old, and old people die.
But what's going to happen to me? you can't keep me here forever.
Stay with me until you find another job or get married.
Later that morning:
Call me FRRANK-AH!
CA-CA!
No! Franca!
NO! CA-CA!
PAM! PAM! PAM
Tell Marianna to post this on the shop door. The wake is this afternoon.
Mrs. Marcella dei Buoi died peacefully on Sunday July 20th, 1942.. The funeral will be on Wednesday at St.Paul's Church, Montanaro at 9 AM.
I can't go to the wake. I have to clean the house.
Then go later when people will be paying respects.
Who will go? No one liked her!
You didn't, but you still cared for her at the hospital.
That's different. She was my boss and you made it easy by letting me use the bicycle.
10.

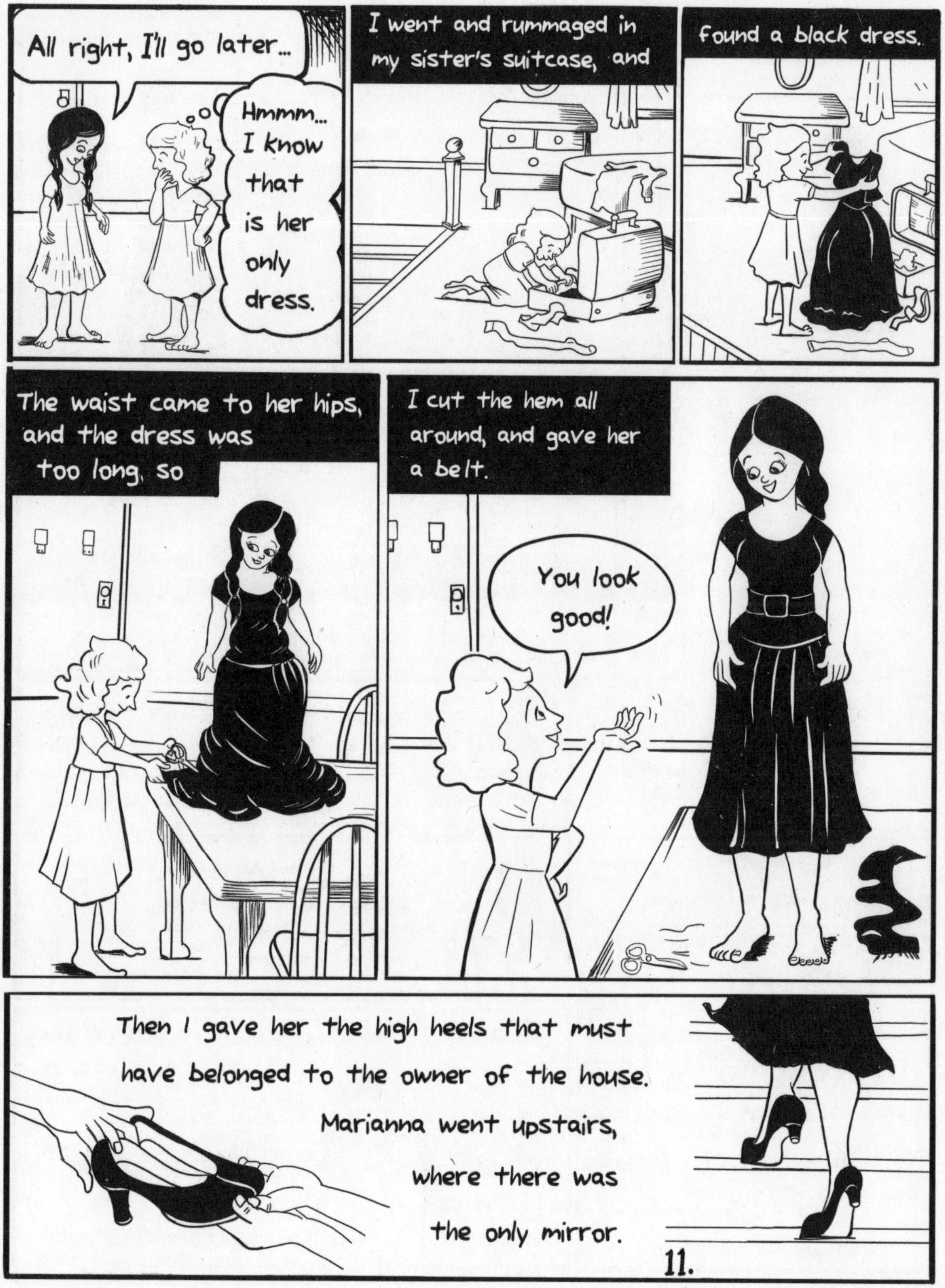
All right, I'll go later...
Hmmm... I know that is her only dress.
I went and rummaged in my sister's suitcase, and
found a black dress.
The waist came to her hips, and the dress was too long, so
I cut the hem all around, and gave her a belt.
You look good!
Then I gave her the high heels that must have belonged to the owner of the house.
Marianna went upstairs,
where there was the only mirror.
11.

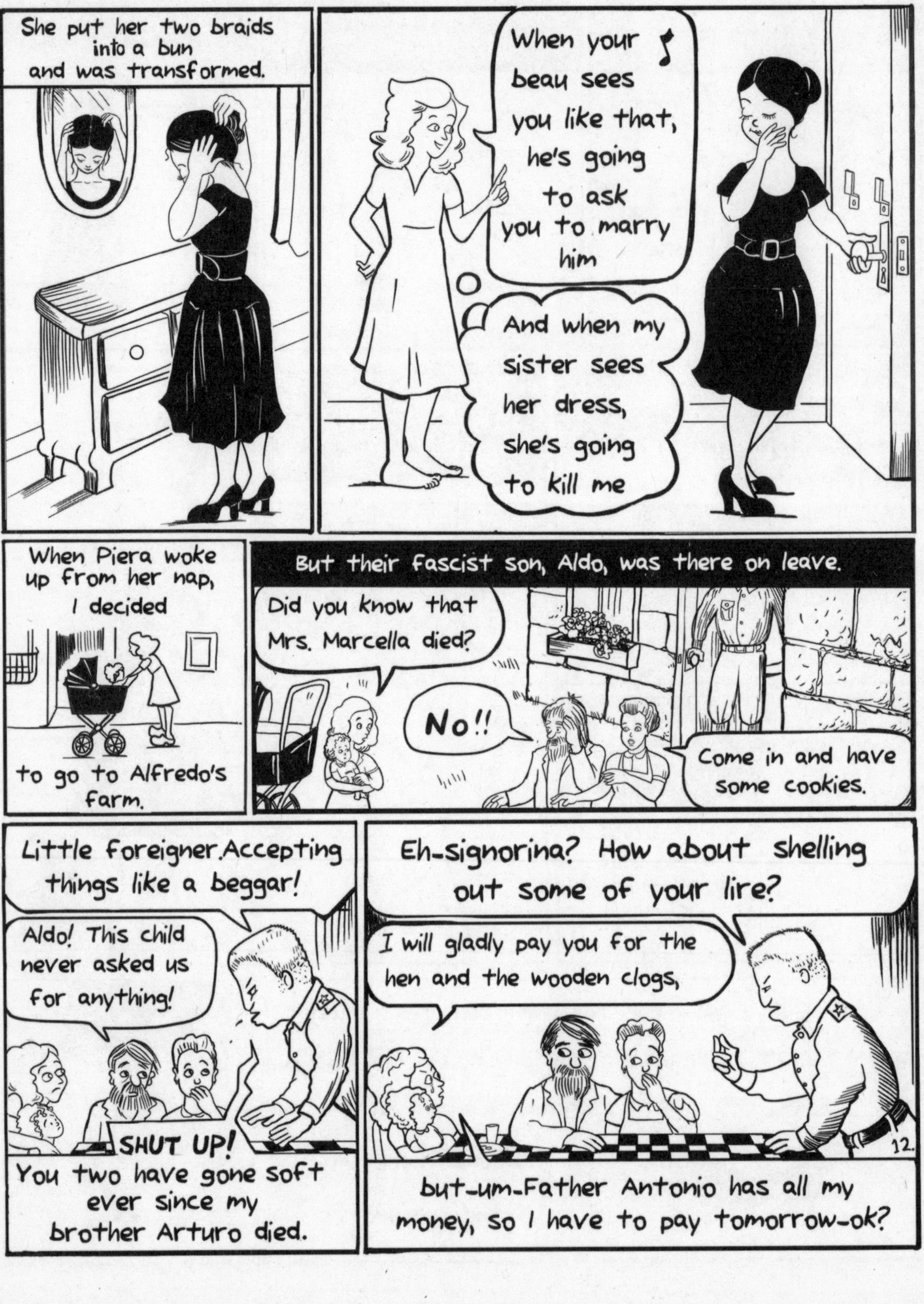
She put her two braids into a bun and was transformed.
When your beau sees you like that, he's going to ask you to marry him
And when my sister sees her dress, she's going to kill me
When Piera woke up from her nap, I decided
to go to Alfredo's farm.
But their fascist son, Aldo, was there on leave.
Did you know that Mrs. Marcella died?
No!!
Come in and have some cookies.
Little foreigner. Accepting things like a beggar!
Aldo! This child never asked us for anything!
SHUT UP!
You two have gone soft ever since my brother Arturo died.
Eh-signorina? How about shelling out some of your lire?
I will gladly pay you for the hen and the wooden clogs,
12.
but-um-Father Antonio has all my money, so I have to pay tomorrow-ok?

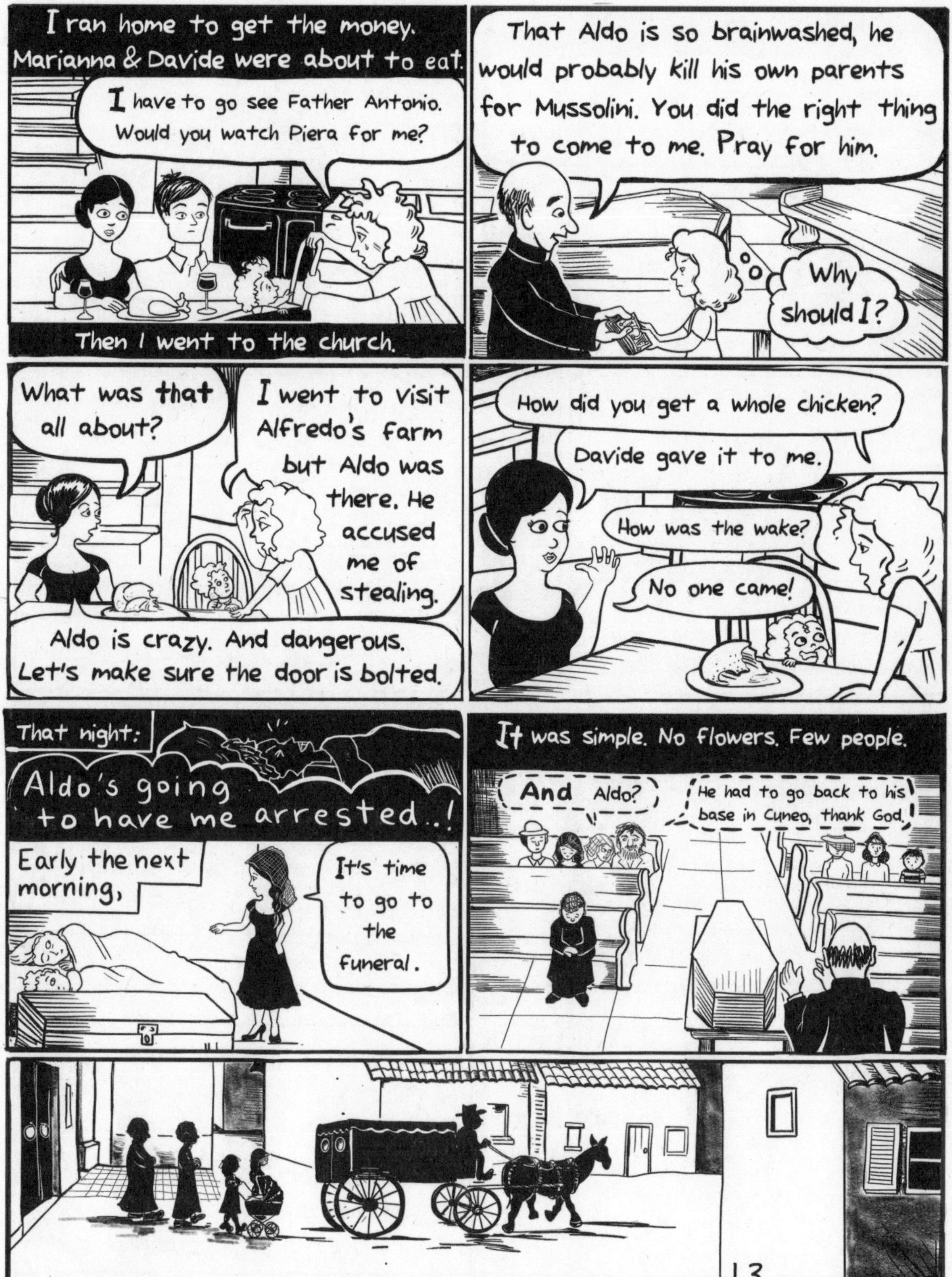
I ran home to get the money. Marianna & Davide were about to eat.
I have to go see Father Antonio. Would you watch Piera for me?
Then I went to the church.
That Aldo is so brainwashed, he would probably kill his own parents for Mussolini. You did the right thing to come to me. Pray for him.
Why should I?
What was that all about?
I went to visit Alfredo's farm but Aldo was there. He accused me of stealing.
Aldo is crazy. And dangerous. Let's make sure the door is bolted.
How did you get a whole chicken?
Davide gave it to me.
How was the wake?
No one came!
That night:
Aldo's going to have me arrested..!
Early the next morning,
It's time to go to the funeral.
It was simple. No flowers. Few people.
And Aldo?
He had to go back to his base in Cuneo, thank God.
13

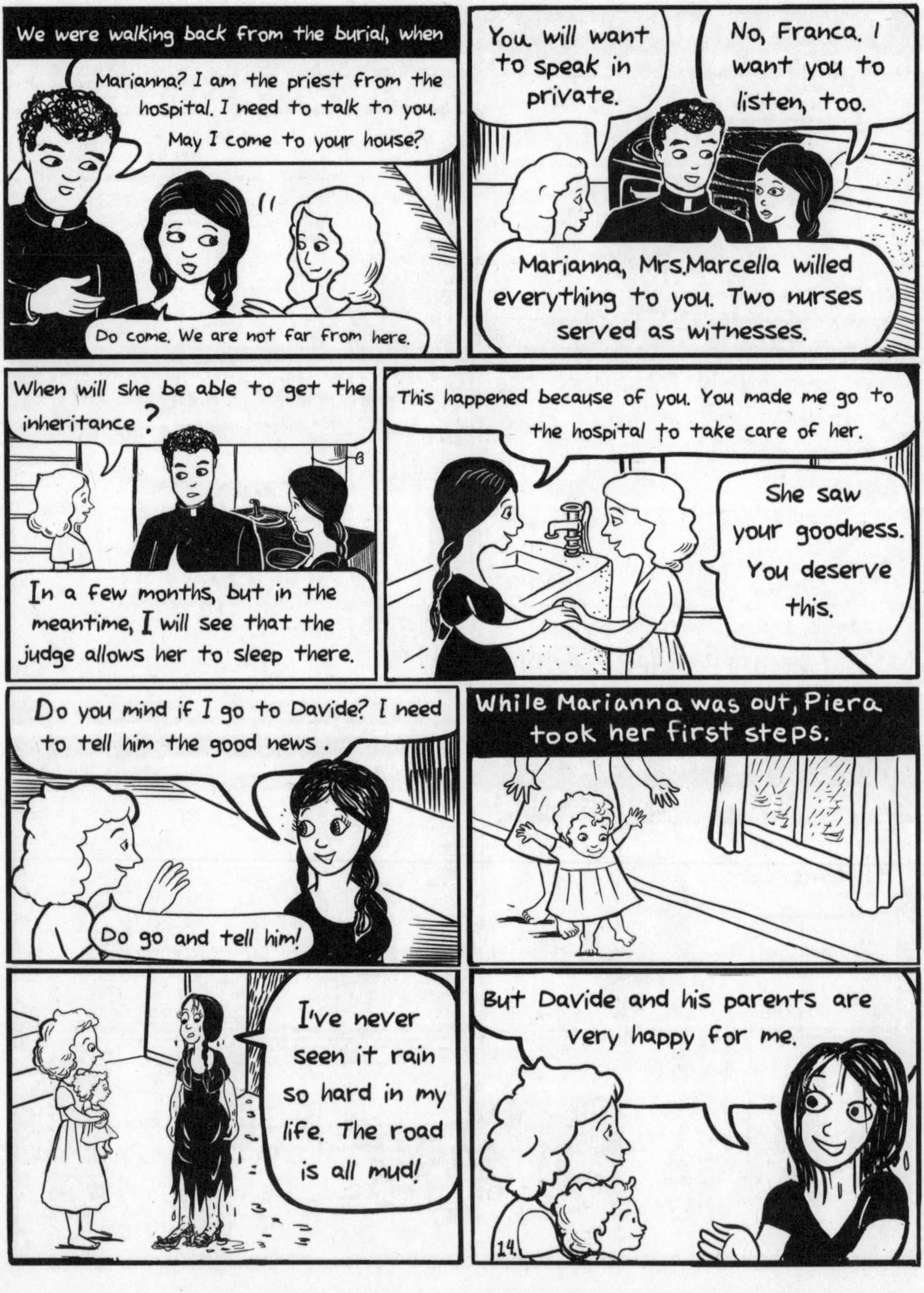

We were walking back from the burial, when
Marianna? I am the priest from the hospital. I need to talk tn you. May I come to your house?
Do come. We are not far from here.
You will want to speak in private.
No, Franca. I want you to listen, too.
Marianna, Mrs.Marcella willed everything to you. Two nurses served as witnesses.
When will she be able to get the inheritance?
In a few months, but in the meantime, I will see that the judge allows her to sleep there.
This happened because of you. You made me go to the hospital to take care of her.
She saw your goodness. You deserve this.
Do you mind if I go to Davide? I need to tell him the good news .
Do go and tell him!
While Marianna was out, Piera took her first steps.
I've never seen it rain so hard in my life. The road is all mud!
But Davide and his parents are very happy for me.
14.

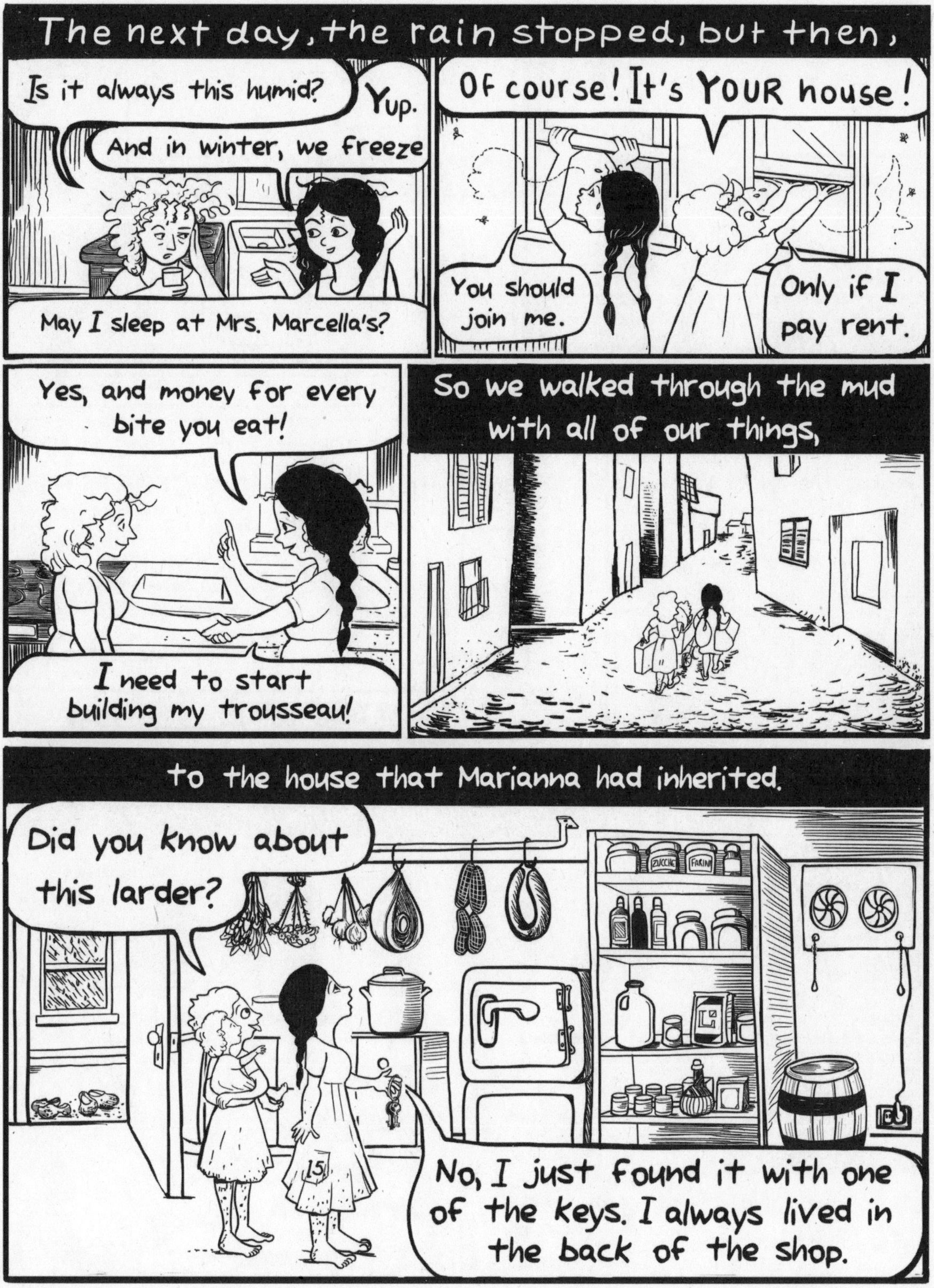
The next day, the rain stopped, but then,
Is it always this humid?
Yup.
And in winter, we freeze
May I sleep at Mrs. Marcella's?
Of course! It's YOUR house!
You should join me.
Only if I pay rent.
Yes, and money for every bite you eat!
I need to start building my trousseau!
So we walked through the mud with all of our things,
to the house that Marianna had inherited.
Did you know about this larder?
ZUCCHE
FARINA
No, I just found it with one of the keys. I always lived in the back of the shop.

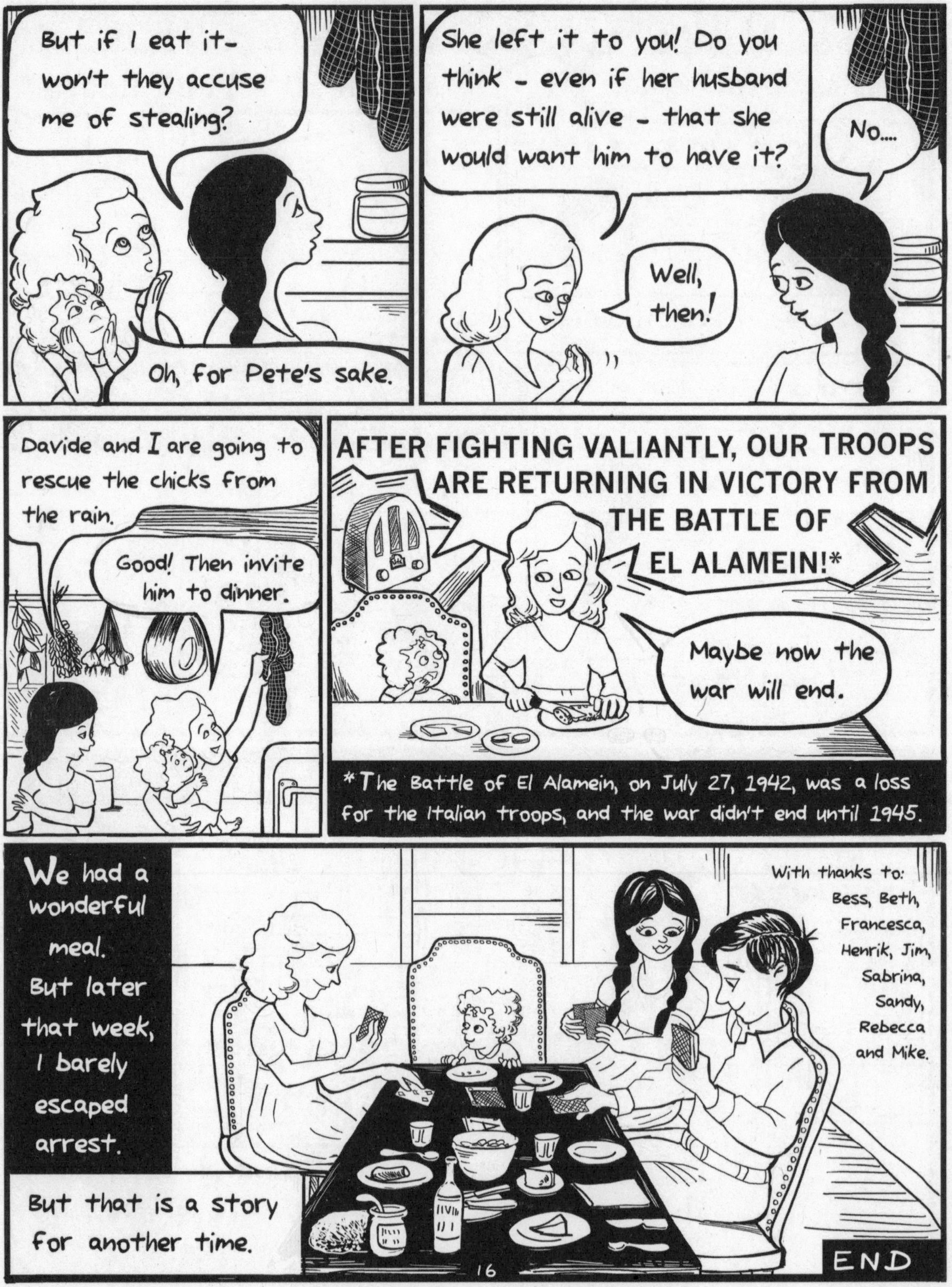

But if I eat it- won't they accuse me of stealing?
Oh, for Pete's sake.
She left it to you! Do you think - even if her husband were still alive - that she would want him to have it?
No....
Well, then!
Davide and I are going to rescue the chicks from the rain.
Good! Then invite him to dinner.
AFTER FIGHTING VALIANTLY, OUR TROOPS ARE RETURNING IN VICTORY FROM THE BATTLE OF EL ALAMEIN!*
Maybe now the war will end.
*The Battle of El Alamein, on July 27, 1942, was a loss for the Italian troops, and the war didn't end until 1945.
We had a wonderful meal. But later that week, I barely escaped arrest.
With thanks to: Bess, Beth, Francesca, Henrik, Jim, Sabrina, Sandy, Rebecca and Mike.
But that is a story for another time.
END
16

Lyari Girls' Club

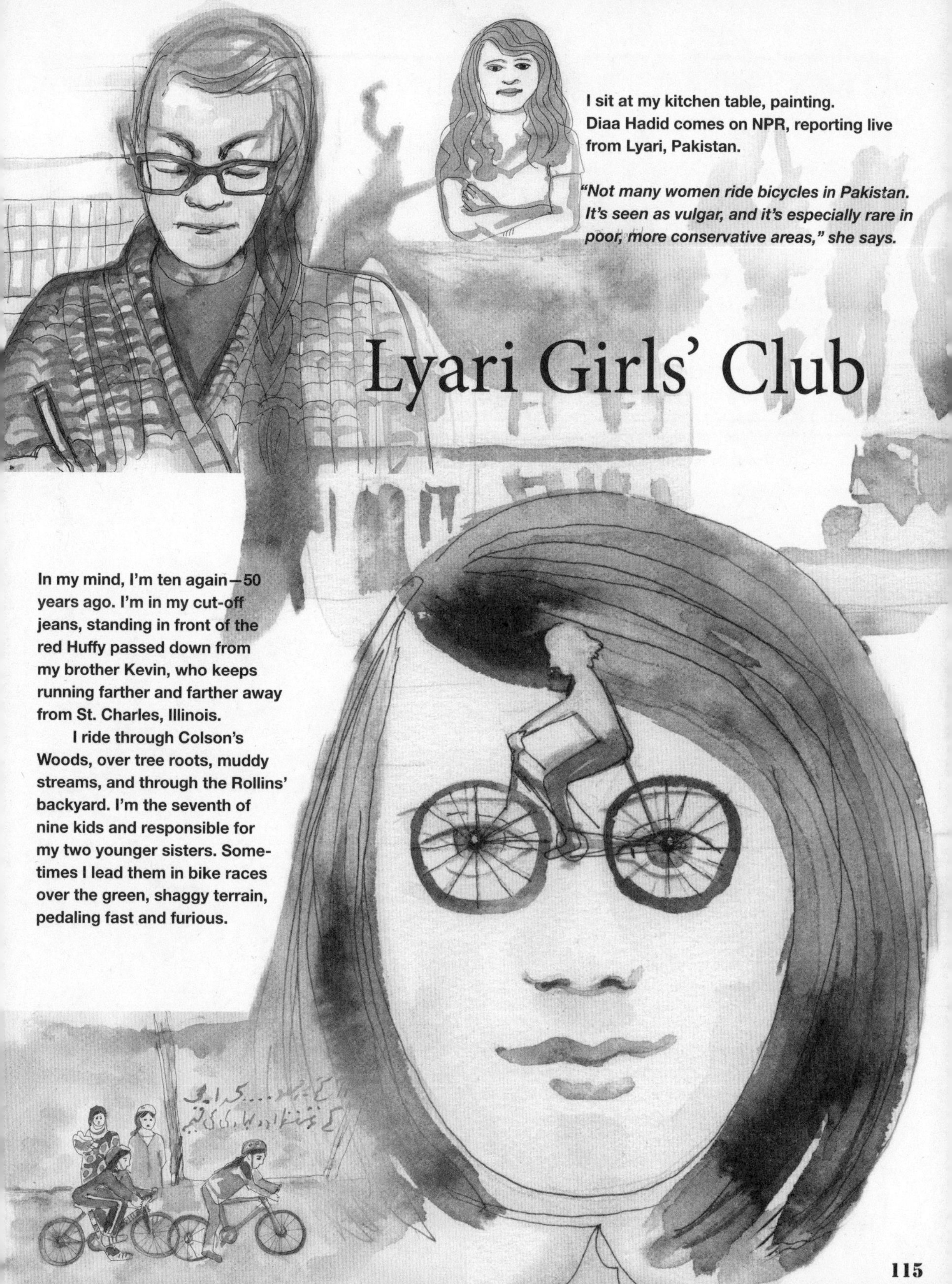

I sit at my kitchen table, painting. Diaa Hadid comes on NPR, reporting live from Lyari, Pakistan.

"Not many women ride bicycles in Pakistan. It's seen as vulgar, and it's especially rare in poor, more conservative areas," she says.

In my mind, I'm ten again—50 years ago. I'm in my cut-off jeans, standing in front of the red Huffy passed down from my brother Kevin, who keeps running farther and farther away from St. Charles, Illinois.

I ride through Colson's Woods, over tree roots, muddy streams, and through the Rollins' backyard. I'm the seventh of nine kids and responsible for my two younger sisters. Sometimes I lead them in bike races over the green, shaggy terrain, pedaling fast and furious.

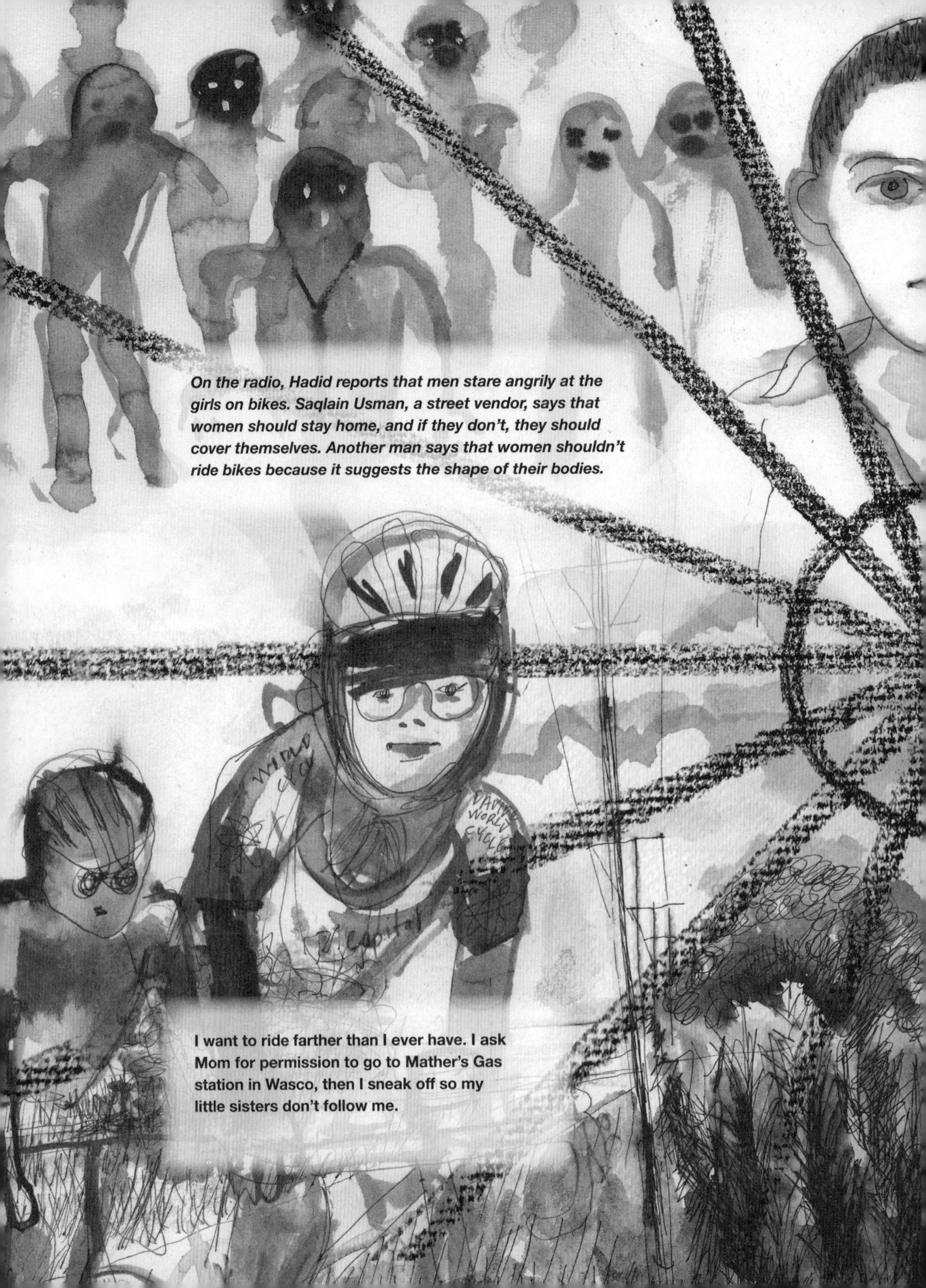
On the radio, Hadid reports that men stare angrily at the girls on bikes. Saqlain Usman, a street vendor, says that women should stay home, and if they don't, they should cover themselves. Another man says that women shouldn't ride bikes because it suggests the shape of their bodies.
I want to ride farther than I ever have. I ask Mom for permission to go to Mather's Gas station in Wasco, then I sneak off so my little sisters don't follow me.

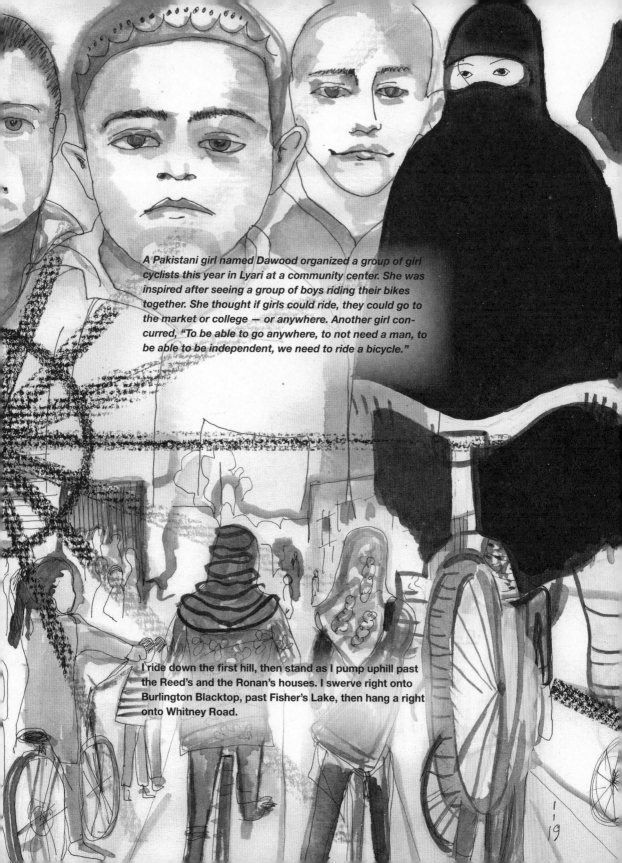

A Pakistani girl named Dawood organized a group of girl cyclists this year in Lyari at a community center. She was inspired after seeing a group of boys riding their bikes together. She thought if girls could ride, they could go to the market or college — or anywhere. Another girl concurred, "To be able to go anywhere, to not need a man, to be able to be independent, we need to ride a bicycle."

I ride down the first hill, then stand as I pump uphill past the Reed's and the Ronan's houses. I swerve right onto Burlington Blacktop, past Fisher's Lake, then hang a right onto Whitney Road.

119

On their first ride, students from an Islamic seminary attack the girls. They surround and try to crush their bikes. After that, Dawood takes the young women to a school enclosed by high walls so men can't see them, but they are still threatened. Eventually, Dawood finds a route that avoids the madrassa. They still get harassed, but not attacked.

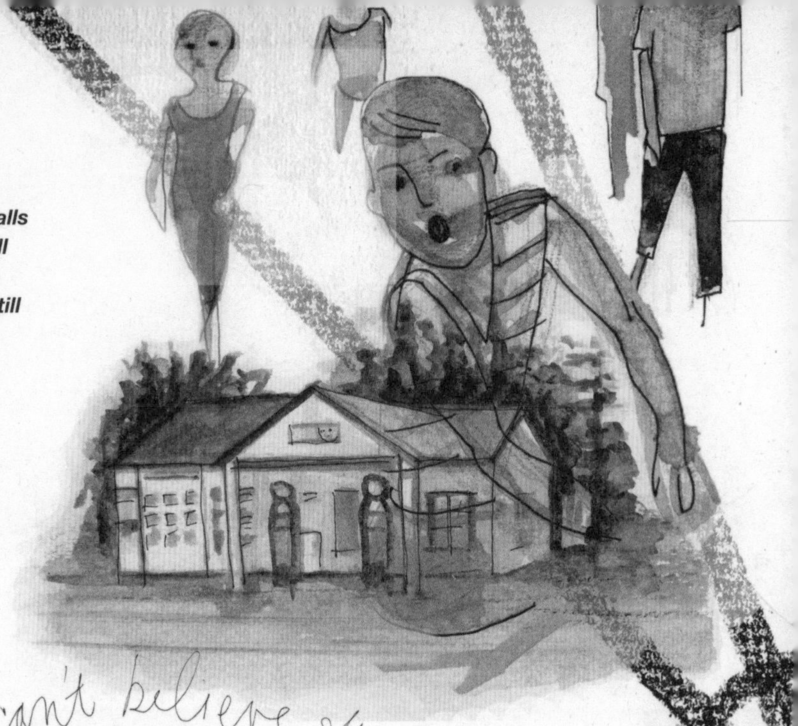

As the road levels off, I pass cornfields to the right, soybean fields to the left. I let go of the breaks, going as fast as I can, the breeze lifting my hair. When I get to Mather's, I buy a 7 Up, then sit on a stoop and swig it.

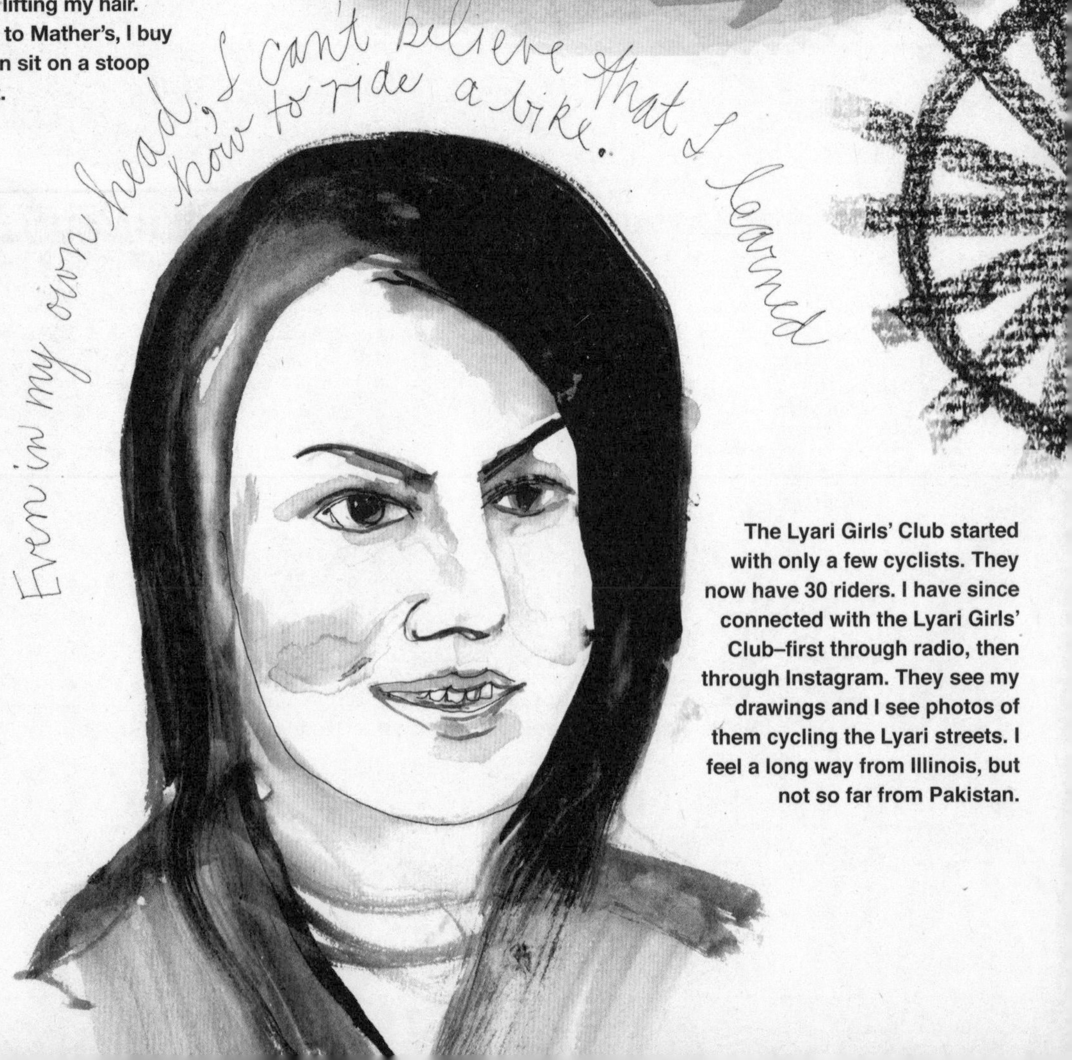
Even in my own head, I can't believe that I learned how to ride a bike.

The Lyari Girls' Club started with only a few cyclists. They now have 30 riders. I have since connected with the Lyari Girls' Club–first through radio, then through Instagram. They see my drawings and I see photos of them cycling the Lyari streets. I feel a long way from Illinois, but not so far from Pakistan.

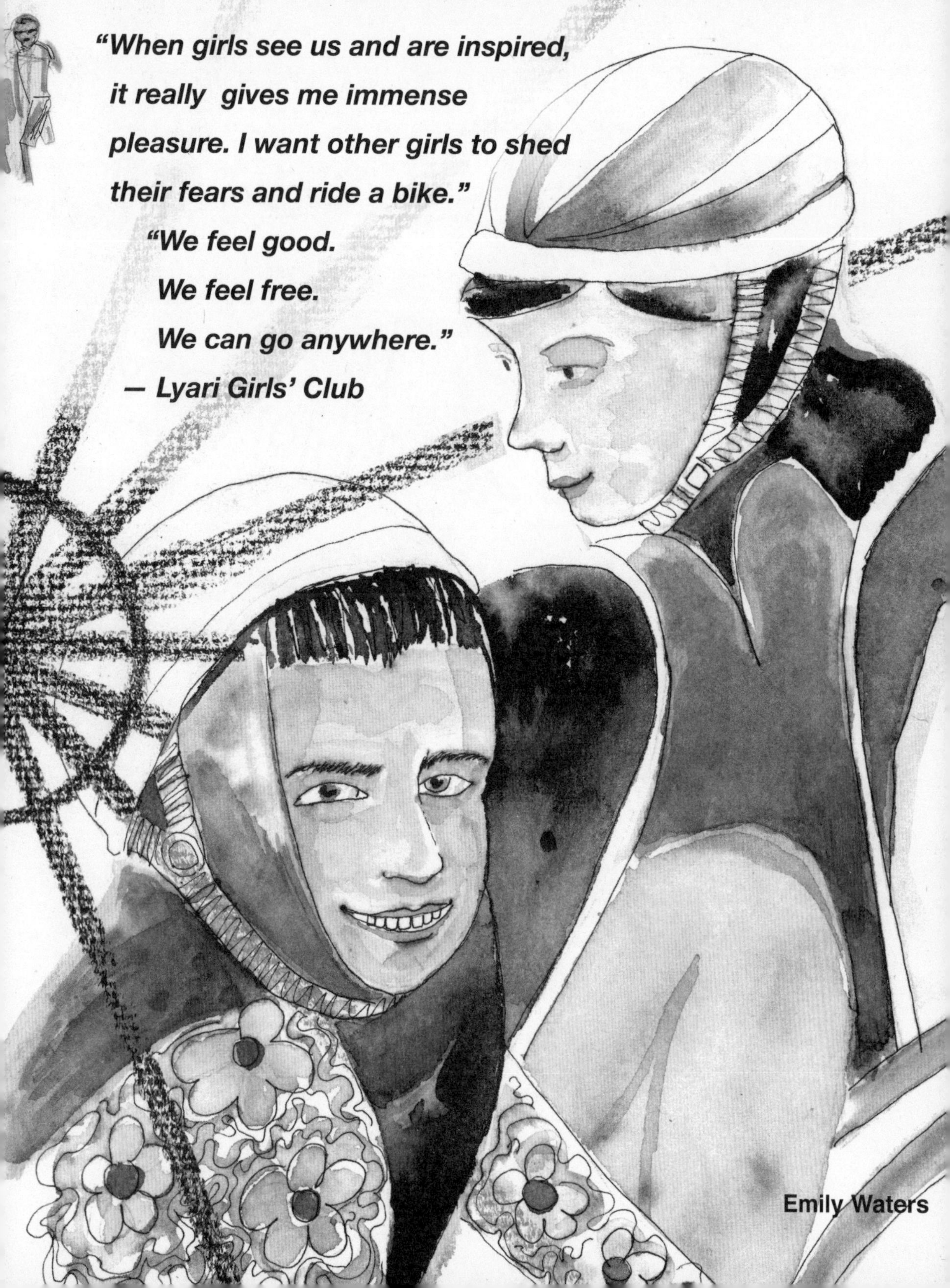
"When girls see us and are inspired, it really gives me immense pleasure. I want other girls to shed their fears and ride a bike."
"We feel good.
We feel free.
We can go anywhere."
— Lyari Girls' Club
Emily Waters

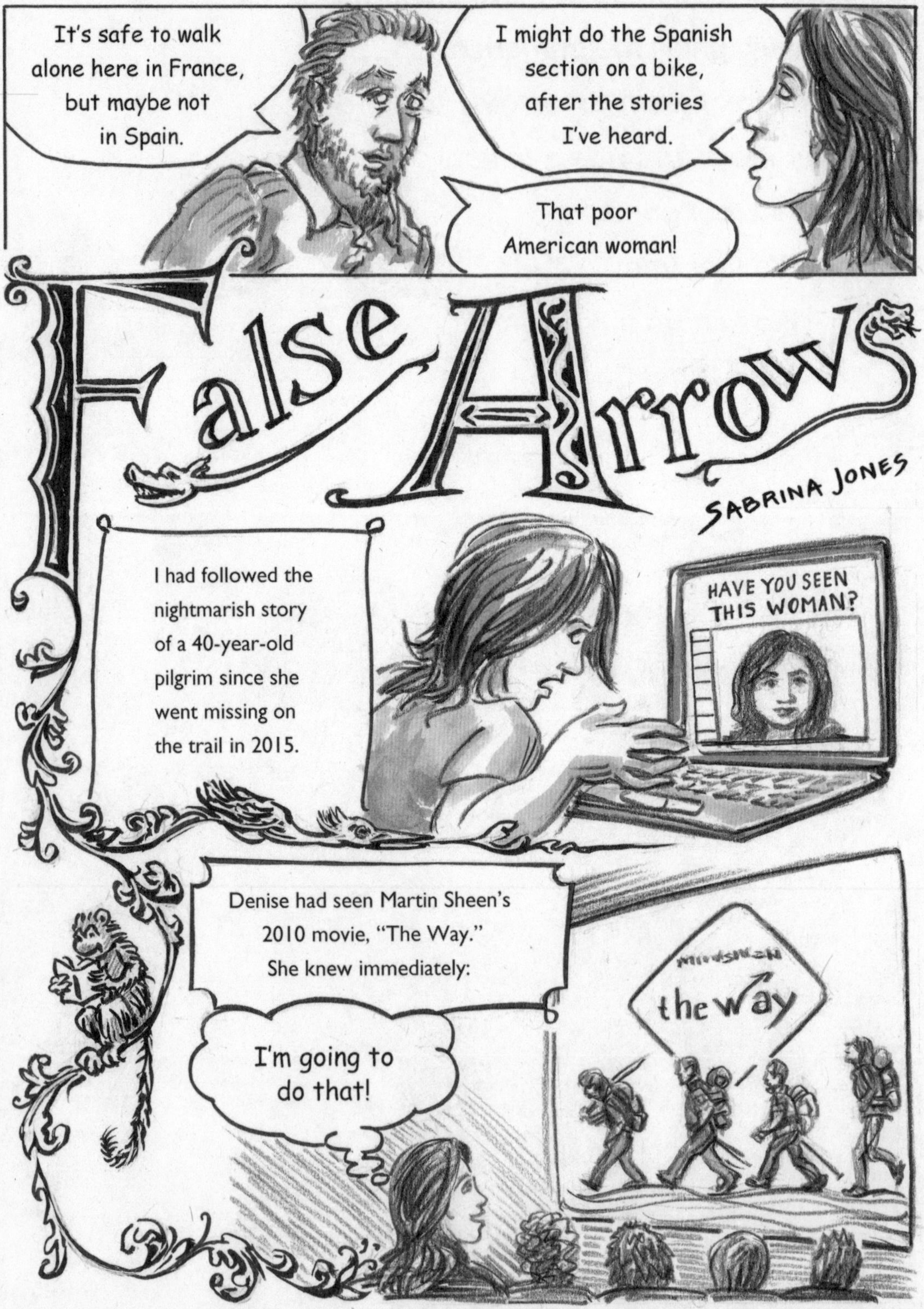
It's safe to walk alone here in France, but maybe not in Spain.
I might do the Spanish section on a bike, after the stories I've heard.
That poor American woman!
False Arrows
SABRINA JONES
I had followed the nightmarish story of a 40-year-old pilgrim since she went missing on the trail in 2015.
HAVE YOU SEEN THIS WOMAN?
Denise had seen Martin Sheen's 2010 movie, "The Way." She knew immediately:
I'm going to do that!
the way

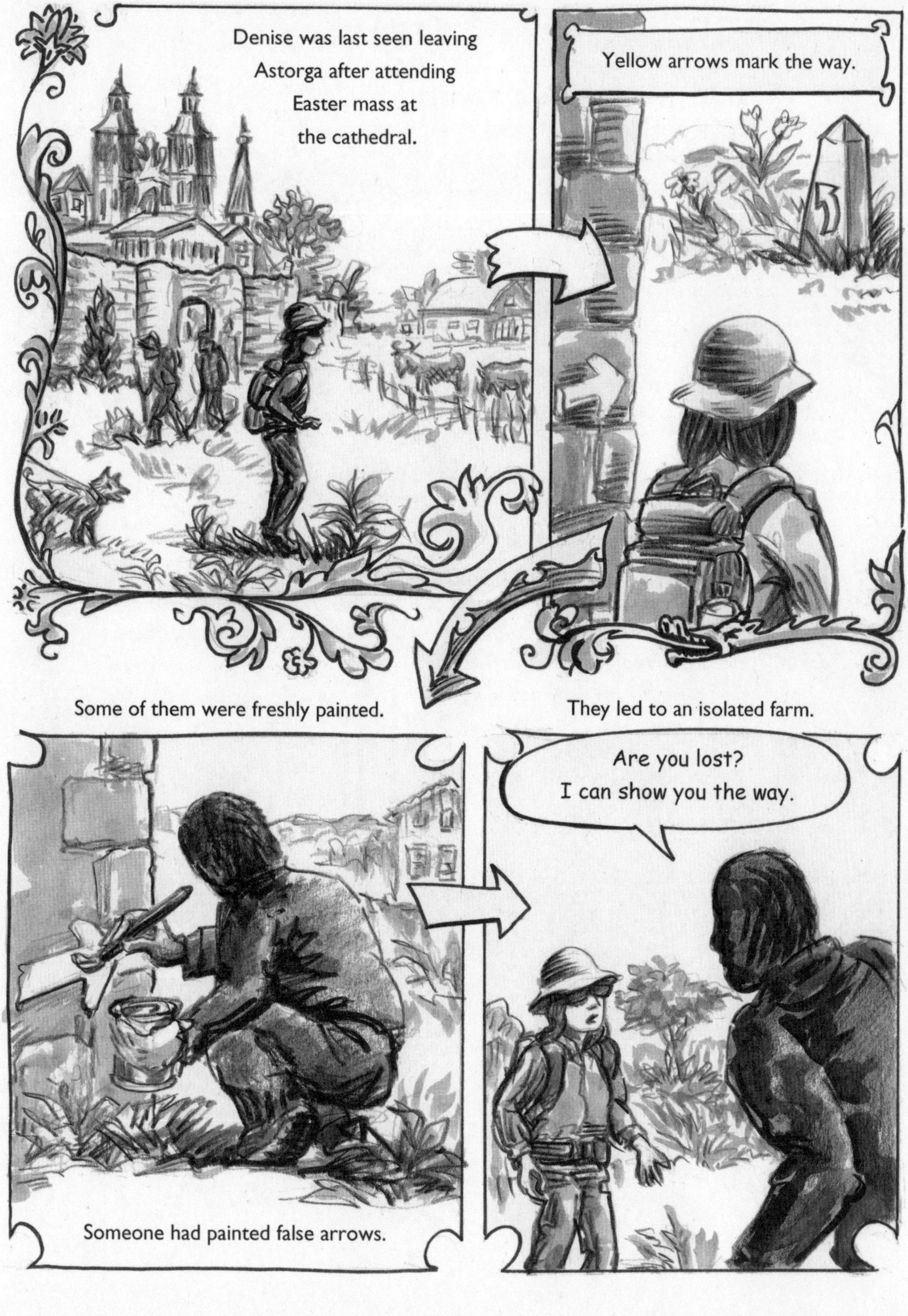

Denise was last seen leaving Astorga after attending Easter mass at the cathedral.
Yellow arrows mark the way.
Some of them were freshly painted.
They led to an isolated farm.
Someone had painted false arrows.
Are you lost? I can show you the way.

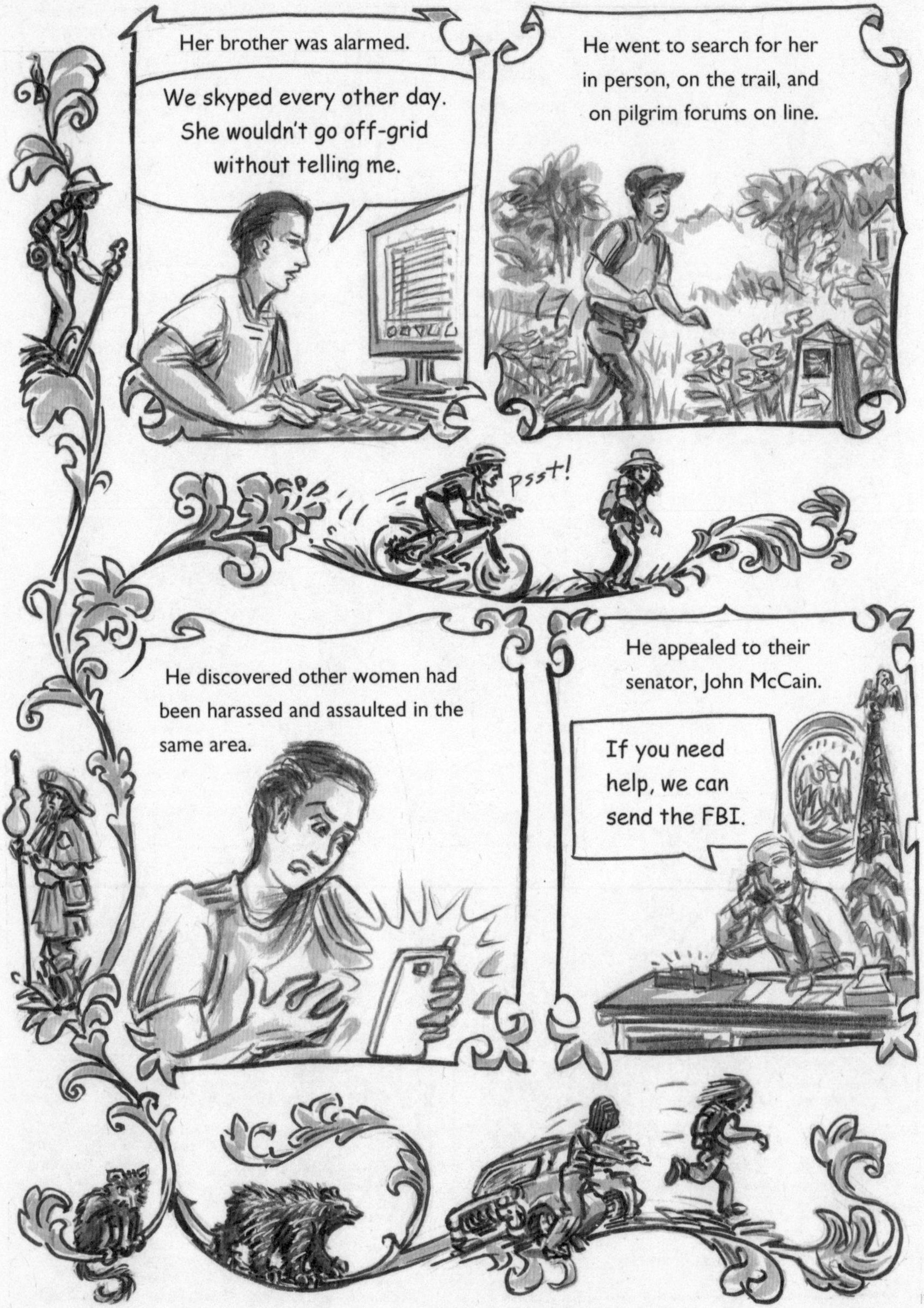
Her brother was alarmed.
We skyped every other day. She wouldn't go off-grid without telling me.
He went to search for her in person, on the trail, and on pilgrim forums on line.
psst!
He discovered other women had been harassed and assaulted in the same area.
He appealed to their senator, John McCain.
If you need help, we can send the FBI.

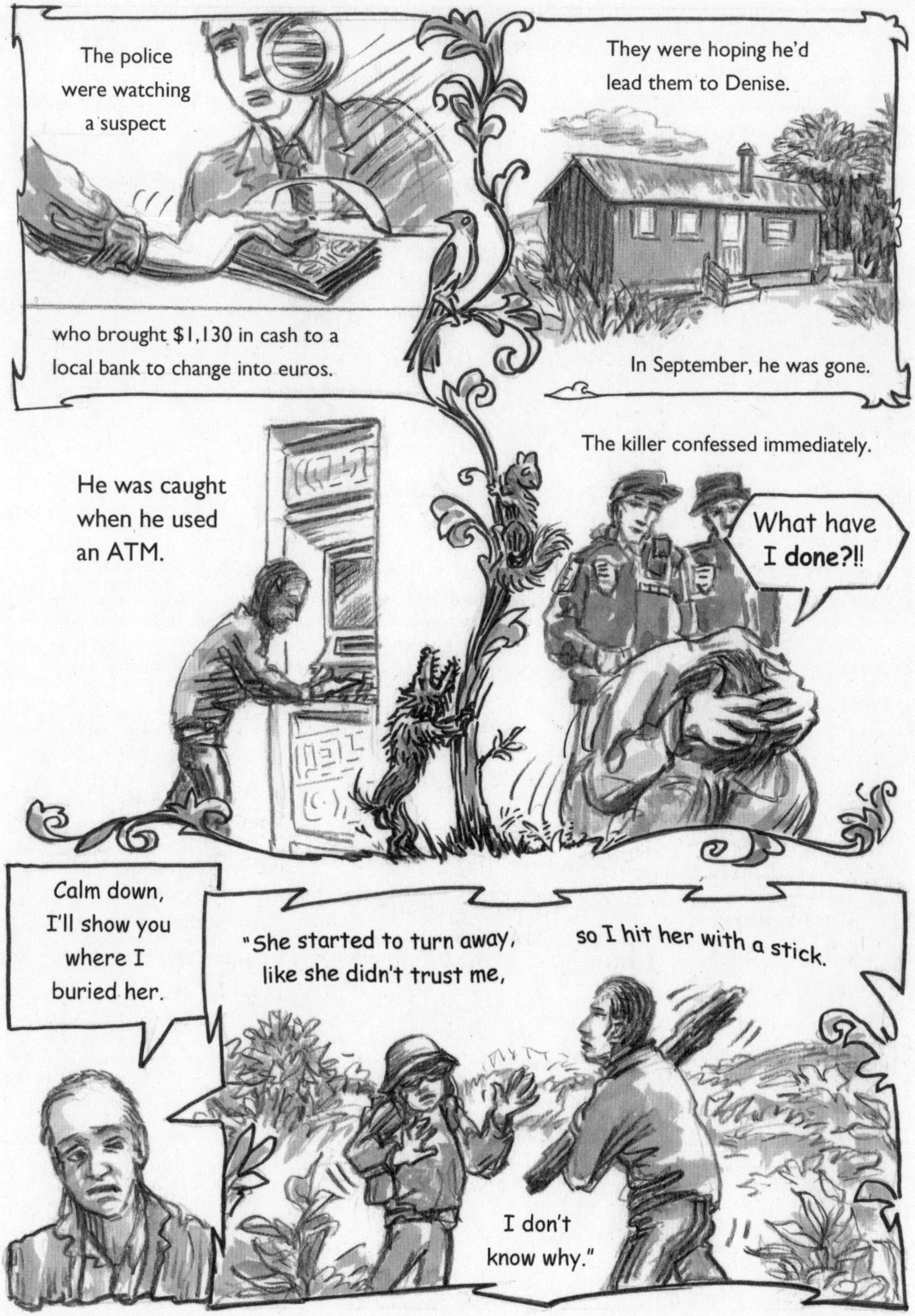

The police were watching a suspect
who brought $1,130 in cash to a local bank to change into euros.
They were hoping he'd lead them to Denise.
In September, he was gone.
He was caught when he used an ATM.
The killer confessed immediately.
What have I **done?!!**
Calm down, I'll show you where I buried her.
"She started to turn away, like she didn't trust me,
so I hit her with a stick.
I don't know why."

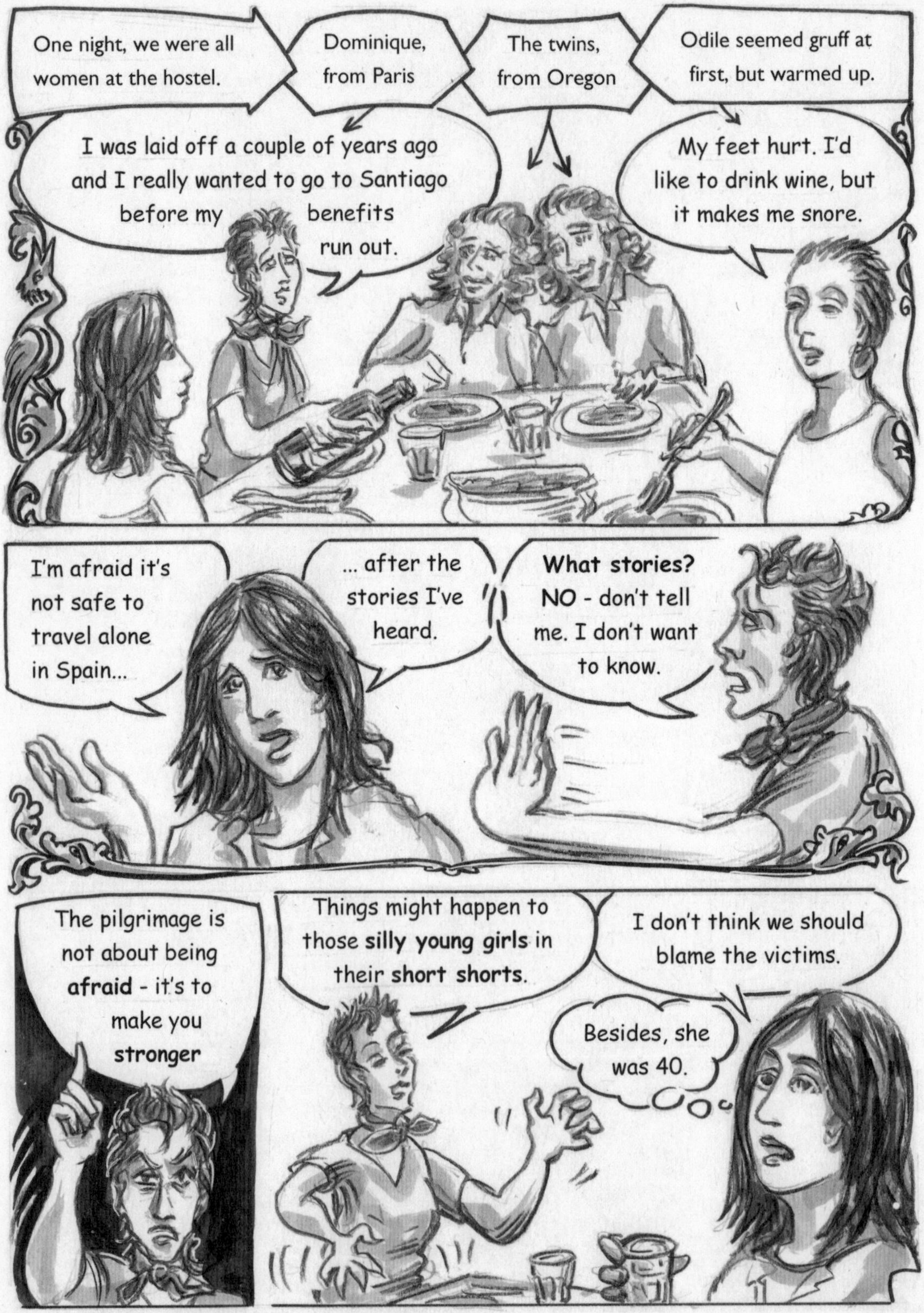
One night, we were all women at the hostel.
Dominique, from Paris
The twins, from Oregon
Odile seemed gruff at first, but warmed up.
I was laid off a couple of years ago and I really wanted to go to Santiago before my benefits run out.
My feet hurt. I'd like to drink wine, but it makes me snore.
I'm afraid it's not safe to travel alone in Spain...
... after the stories I've heard.
What stories? NO - don't tell me. I don't want to know.
The pilgrimage is not about being afraid - it's to make you stronger
Things might happen to those silly young girls in their short shorts.
I don't think we should blame the victims.
Besides, she was 40.

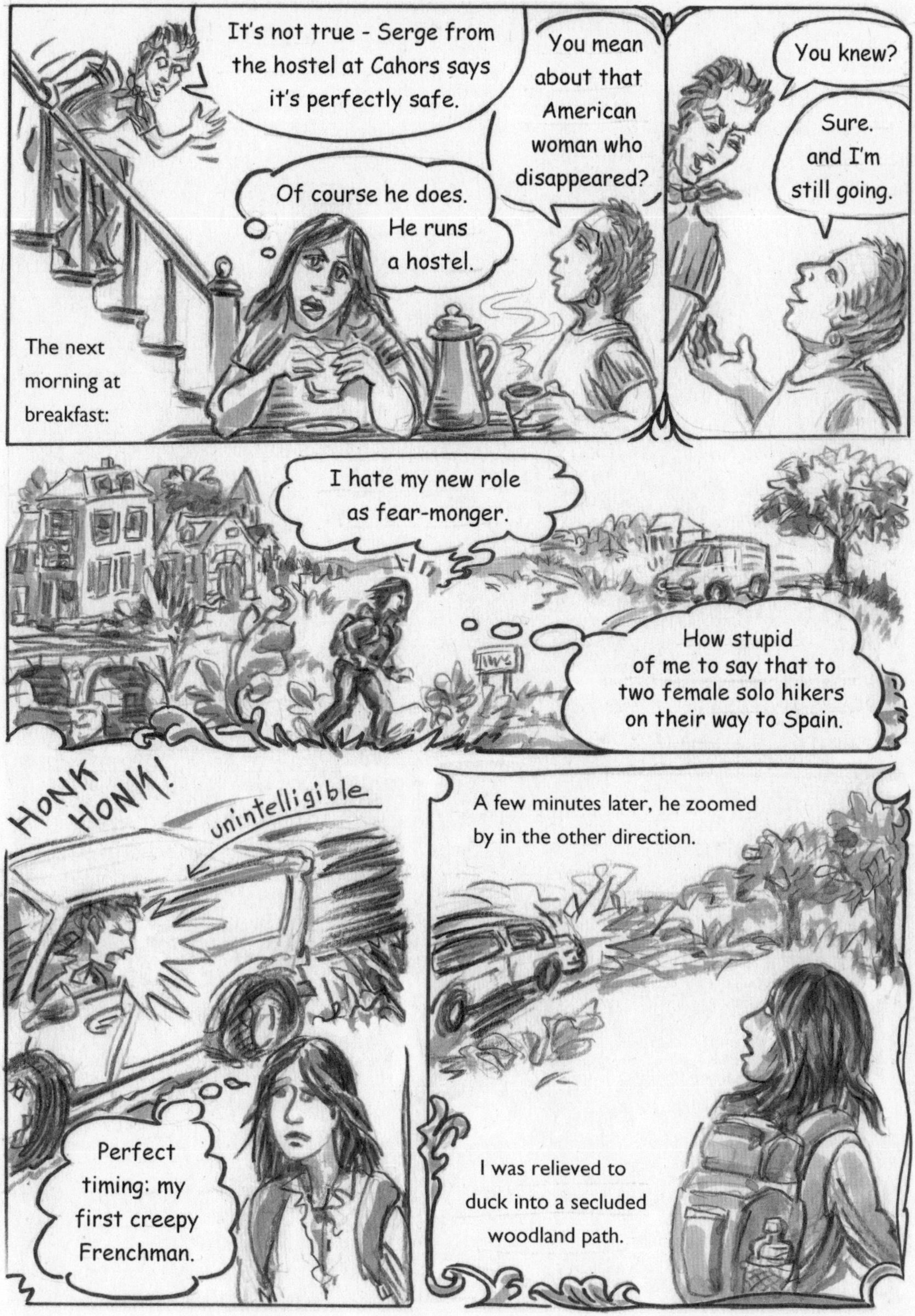
The next morning at breakfast:
It's not true - Serge from the hostel at Cahors says it's perfectly safe.
Of course he does. He runs a hostel.
You mean about that American woman who disappeared?
You knew?
Sure. and I'm still going.
I hate my new role as fear-monger.
How stupid of me to say that to two female solo hikers on their way to Spain.
HONK HONK!
unintelligible
Perfect timing: my first creepy Frenchman.
A few minutes later, he zoomed by in the other direction.
I was relieved to duck into a secluded woodland path.

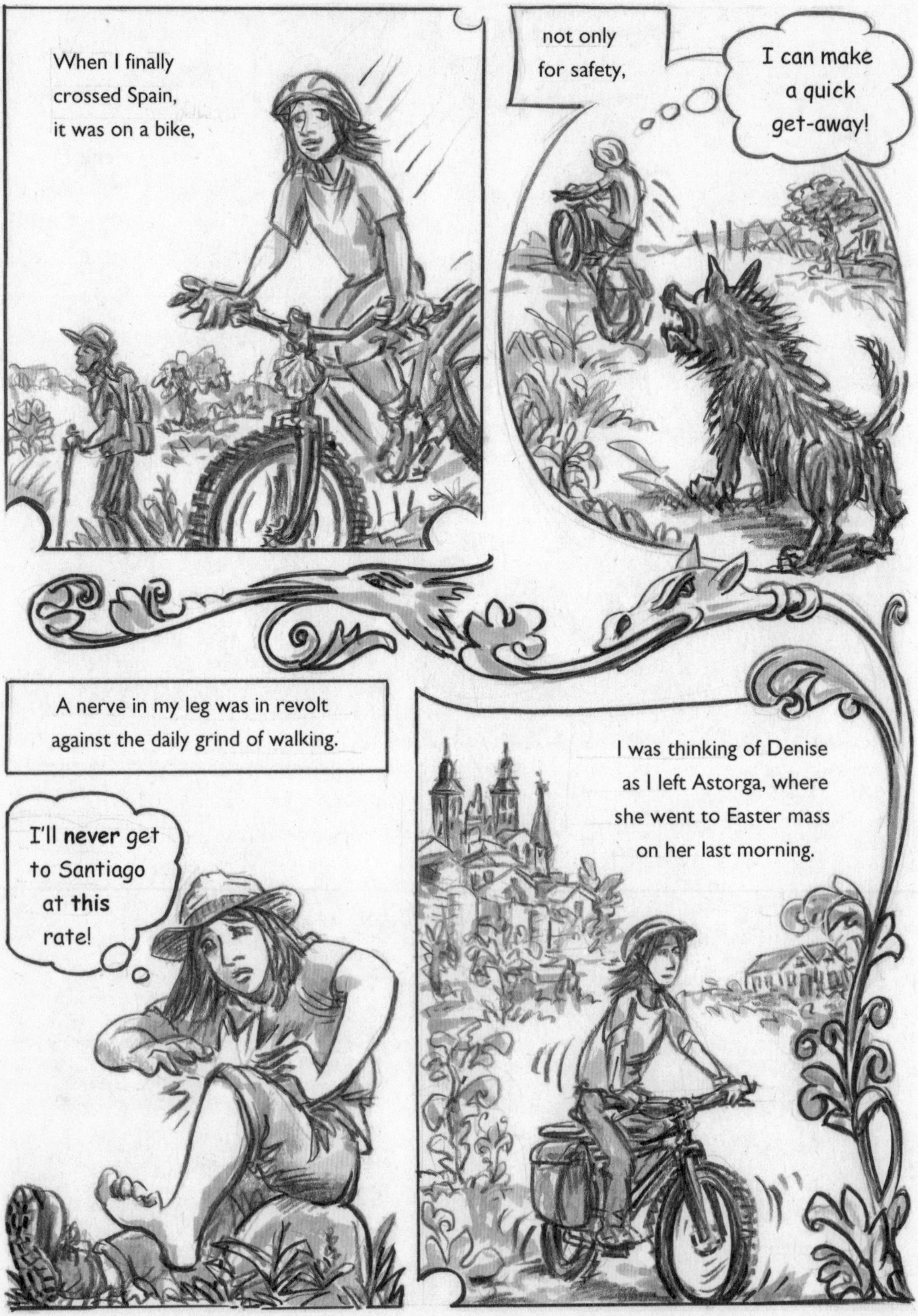
When I finally crossed Spain, it was on a bike,
not only for safety,
I can make a quick get-away!
A nerve in my leg was in revolt against the daily grind of walking.
I'll **never** get to Santiago at **this** rate!
I was thinking of Denise as I left Astorga, where she went to Easter mass on her last morning.

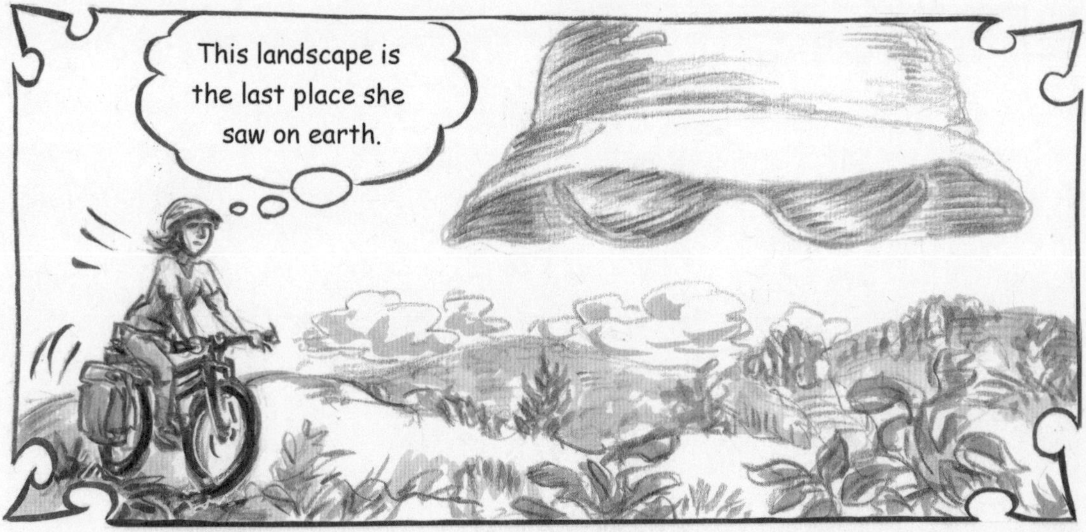
This landscape is the last place she saw on earth.

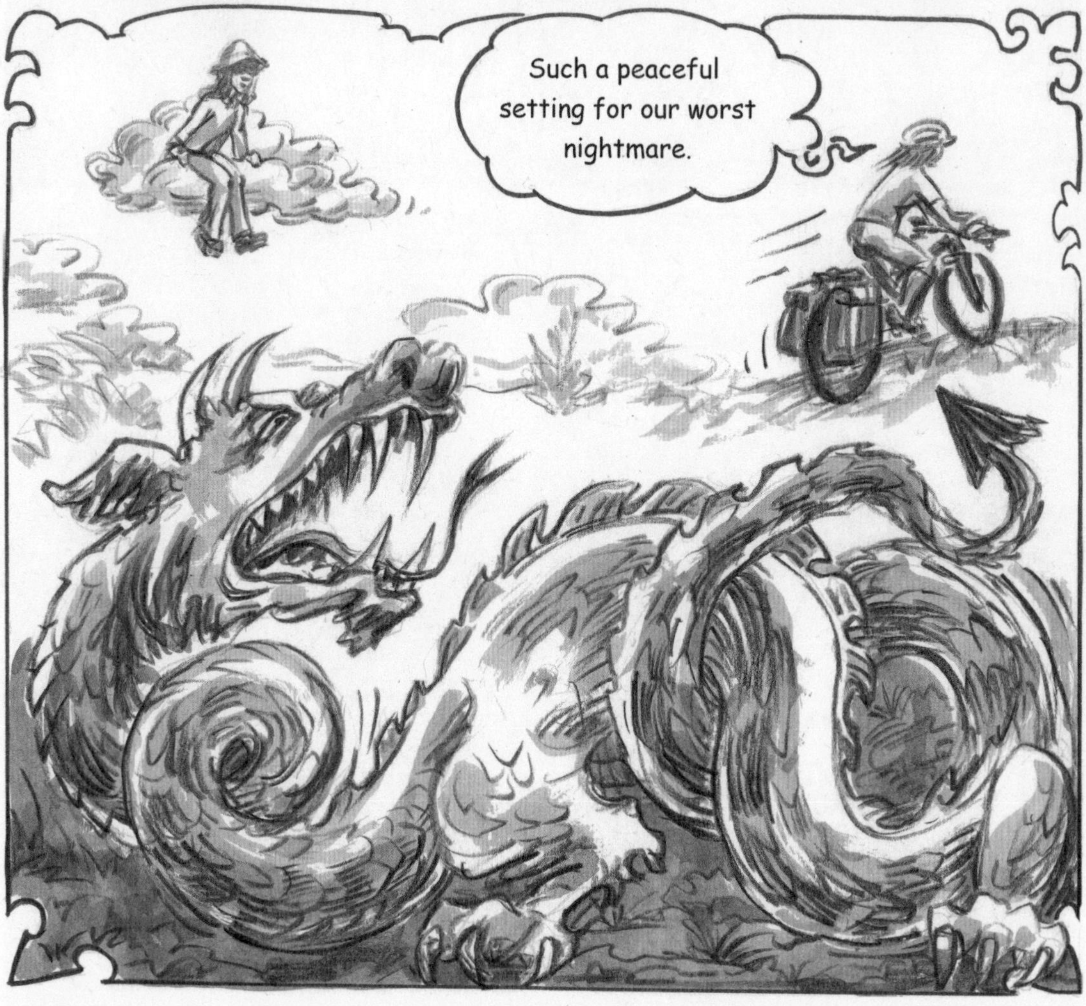
Such a peaceful setting for our worst nightmare.

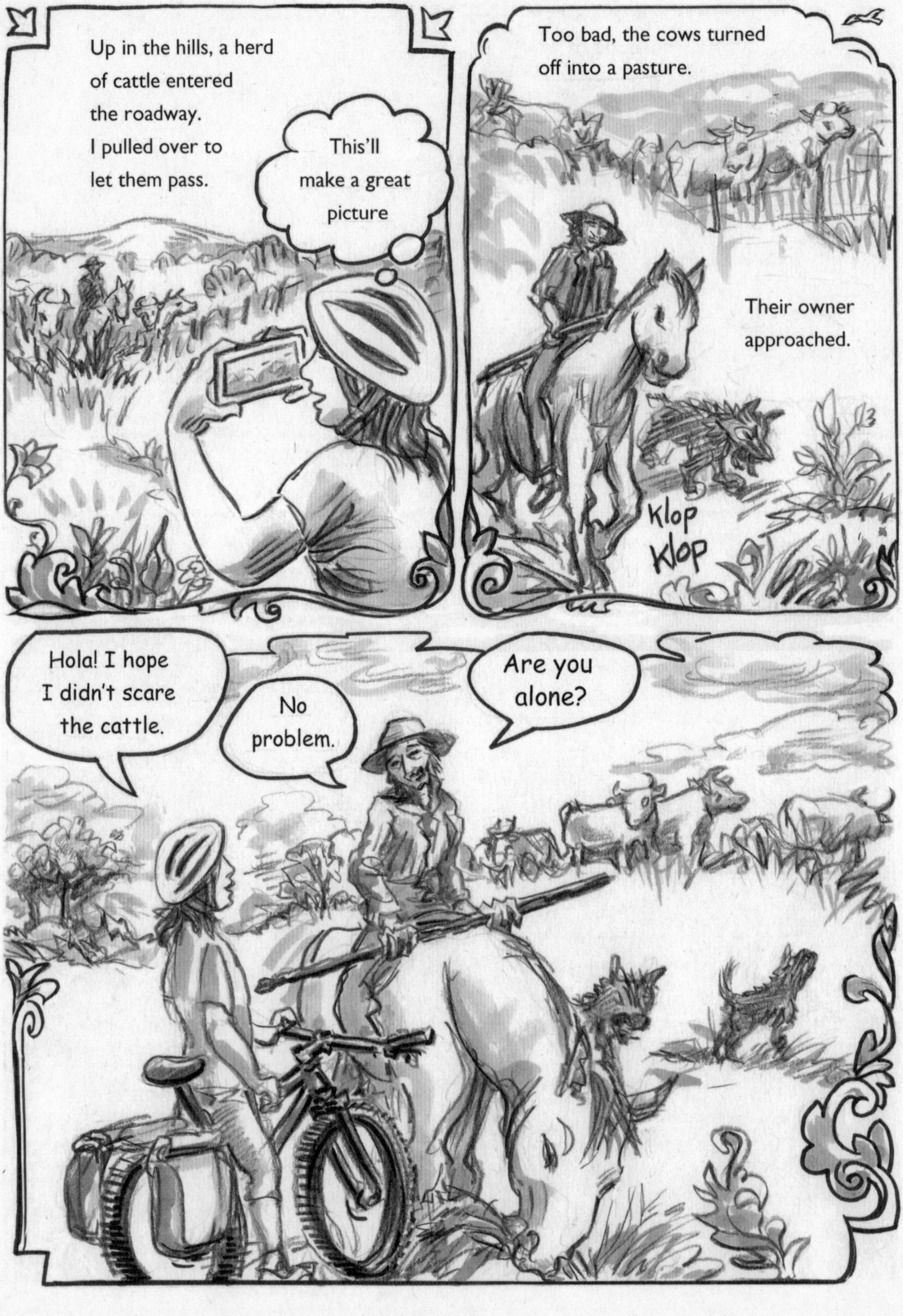
Up in the hills, a herd of cattle entered the roadway.
I pulled over to let them pass.
This'll make a great picture
Too bad, the cows turned off into a pasture.
Their owner approached.
Klop Klop
Hola! I hope I didn't scare the cattle.
No problem.
Are you alone?

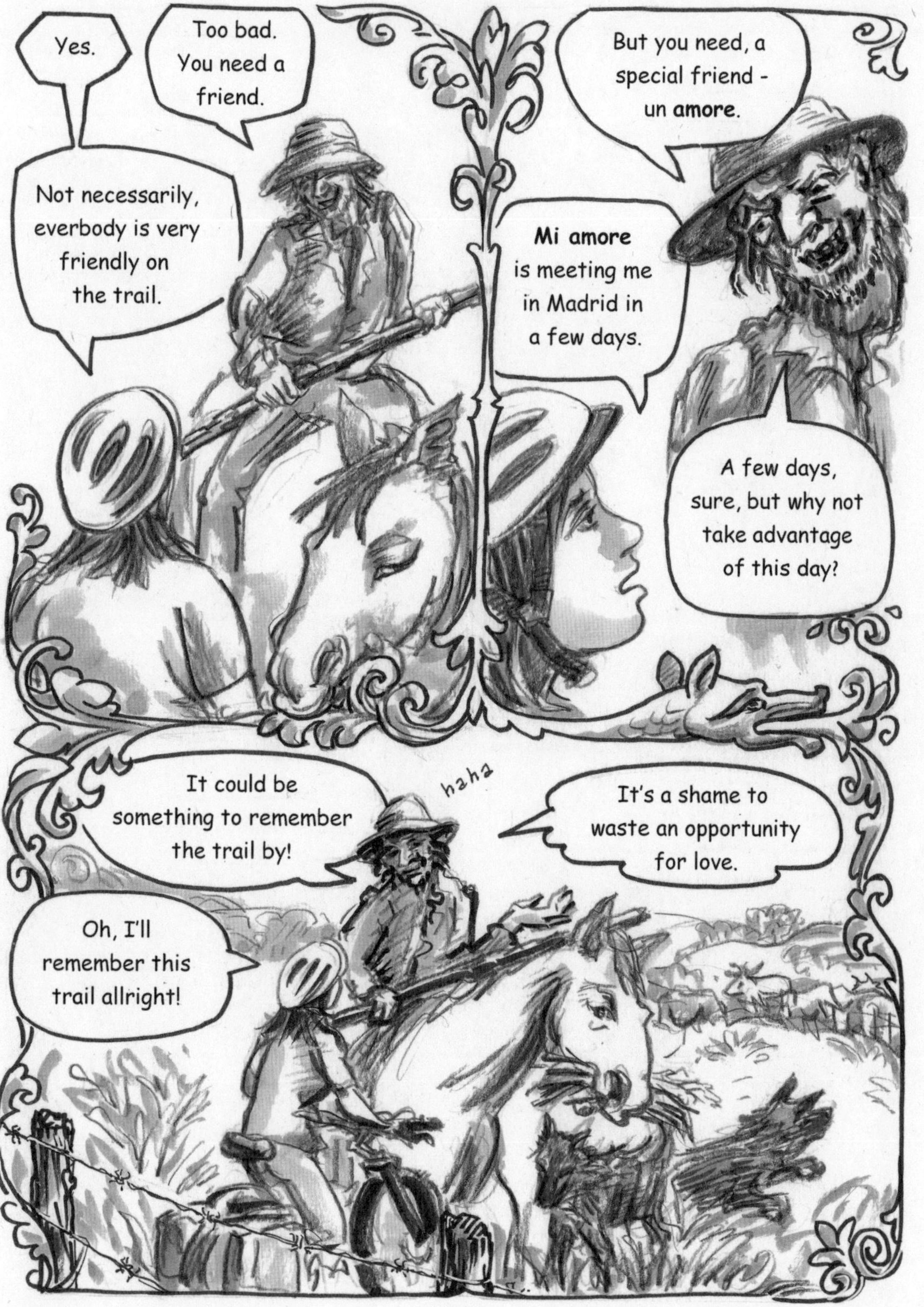
Yes.
Too bad. You need a friend.
Not necessarily, everbody is very friendly on the trail.
But you need, a special friend - un **amore**.
Mi amore is meeting me in Madrid in a few days.
A few days, sure, but why not take advantage of this day?
It could be something to remember the trail by!
haha
It's a shame to waste an opportunity for love.
Oh, I'll remember this trail allright!

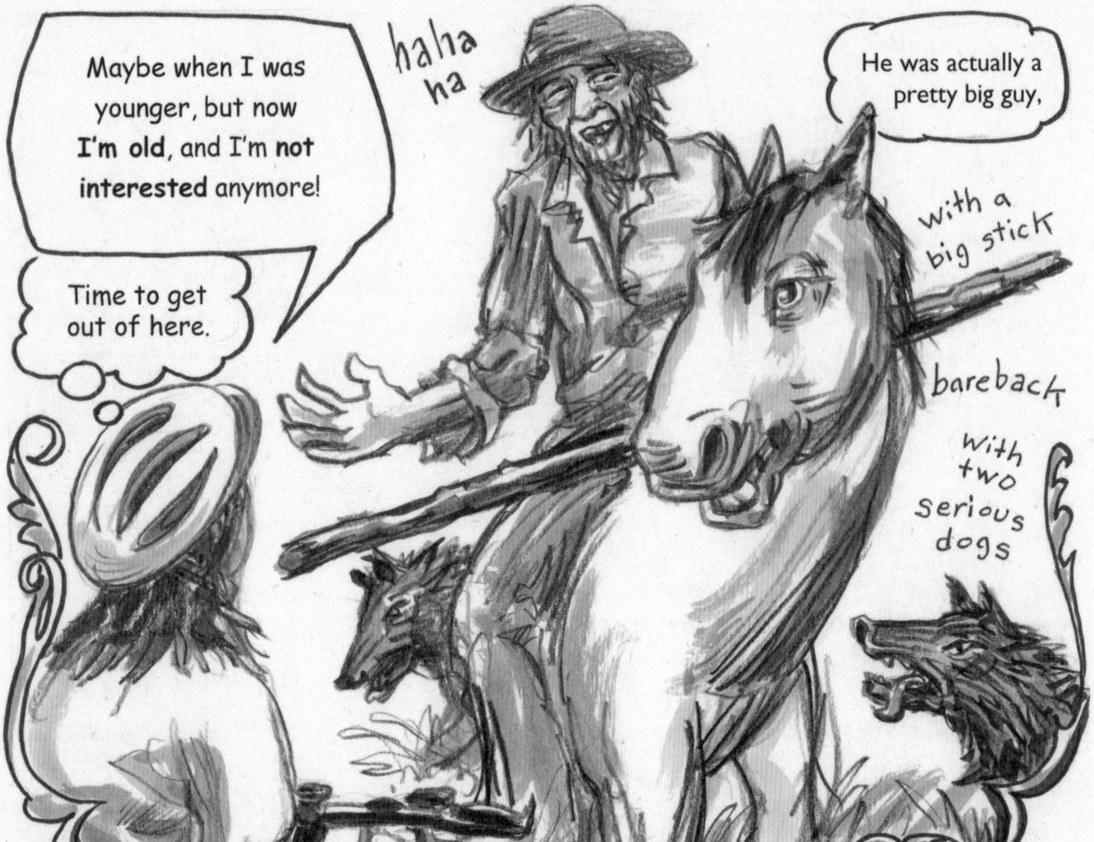
Maybe when I was younger, but now **I'm old**, and I'm **not interested** anymore!
haha ha
He was actually a pretty big guy,
with a big stick
bareback
with two serious dogs
Time to get out of here.

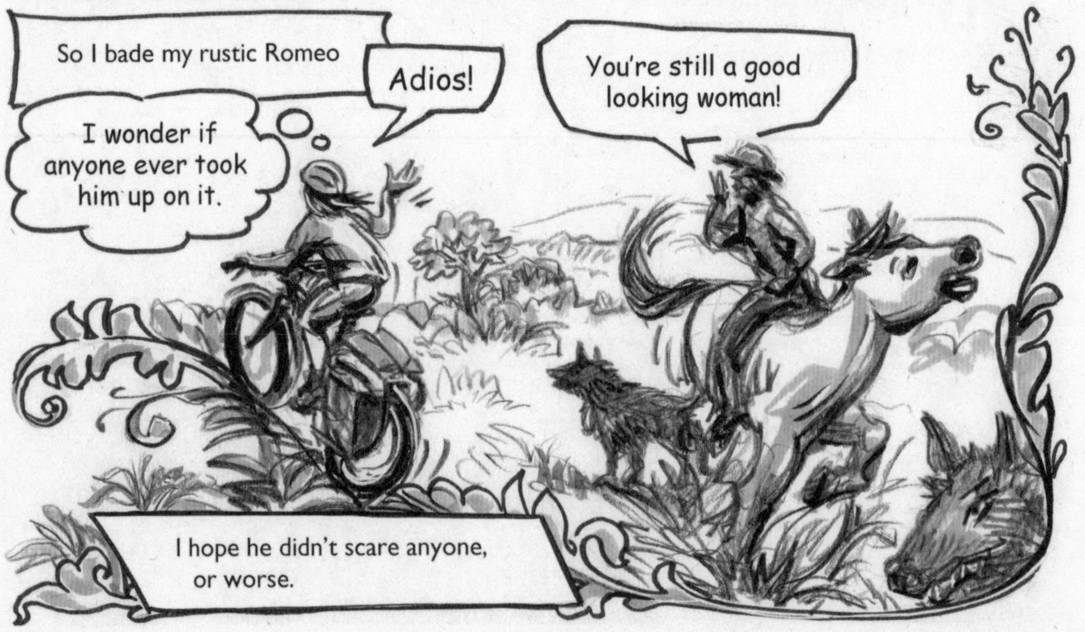
So I bade my rustic Romeo
Adios!
You're still a good looking woman!
I wonder if anyone ever took him up on it.
I hope he didn't scare anyone, or worse.

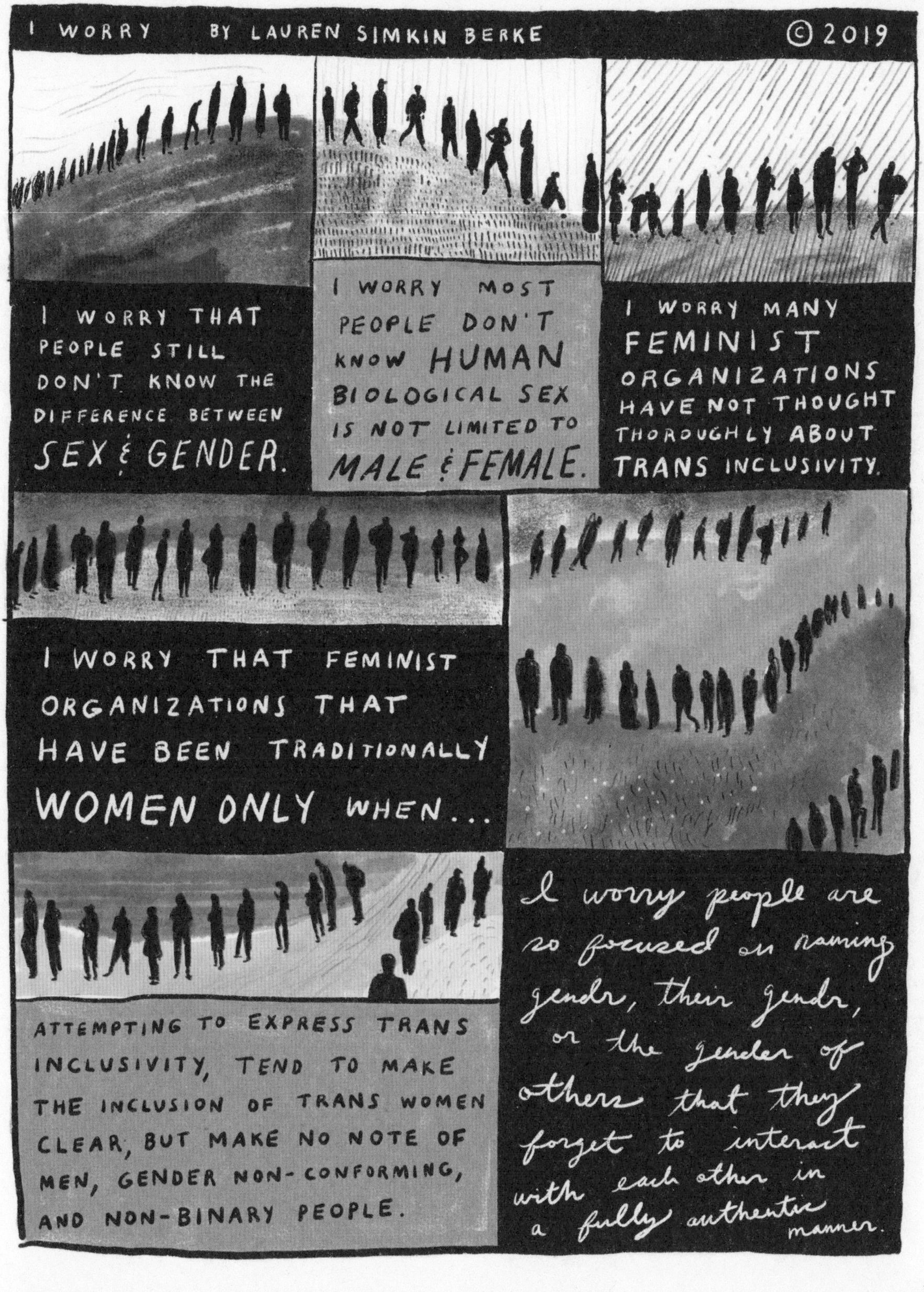
I WORRY BY LAUREN SIMKIN BERKE ©2019
I WORRY THAT PEOPLE STILL DON'T KNOW THE DIFFERENCE BETWEEN SEX & GENDER.
I WORRY MOST PEOPLE DON'T KNOW HUMAN BIOLOGICAL SEX IS NOT LIMITED TO MALE & FEMALE.
I WORRY MANY FEMINIST ORGANIZATIONS HAVE NOT THOUGHT THOROUGHLY ABOUT TRANS INCLUSIVITY.
I WORRY THAT FEMINIST ORGANIZATIONS THAT HAVE BEEN TRADITIONALLY WOMEN ONLY WHEN...
ATTEMPTING TO EXPRESS TRANS INCLUSIVITY, TEND TO MAKE THE INCLUSION OF TRANS WOMEN CLEAR, BUT MAKE NO NOTE OF MEN, GENDER NON-CONFORMING, AND NON-BINARY PEOPLE.
I worry people are so focused on naming gender, their gender, or the gender of others that they forget to interact with each other in a fully authentic manner.

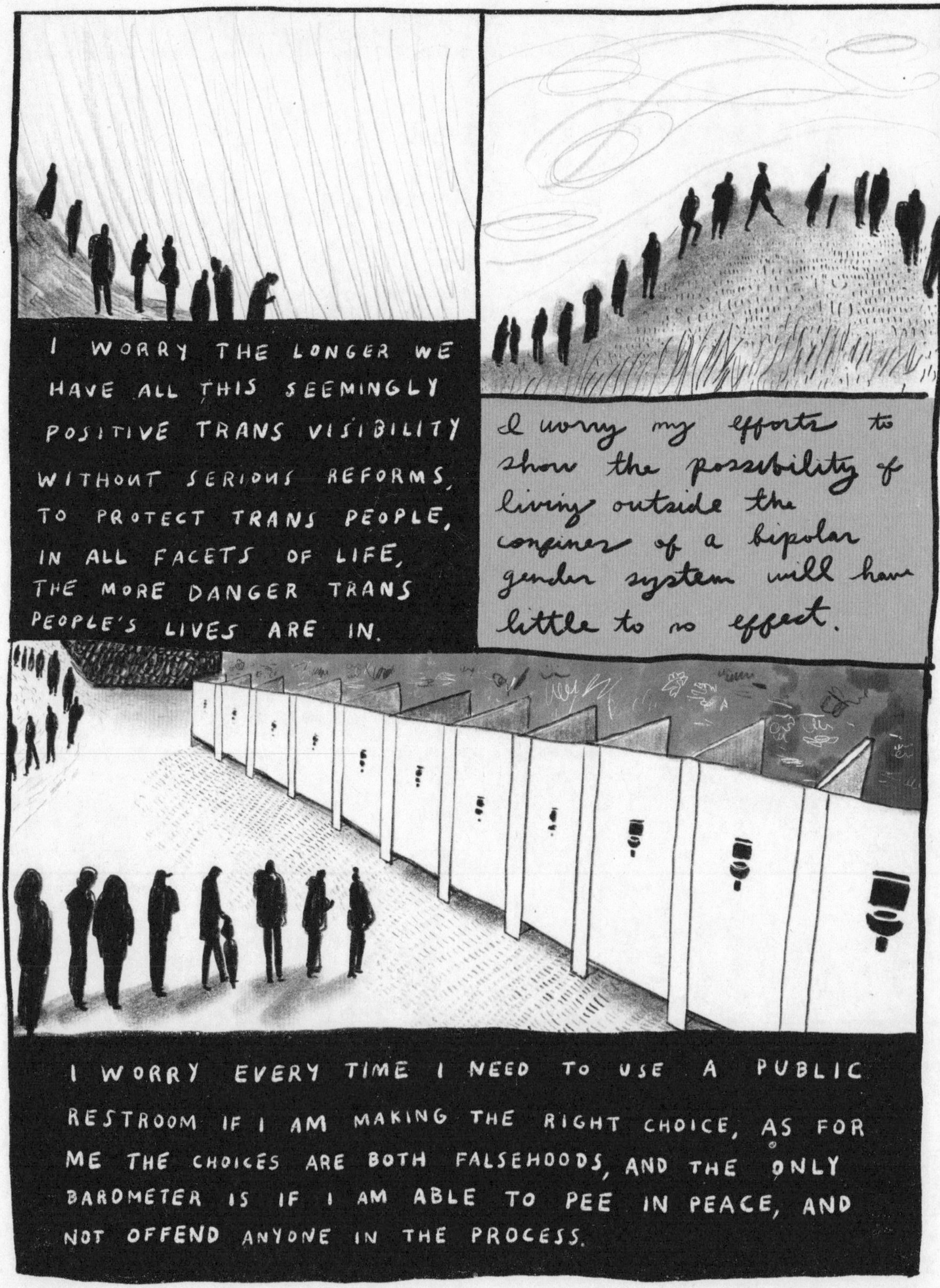
I WORRY THE LONGER WE HAVE ALL THIS SEEMINGLY POSITIVE TRANS VISIBILITY WITHOUT SERIOUS REFORMS, TO PROTECT TRANS PEOPLE, IN ALL FACETS OF LIFE, THE MORE DANGER TRANS PEOPLE'S LIVES ARE IN.
I worry my efforts to show the possibility of living outside the confines of a bipolar gender system will have little to no effect.
I WORRY EVERY TIME I NEED TO USE A PUBLIC RESTROOM IF I AM MAKING THE RIGHT CHOICE, AS FOR ME THE CHOICES ARE BOTH FALSEHOODS, AND THE ONLY BAROMETER IS IF I AM ABLE TO PEE IN PEACE, AND NOT OFFEND ANYONE IN THE PROCESS.

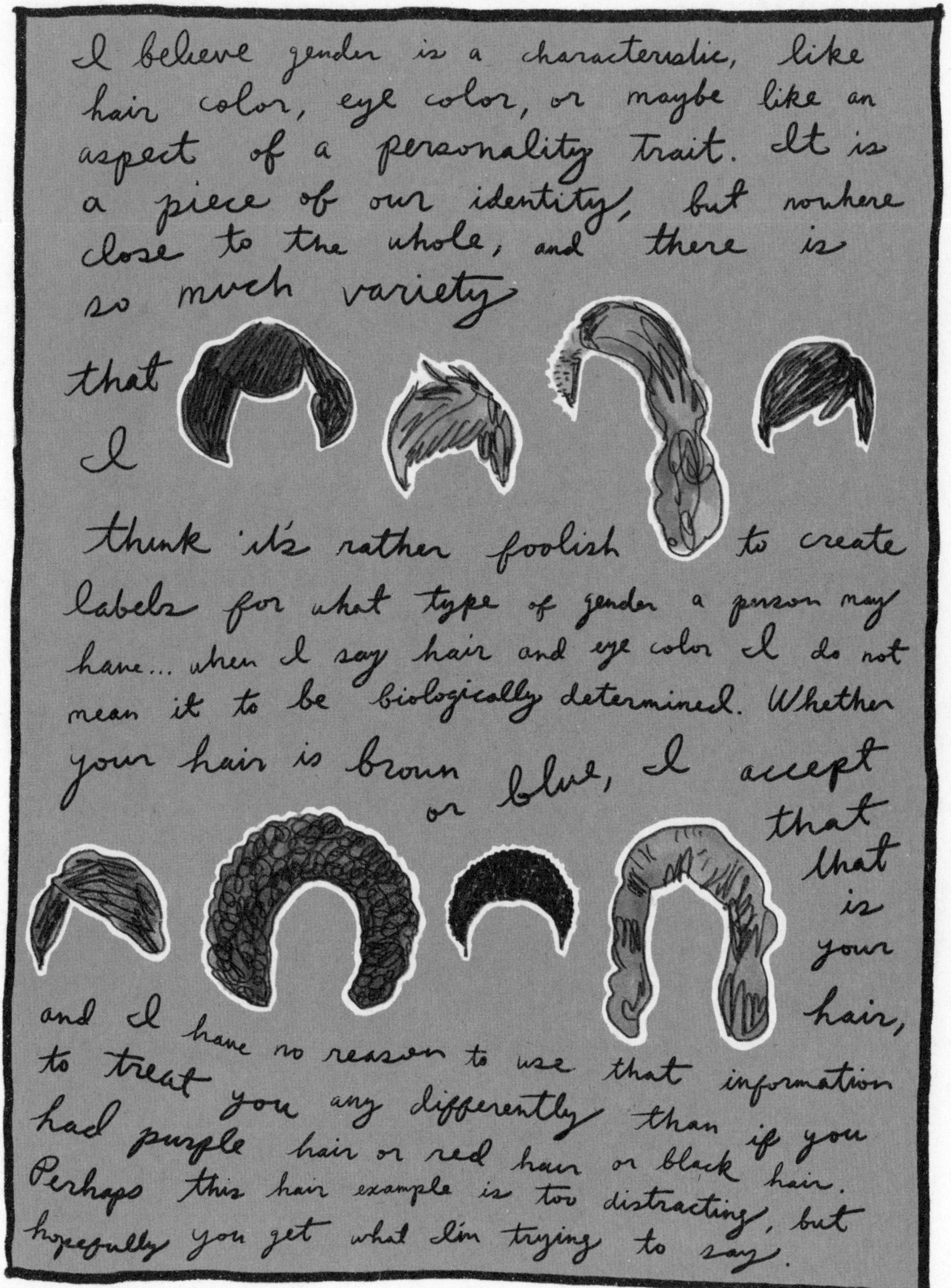
I believe gender is a characteristic, like hair color, eye color, or maybe like an aspect of a personality trait. It is a piece of our identity, but nowhere close to the whole, and there is so much variety that I think it's rather foolish to create labels for what type of gender a person may have... when I say hair and eye color I do not mean it to be biologically determined. Whether your hair is brown or blue, I accept that that is your hair, and I have no reason to use that information to treat you any differently than if you had purple hair or red hair or black hair. Perhaps this hair example is too distracting, but hopefully you get what I'm trying to say.

I dream of living in a society...

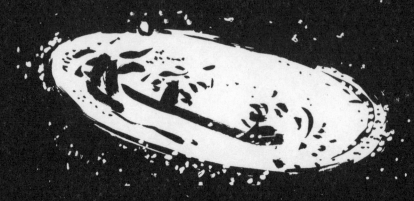

where gender is not embedded into the language, where the mask of fixed and limited genders is lifted, and we get to see how human expression flourishes unbound and open to all the universe has to offer.

Alternatively, I dream of a world where all the cisgendered men are quarantined on a remote island, or perhaps a small continent, with all the guns and bombs they've created, so we could see what happens when we get to rebuild our house without patriarchy breathing down our necks.

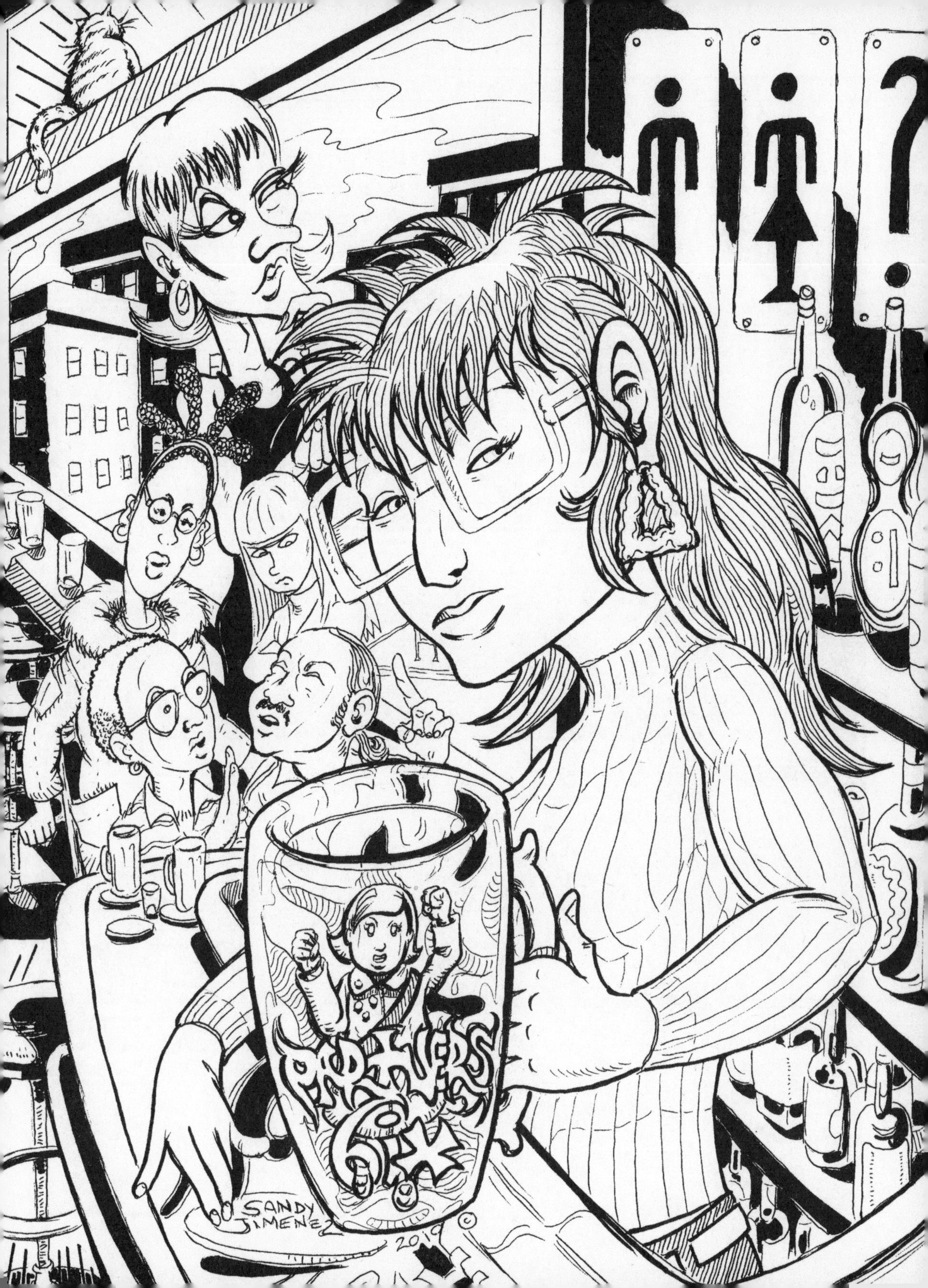
SANDY JIMENEZ
2019 ©

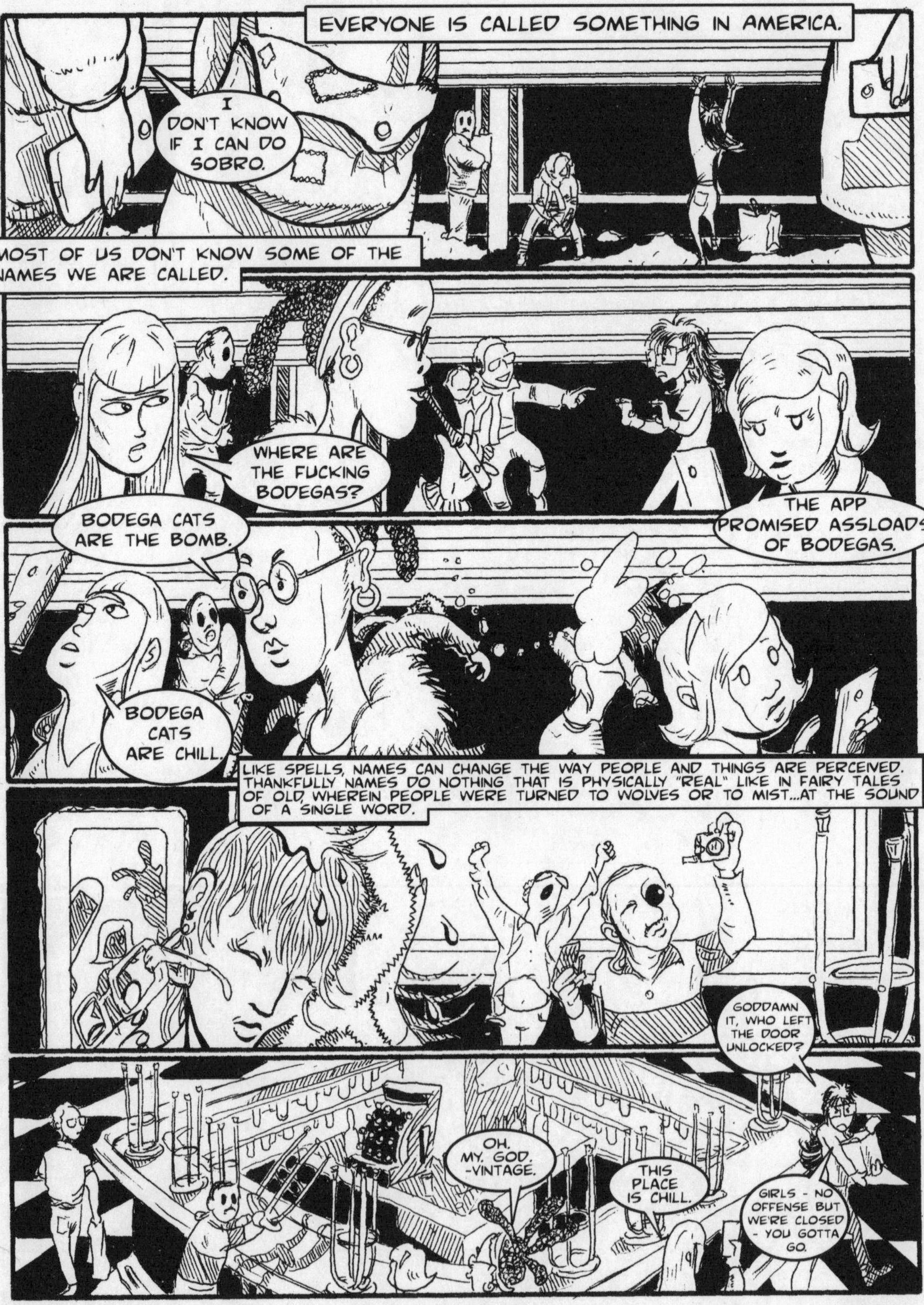
EVERYONE IS CALLED SOMETHING IN AMERICA.
I DON'T KNOW IF I CAN DO SOBRO.
MOST OF US DON'T KNOW SOME OF THE NAMES WE ARE CALLED.
WHERE ARE THE FUCKING BODEGAS?
THE APP PROMISED ASSLOADS OF BODEGAS.
BODEGA CATS ARE THE BOMB.
BODEGA CATS ARE CHILL.
LIKE SPELLS, NAMES CAN CHANGE THE WAY PEOPLE AND THINGS ARE PERCEIVED. THANKFULLY NAMES DO NOTHING THAT IS PHYSICALLY "REAL" LIKE IN FAIRY TALES OF OLD, WHEREIN PEOPLE WERE TURNED TO WOLVES OR TO MIST...AT THE SOUND OF A SINGLE WORD.
GODDAMN IT, WHO LEFT THE DOOR UNLOCKED?
OH. MY. GOD. -VINTAGE.
THIS PLACE IS CHILL.
GIRLS - NO OFFENSE BUT WE'RE CLOSED - YOU GOTTA GO.

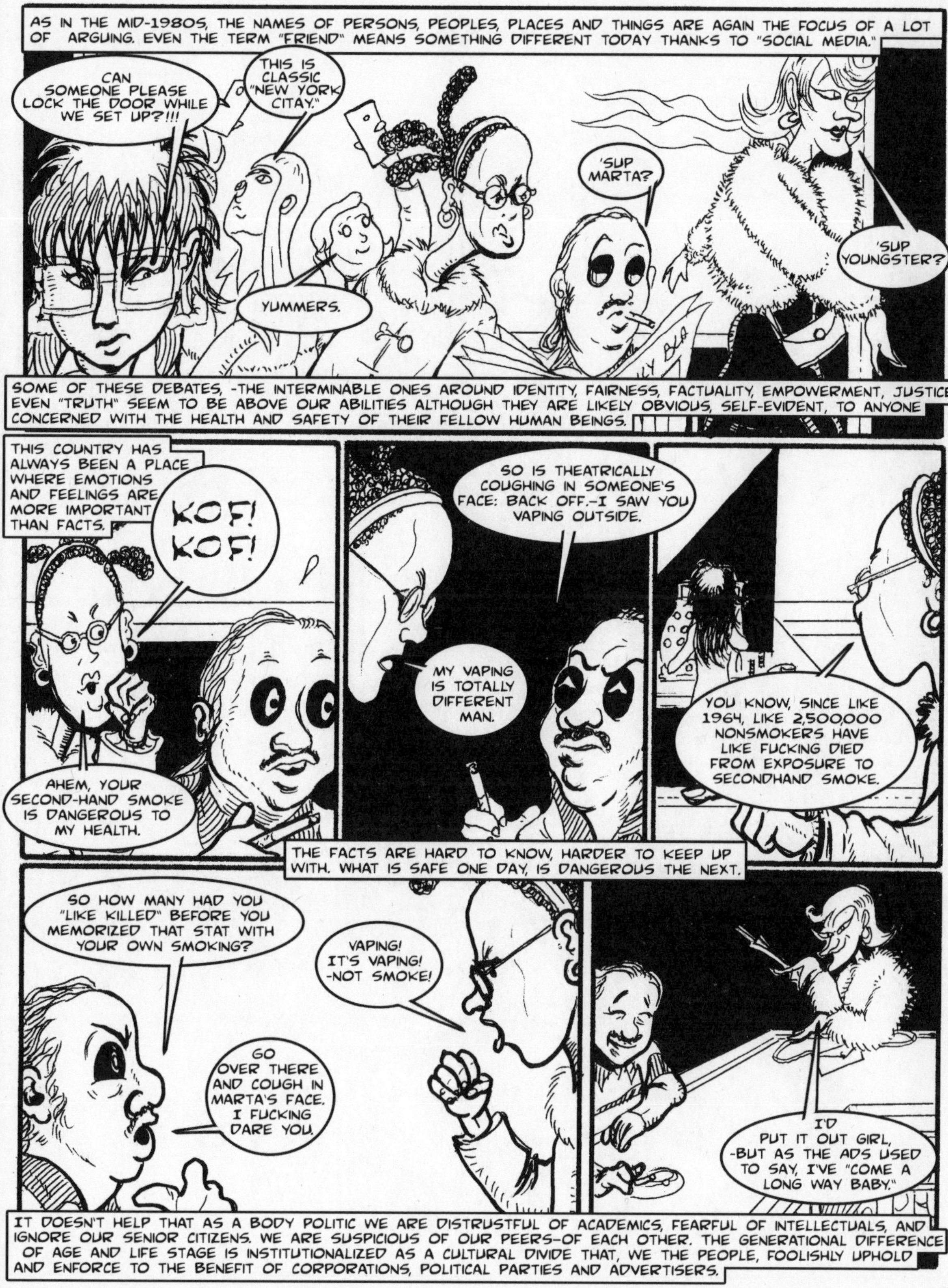
AS IN THE MID-1980S, THE NAMES OF PERSONS, PEOPLES, PLACES AND THINGS ARE AGAIN THE FOCUS OF A LOT OF ARGUING. EVEN THE TERM "FRIEND" MEANS SOMETHING DIFFERENT TODAY THANKS TO "SOCIAL MEDIA."
CAN SOMEONE PLEASE LOCK THE DOOR WHILE WE SET UP?!!!
THIS IS CLASSIC "NEW YORK CITAY."
YUMMERS.
'SUP MARTA?
'SUP YOUNGSTER?
SOME OF THESE DEBATES, -THE INTERMINABLE ONES AROUND IDENTITY, FAIRNESS, FACTUALITY, EMPOWERMENT, JUSTICE, EVEN "TRUTH" SEEM TO BE ABOVE OUR ABILITIES ALTHOUGH THEY ARE LIKELY OBVIOUS, SELF-EVIDENT, TO ANYONE CONCERNED WITH THE HEALTH AND SAFETY OF THEIR FELLOW HUMAN BEINGS.
THIS COUNTRY HAS ALWAYS BEEN A PLACE WHERE EMOTIONS AND FEELINGS ARE MORE IMPORTANT THAN FACTS.
KOF! KOF!
AHEM, YOUR SECOND-HAND SMOKE IS DANGEROUS TO MY HEALTH.
SO IS THEATRICALLY COUGHING IN SOMEONE'S FACE: BACK OFF.-I SAW YOU VAPING OUTSIDE.
MY VAPING IS TOTALLY DIFFERENT MAN.
YOU KNOW, SINCE LIKE 1964, LIKE 2,500,000 NONSMOKERS HAVE LIKE FUCKING DIED FROM EXPOSURE TO SECONDHAND SMOKE.
THE FACTS ARE HARD TO KNOW, HARDER TO KEEP UP WITH. WHAT IS SAFE ONE DAY, IS DANGEROUS THE NEXT.
SO HOW MANY HAD YOU "LIKE KILLED" BEFORE YOU MEMORIZED THAT STAT WITH YOUR OWN SMOKING?
VAPING! IT'S VAPING! -NOT SMOKE!
GO OVER THERE AND COUGH IN MARTA'S FACE. I FUCKING DARE YOU.
I'D PUT IT OUT GIRL, -BUT AS THE ADS USED TO SAY, I'VE "COME A LONG WAY BABY."
IT DOESN'T HELP THAT AS A BODY POLITIC WE ARE DISTRUSTFUL OF ACADEMICS, FEARFUL OF INTELLECTUALS, AND IGNORE OUR SENIOR CITIZENS. WE ARE SUSPICIOUS OF OUR PEERS-OF EACH OTHER. THE GENERATIONAL DIFFERENCE OF AGE AND LIFE STAGE IS INSTITUTIONALIZED AS A CULTURAL DIVIDE THAT, WE THE PEOPLE, FOOLISHLY UPHOLD AND ENFORCE TO THE BENEFIT OF CORPORATIONS, POLITICAL PARTIES AND ADVERTISERS.

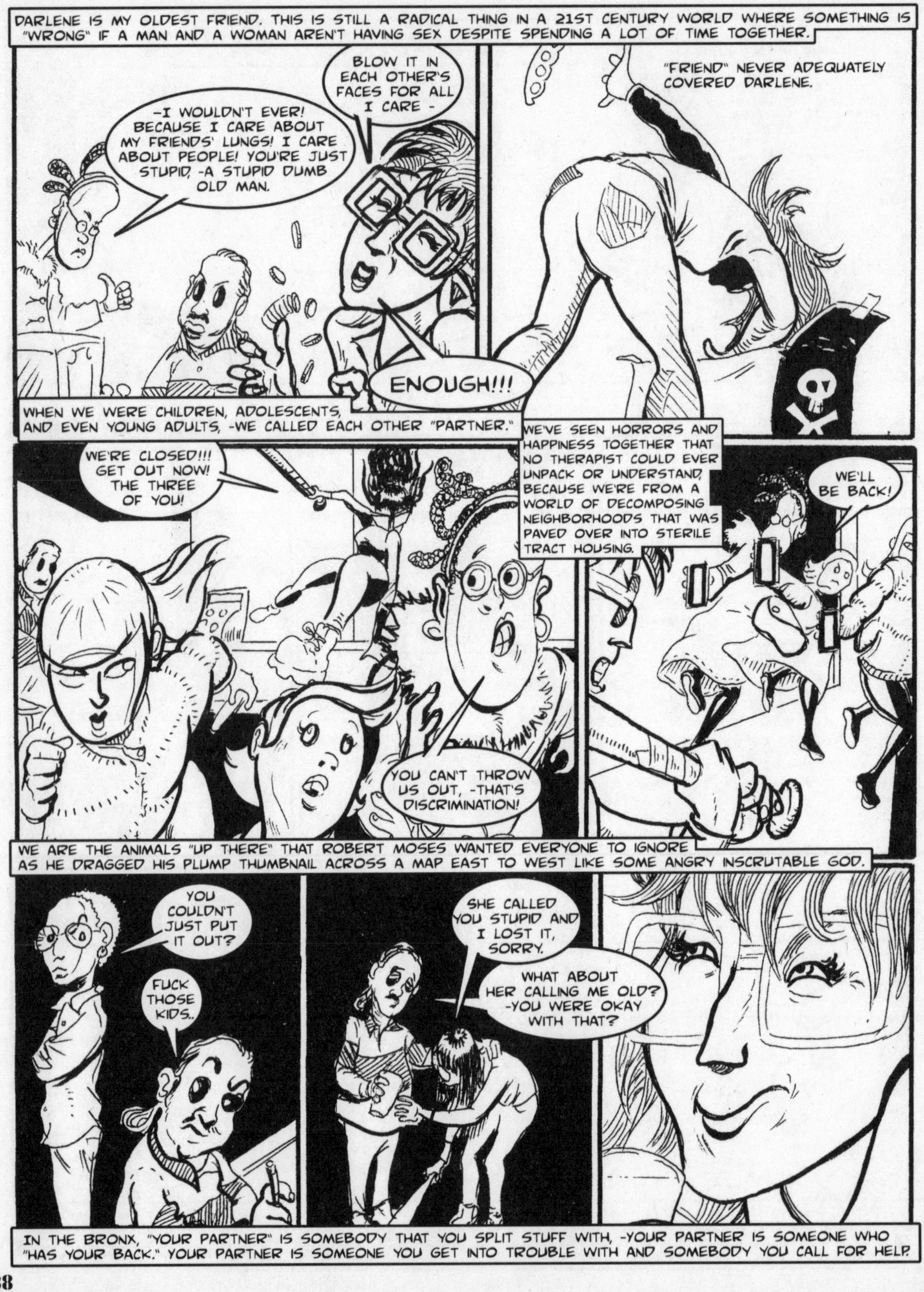

DARLENE IS MY OLDEST FRIEND. THIS IS STILL A RADICAL THING IN A 21ST CENTURY WORLD WHERE SOMETHING IS "WRONG" IF A MAN AND A WOMAN AREN'T HAVING SEX DESPITE SPENDING A LOT OF TIME TOGETHER.
-I WOULDN'T EVER! BECAUSE I CARE ABOUT MY FRIENDS' LUNGS! I CARE ABOUT PEOPLE! YOU'RE JUST STUPID, -A STUPID DUMB OLD MAN.
BLOW IT IN EACH OTHER'S FACES FOR ALL I CARE -
ENOUGH!!!
WHEN WE WERE CHILDREN, ADOLESCENTS, AND EVEN YOUNG ADULTS, -WE CALLED EACH OTHER "PARTNER."
"FRIEND" NEVER ADEQUATELY COVERED DARLENE.
WE'VE SEEN HORRORS AND HAPPINESS TOGETHER THAT NO THERAPIST COULD EVER UNPACK OR UNDERSTAND, BECAUSE WE'RE FROM A WORLD OF DECOMPOSING NEIGHBORHOODS THAT WAS PAVED OVER INTO STERILE TRACT HOUSING.
WE'RE CLOSED!!! GET OUT NOW! THE THREE OF YOU!
YOU CAN'T THROW US OUT, -THAT'S DISCRIMINATION!
WE'LL BE BACK!
WE ARE THE ANIMALS "UP THERE" THAT ROBERT MOSES WANTED EVERYONE TO IGNORE AS HE DRAGGED HIS PLUMP THUMBNAIL ACROSS A MAP EAST TO WEST LIKE SOME ANGRY INSCRUTABLE GOD.
YOU COULDN'T JUST PUT IT OUT?
FUCK THOSE KIDS..
SHE CALLED YOU STUPID AND I LOST IT, SORRY.
WHAT ABOUT HER CALLING ME OLD? -YOU WERE OKAY WITH THAT?
IN THE BRONX, "YOUR PARTNER" IS SOMEBODY THAT YOU SPLIT STUFF WITH, -YOUR PARTNER IS SOMEONE WHO "HAS YOUR BACK." YOUR PARTNER IS SOMEONE YOU GET INTO TROUBLE WITH AND SOMEBODY YOU CALL FOR HELP.

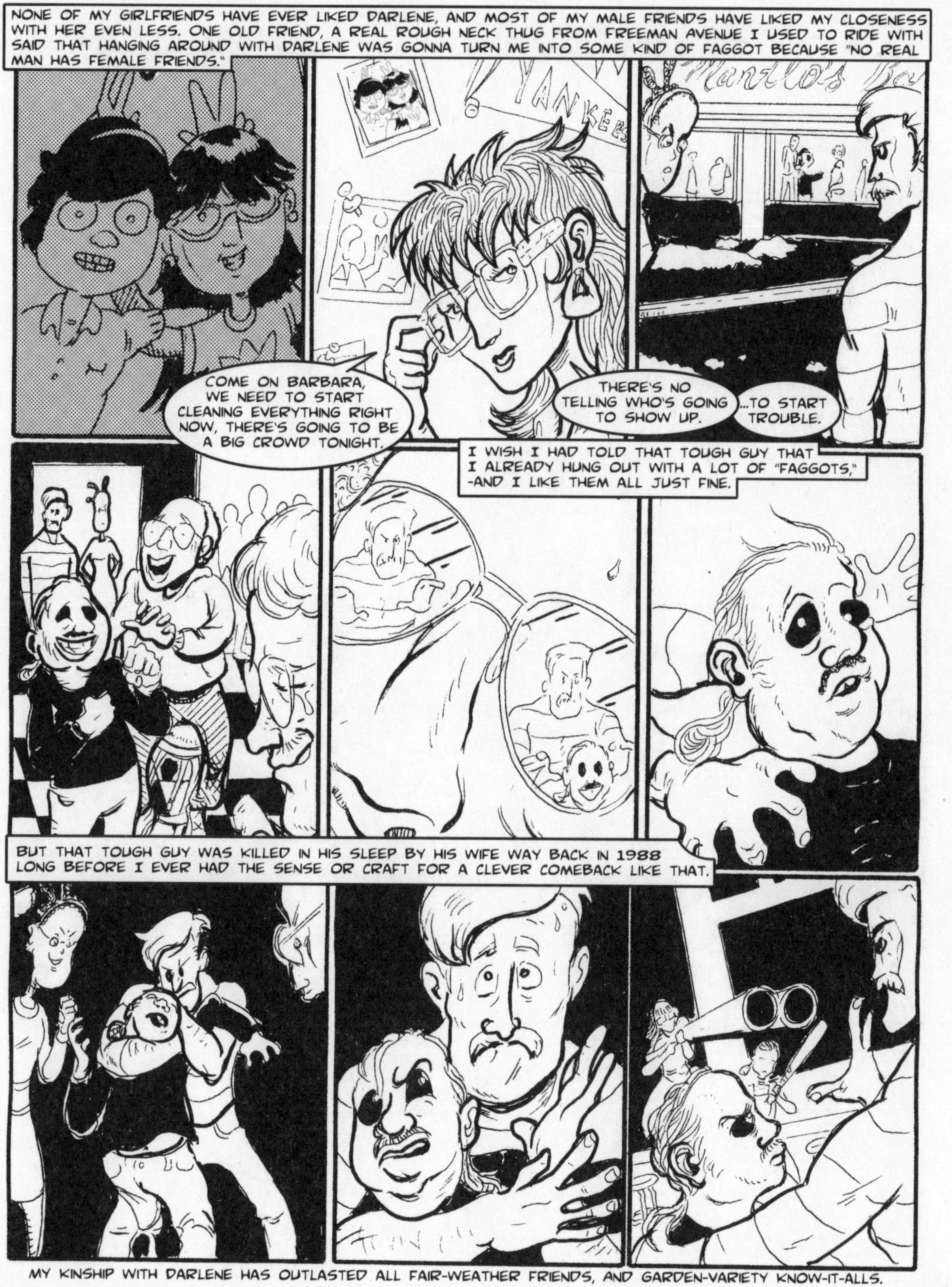
NONE OF MY GIRLFRIENDS HAVE EVER LIKED DARLENE, AND MOST OF MY MALE FRIENDS HAVE LIKED MY CLOSENESS WITH HER EVEN LESS. ONE OLD FRIEND, A REAL ROUGH NECK THUG FROM FREEMAN AVENUE I USED TO RIDE WITH SAID THAT HANGING AROUND WITH DARLENE WAS GONNA TURN ME INTO SOME KIND OF FAGGOT BECAUSE "NO REAL MAN HAS FEMALE FRIENDS."
YANKEES
COME ON BARBARA, WE NEED TO START CLEANING EVERYTHING RIGHT NOW, THERE'S GOING TO BE A BIG CROWD TONIGHT.
THERE'S NO TELLING WHO'S GOING TO SHOW UP.
...TO START TROUBLE.
I WISH I HAD TOLD THAT TOUGH GUY THAT I ALREADY HUNG OUT WITH A LOT OF "FAGGOTS," -AND I LIKE THEM ALL JUST FINE.
BUT THAT TOUGH GUY WAS KILLED IN HIS SLEEP BY HIS WIFE WAY BACK IN 1988 LONG BEFORE I EVER HAD THE SENSE OR CRAFT FOR A CLEVER COMEBACK LIKE THAT.

MY KINSHIP WITH DARLENE HAS OUTLASTED ALL FAIR-WEATHER FRIENDS, AND GARDEN-VARIETY KNOW-IT-ALLS.

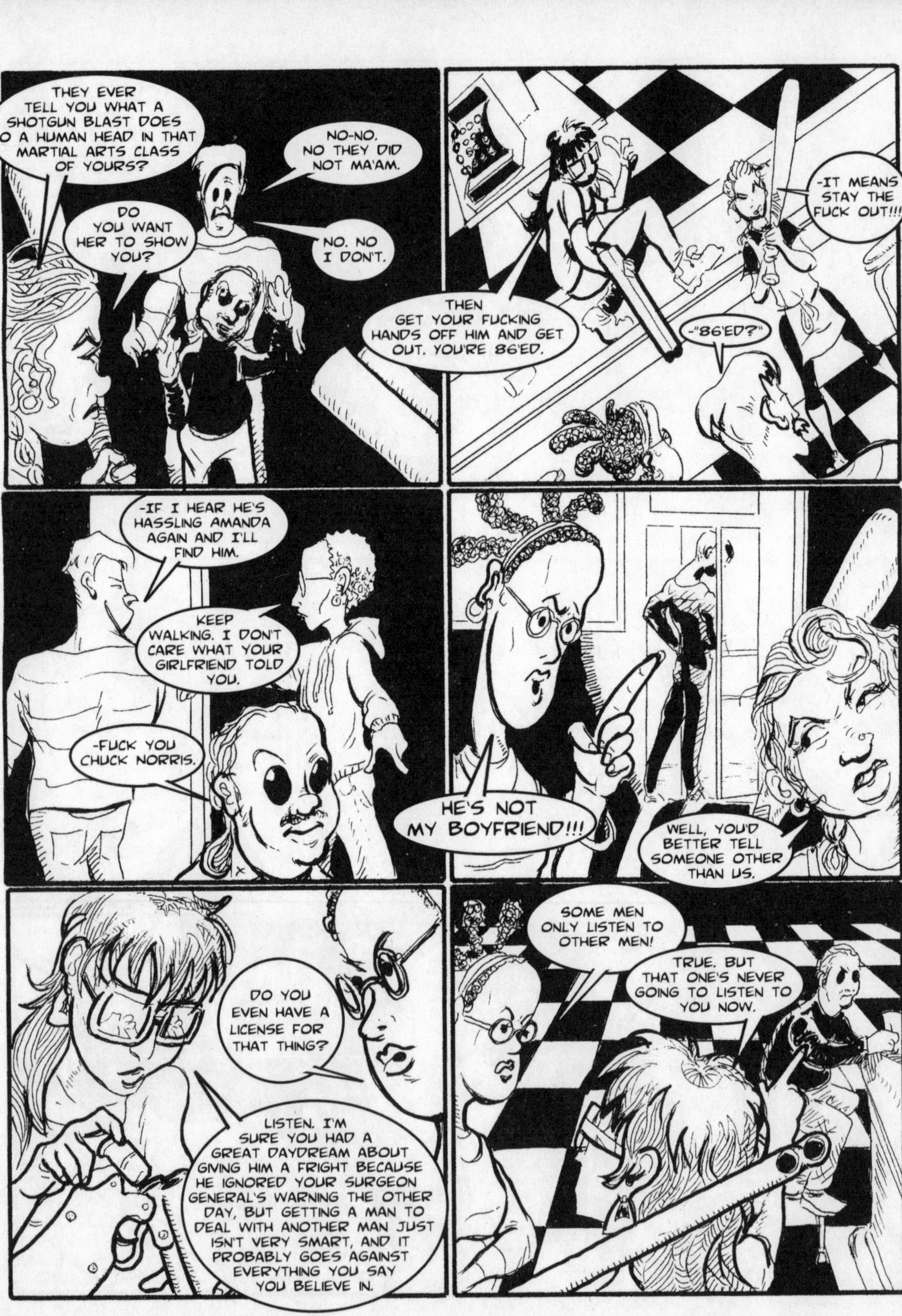
THEY EVER TELL YOU WHAT A SHOTGUN BLAST DOES TO A HUMAN HEAD IN THAT MARTIAL ARTS CLASS OF YOURS?
NO-NO. NO THEY DID NOT MA'AM.
DO YOU WANT HER TO SHOW YOU?
NO. NO I DON'T.
-IT MEANS STAY THE FUCK OUT!!!
THEN GET YOUR FUCKING HANDS OFF HIM AND GET OUT. YOU'RE 86'ED.
-"86'ED?"
-IF I HEAR HE'S HASSLING AMANDA AGAIN AND I'LL FIND HIM.
KEEP WALKING. I DON'T CARE WHAT YOUR GIRLFRIEND TOLD YOU.
-FUCK YOU CHUCK NORRIS.
HE'S NOT MY BOYFRIEND!!!
WELL, YOU'D BETTER TELL SOMEONE OTHER THAN US.
DO YOU EVEN HAVE A LICENSE FOR THAT THING?
LISTEN. I'M SURE YOU HAD A GREAT DAYDREAM ABOUT GIVING HIM A FRIGHT BECAUSE HE IGNORED YOUR SURGEON GENERAL'S WARNING THE OTHER DAY, BUT GETTING A MAN TO DEAL WITH ANOTHER MAN JUST ISN'T VERY SMART, AND IT PROBABLY GOES AGAINST EVERYTHING YOU SAY YOU BELIEVE IN.
SOME MEN ONLY LISTEN TO OTHER MEN!
TRUE. BUT THAT ONE'S NEVER GOING TO LISTEN TO YOU NOW.

ONE WEEK LATER

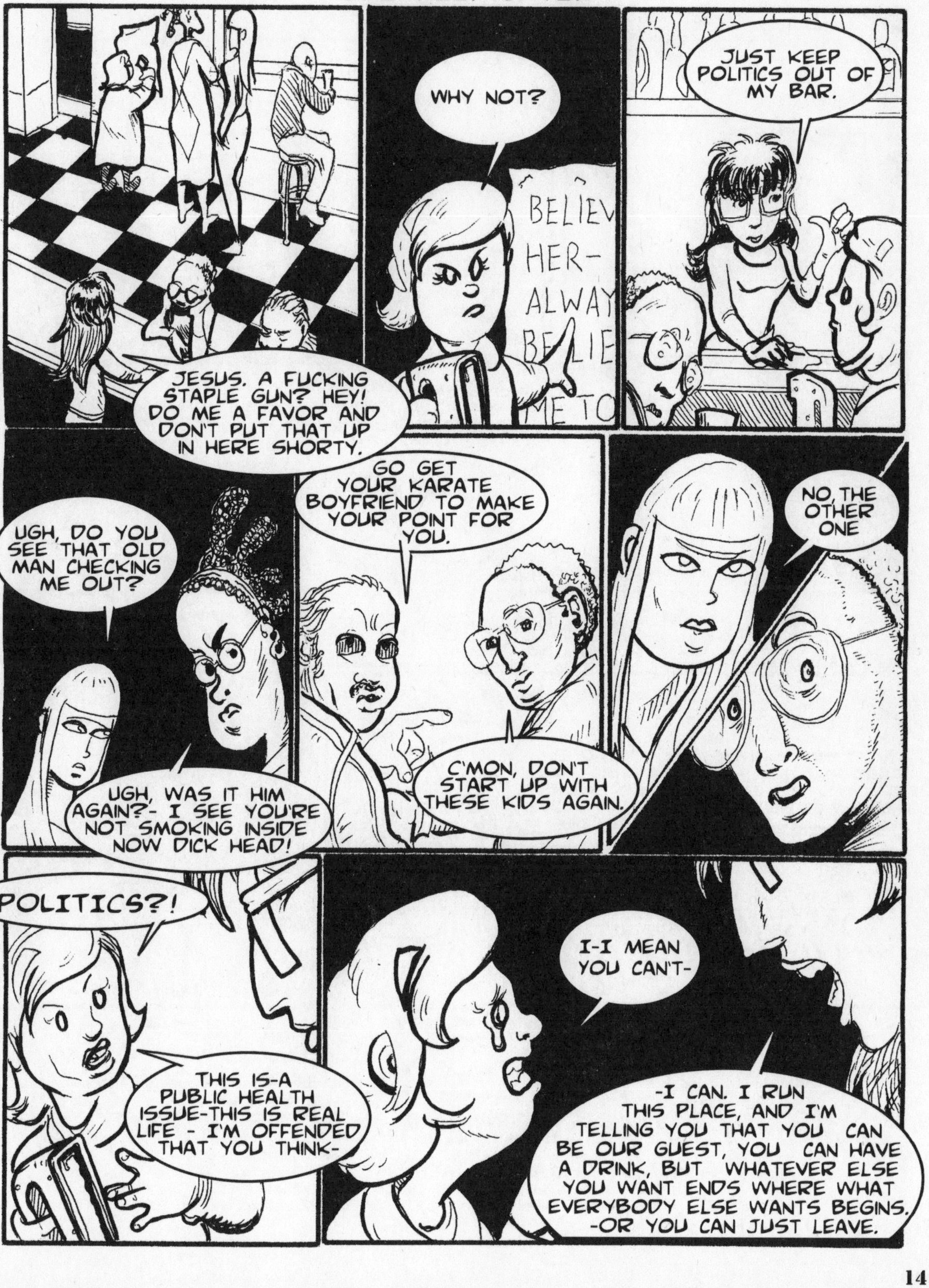

JESUS. A FUCKING STAPLE GUN? HEY! DO ME A FAVOR AND DON'T PUT THAT UP IN HERE SHORTY.
WHY NOT?
BELIEV HER- ALWAY BELIE ME TO
JUST KEEP POLITICS OUT OF MY BAR.
UGH, DO YOU SEE THAT OLD MAN CHECKING ME OUT?
UGH, WAS IT HIM AGAIN?- I SEE YOU'RE NOT SMOKING INSIDE NOW DICK HEAD!
GO GET YOUR KARATE BOYFRIEND TO MAKE YOUR POINT FOR YOU.
C'MON, DON'T START UP WITH THESE KIDS AGAIN.
NO, THE OTHER ONE
POLITICS?!
THIS IS-A PUBLIC HEALTH ISSUE-THIS IS REAL LIFE - I'M OFFENDED THAT YOU THINK-
I-I MEAN YOU CAN'T-
-I CAN. I RUN THIS PLACE, AND I'M TELLING YOU THAT YOU CAN BE OUR GUEST, YOU CAN HAVE A DRINK, BUT WHATEVER ELSE YOU WANT ENDS WHERE WHAT EVERYBODY ELSE WANTS BEGINS. -OR YOU CAN JUST LEAVE.

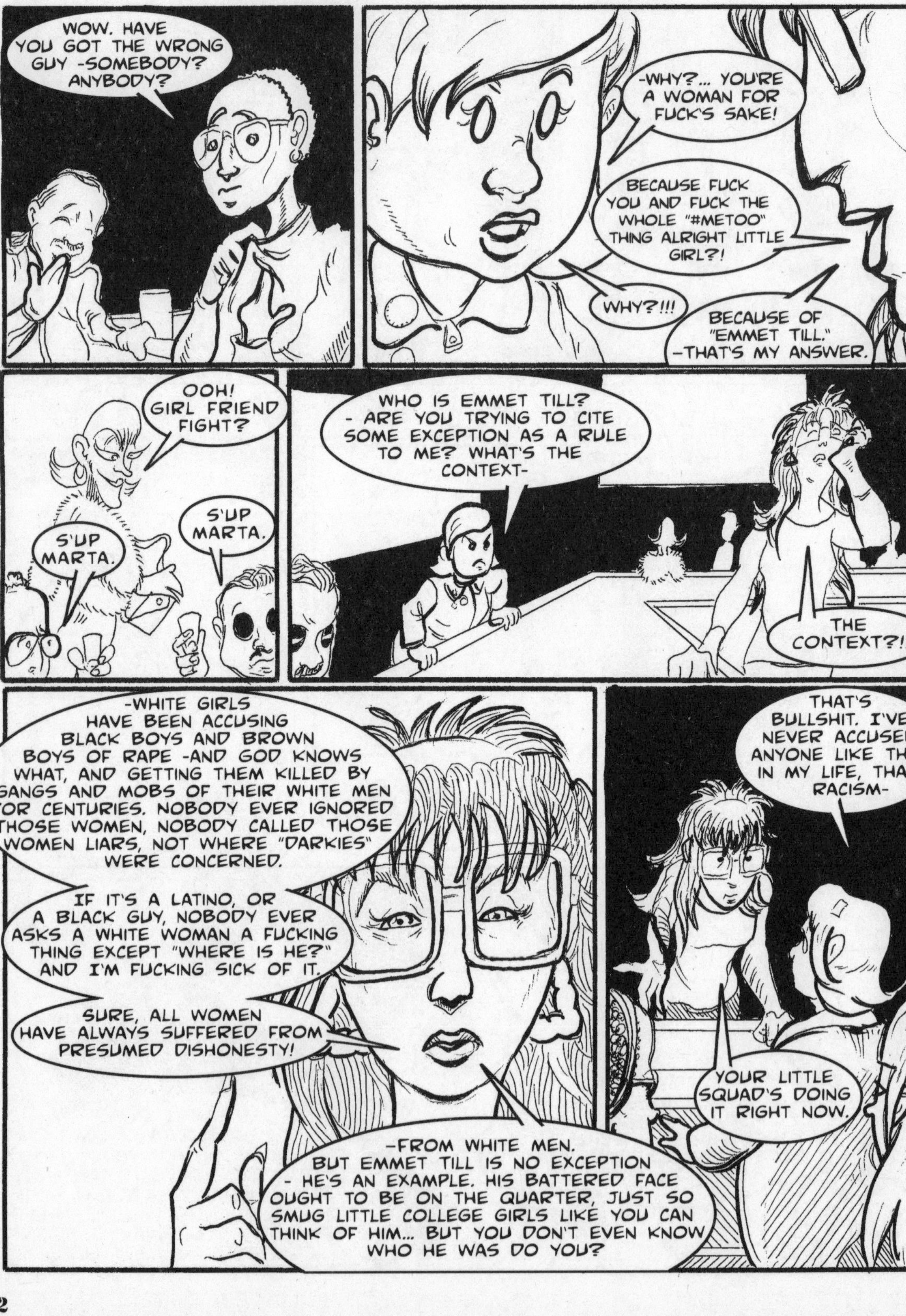
WOW. HAVE YOU GOT THE WRONG GUY -SOMEBODY? ANYBODY?
-WHY?... YOU'RE A WOMAN FOR FUCK'S SAKE!
WHY?!!!
BECAUSE FUCK YOU AND FUCK THE WHOLE "#METOO" THING ALRIGHT LITTLE GIRL?!
BECAUSE OF "EMMET TILL." -THAT'S MY ANSWER.
OOH! GIRL FRIEND FIGHT?
S'UP MARTA.
S'UP MARTA.
WHO IS EMMET TILL? - ARE YOU TRYING TO CITE SOME EXCEPTION AS A RULE TO ME? WHAT'S THE CONTEXT-
THE CONTEXT?!!!
-WHITE GIRLS HAVE BEEN ACCUSING BLACK BOYS AND BROWN BOYS OF RAPE -AND GOD KNOWS WHAT, AND GETTING THEM KILLED BY GANGS AND MOBS OF THEIR WHITE MEN FOR CENTURIES. NOBODY EVER IGNORED THOSE WOMEN, NOBODY CALLED THOSE WOMEN LIARS, NOT WHERE "DARKIES" WERE CONCERNED.
IF IT'S A LATINO, OR A BLACK GUY, NOBODY EVER ASKS A WHITE WOMAN A FUCKING THING EXCEPT "WHERE IS HE?" AND I'M FUCKING SICK OF IT.
SURE, ALL WOMEN HAVE ALWAYS SUFFERED FROM PRESUMED DISHONESTY!
-FROM WHITE MEN. BUT EMMET TILL IS NO EXCEPTION - HE'S AN EXAMPLE. HIS BATTERED FACE OUGHT TO BE ON THE QUARTER, JUST SO SMUG LITTLE COLLEGE GIRLS LIKE YOU CAN THINK OF HIM... BUT YOU DON'T EVEN KNOW WHO HE WAS DO YOU?
THAT'S BULLSHIT. I'VE NEVER ACCUSED ANYONE LIKE THAT IN MY LIFE, THAT'S RACISM-
YOUR LITTLE SQUAD'S DOING IT RIGHT NOW.

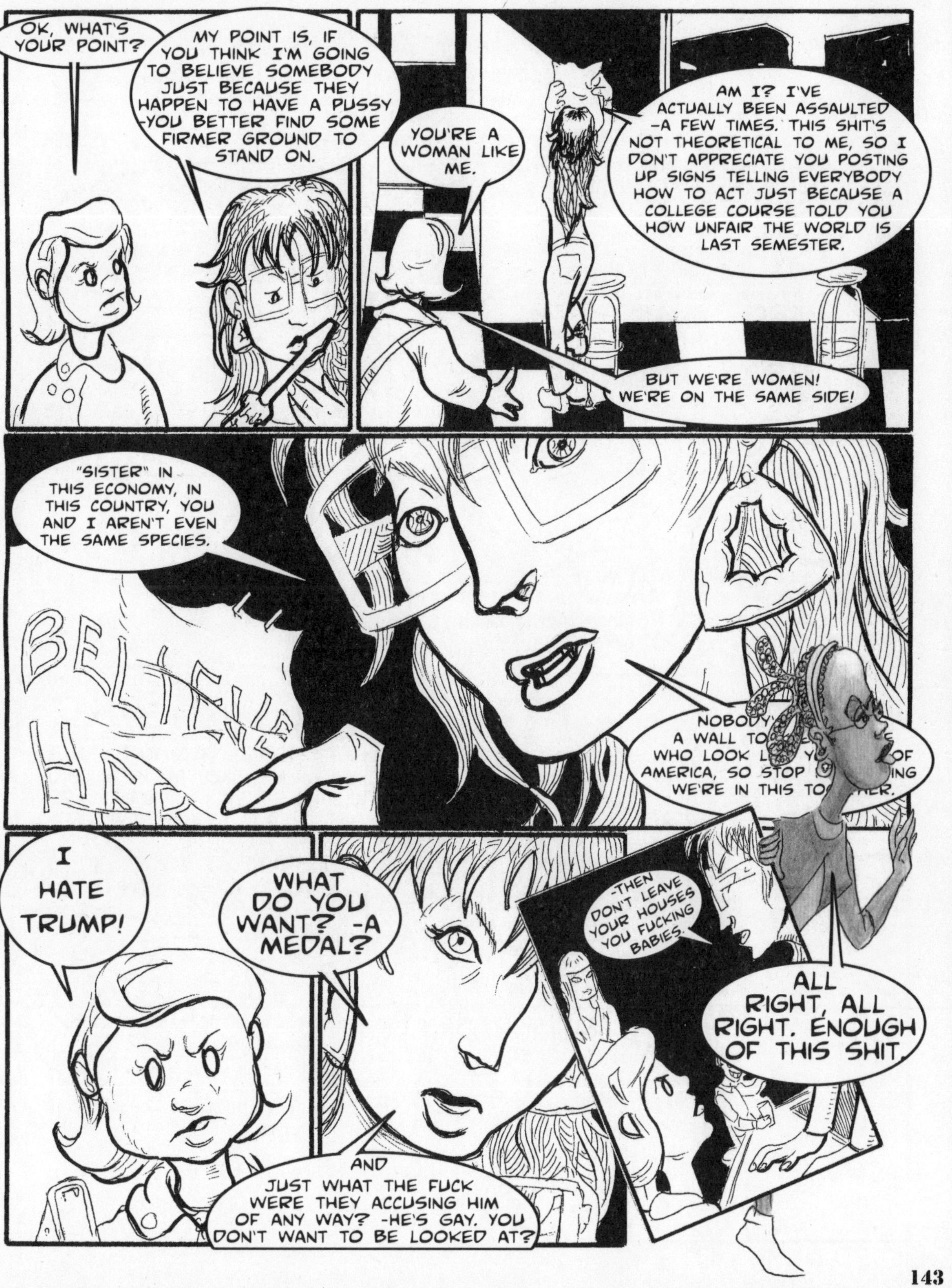
OK, WHAT'S YOUR POINT?
MY POINT IS, IF YOU THINK I'M GOING TO BELIEVE SOMEBODY JUST BECAUSE THEY HAPPEN TO HAVE A PUSSY -YOU BETTER FIND SOME FIRMER GROUND TO STAND ON.
YOU'RE A WOMAN LIKE ME.
AM I? I'VE ACTUALLY BEEN ASSAULTED -A FEW TIMES. THIS SHIT'S NOT THEORETICAL TO ME, SO I DON'T APPRECIATE YOU POSTING UP SIGNS TELLING EVERYBODY HOW TO ACT JUST BECAUSE A COLLEGE COURSE TOLD YOU HOW UNFAIR THE WORLD IS LAST SEMESTER.
BUT WE'RE WOMEN! WE'RE ON THE SAME SIDE!
"SISTER" IN THIS ECONOMY, IN THIS COUNTRY, YOU AND I AREN'T EVEN THE SAME SPECIES.
BELIEVE HER
NOBODY
A WALL TO
WHO LOOK L
AMERICA, SO STOP
WE'RE IN THIS TO
I HATE TRUMP!
WHAT DO YOU WANT? -A MEDAL?
-THEN DON'T LEAVE YOUR HOUSES YOU FUCKING BABIES.
ALL RIGHT, ALL RIGHT. ENOUGH OF THIS SHIT.
AND JUST WHAT THE FUCK WERE THEY ACCUSING HIM OF ANY WAY? -HE'S GAY. YOU DON'T WANT TO BE LOOKED AT?

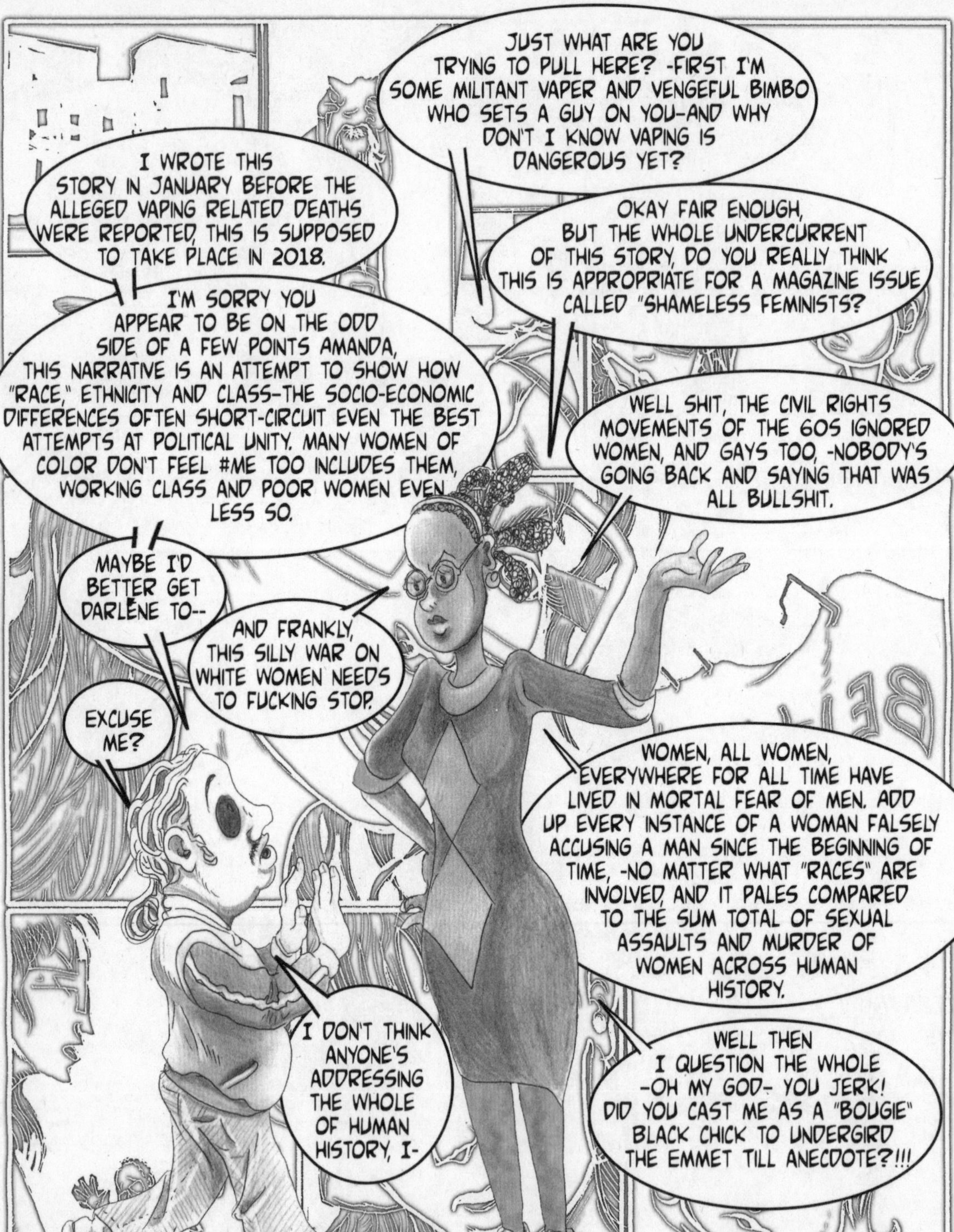

JUST WHAT ARE YOU TRYING TO PULL HERE? -FIRST I'M SOME MILITANT VAPER AND VENGEFUL BIMBO WHO SETS A GUY ON YOU–AND WHY DON'T I KNOW VAPING IS DANGEROUS YET?
I WROTE THIS STORY IN JANUARY BEFORE THE ALLEGED VAPING RELATED DEATHS WERE REPORTED, THIS IS SUPPOSED TO TAKE PLACE IN 2018.
OKAY FAIR ENOUGH, BUT THE WHOLE UNDERCURRENT OF THIS STORY, DO YOU REALLY THINK THIS IS APPROPRIATE FOR A MAGAZINE ISSUE CALLED "SHAMELESS FEMINISTS?
I'M SORRY YOU APPEAR TO BE ON THE ODD SIDE OF A FEW POINTS AMANDA, THIS NARRATIVE IS AN ATTEMPT TO SHOW HOW "RACE," ETHNICITY AND CLASS–THE SOCIO-ECONOMIC DIFFERENCES OFTEN SHORT-CIRCUIT EVEN THE BEST ATTEMPTS AT POLITICAL UNITY. MANY WOMEN OF COLOR DON'T FEEL #ME TOO INCLUDES THEM, WORKING CLASS AND POOR WOMEN EVEN LESS SO.
WELL SHIT, THE CIVIL RIGHTS MOVEMENTS OF THE 60S IGNORED WOMEN, AND GAYS TOO, -NOBODY'S GOING BACK AND SAYING THAT WAS ALL BULLSHIT.
MAYBE I'D BETTER GET DARLENE TO--
AND FRANKLY, THIS SILLY WAR ON WHITE WOMEN NEEDS TO FUCKING STOP.
EXCUSE ME?
WOMEN, ALL WOMEN, EVERYWHERE FOR ALL TIME HAVE LIVED IN MORTAL FEAR OF MEN. ADD UP EVERY INSTANCE OF A WOMAN FALSELY ACCUSING A MAN SINCE THE BEGINNING OF TIME, -NO MATTER WHAT "RACES" ARE INVOLVED, AND IT PALES COMPARED TO THE SUM TOTAL OF SEXUAL ASSAULTS AND MURDER OF WOMEN ACROSS HUMAN HISTORY.
I DON'T THINK ANYONE'S ADDRESSING THE WHOLE OF HUMAN HISTORY, I-
WELL THEN I QUESTION THE WHOLE -OH MY GOD- YOU JERK! DID YOU CAST ME AS A "BOUGIE" BLACK CHICK TO UNDERGIRD THE EMMET TILL ANECDOTE?!!!

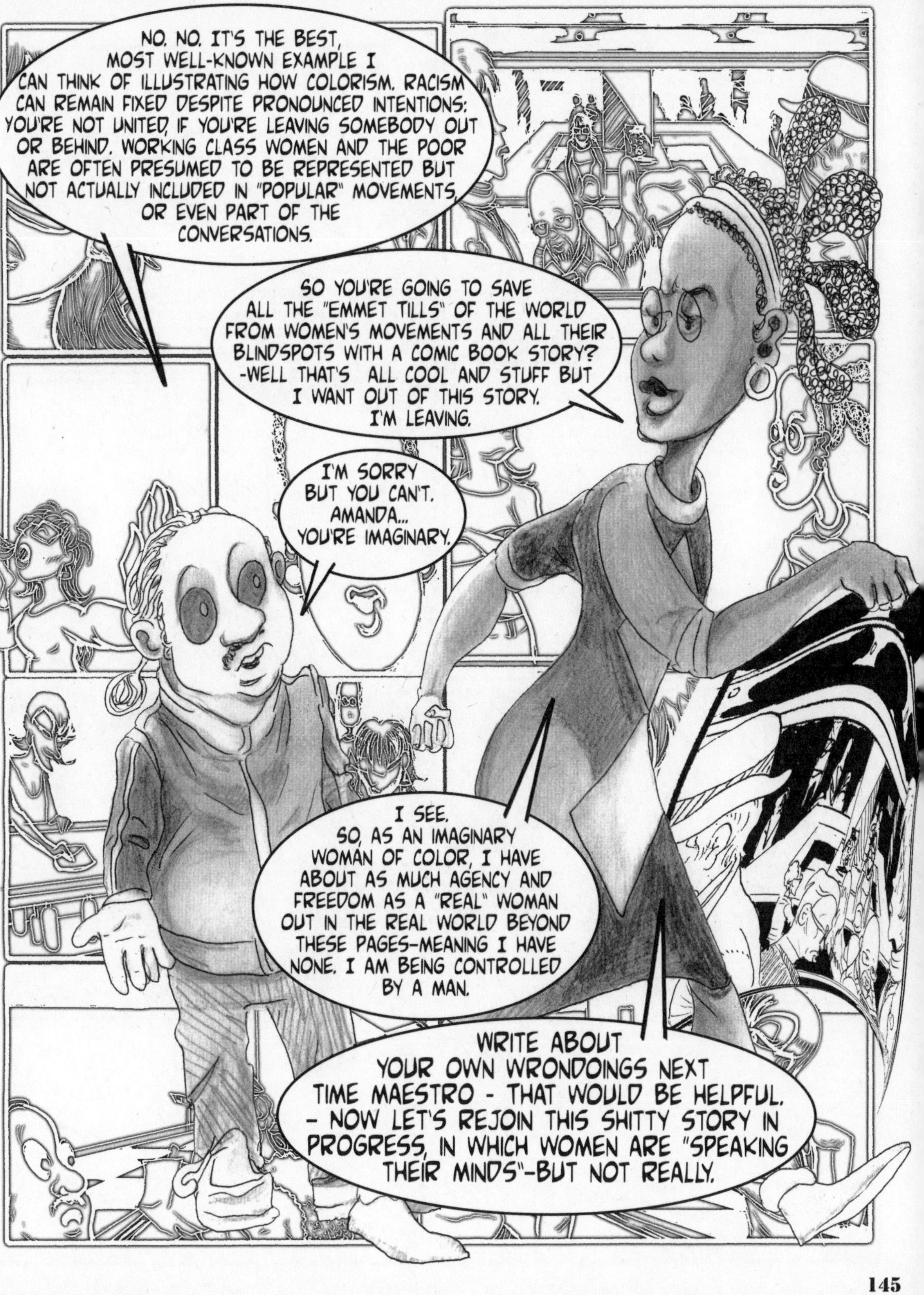
NO. NO. IT'S THE BEST, MOST WELL-KNOWN EXAMPLE I CAN THINK OF ILLUSTRATING HOW COLORISM. RACISM CAN REMAIN FIXED DESPITE PRONOUNCED INTENTIONS: YOU'RE NOT UNITED, IF YOU'RE LEAVING SOMEBODY OUT OR BEHIND. WORKING CLASS WOMEN AND THE POOR ARE OFTEN PRESUMED TO BE REPRESENTED BUT NOT ACTUALLY INCLUDED IN "POPULAR" MOVEMENTS, OR EVEN PART OF THE CONVERSATIONS.
SO YOU'RE GOING TO SAVE ALL THE "EMMET TILLS" OF THE WORLD FROM WOMEN'S MOVEMENTS AND ALL THEIR BLINDSPOTS WITH A COMIC BOOK STORY? -WELL THAT'S ALL COOL AND STUFF BUT I WANT OUT OF THIS STORY. I'M LEAVING.
I'M SORRY BUT YOU CAN'T. AMANDA... YOU'RE IMAGINARY.
I SEE. SO, AS AN IMAGINARY WOMAN OF COLOR, I HAVE ABOUT AS MUCH AGENCY AND FREEDOM AS A "REAL" WOMAN OUT IN THE REAL WORLD BEYOND THESE PAGES–MEANING I HAVE NONE. I AM BEING CONTROLLED BY A MAN.
WRITE ABOUT YOUR OWN WRONDOINGS NEXT TIME MAESTRO - THAT WOULD BE HELPFUL. - NOW LET'S REJOIN THIS SHITTY STORY IN PROGRESS, IN WHICH WOMEN ARE "SPEAKING THEIR MINDS"–BUT NOT REALLY.

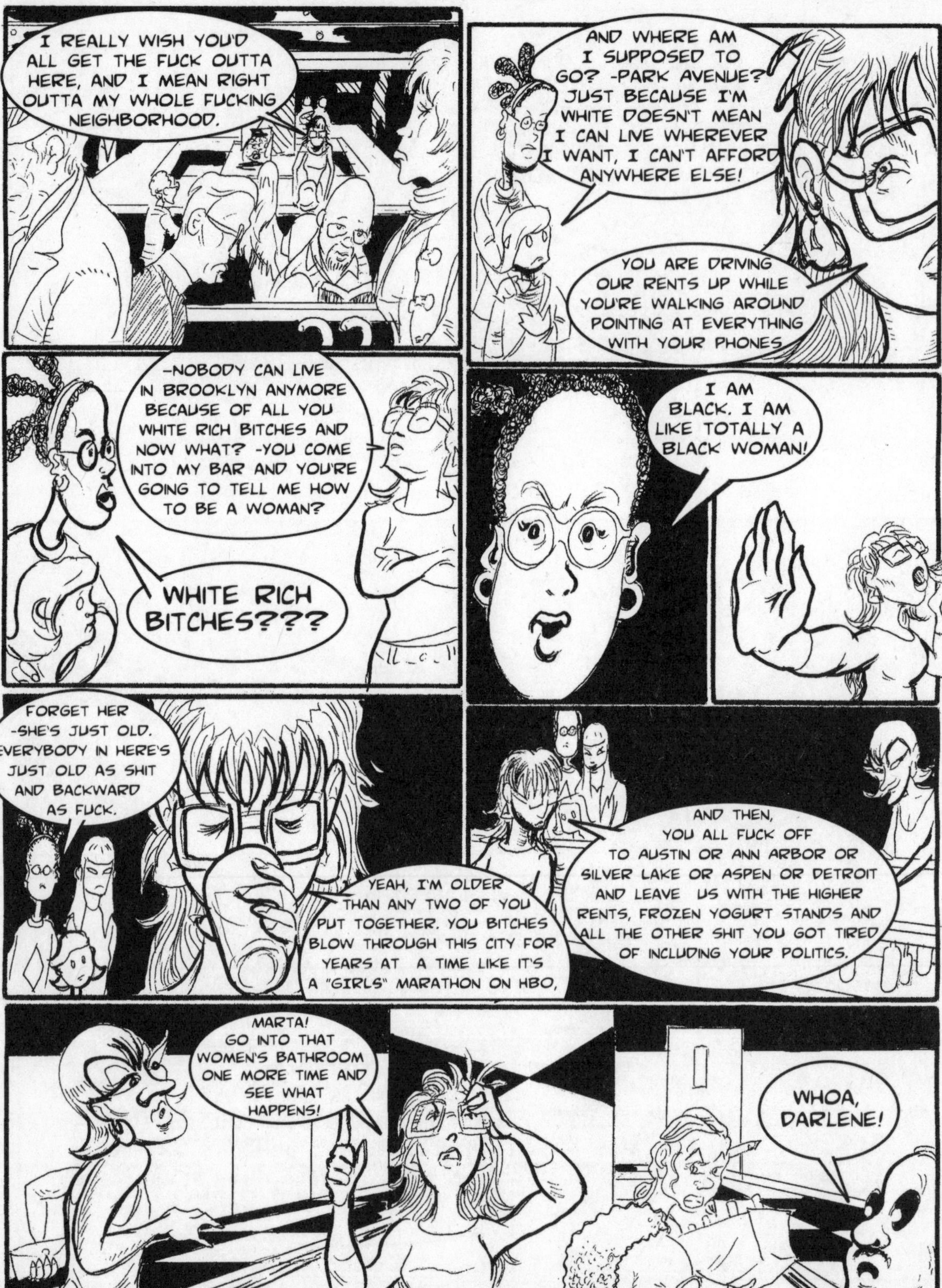

I REALLY WISH YOU'D ALL GET THE FUCK OUTTA HERE, AND I MEAN RIGHT OUTTA MY WHOLE FUCKING NEIGHBORHOOD.
AND WHERE AM I SUPPOSED TO GO? -PARK AVENUE? JUST BECAUSE I'M WHITE DOESN'T MEAN I CAN LIVE WHEREVER I WANT, I CAN'T AFFORD ANYWHERE ELSE!
YOU ARE DRIVING OUR RENTS UP WHILE YOU'RE WALKING AROUND POINTING AT EVERYTHING WITH YOUR PHONES
-NOBODY CAN LIVE IN BROOKLYN ANYMORE BECAUSE OF ALL YOU WHITE RICH BITCHES AND NOW WHAT? -YOU COME INTO MY BAR AND YOU'RE GOING TO TELL ME HOW TO BE A WOMAN?
WHITE RICH BITCHES???
I AM BLACK. I AM LIKE TOTALLY A BLACK WOMAN!
FORGET HER -SHE'S JUST OLD. EVERYBODY IN HERE'S JUST OLD AS SHIT AND BACKWARD AS FUCK.
YEAH, I'M OLDER THAN ANY TWO OF YOU PUT TOGETHER. YOU BITCHES BLOW THROUGH THIS CITY FOR YEARS AT A TIME LIKE IT'S A "GIRLS" MARATHON ON HBO,
AND THEN, YOU ALL FUCK OFF TO AUSTIN OR ANN ARBOR OR SILVER LAKE OR ASPEN OR DETROIT AND LEAVE US WITH THE HIGHER RENTS, FROZEN YOGURT STANDS AND ALL THE OTHER SHIT YOU GOT TIRED OF INCLUDING YOUR POLITICS.
MARTA! GO INTO THAT WOMEN'S BATHROOM ONE MORE TIME AND SEE WHAT HAPPENS!
WHOA, DARLENE!

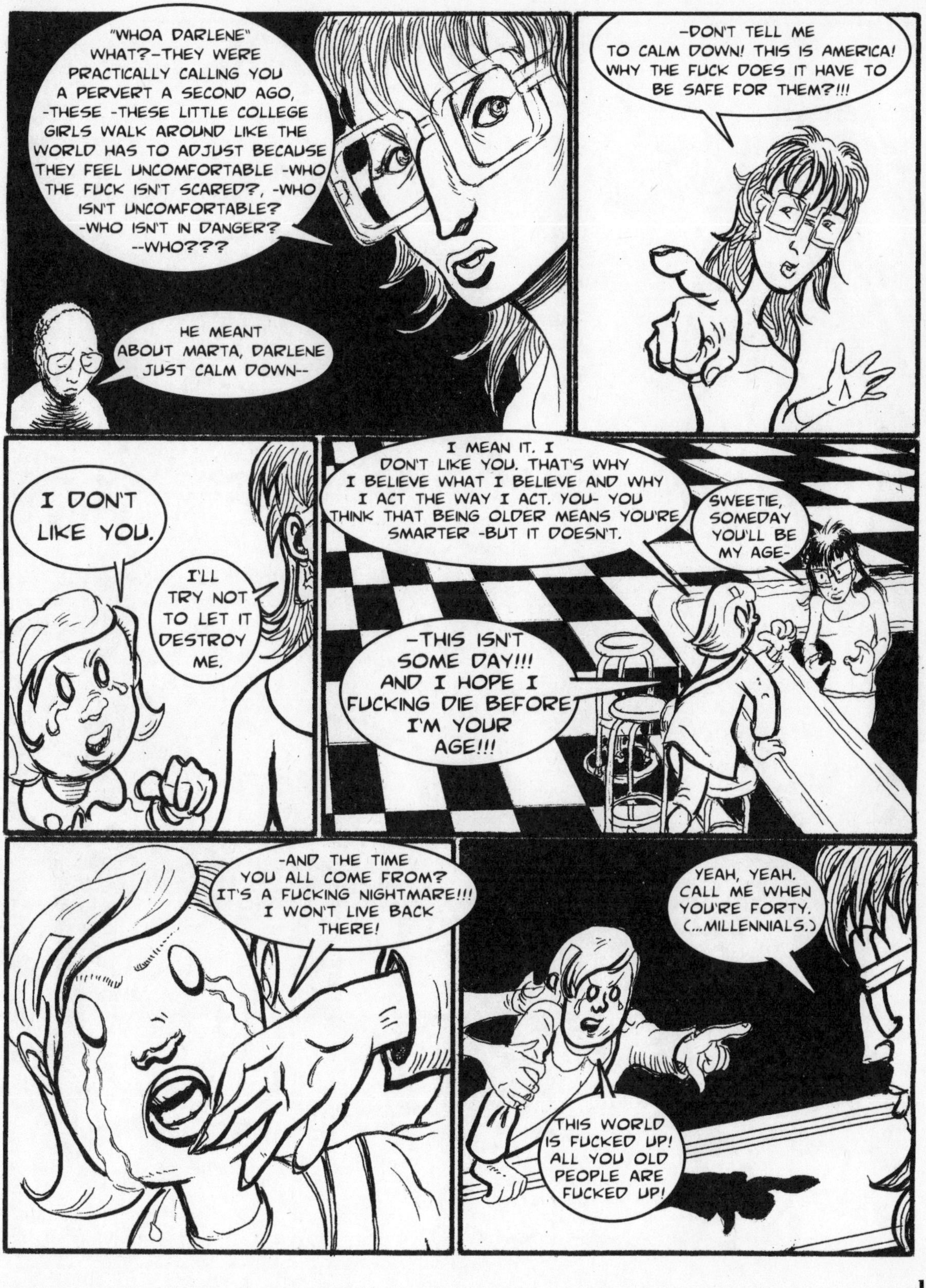

"WHOA DARLENE" WHAT?–THEY WERE PRACTICALLY CALLING YOU A PERVERT A SECOND AGO, -THESE -THESE LITTLE COLLEGE GIRLS WALK AROUND LIKE THE WORLD HAS TO ADJUST BECAUSE THEY FEEL UNCOMFORTABLE -WHO THE FUCK ISN'T SCARED?, -WHO ISN'T UNCOMFORTABLE? -WHO ISN'T IN DANGER? --WHO???
HE MEANT ABOUT MARTA, DARLENE JUST CALM DOWN--
–DON'T TELL ME TO CALM DOWN! THIS IS AMERICA! WHY THE FUCK DOES IT HAVE TO BE SAFE FOR THEM?!!!
I DON'T LIKE YOU.
I'LL TRY NOT TO LET IT DESTROY ME.
I MEAN IT. I DON'T LIKE YOU. THAT'S WHY I BELIEVE WHAT I BELIEVE AND WHY I ACT THE WAY I ACT. YOU- YOU THINK THAT BEING OLDER MEANS YOU'RE SMARTER -BUT IT DOESN'T.
SWEETIE, SOMEDAY YOU'LL BE MY AGE-
–THIS ISN'T SOME DAY!!! AND I HOPE I FUCKING DIE BEFORE I'M YOUR AGE!!!
-AND THE TIME YOU ALL COME FROM? IT'S A FUCKING NIGHTMARE!!! I WON'T LIVE BACK THERE!
YEAH, YEAH. CALL ME WHEN YOU'RE FORTY. (...MILLENNIALS.)
THIS WORLD IS FUCKED UP! ALL YOU OLD PEOPLE ARE FUCKED UP!

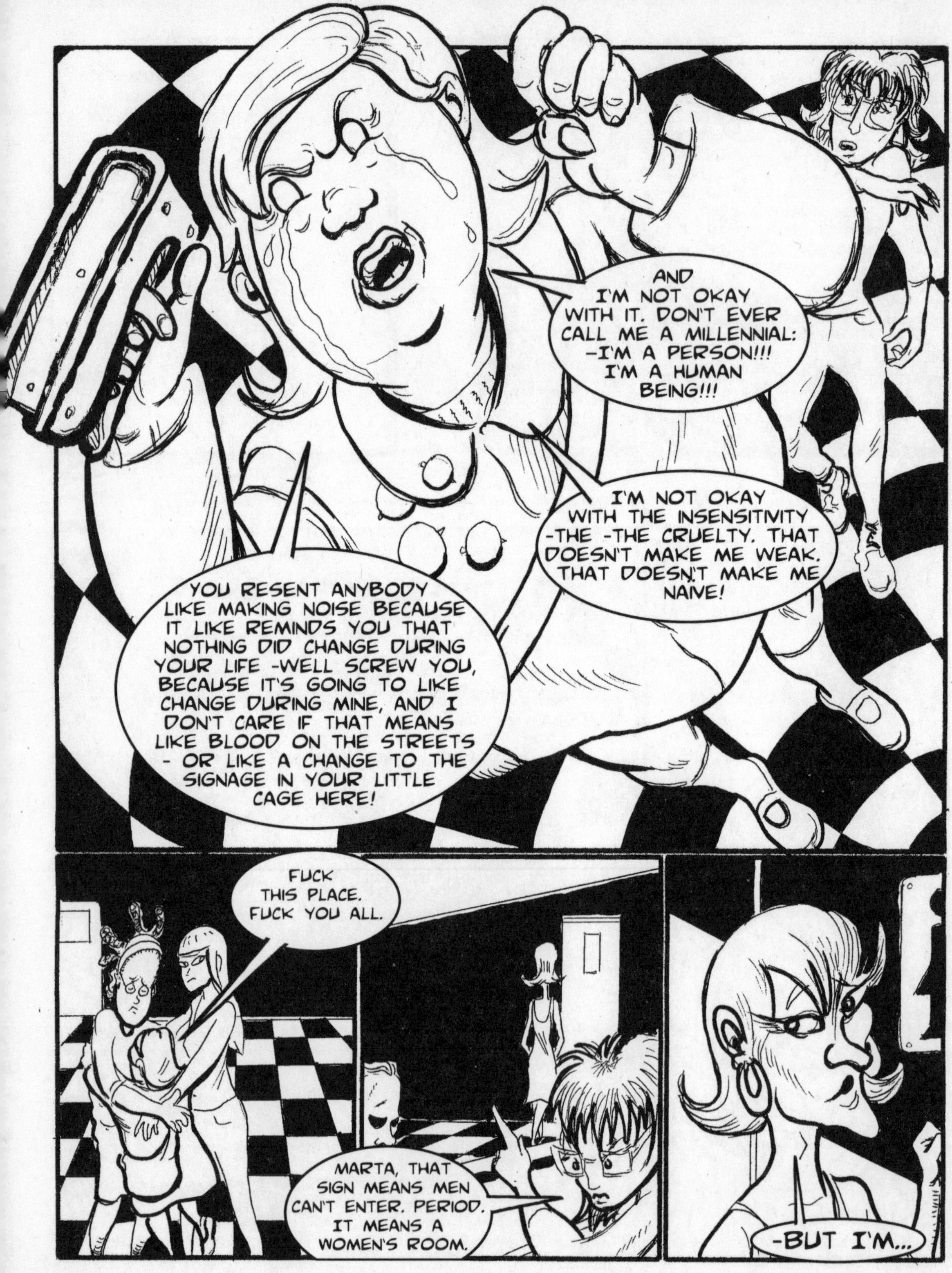
AND I'M NOT OKAY WITH IT. DON'T EVER CALL ME A MILLENNIAL: -I'M A PERSON!!! I'M A HUMAN BEING!!!
I'M NOT OKAY WITH THE INSENSITIVITY -THE -THE CRUELTY. THAT DOESN'T MAKE ME WEAK. THAT DOESN'T MAKE ME NAIVE!
YOU RESENT ANYBODY LIKE MAKING NOISE BECAUSE IT LIKE REMINDS YOU THAT NOTHING DID CHANGE DURING YOUR LIFE -WELL SCREW YOU, BECAUSE IT'S GOING TO LIKE CHANGE DURING MINE, AND I DON'T CARE IF THAT MEANS LIKE BLOOD ON THE STREETS - OR LIKE A CHANGE TO THE SIGNAGE IN YOUR LITTLE CAGE HERE!
FUCK THIS PLACE. FUCK YOU ALL.
MARTA, THAT SIGN MEANS MEN CAN'T ENTER. PERIOD. IT MEANS A WOMEN'S ROOM.
-BUT I'M...

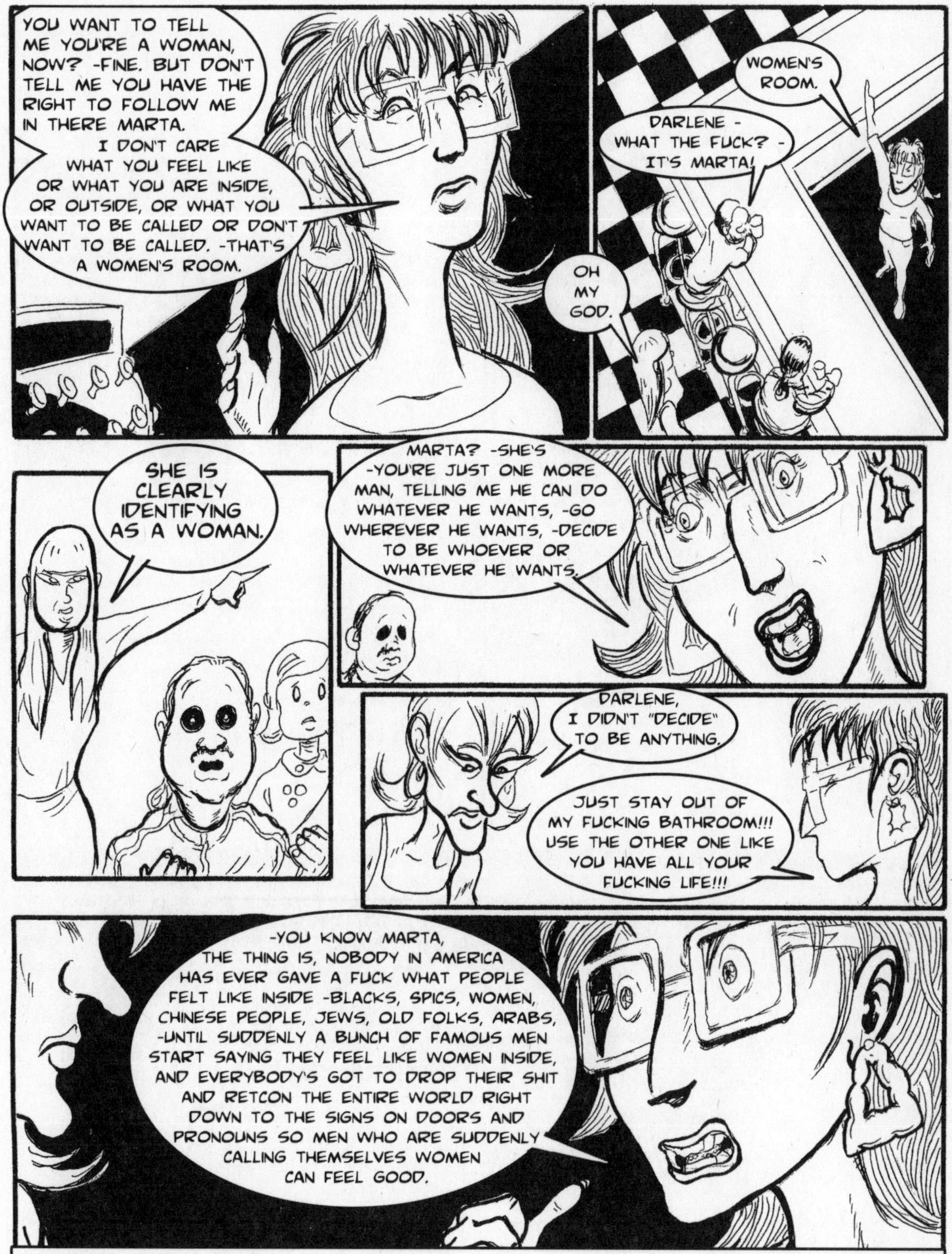
YOU WANT TO TELL ME YOU'RE A WOMAN, NOW? -FINE. BUT DON'T TELL ME YOU HAVE THE RIGHT TO FOLLOW ME IN THERE MARTA. I DON'T CARE WHAT YOU FEEL LIKE OR WHAT YOU ARE INSIDE, OR OUTSIDE, OR WHAT YOU WANT TO BE CALLED OR DON'T WANT TO BE CALLED. -THAT'S A WOMEN'S ROOM.
WOMEN'S ROOM.
DARLENE - WHAT THE FUCK? - IT'S MARTA!
OH MY GOD.
SHE IS CLEARLY IDENTIFYING AS A WOMAN.
MARTA? -SHE'S -YOU'RE JUST ONE MORE MAN, TELLING ME HE CAN DO WHATEVER HE WANTS, -GO WHEREVER HE WANTS, -DECIDE TO BE WHOEVER OR WHATEVER HE WANTS.
DARLENE, I DIDN'T "DECIDE" TO BE ANYTHING.
JUST STAY OUT OF MY FUCKING BATHROOM!!! USE THE OTHER ONE LIKE YOU HAVE ALL YOUR FUCKING LIFE!!!
-YOU KNOW MARTA, THE THING IS, NOBODY IN AMERICA HAS EVER GAVE A FUCK WHAT PEOPLE FELT LIKE INSIDE -BLACKS, SPICS, WOMEN, CHINESE PEOPLE, JEWS, OLD FOLKS, ARABS, -UNTIL SUDDENLY A BUNCH OF FAMOUS MEN START SAYING THEY FEEL LIKE WOMEN INSIDE, AND EVERYBODY'S GOT TO DROP THEIR SHIT AND RETCON THE ENTIRE WORLD RIGHT DOWN TO THE SIGNS ON DOORS AND PRONOUNS SO MEN WHO ARE SUDDENLY CALLING THEMSELVES WOMEN CAN FEEL GOOD.
EVEN WITH MY OWN BIG MOUTH, I DID NOT KNOW WHAT TO SAY IN THAT MOMENT. I WAS USELESS UP AGAINST DARLENE'S ANGER.

HOW'S THAT FOR FEMINISM?!! AM I A FEMINIST NOW?!!

DARLENE HAD DONE AND SAID THINGS TO EMBARRASS ME ALL OF MY LIFE. DARLENE HAD ALWAYS BEEN LOUD, BRUSQUELY OPINIONATED, AND EVEN "CATHOLICALLY" NARROW-MINDED AT TIMES—DARLENE WAS THE KIND OF BRONX GIRL THAT COULD MAKE YOU WANT TO GET OFF OF A BUS IF SHE WAS LOUD ENOUGH, CRASS ENOUGH. BUT FOR THE FIRST TIME IN MY LIFE, MY OLD DEFENDER ONE OF MY OLDEST FRIENDS—LOOKED LIKE A DINOSAUR TO ME. SHE LOOKED SLOW, PLODDING, AND AS MINDLESSLY DANGEROUS AS ANY ARCHETYPAL BIGOT FROM MY EXPERIENCE OR IMAGINATION. HER POINT:—THAT WOMEN'S REST ROOMS ARE THE LAST REFUGE IN A BAR WHERE A WOMAN CAN ESCAPE A MAN, –A DANGEROUS MAN, –A MAN WHO IS DRUNK, –OR VIOLENT, AND MAYBE MAKE A PLAN OF ESCAPE WITH ANOTHER WOMAN, OR JUST PUT SOME DISTANCE BETWEEN THEMSELVES AND AN UNWANTED, INSISTENT SELF-PRESUMED SUITOR –WAS RATHER LOST IN HER BILE AND RAGE.

OH, YOU'RE NOT A FEMINIST DARLENE; YOU'RE AN ASSHOLE.

I WANTED TO ASK DARLENE, WHAT EXACTLY WOULD IT COST HER TO SAY MARTA WAS JUST A WOMAN NOT UNLIKE HERSELF? WHAT LOSS WAS SO GREAT THAT THE WORDS WERE TANTAMOUNT TO SUICIDE, SELF-IMMOLATION?

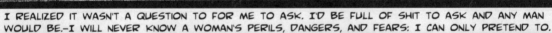

I REALIZED IT WASN'T A QUESTION TO FOR ME TO ASK. I'D BE FULL OF SHIT TO ASK AND ANY MAN WOULD BE.–I WILL NEVER KNOW A WOMAN'S PERILS, DANGERS, AND FEARS: I CAN ONLY PRETEND TO.

–LOOK DARLENE, I GET IT BY THE WAY I REALLY DO.

THE MOST IMPORTANT THING THAT MEN CAN DO FOR WOMEN IS ADMIT THAT WE ARE THEIR PROBLEM...

–WHO AM I TO ASK ANY WOMAN A QUESTION ABOUT HOW SHE IS DEALING WITH THE REALITIES OF A WORLD THAT WOULD SOONER SEE HER DEAD, THAN ADMIT HER EQUALITY?

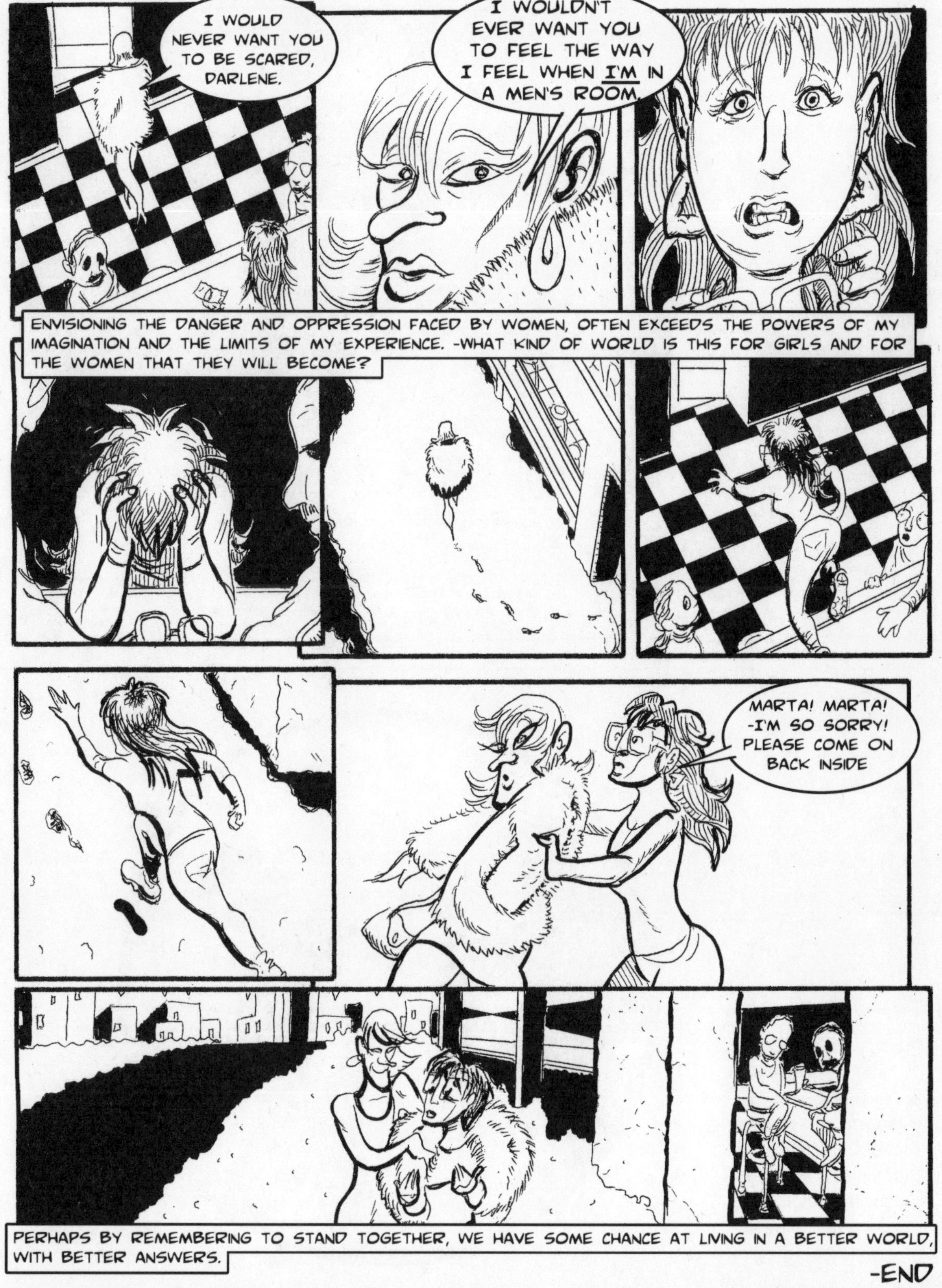
I WOULD NEVER WANT YOU TO BE SCARED, DARLENE.
I WOULDN'T EVER WANT YOU TO FEEL THE WAY I FEEL WHEN I'M IN A MEN'S ROOM.
ENVISIONING THE DANGER AND OPPRESSION FACED BY WOMEN, OFTEN EXCEEDS THE POWERS OF MY IMAGINATION AND THE LIMITS OF MY EXPERIENCE. -WHAT KIND OF WORLD IS THIS FOR GIRLS AND FOR THE WOMEN THAT THEY WILL BECOME?
MARTA! MARTA! -I'M SO SORRY! PLEASE COME ON BACK INSIDE
PERHAPS BY REMEMBERING TO STAND TOGETHER, WE HAVE SOME CHANCE AT LIVING IN A BETTER WORLD, WITH BETTER ANSWERS.

-END

Life Lines

by Rebecca Migdal

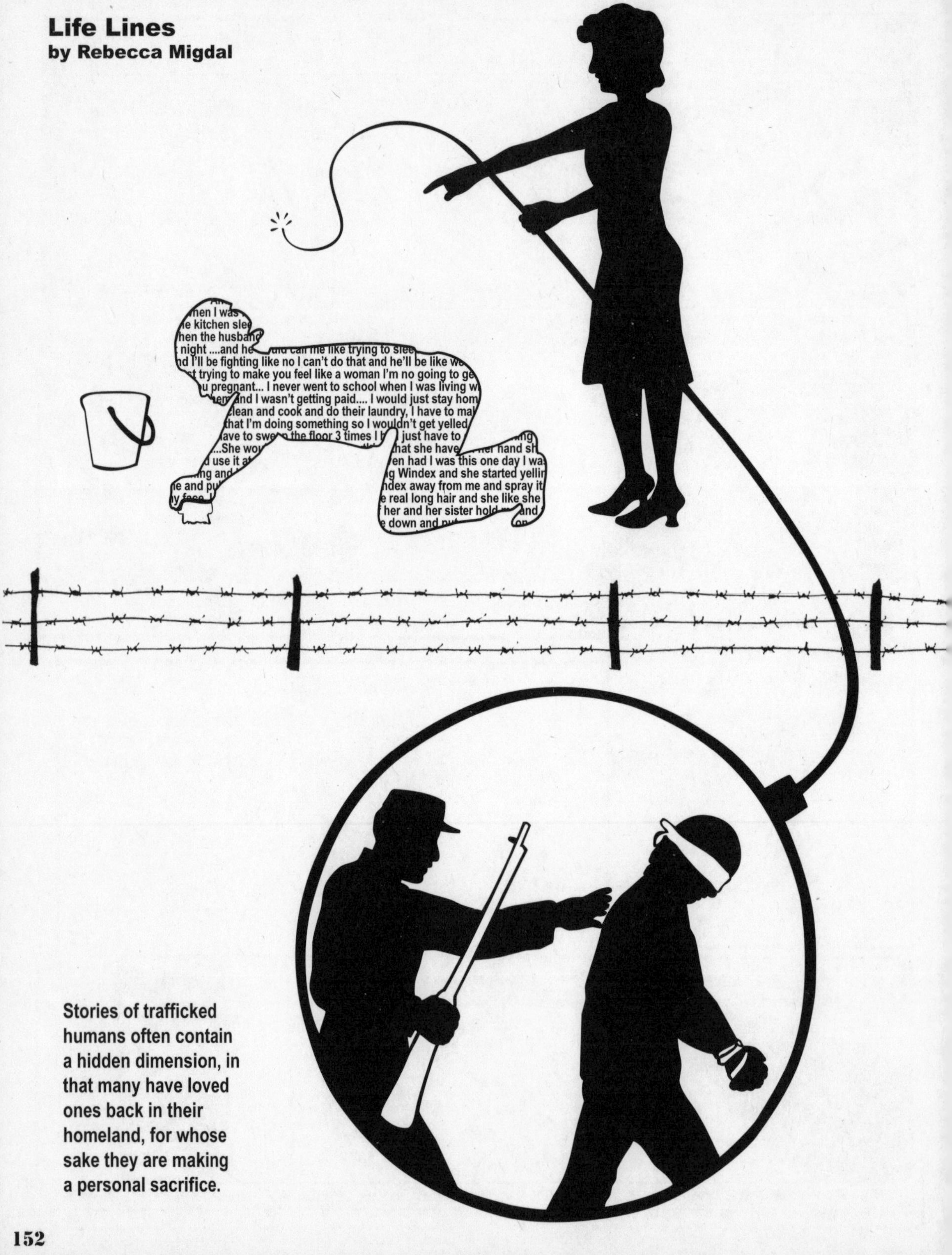

hen I wa
e kitchen sle
hen the husba
night ....and he
d I'll be fighting like no I can't do that and he'll be like w
t trying to make you feel like a woman I'm no going to ge
u pregnant... I never went to school when I was living w
nd I wasn't getting paid.... I would just stay hom
lean and cook and do their laundry, I have to ma
that I'm doing something so I wouldn't get yelled
ave to swe the floor 3 times I just have to
...She wo
hat she have
d use it a
en had I was this one day I wa
ng and
g Windex and she started yelli
e and p
ndex away from me and spray it
e real long hair and she like she
her and her sister hold and
e down and

Stories of trafficked humans often contain a hidden dimension, in that many have loved ones back in their homeland, for whose sake they are making a personal sacrifice.

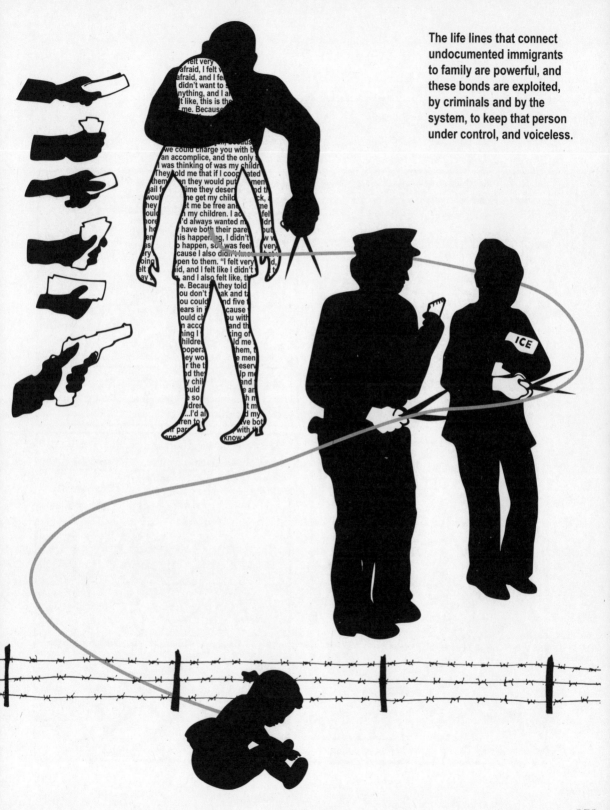

The life lines that connect undocumented immigrants to family are powerful, and these bonds are exploited, by criminals and by the system, to keep that person under control, and voiceless.

Pinned

words by Joanne Starer
pictures by Ellen Lindner

SOME NAMES HAVE BEEN CHANGED BECAUSE OUR LAWYERS MADE US!

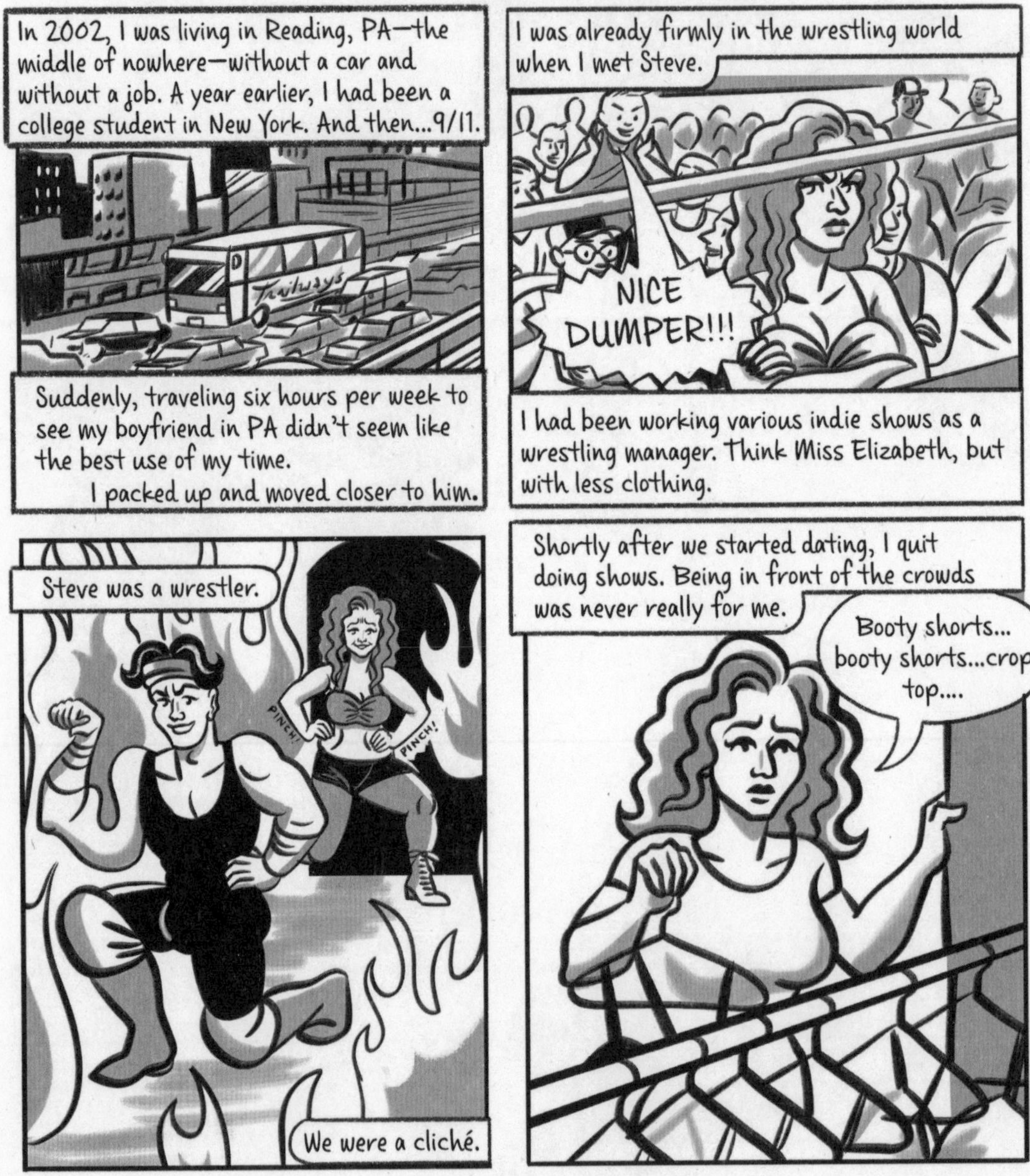
In 2002, I was living in Reading, PA—the middle of nowhere—without a car and without a job. A year earlier, I had been a college student in New York. And then...9/11.
Trailways
Suddenly, traveling six hours per week to see my boyfriend in PA didn't seem like the best use of my time.
I packed up and moved closer to him.
I was already firmly in the wrestling world when I met Steve.
NICE DUMPER!!!
I had been working various indie shows as a wrestling manager. Think Miss Elizabeth, but with less clothing.
Steve was a wrestler.
PINCH!
PINCH!
We were a cliché.
Shortly after we started dating, I quit doing shows. Being in front of the crowds was never really for me.
Booty shorts... booty shorts...crop top....

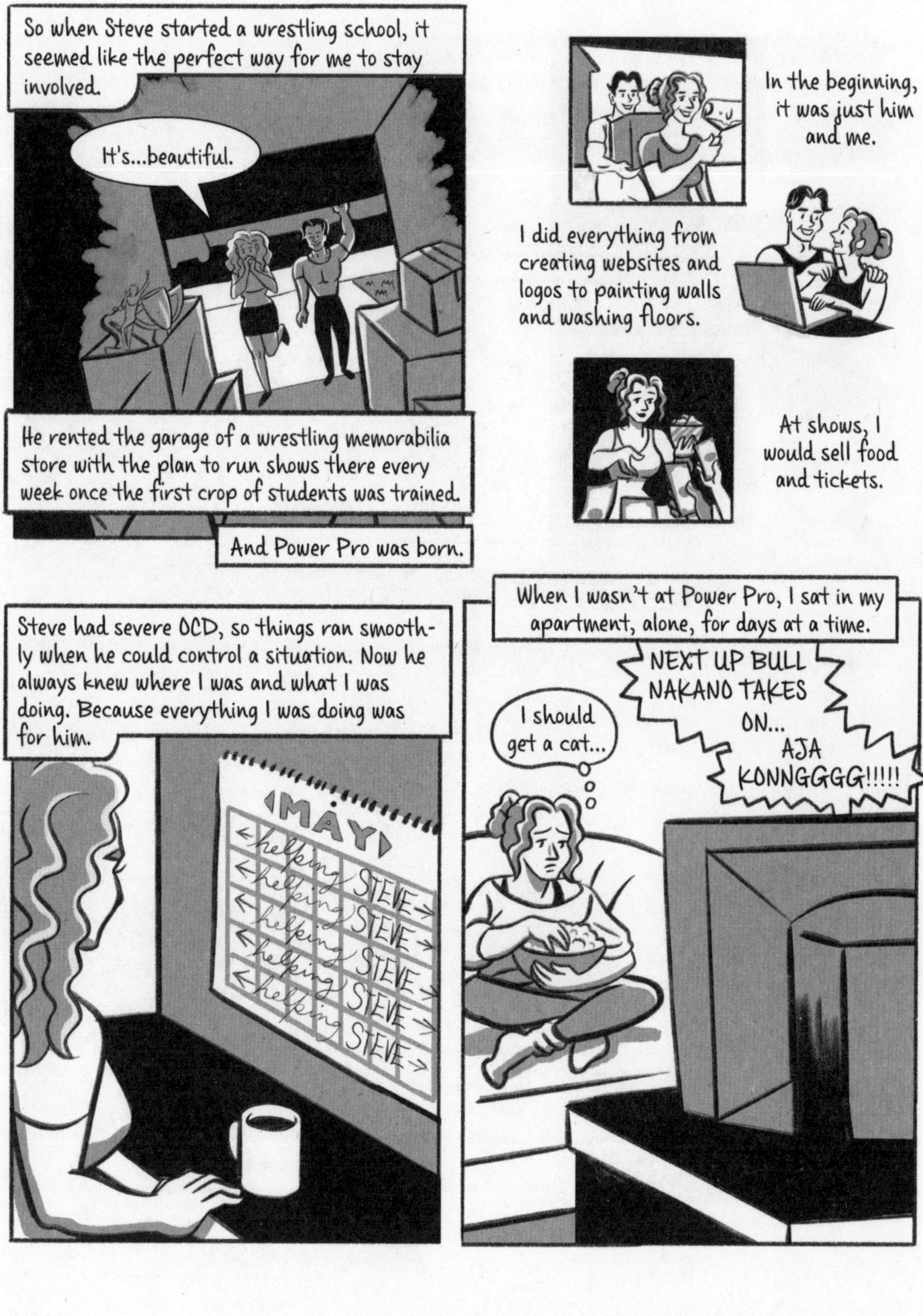
So when Steve started a wrestling school, it seemed like the perfect way for me to stay involved.
It's...beautiful.
He rented the garage of a wrestling memorabilia store with the plan to run shows there every week once the first crop of students was trained.
And Power Pro was born.
In the beginning, it was just him and me.
I did everything from creating websites and logos to painting walls and washing floors.
At shows, I would sell food and tickets.
Steve had severe OCD, so things ran smoothly when he could control a situation. Now he always knew where I was and what I was doing. Because everything I was doing was for him.
MAY
helping STEVE
helping STEVE
helping STEVE
helping STEVE
helping STEVE
helping STEVE
When I wasn't at Power Pro, I sat in my apartment, alone, for days at a time.
I should get a cat...
NEXT UP BULL NAKANO TAKES ON... AJA KONNGGGG!!!!!

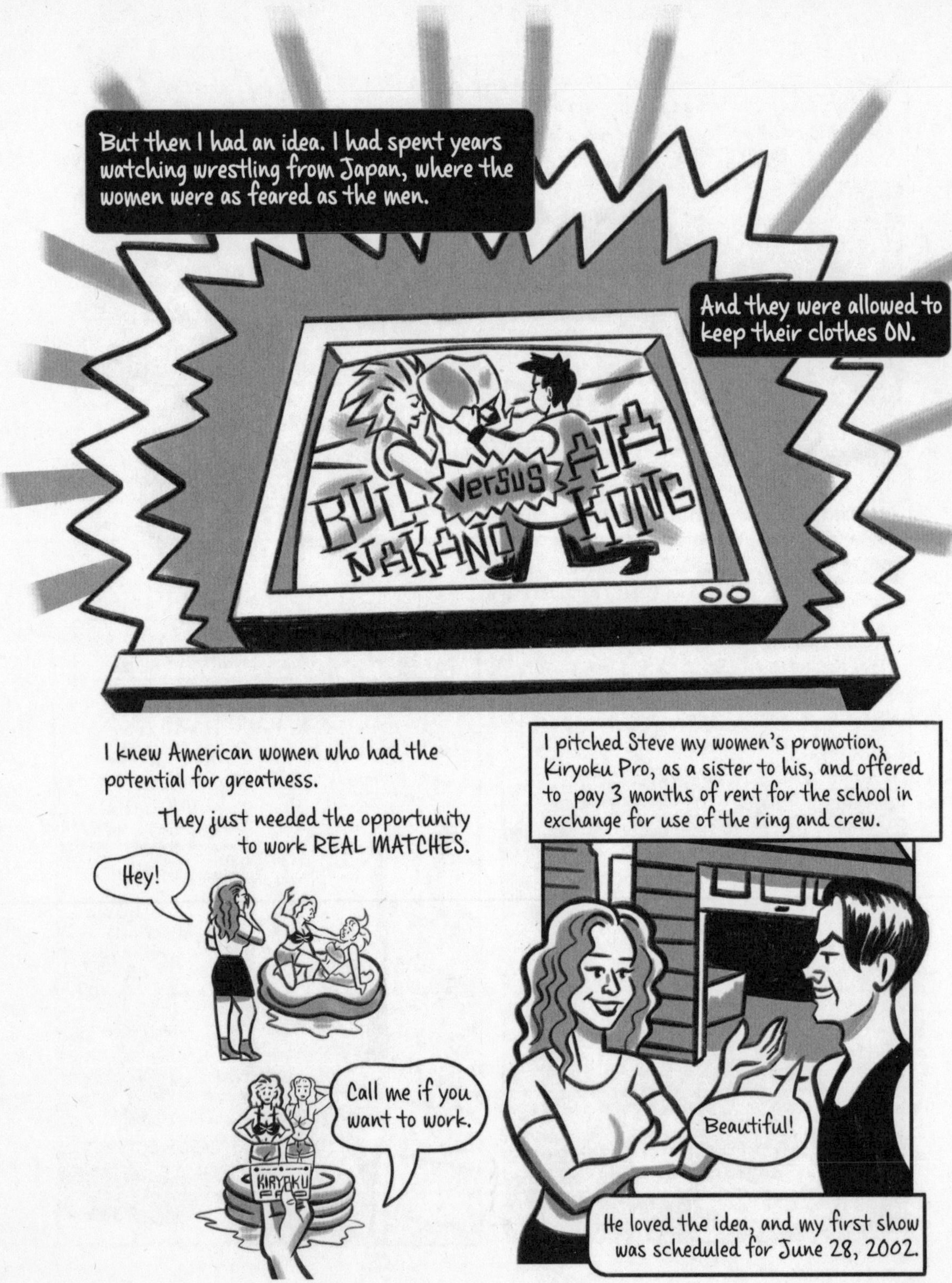
But then I had an idea. I had spent years watching wrestling from Japan, where the women were as feared as the men.
And they were allowed to keep their clothes ON.
BULL NAKANO VERSUS AJA KONG
I knew American women who had the potential for greatness.
They just needed the opportunity to work REAL MATCHES.
Hey!
Call me if you want to work.
KIRYOKU PRO
I pitched Steve my women's promotion, Kiryoku Pro, as a sister to his, and offered to pay 3 months of rent for the school in exchange for use of the ring and crew.
Beautiful!
He loved the idea, and my first show was scheduled for June 28, 2002.

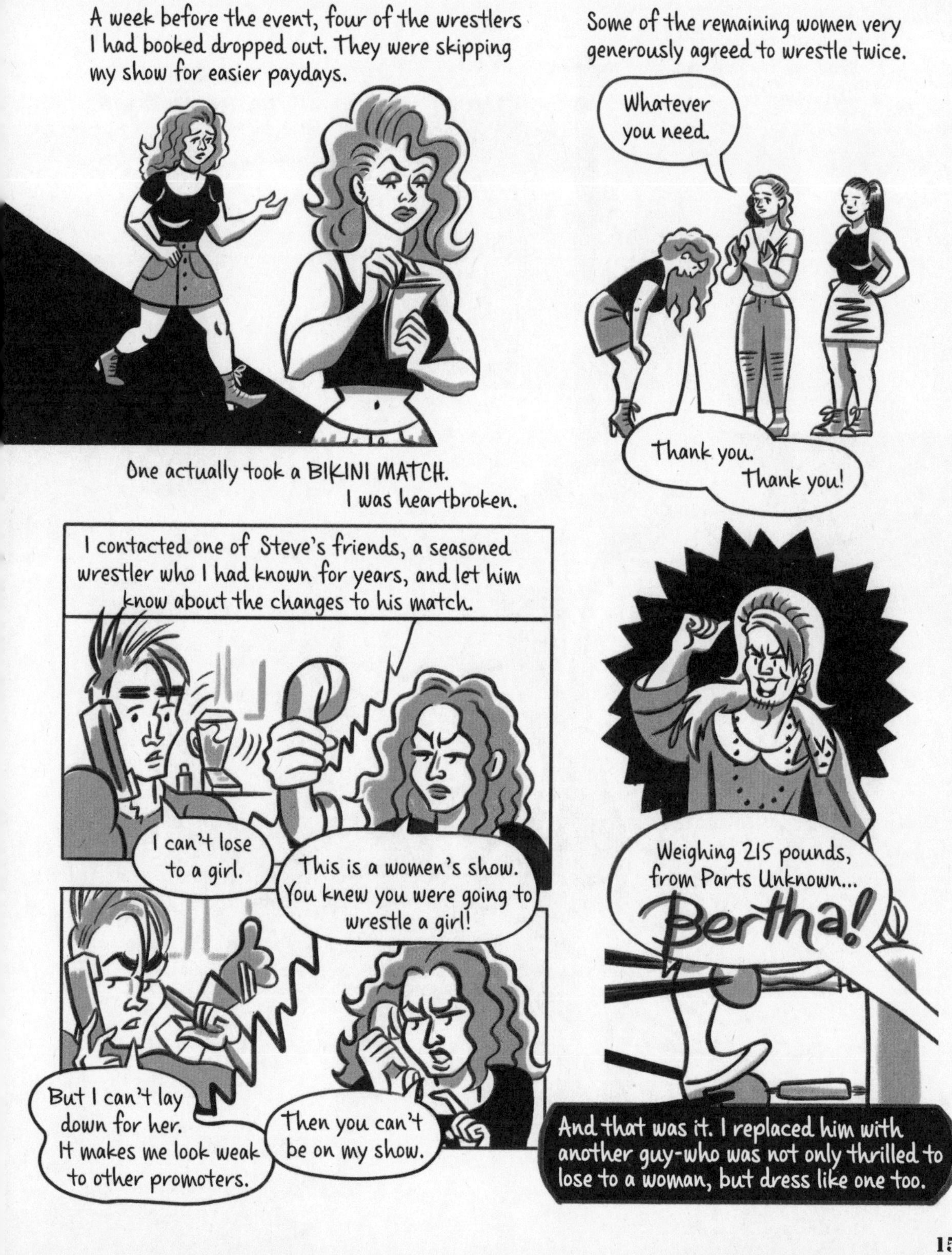
A week before the event, four of the wrestlers I had booked dropped out. They were skipping my show for easier paydays.
One actually took a BIKINI MATCH. I was heartbroken.
Some of the remaining women very generously agreed to wrestle twice.
Whatever you need.
Thank you. Thank you!
I contacted one of Steve's friends, a seasoned wrestler who I had known for years, and let him know about the changes to his match.
I can't lose to a girl.
This is a women's show. You knew you were going to wrestle a girl!
But I can't lay down for her. It makes me look weak to other promoters.
Then you can't be on my show.
Weighing 215 pounds, from Parts Unknown...
Bertha!
And that was it. I replaced him with another guy-who was not only thrilled to lose to a woman, but dress like one too.

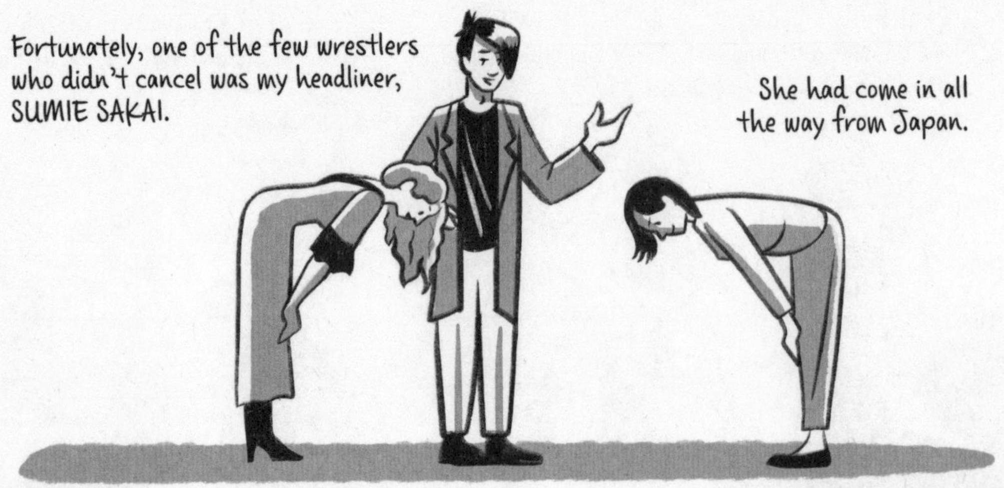
Fortunately, one of the few wrestlers who didn't cancel was my headliner, SUMIE SAKAI.
She had come in all the way from Japan.

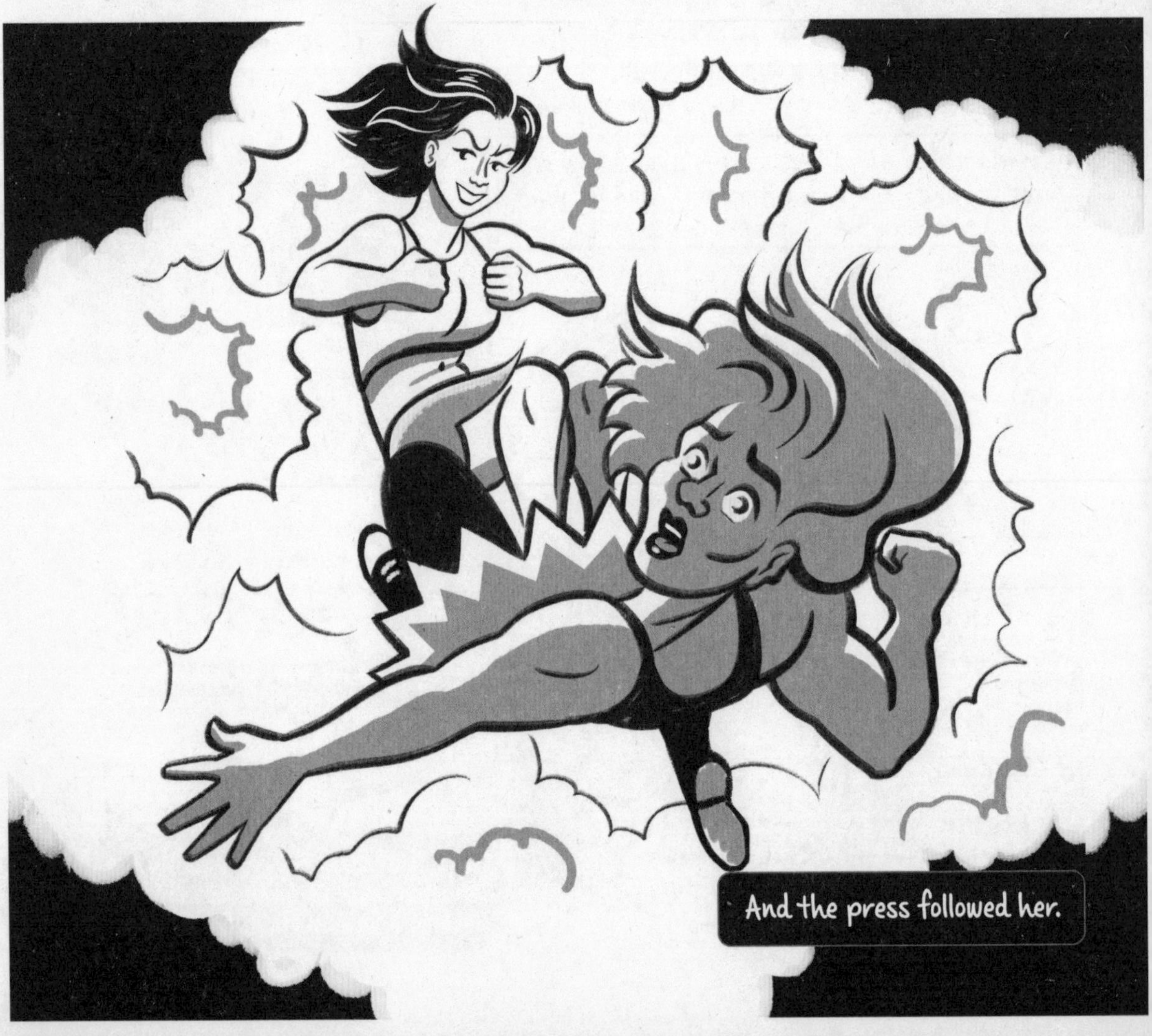
And the press followed her.

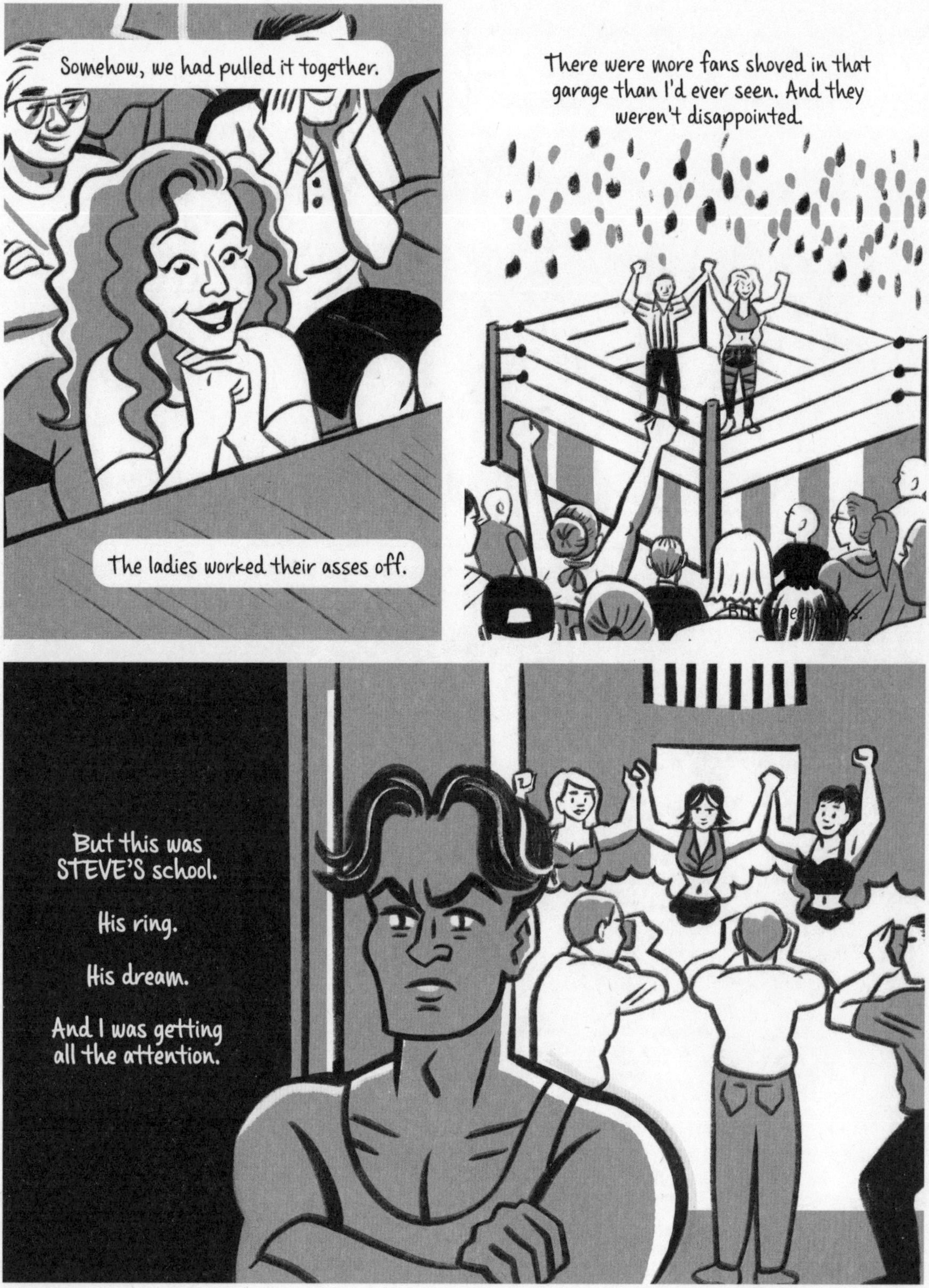
Somehow, we had pulled it together.
The ladies worked their asses off.
There were more fans shoved in that garage than I'd ever seen. And they weren't disappointed.
But this was STEVE'S school.
His ring.
His dream.
And I was getting all the attention.

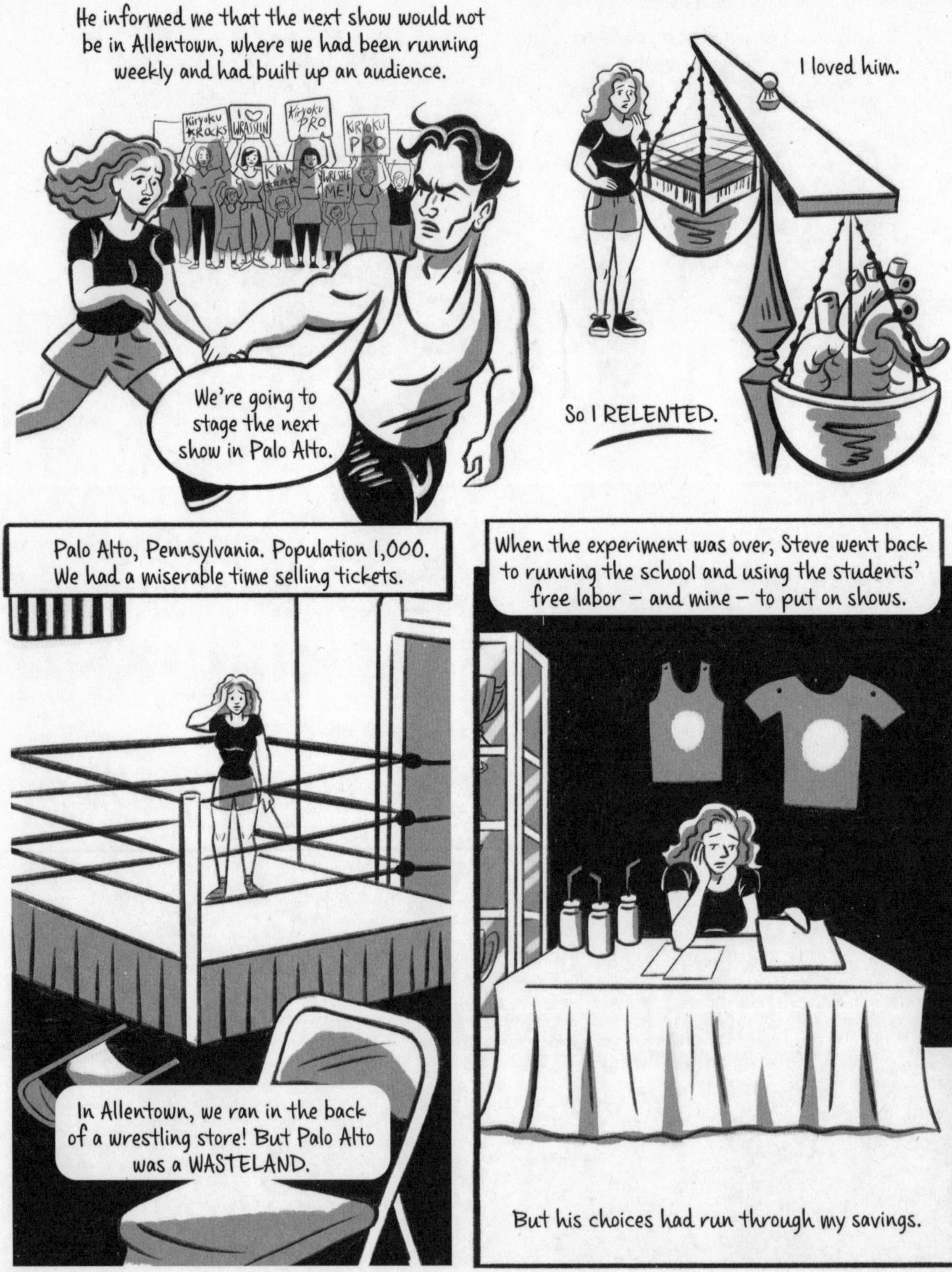
He informed me that the next show would not be in Allentown, where we had been running weekly and had built up an audience.
Kiryoku ★ROCKS
I ♥ WRASSLIN
Kiryoku PRO
KIRYOKU PRO
KPW
WRESTLE ME!
We're going to stage the next show in Palo Alto.
I loved him.
So I RELENTED.
Palo Alto, Pennsylvania. Population 1,000. We had a miserable time selling tickets.
In Allentown, we ran in the back of a wrestling store! But Palo Alto was a WASTELAND.
When the experiment was over, Steve went back to running the school and using the students' free labor – and mine – to put on shows.
But his choices had run through my savings.

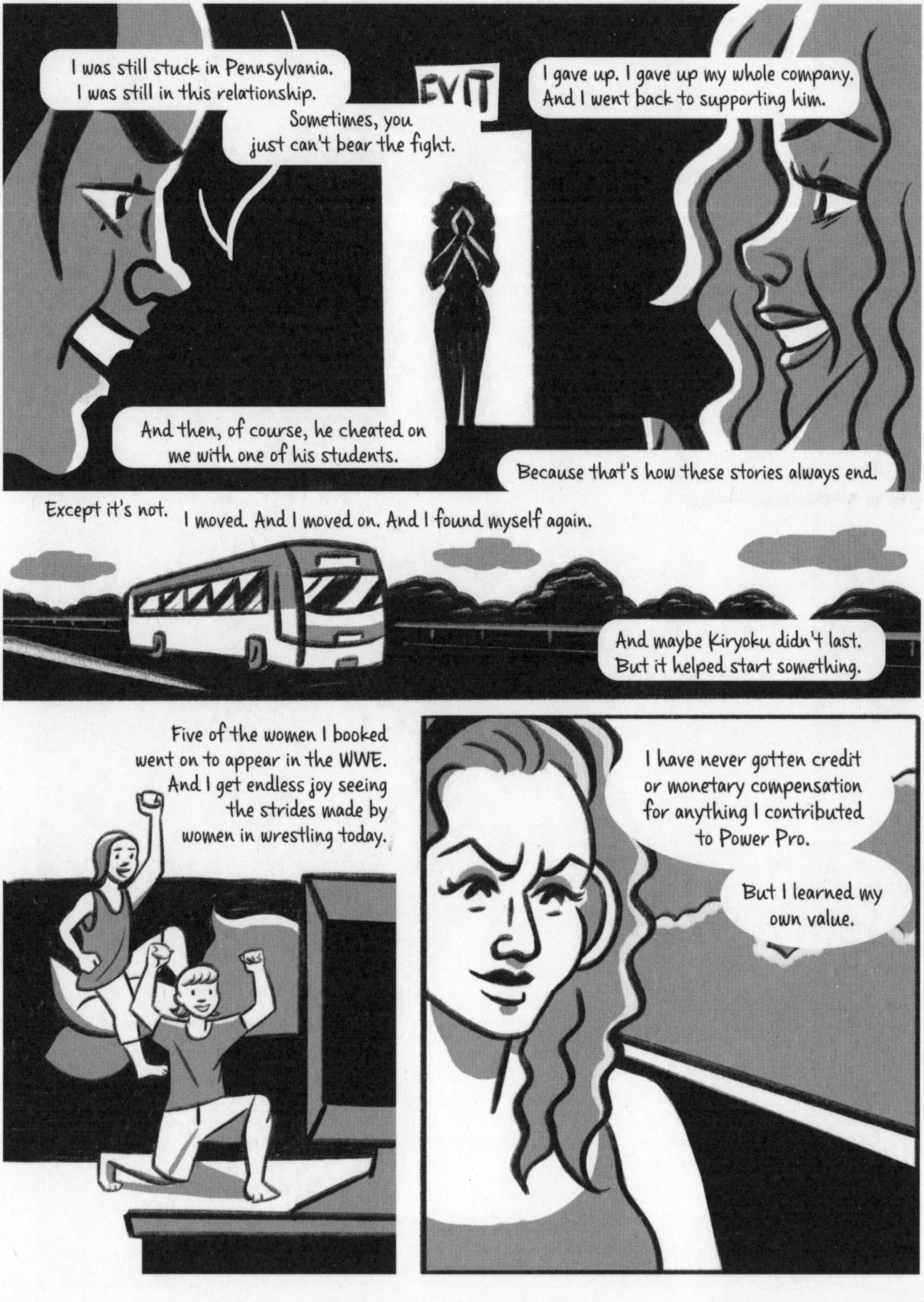
I was still stuck in Pennsylvania.
I was still in this relationship.
Sometimes, you just can't bear the fight.
EXIT
I gave up. I gave up my whole company. And I went back to supporting him.
And then, of course, he cheated on me with one of his students.
Because that's how these stories always end.
Except it's not.
I moved. And I moved on. And I found myself again.
And maybe Kiryoku didn't last. But it helped start something.
Five of the women I booked went on to appear in the WWE. And I get endless joy seeing the strides made by women in wrestling today.
I have never gotten credit or monetary compensation for anything I contributed to Power Pro.
But I learned my own value.

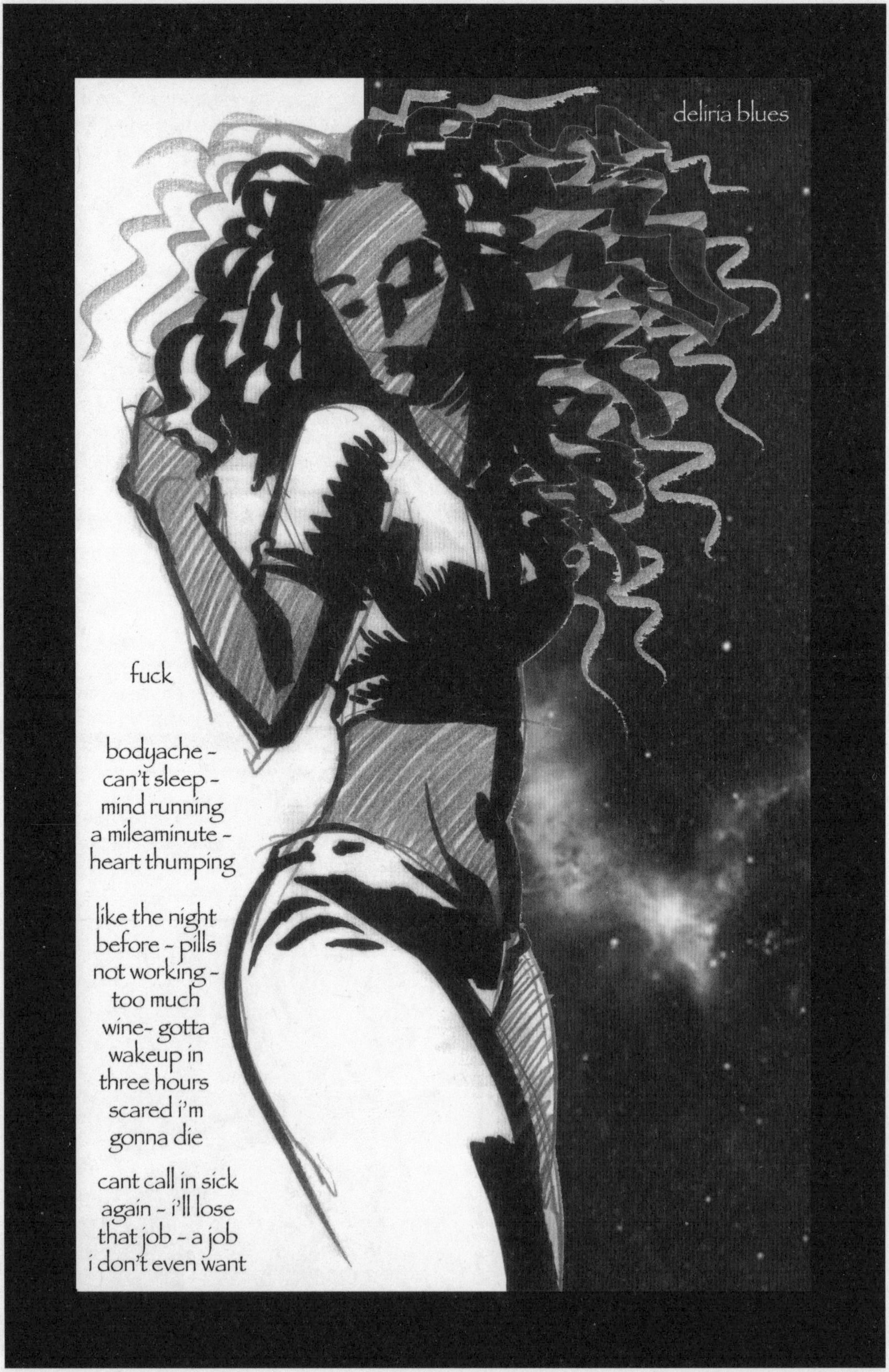
deliria blues
fuck
bodyache - can't sleep - mind running a mileaminute - heart thumping
like the night before - pills not working - too much wine- gotta wakeup in three hours scared i'm gonna die
cant call in sick again - i'll lose that job - a job i don't even want

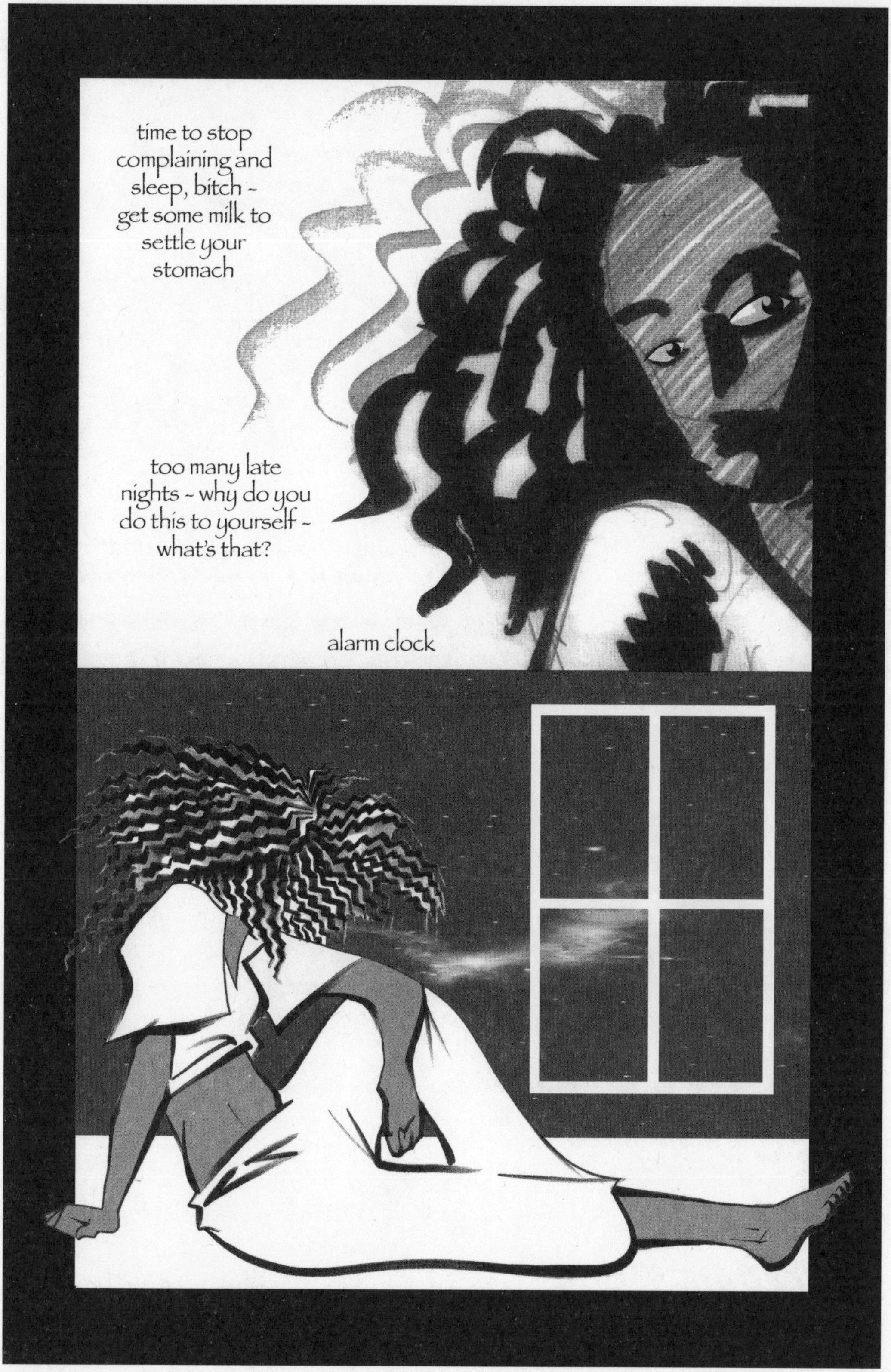

time to stop complaining and sleep, bitch - get some milk to settle your stomach
too many late nights - why do you do this to yourself - what's that?
alarm clock

sane energy project.org

we win campaigns • we share our skills •
we build community • we do our work with joy

@sane energy   @sane energyproject

Zines for a liberated future.

Booklyn

shop.booklyn.org

THE MUSEUM OF RECLAIMED URBAN SPACE

A living archive of
the Lower East Side's
radical activist history

C-Squat, 155 Avenue C, NYC, NY, 10009
open Tuesdays and Thursday through
Sunday, 11am-7pm
www.morusnyc.org

REBECCA MIGDAL

INTIMATE PARTNER VIOLENCE
Escape Room

FROM ABUSE TO FREEDOM,
SURVIVORS TELL THEIR STORIES

A beautiful, 60 page illustrated guide for
women, survivors and their communities,
on sale now at **bookandpuppet.com**

• RETAIL AND WHOLESALE PRICING AVAILABLE •
EMAIL SALES@BOOKANDPUPPET.COM FOR INFO

FIVE: 30 PM – FOUR AM

120 Orchard

MAX FISH

CUTTING

By Charly Shooster

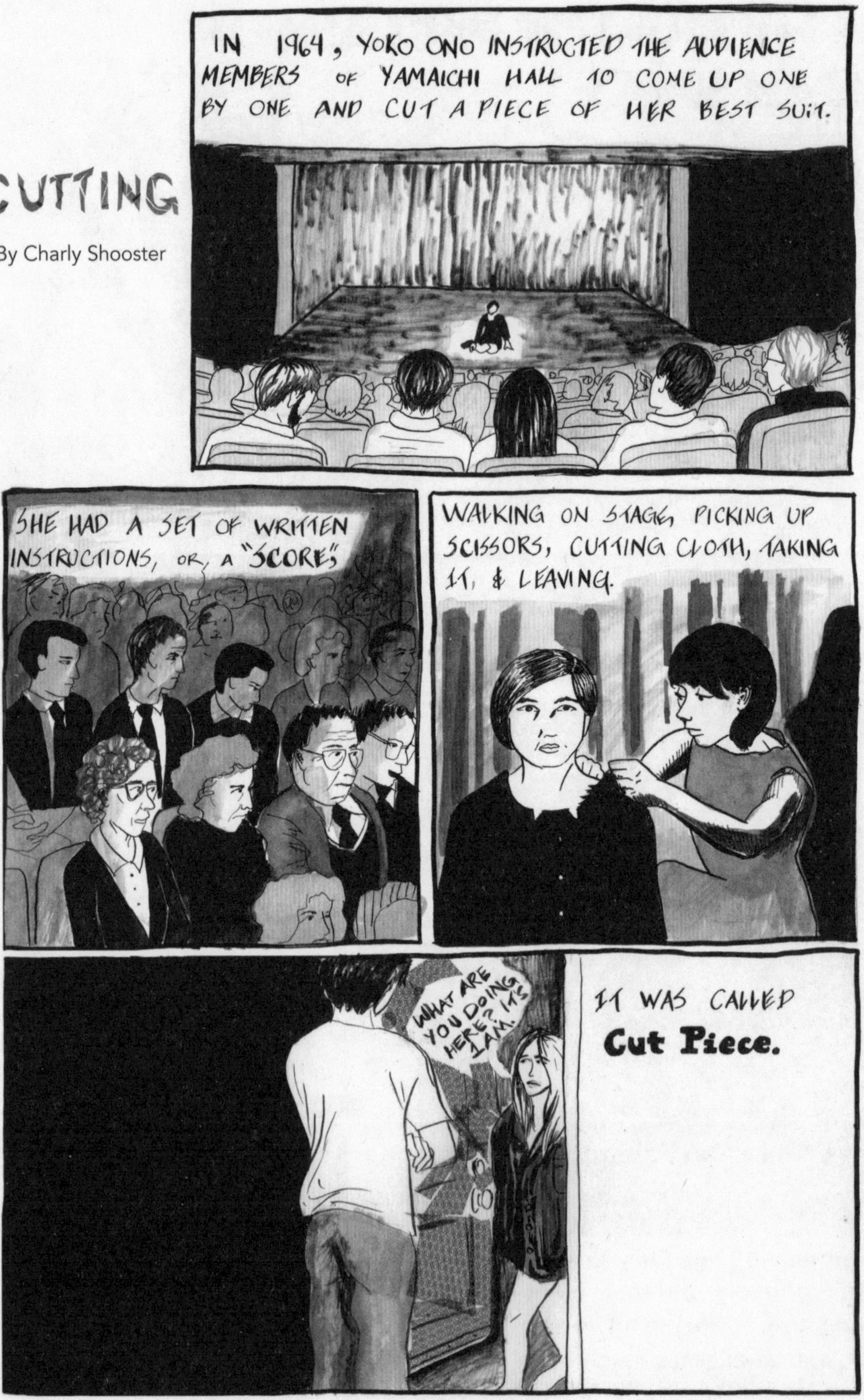
IN 1964, YOKO ONO INSTRUCTED THE AUDIENCE MEMBERS OF YAMAICHI HALL TO COME UP ONE BY ONE AND CUT A PIECE OF HER BEST SUIT.
SHE HAD A SET OF WRITTEN INSTRUCTIONS, OR, A "SCORE,"
WALKING ON STAGE, PICKING UP SCISSORS, CUTTING CLOTH, TAKING IT, & LEAVING.
WHAT ARE YOU DOING HERE? IT'S 1AM.
IT WAS CALLED
Cut Piece.

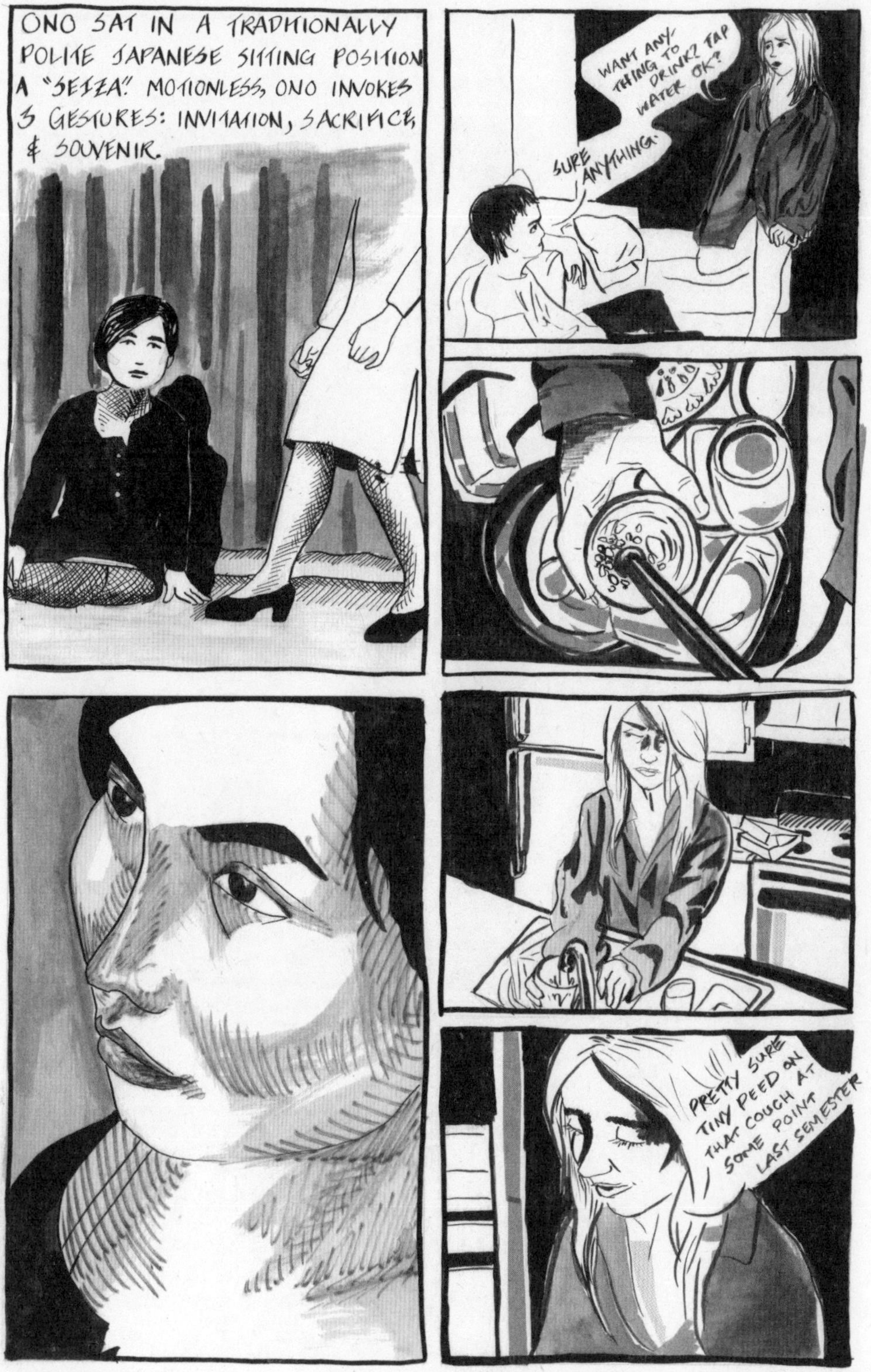
ONO SAT IN A TRADITIONALLY POLITE JAPANESE SITTING POSITION A "SEIZA." MOTIONLESS, ONO INVOKES 3 GESTURES: INVITATION, SACRIFICE, & SOUVENIR.
WANT ANYTHING TO DRINK? TAP WATER OK?
SURE ANYTHING.
PRETTY SURE TINY PEED ON THAT COUCH AT SOME POINT LAST SEMESTER

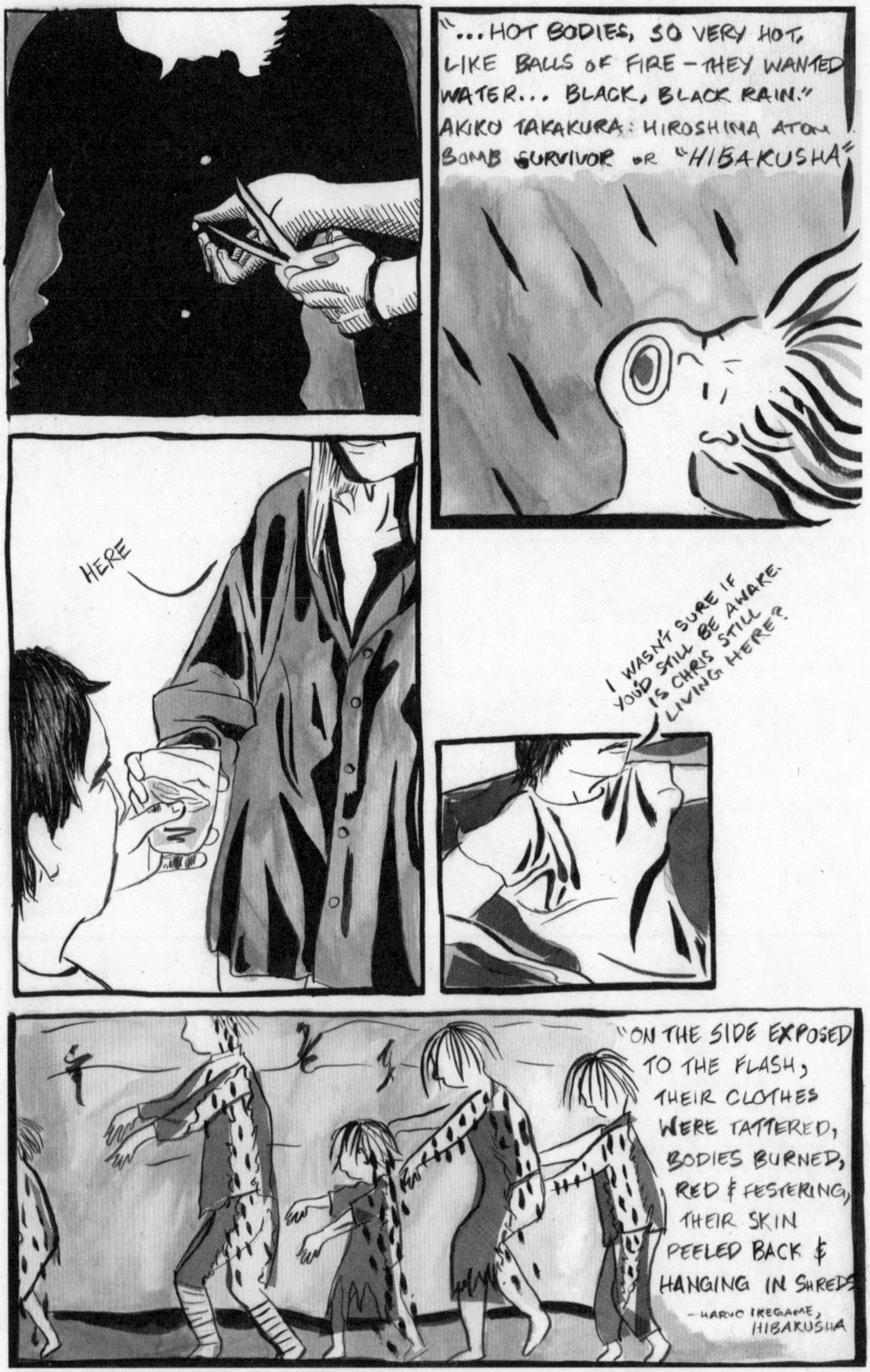
"...HOT BODIES, SO VERY HOT, LIKE BALLS OF FIRE - THEY WANTED WATER... BLACK, BLACK RAIN." AKIKO TAKAKURA: HIROSHIMA ATOM BOMB SURVIVOR OR "HIBAKUSHA"
HERE
I WASN'T SURE IF YOU'D STILL BE AWAKE. IS CHRIS STILL LIVING HERE?
"ON THE SIDE EXPOSED TO THE FLASH, THEIR CLOTHES WERE TATTERED, BODIES BURNED, RED & FESTERING, THEIR SKIN PEELED BACK & HANGING IN SHREDS"
-HARUO IKEGAME, HIBAKUSHA

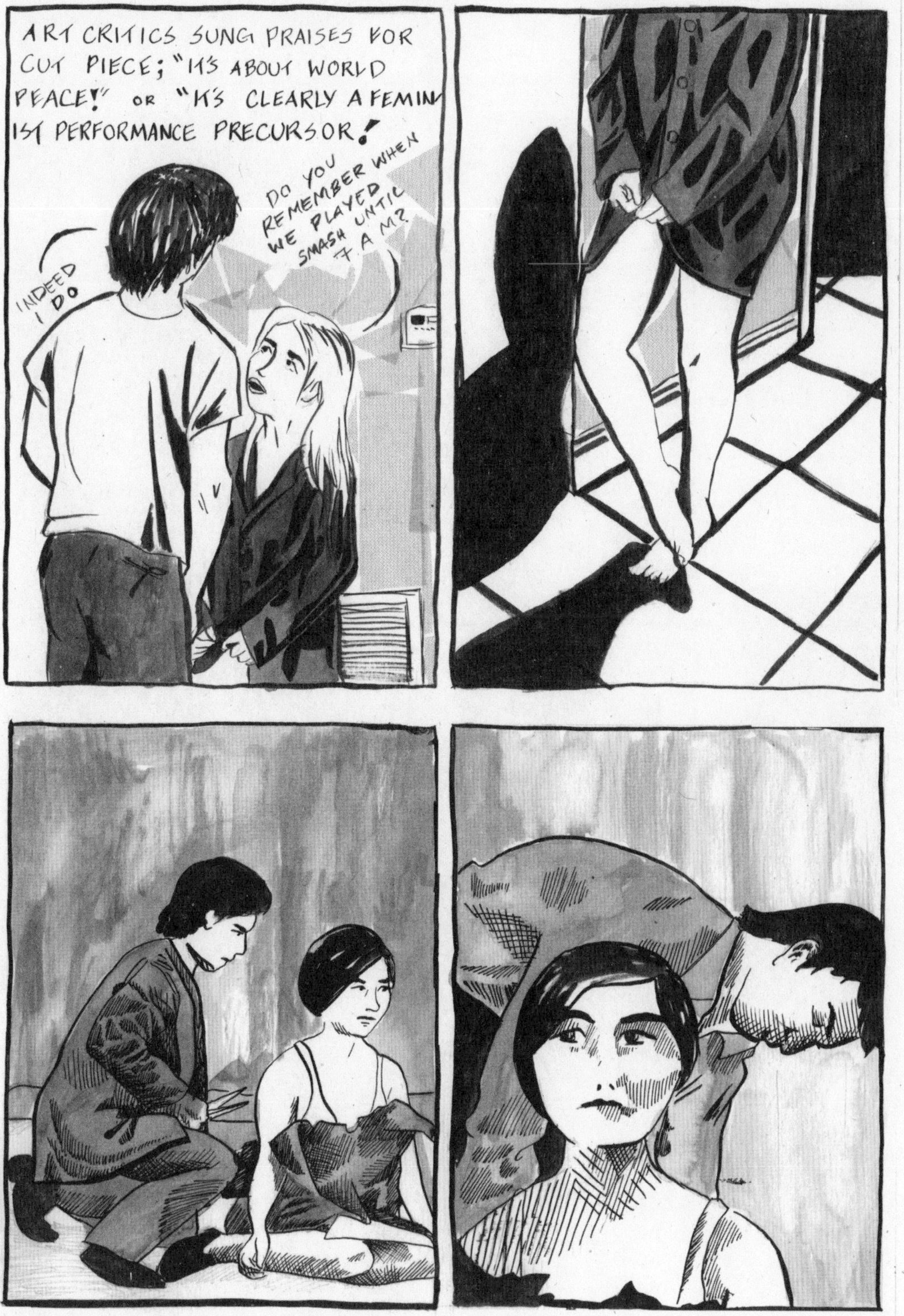
ART CRITICS SUNG PRAISES FOR CUT PIECE; "IT'S ABOUT WORLD PEACE!" OR "IT'S CLEARLY A FEMINIST PERFORMANCE PRECURSOR!
DO YOU REMEMBER WHEN WE PLAYED SMASH UNTIL 7 A.M?
INDEED I DO

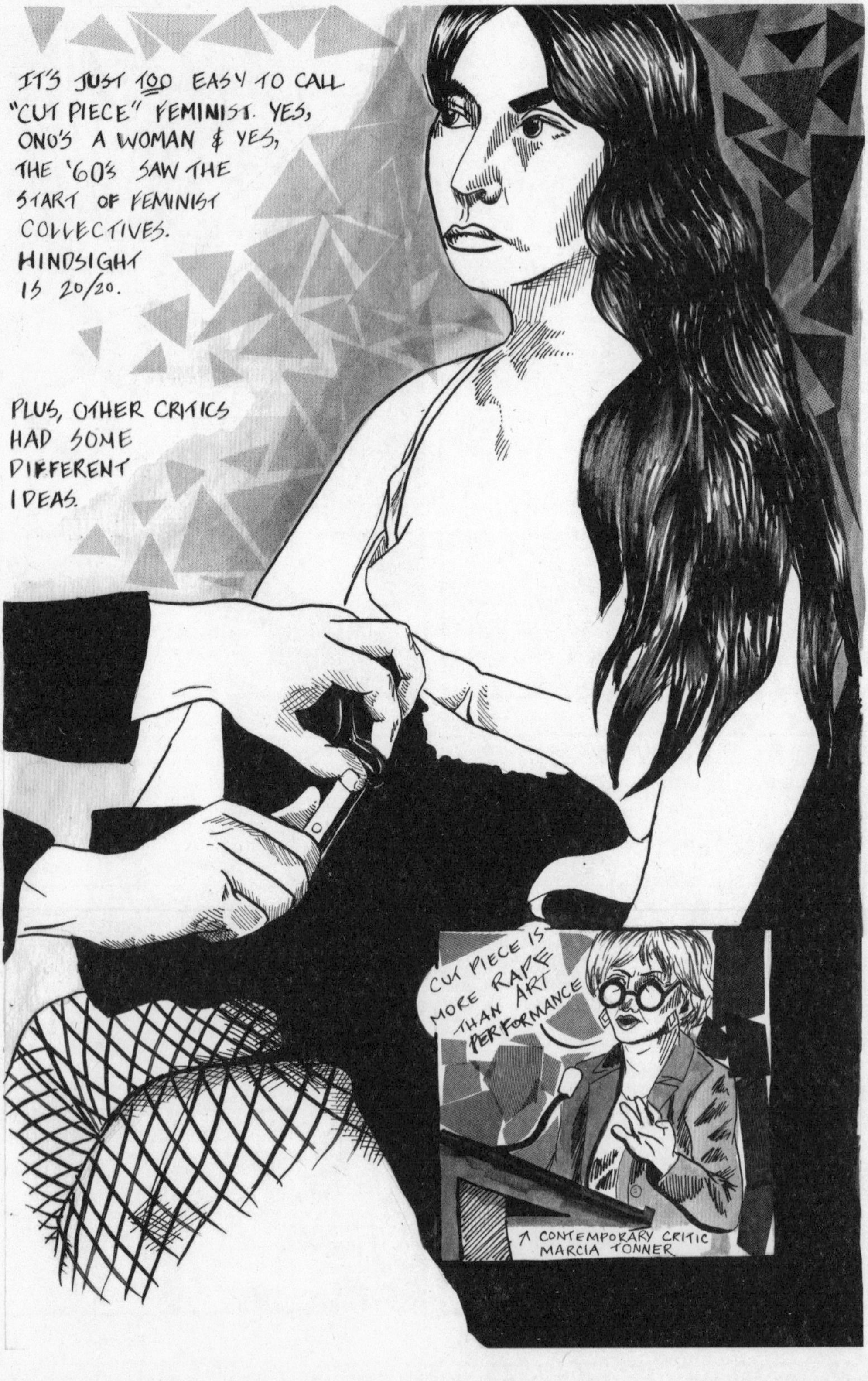
IT'S JUST TOO EASY TO CALL "CUT PIECE" FEMINIST. YES, ONO'S A WOMAN & YES, THE '60'S SAW THE START OF FEMINIST COLLECTIVES. HINDSIGHT IS 20/20.
PLUS, OTHER CRITICS HAD SOME DIFFERENT IDEAS.
CUT PIECE IS MORE RAPE THAN ART PERFORMANCE
↑ CONTEMPORARY CRITIC MARCIA TONNER

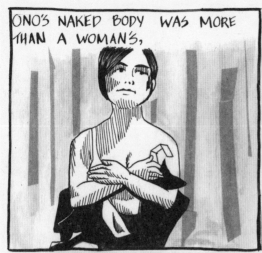

ONO'S NAKED BODY WAS MORE THAN A WOMAN'S,

I DIDN'T CARE MUCH WHEN YOU KISSED ALLIE...

IT WAS A NAKED BODY IN JAPAN IN 1964.

A NAKED BODY

ADORNED IN RIPPED & RAGGED CLOTHING, HANGING, PEELED BACK.

THOUGH IT WAS READ BY SOME CONTEMPORARIES AS A WORK LAYING CLAIM TO VIOLENCE AGAINST WOMEN, "CUT PIECE" UNDERSTANDS ITSELF AS EXPLICITLY POSTWAR. ONO'S BODY MADE FOR MORE THAN A GENDERED READING. WHAT ABOUT RACE & NATIONAL VIOLENCE?

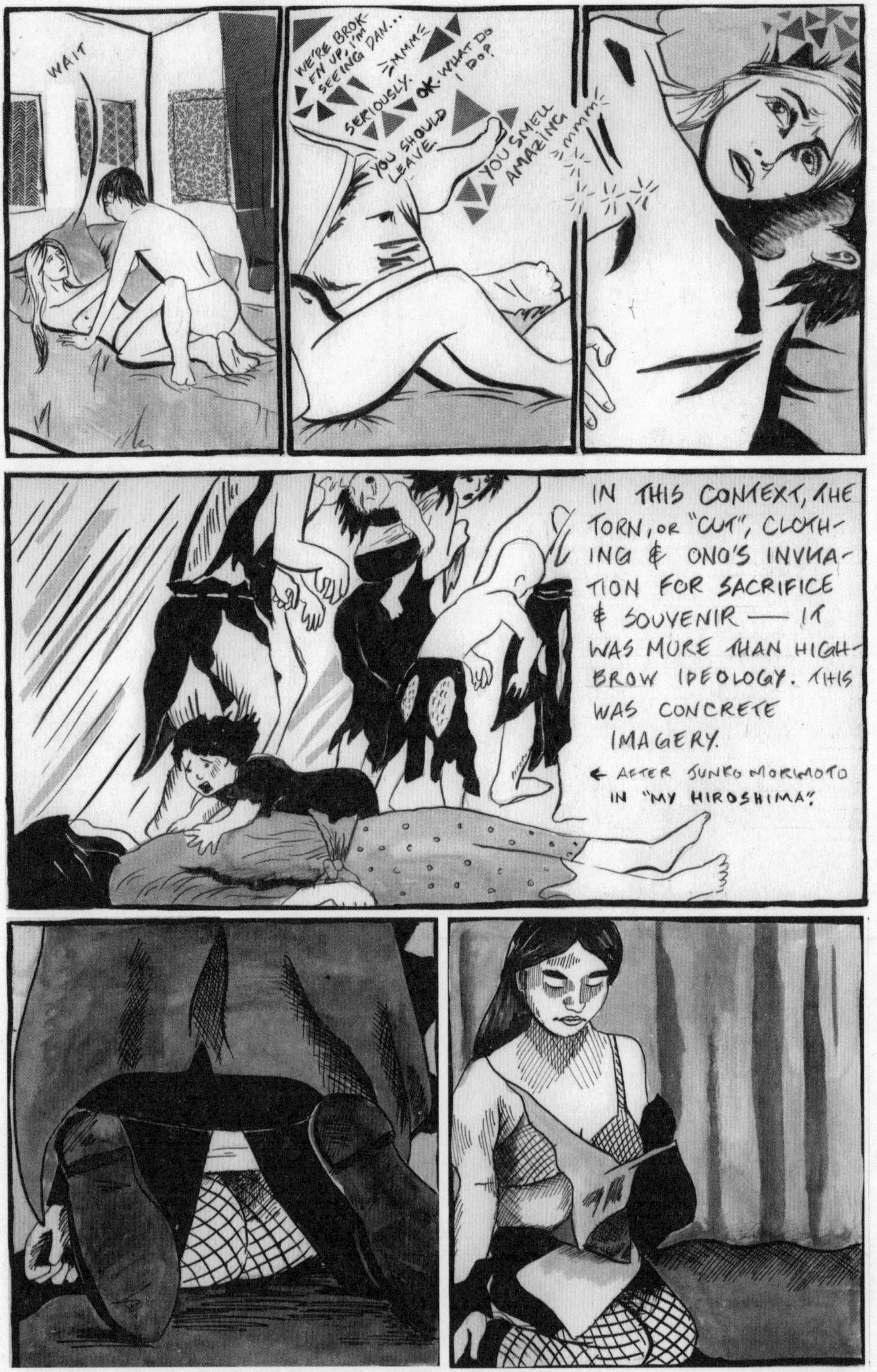

WAIT
WE'RE BROKEN UP, I'M SEEING DAN...
MMM
SERIOUSLY.
OK. WHAT DO I DO?
YOU SHOULD LEAVE.
YOU SMELL AMAZING
MMM
IN THIS CONTEXT, THE TORN, OR "CUT", CLOTHING & ONO'S INVITATION FOR SACRIFICE & SOUVENIR — IT WAS MORE THAN HIGHBROW IDEOLOGY. THIS WAS CONCRETE IMAGERY.
← AFTER JUNKO MORIMOTO IN "MY HIROSHIMA".

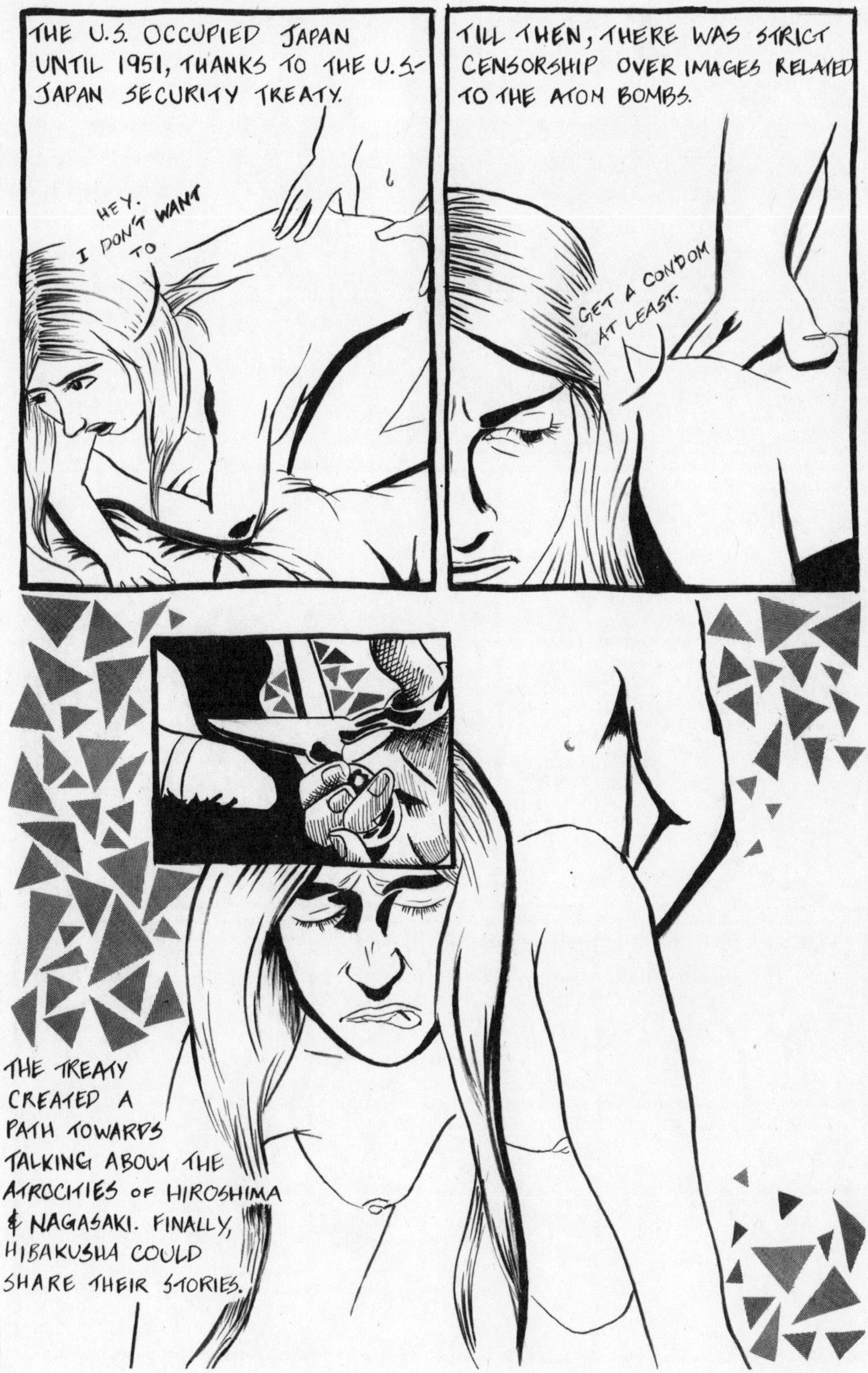
THE U.S. OCCUPIED JAPAN UNTIL 1951, THANKS TO THE U.S.-JAPAN SECURITY TREATY.
HEY. I DON'T WANT TO
TILL THEN, THERE WAS STRICT CENSORSHIP OVER IMAGES RELATED TO THE ATOM BOMBS.
GET A CONDOM AT LEAST.
THE TREATY CREATED A PATH TOWARDS TALKING ABOUT THE ATROCITIES OF HIROSHIMA & NAGASAKI. FINALLY, HIBAKUSHA COULD SHARE THEIR STORIES.

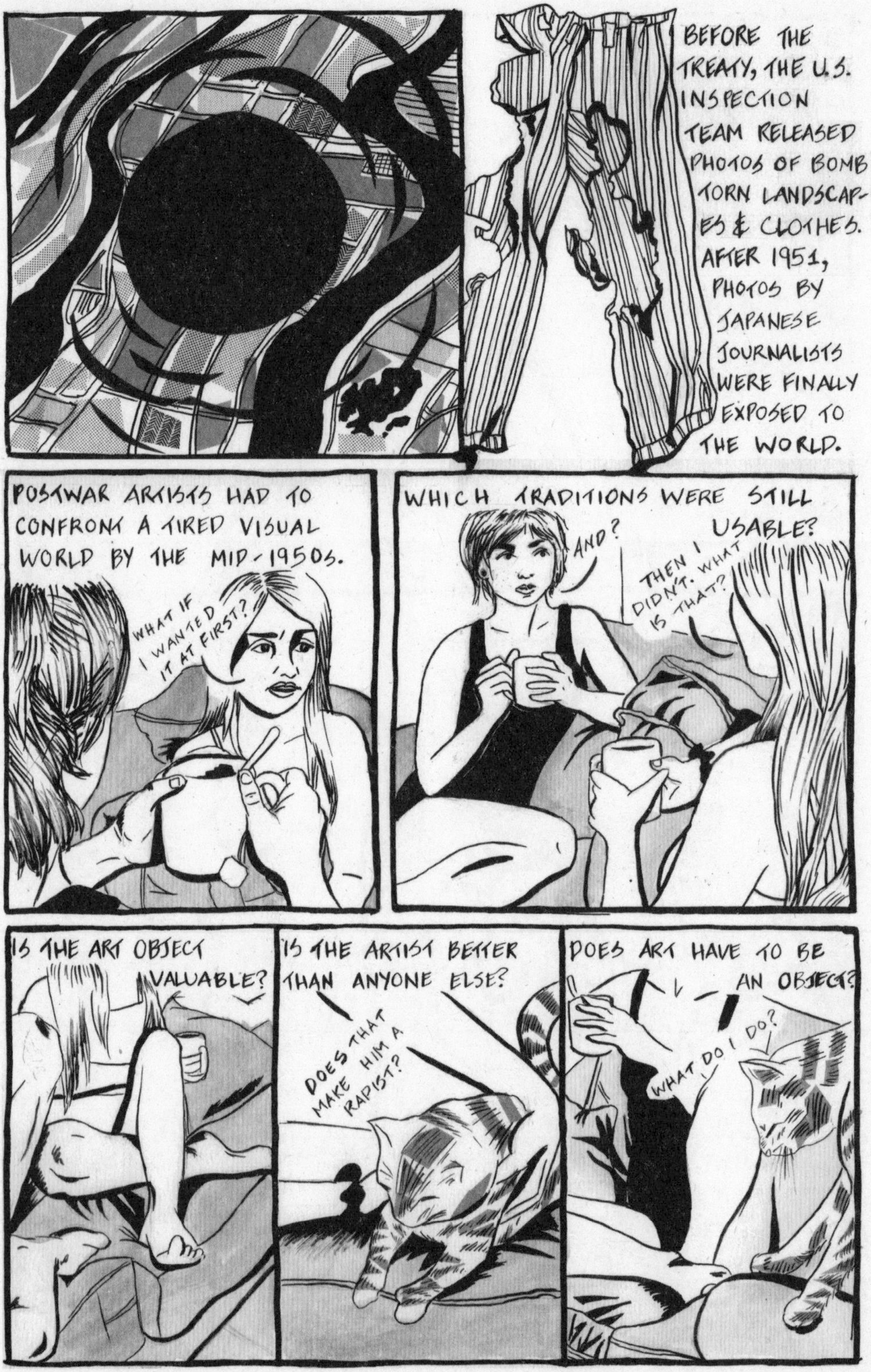
BEFORE THE TREATY, THE U.S. INSPECTION TEAM RELEASED PHOTOS OF BOMB TORN LANDSCAPES & CLOTHES. AFTER 1951, PHOTOS BY JAPANESE JOURNALISTS WERE FINALLY EXPOSED TO THE WORLD.
POSTWAR ARTISTS HAD TO CONFRONT A TIRED VISUAL WORLD BY THE MID-1950s.
WHAT IF I WANTED IT AT FIRST?
WHICH TRADITIONS WERE STILL USABLE?
AND?
THEN I DIDN'T. WHAT IS THAT?
IS THE ART OBJECT VALUABLE?
IS THE ARTIST BETTER THAN ANYONE ELSE?
DOES THAT MAKE HIM A RAPIST?
DOES ART HAVE TO BE AN OBJECT?
WHAT DO I DO?

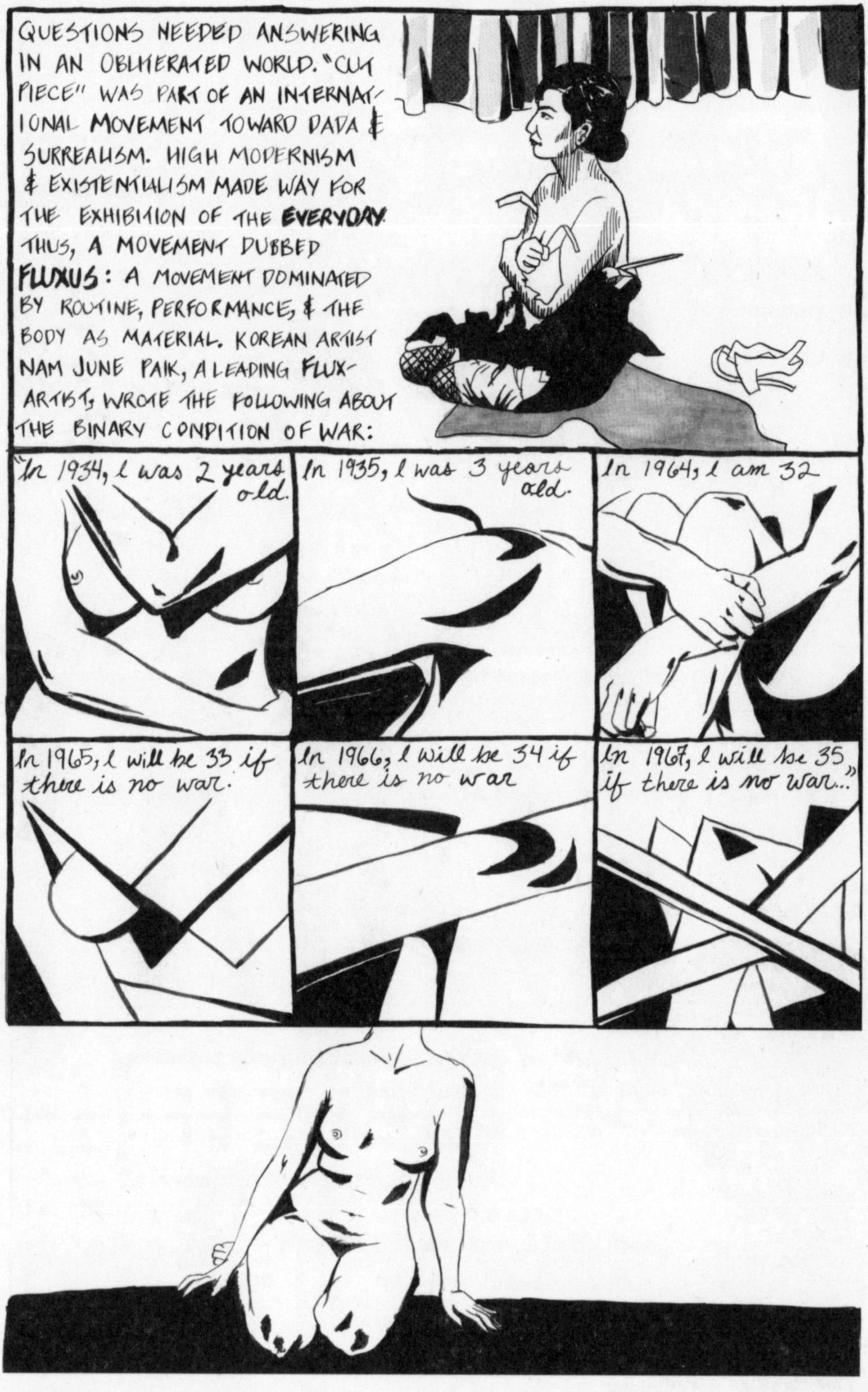
QUESTIONS NEEDED ANSWERING IN AN OBLITERATED WORLD. "CUT PIECE" WAS PART OF AN INTERNATIONAL MOVEMENT TOWARD DADA & SURREALISM. HIGH MODERNISM & EXISTENTIALISM MADE WAY FOR THE EXHIBITION OF THE EVERYDAY. THUS, A MOVEMENT DUBBED FLUXUS: A MOVEMENT DOMINATED BY ROUTINE, PERFORMANCE, & THE BODY AS MATERIAL. KOREAN ARTIST NAM JUNE PAIK, A LEADING FLUX-ARTIST, WROTE THE FOLLOWING ABOUT THE BINARY CONDITION OF WAR:
"In 1934, I was 2 years old.
In 1935, I was 3 years old.
In 1964, I am 32
In 1965, I will be 33 if there is no war.
In 1966, I will be 34 if there is no war
In 1967, I will be 35 if there is no war..."

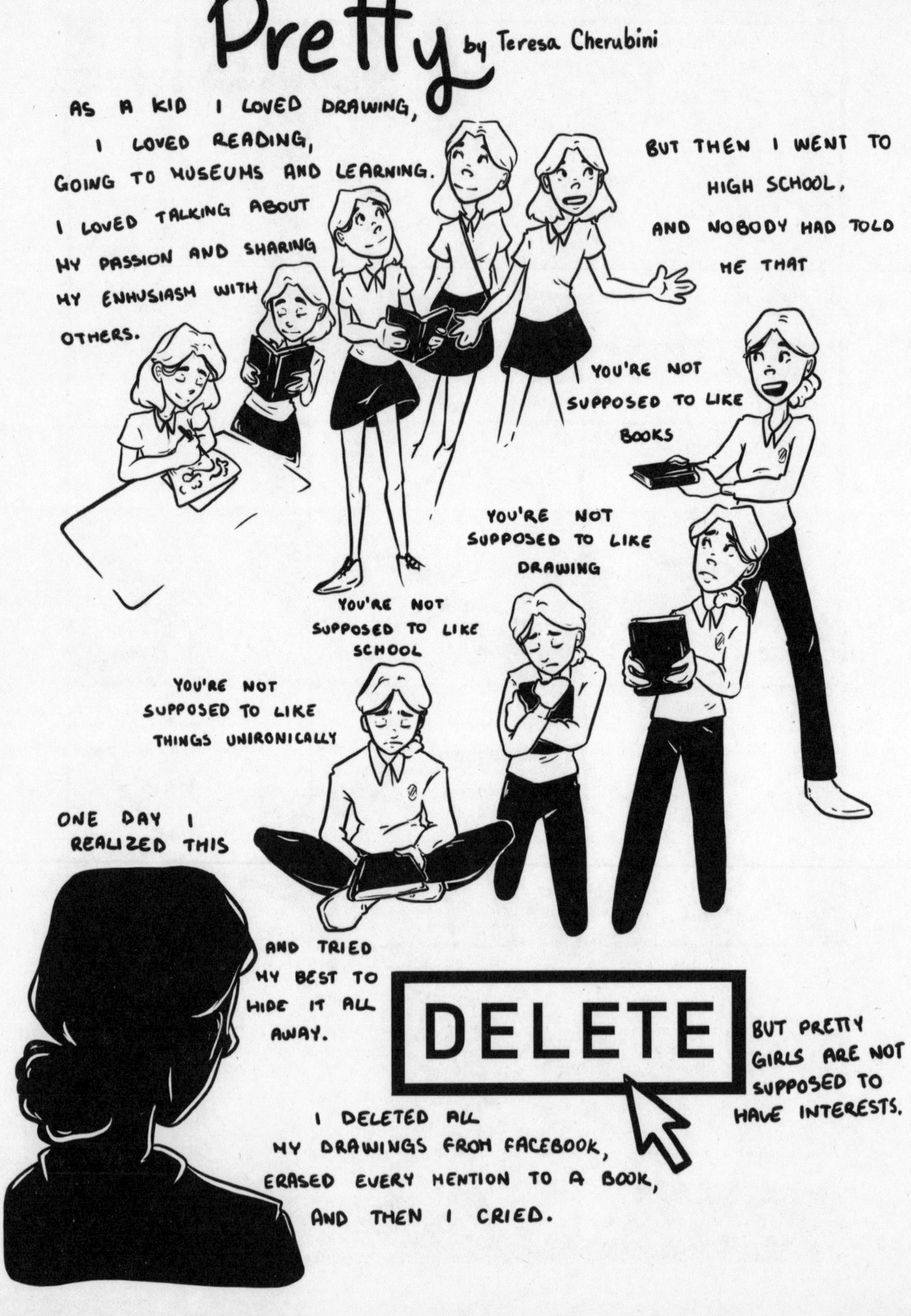
Pretty
by Teresa Cherubini
AS A KID I LOVED DRAWING,
I LOVED READING,
GOING TO MUSEUMS AND LEARNING.
I LOVED TALKING ABOUT
MY PASSION AND SHARING
MY ENHUSIASM WITH
OTHERS.
BUT THEN I WENT TO
HIGH SCHOOL,
AND NOBODY HAD TOLD
ME THAT
YOU'RE NOT
SUPPOSED TO LIKE
BOOKS
YOU'RE NOT
SUPPOSED TO LIKE
DRAWING
YOU'RE NOT
SUPPOSED TO LIKE
SCHOOL
YOU'RE NOT
SUPPOSED TO LIKE
THINGS UNIRONICALLY
ONE DAY I
REALIZED THIS
AND TRIED
MY BEST TO
HIDE IT ALL
AWAY.
DELETE
BUT PRETTY
GIRLS ARE NOT
SUPPOSED TO
HAVE INTERESTS.
I DELETED ALL
MY DRAWINGS FROM FACEBOOK,
ERASED EVERY MENTION TO A BOOK,
AND THEN I CRIED.

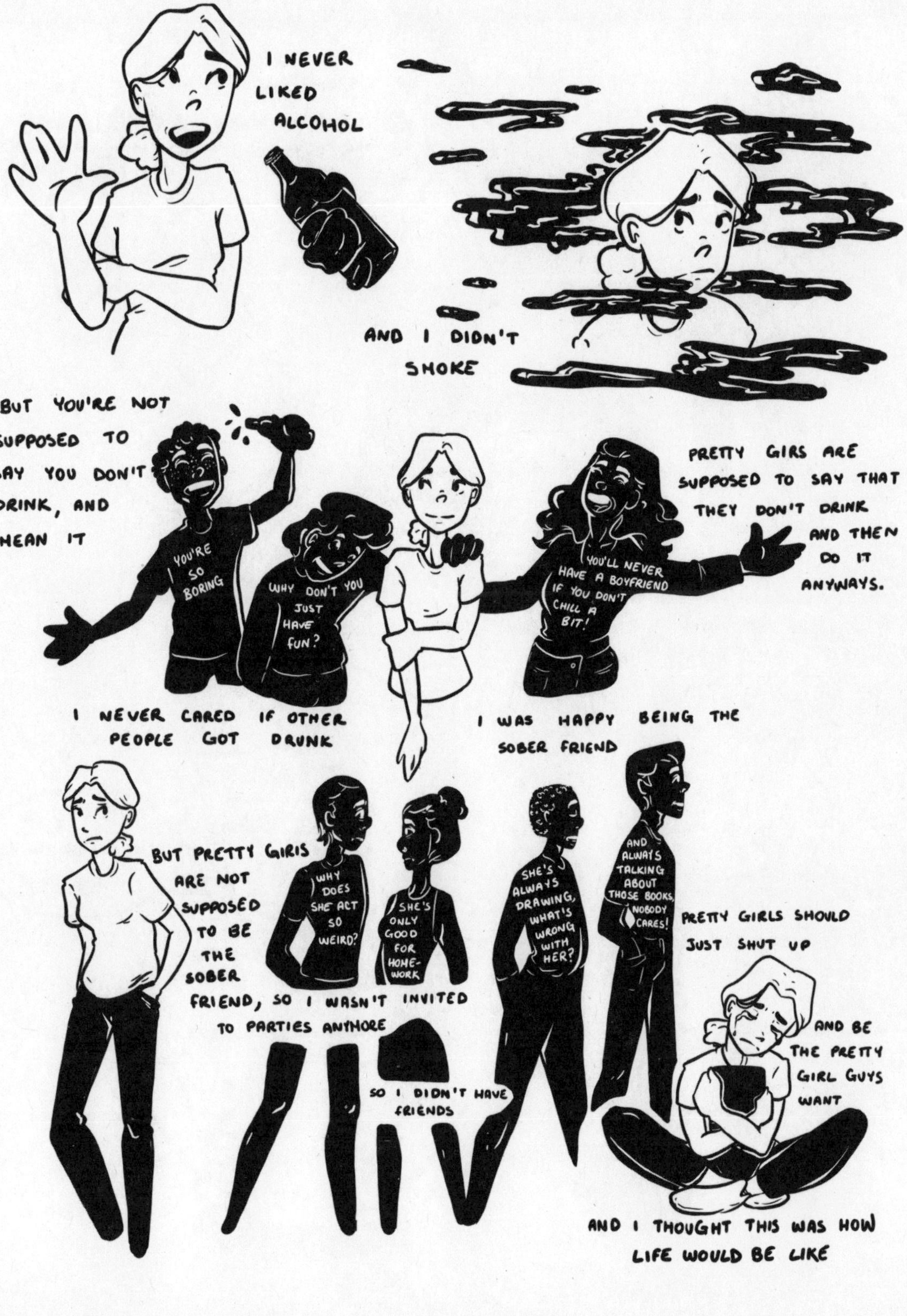
I NEVER LIKED ALCOHOL
AND I DIDN'T SMOKE
BUT YOU'RE NOT SUPPOSED TO SAY YOU DON'T DRINK, AND MEAN IT
YOU'RE SO BORING
WHY DON'T YOU JUST HAVE FUN?
YOU'LL NEVER HAVE A BOYFRIEND IF YOU DON'T CHILL A BIT!
PRETTY GIRS ARE SUPPOSED TO SAY THAT THEY DON'T DRINK AND THEN DO IT ANYWAYS.
I NEVER CARED IF OTHER PEOPLE GOT DRUNK
I WAS HAPPY BEING THE SOBER FRIEND
BUT PRETTY GIRLS ARE NOT SUPPOSED TO BE THE SOBER FRIEND, SO I WASN'T INVITED TO PARTIES ANYMORE
WHY DOES SHE ACT SO WEIRD?
SHE'S ONLY GOOD FOR HOME-WORK
SHE'S ALWAYS DRAWING, WHAT'S WRONG WITH HER?
AND ALWAYS TALKING ABOUT THOSE BOOKS, NOBODY CARES!
SO I DIDN'T HAVE FRIENDS
PRETTY GIRLS SHOULD JUST SHUT UP
AND BE THE PRETTY GIRL GUYS WANT
AND I THOUGHT THIS WAS HOW LIFE WOULD BE LIKE

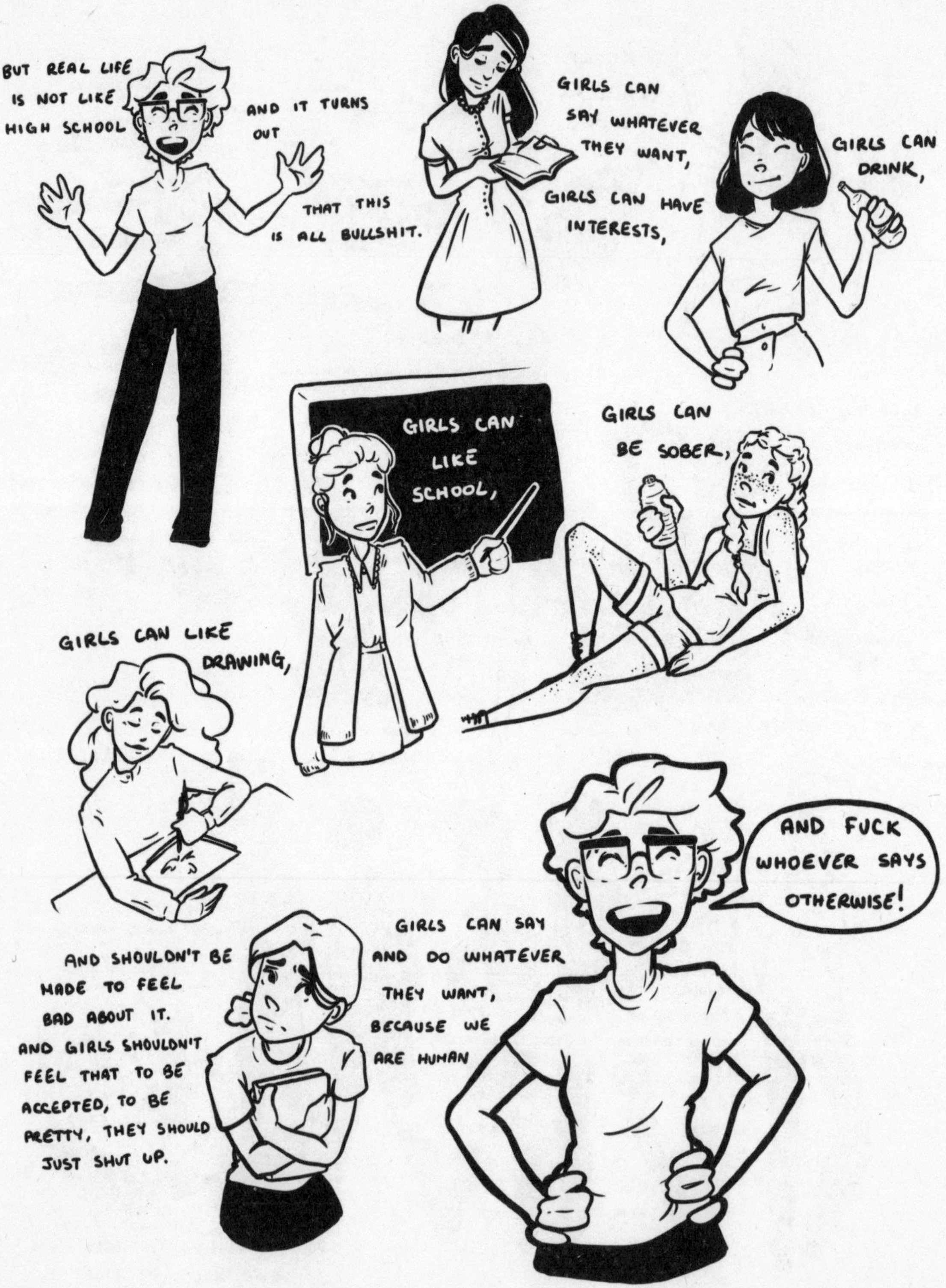
BUT REAL LIFE IS NOT LIKE HIGH SCHOOL
AND IT TURNS OUT
THAT THIS IS ALL BULLSHIT.
GIRLS CAN SAY WHATEVER THEY WANT,
GIRLS CAN HAVE INTERESTS,
GIRLS CAN DRINK,
GIRLS CAN LIKE SCHOOL,
GIRLS CAN BE SOBER,
GIRLS CAN LIKE DRAWING,
AND SHOULDN'T BE MADE TO FEEL BAD ABOUT IT.
AND GIRLS SHOULDN'T FEEL THAT TO BE ACCEPTED, TO BE PRETTY, THEY SHOULD JUST SHUT UP.
GIRLS CAN SAY AND DO WHATEVER THEY WANT, BECAUSE WE ARE HUMAN
AND FUCK WHOEVER SAYS OTHERWISE!

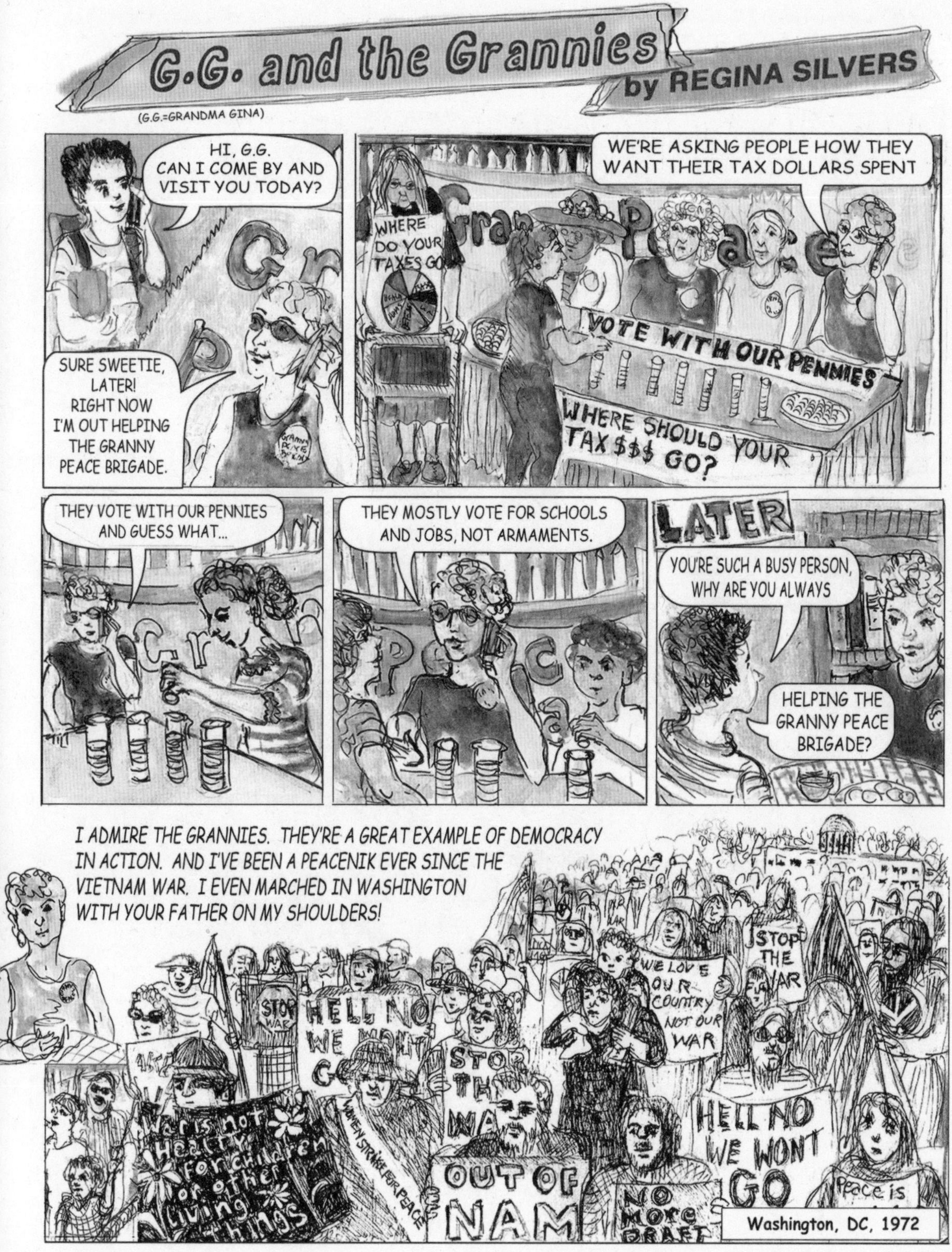
G.G. and the Grannies
by REGINA SILVERS
(G.G.=GRANDMA GINA)
HI, G.G. CAN I COME BY AND VISIT YOU TODAY?
SURE SWEETIE, LATER! RIGHT NOW I'M OUT HELPING THE GRANNY PEACE BRIGADE.
WE'RE ASKING PEOPLE HOW THEY WANT THEIR TAX DOLLARS SPENT
WHERE DO YOUR TAXES GO
VOTE WITH OUR PENNIES
WHERE SHOULD YOUR TAX $$$ GO?
THEY VOTE WITH OUR PENNIES AND GUESS WHAT...
THEY MOSTLY VOTE FOR SCHOOLS AND JOBS, NOT ARMAMENTS.
LATER
YOU'RE SUCH A BUSY PERSON, WHY ARE YOU ALWAYS
HELPING THE GRANNY PEACE BRIGADE?
I ADMIRE THE GRANNIES. THEY'RE A GREAT EXAMPLE OF DEMOCRACY IN ACTION. AND I'VE BEEN A PEACENIK EVER SINCE THE VIETNAM WAR. I EVEN MARCHED IN WASHINGTON WITH YOUR FATHER ON MY SHOULDERS!
STOP WAR
HELL NO WE WONT GO
STOP THE WAR
WE LOVE OUR COUNTRY NOT OUR WAR
STOP THE WA
War is not Healthy for children or other living things
WOMEN STRIKE FOR PEACE
OUT OF NAM
NO more DRAFT
HELL NO WE WONT GO
Peace is
Washington, DC, 1972

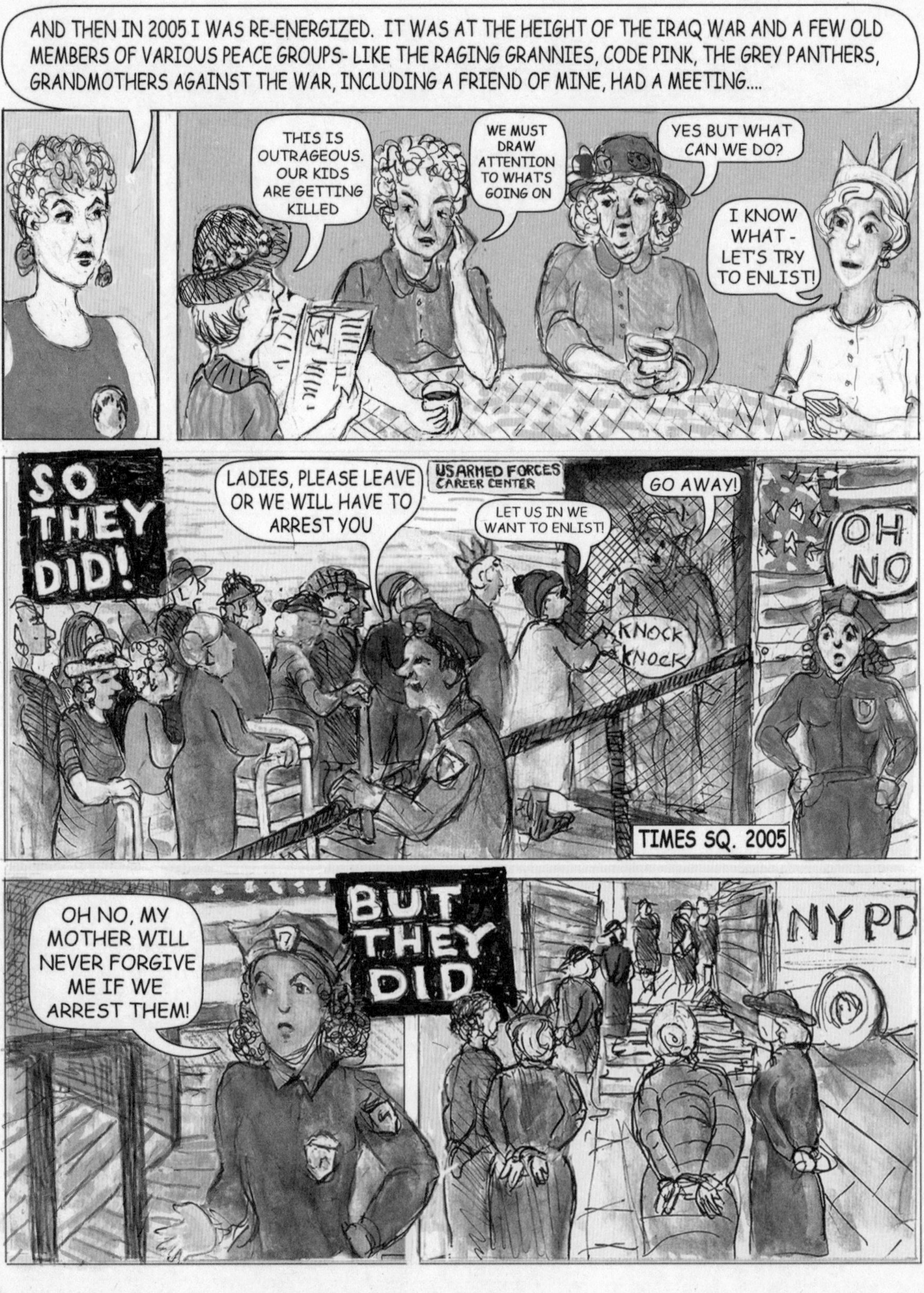
AND THEN IN 2005 I WAS RE-ENERGIZED. IT WAS AT THE HEIGHT OF THE IRAQ WAR AND A FEW OLD MEMBERS OF VARIOUS PEACE GROUPS- LIKE THE RAGING GRANNIES, CODE PINK, THE GREY PANTHERS, GRANDMOTHERS AGAINST THE WAR, INCLUDING A FRIEND OF MINE, HAD A MEETING....
THIS IS OUTRAGEOUS. OUR KIDS ARE GETTING KILLED
WE MUST DRAW ATTENTION TO WHAT'S GOING ON
YES BUT WHAT CAN WE DO?
I KNOW WHAT - LET'S TRY TO ENLIST!
SO THEY DID!
LADIES, PLEASE LEAVE OR WE WILL HAVE TO ARREST YOU
US ARMED FORCES CAREER CENTER
GO AWAY!
LET US IN WE WANT TO ENLIST!
KNOCK KNOCK
OH NO
TIMES SQ. 2005
OH NO, MY MOTHER WILL NEVER FORGIVE ME IF WE ARREST THEM!
BUT THEY DID
NYPD

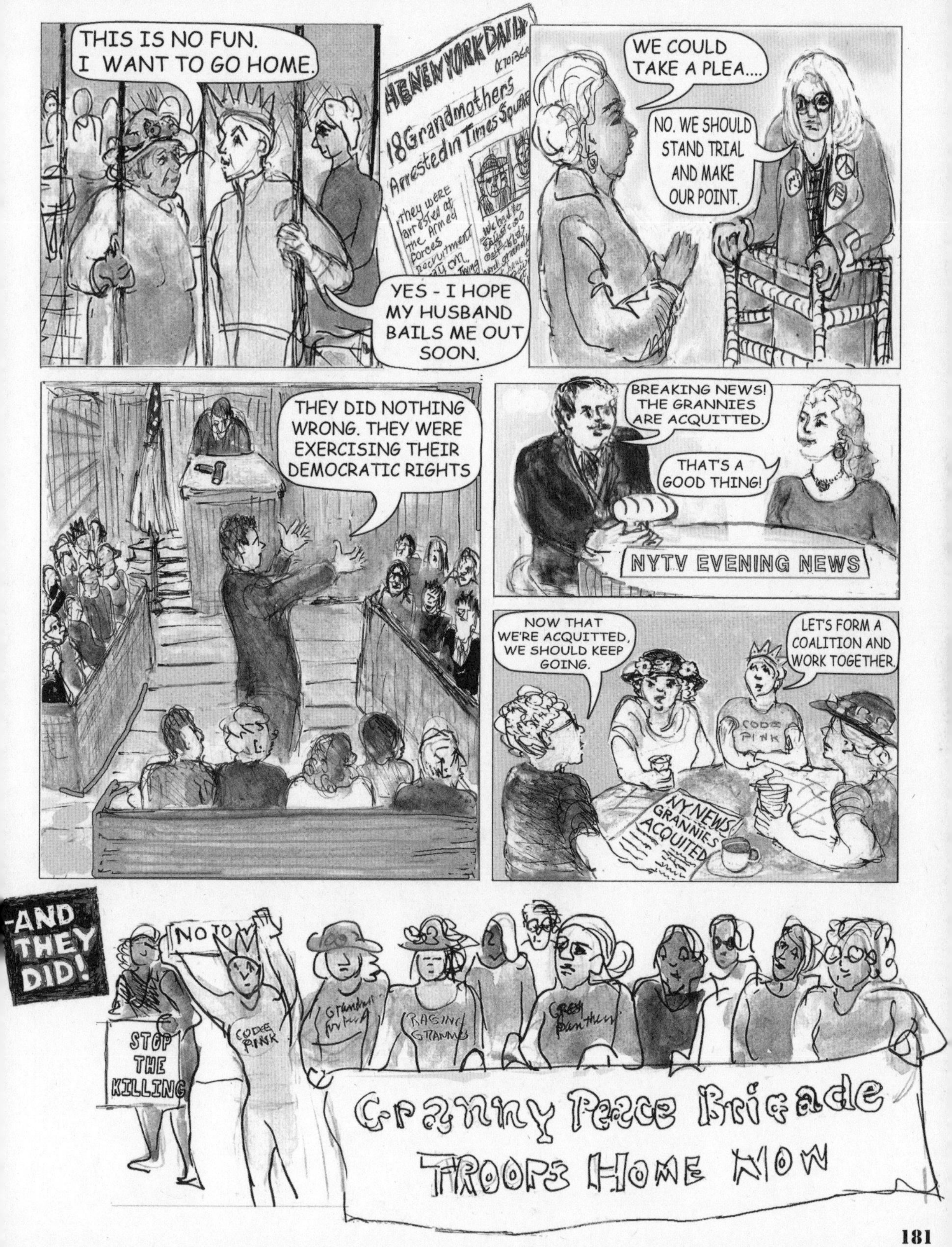
THIS IS NO FUN. I WANT TO GO HOME.
YES - I HOPE MY HUSBAND BAILS ME OUT SOON.
18 Grandmothers Arrested in Times Square
WE COULD TAKE A PLEA....
NO. WE SHOULD STAND TRIAL AND MAKE OUR POINT.
THEY DID NOTHING WRONG. THEY WERE EXERCISING THEIR DEMOCRATIC RIGHTS
BREAKING NEWS! THE GRANNIES ARE ACQUITTED.
THAT'S A GOOD THING!
NYTV EVENING NEWS
NOW THAT WE'RE ACQUITTED, WE SHOULD KEEP GOING.
LET'S FORM A COALITION AND WORK TOGETHER.
CODE PINK
NY NEWS GRANNIES ACQUITED
-AND THEY DID!
STOP THE KILLING
CODE PINK
RAGING GRANNIES
Granny Peace Brigade
TROOPS HOME NOW

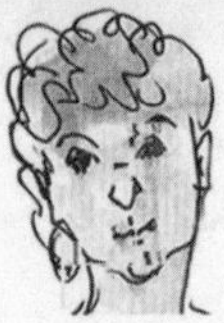

SO I STARTED FOLLOWING THE GRANNY PEACE BRIGADE. I TOOK PHOTOS WHILE MARCHING WITH THEM. AND AFTER A WHILE I BEGAN MAKING PAINTINGS FROM MY PHOTOS.

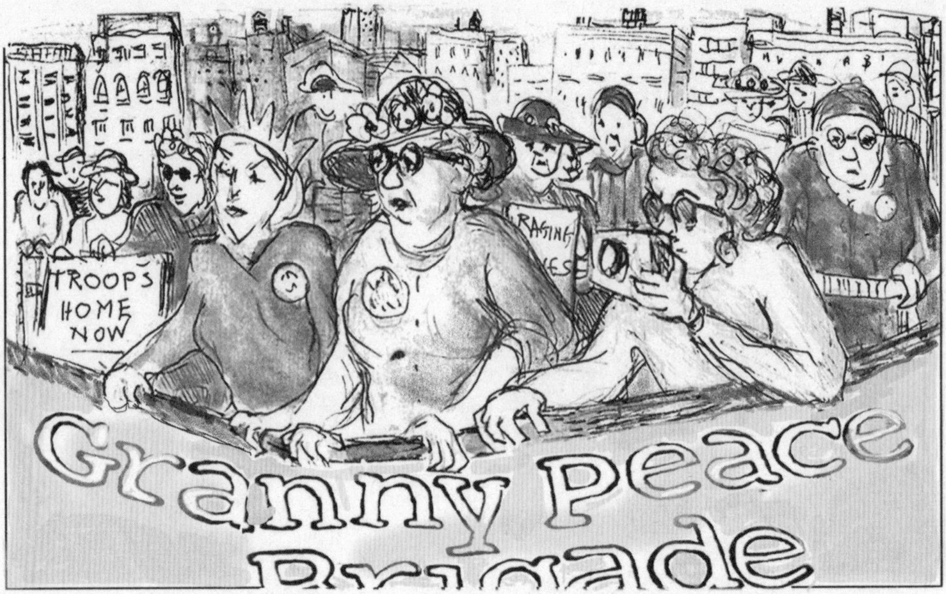
TROOPS HOME NOW
Granny Peace Brigade

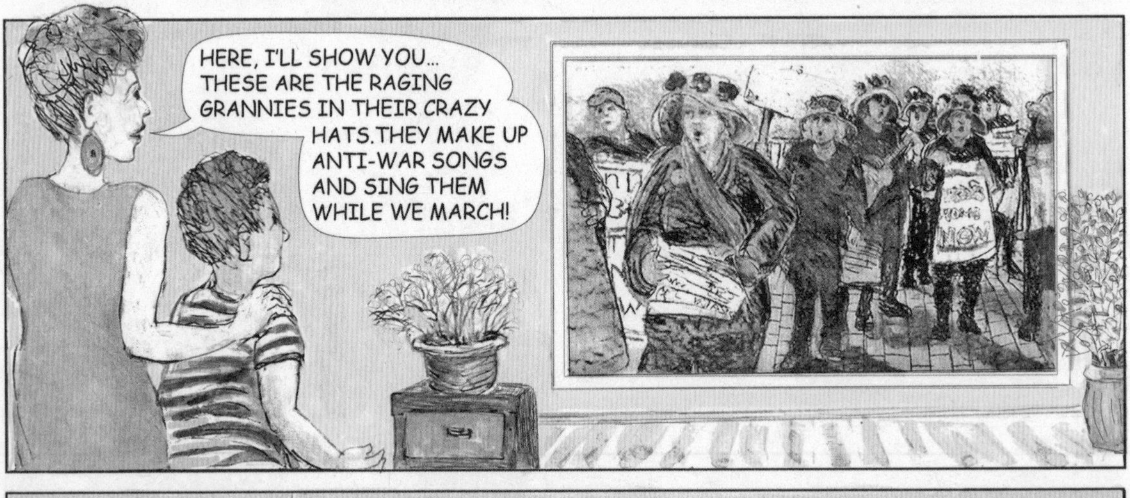
HERE, I'LL SHOW YOU... THESE ARE THE RAGING GRANNIES IN THEIR CRAZY HATS.THEY MAKE UP ANTI-WAR SONGS AND SING THEM WHILE WE MARCH!

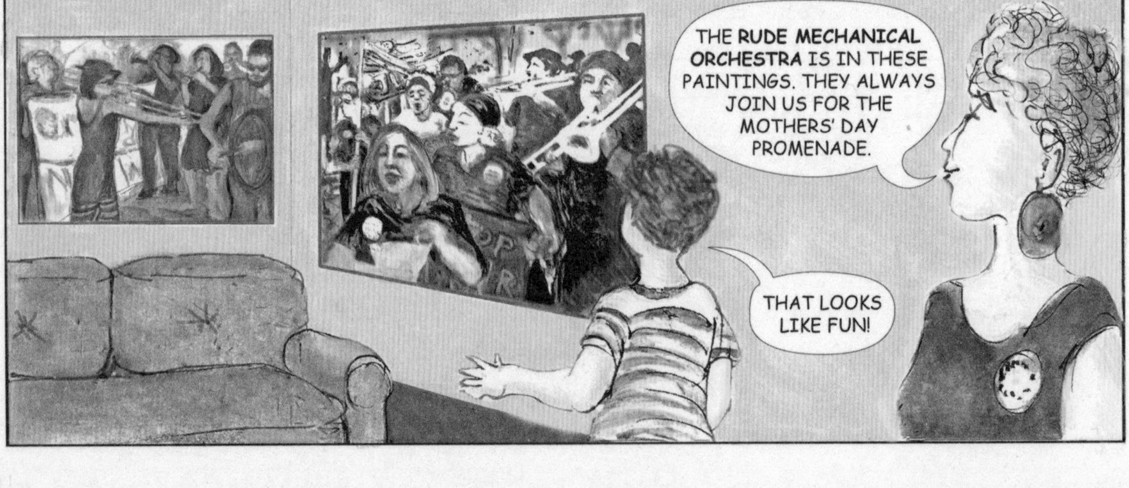
THE RUDE MECHANICAL ORCHESTRA IS IN THESE PAINTINGS. THEY ALWAYS JOIN US FOR THE MOTHERS' DAY PROMENADE.
THAT LOOKS LIKE FUN!

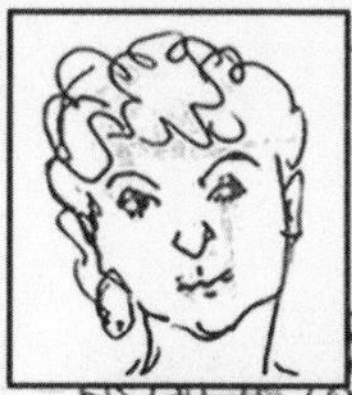

I ALWAYS LOVE THIS EVENT. ACCOMPANIED BY THE RUDE MECHANICAL ORCHESTRA THE GRANNIES DISTRIBUTE JULIA WARD HOWE'S PROCLAMATION FROM 1870, AND TEACH FOLKS THE **REAL** ORIGINS OF MOTHERS DAY.

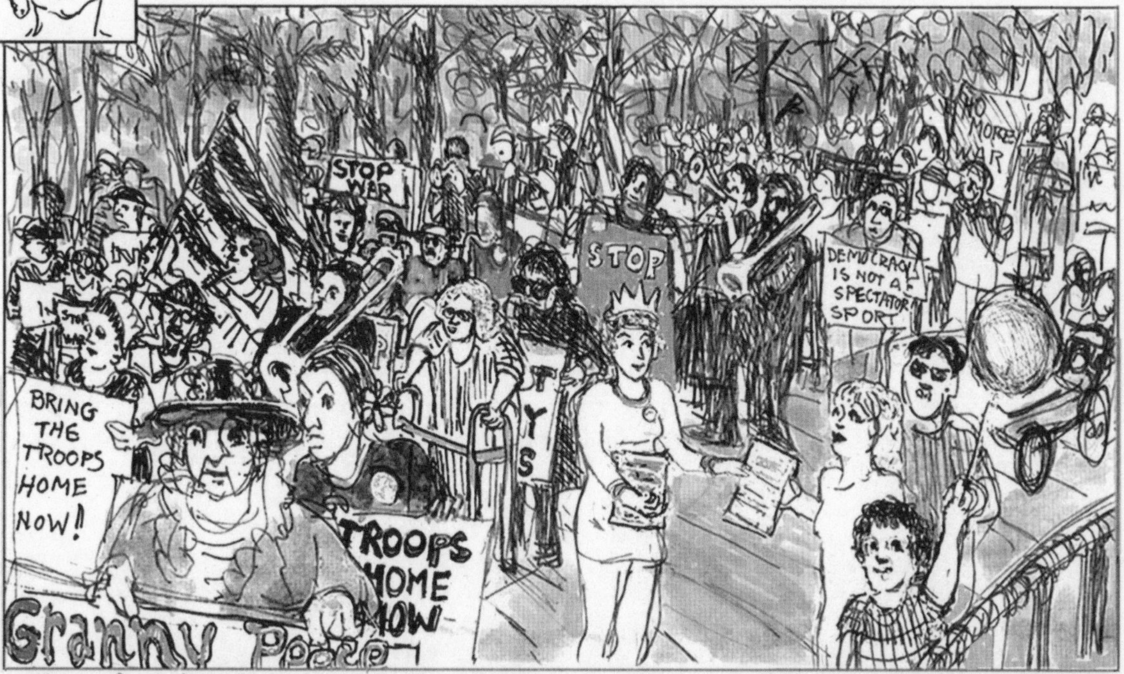
STOP WAR
NO MORE WAR
STOP
DEMOCRACY IS NOT A SPECTATOR SPORT
BRING THE TROOPS HOME NOW!
TROOPS HOME NOW
Granny

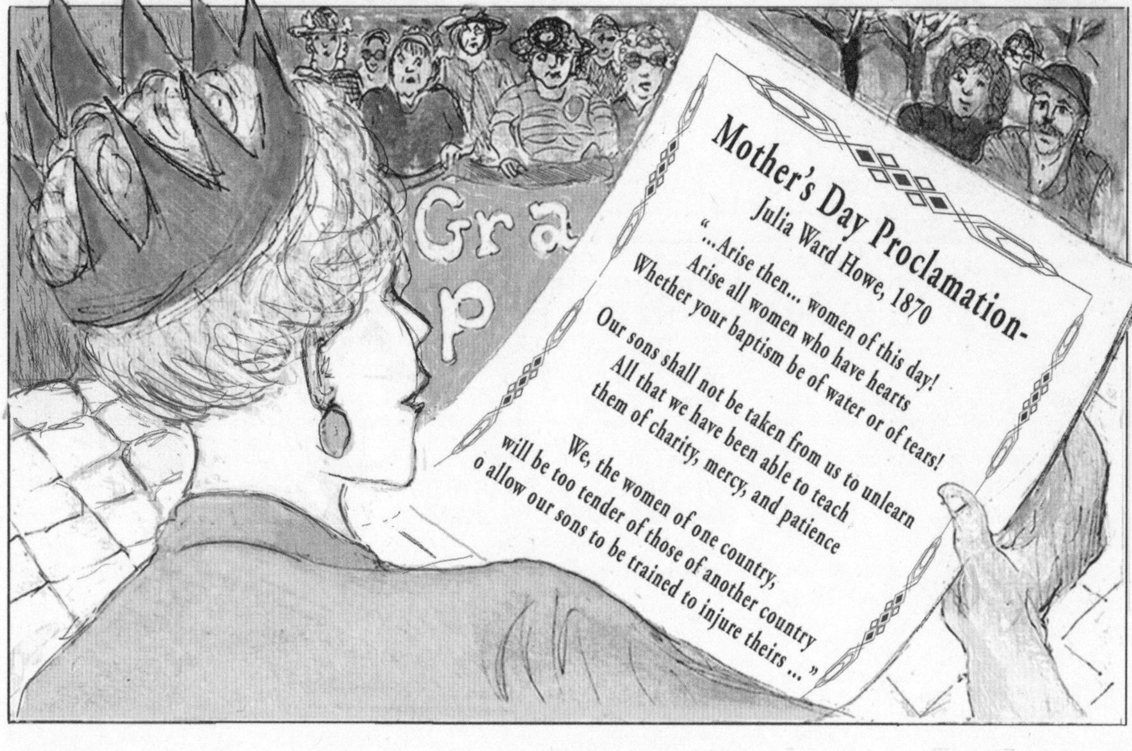
Mother's Day Proclamation-
Julia Ward Howe, 1870
"...Arise then... women of this day!
Arise all women who have hearts
Whether your baptism be of water or of tears!
Our sons shall not be taken from us to unlearn
All that we have been able to teach
them of charity, mercy, and patience
We, the women of one country,
will be too tender of those of another country
o allow our sons to be trained to injure theirs ..."

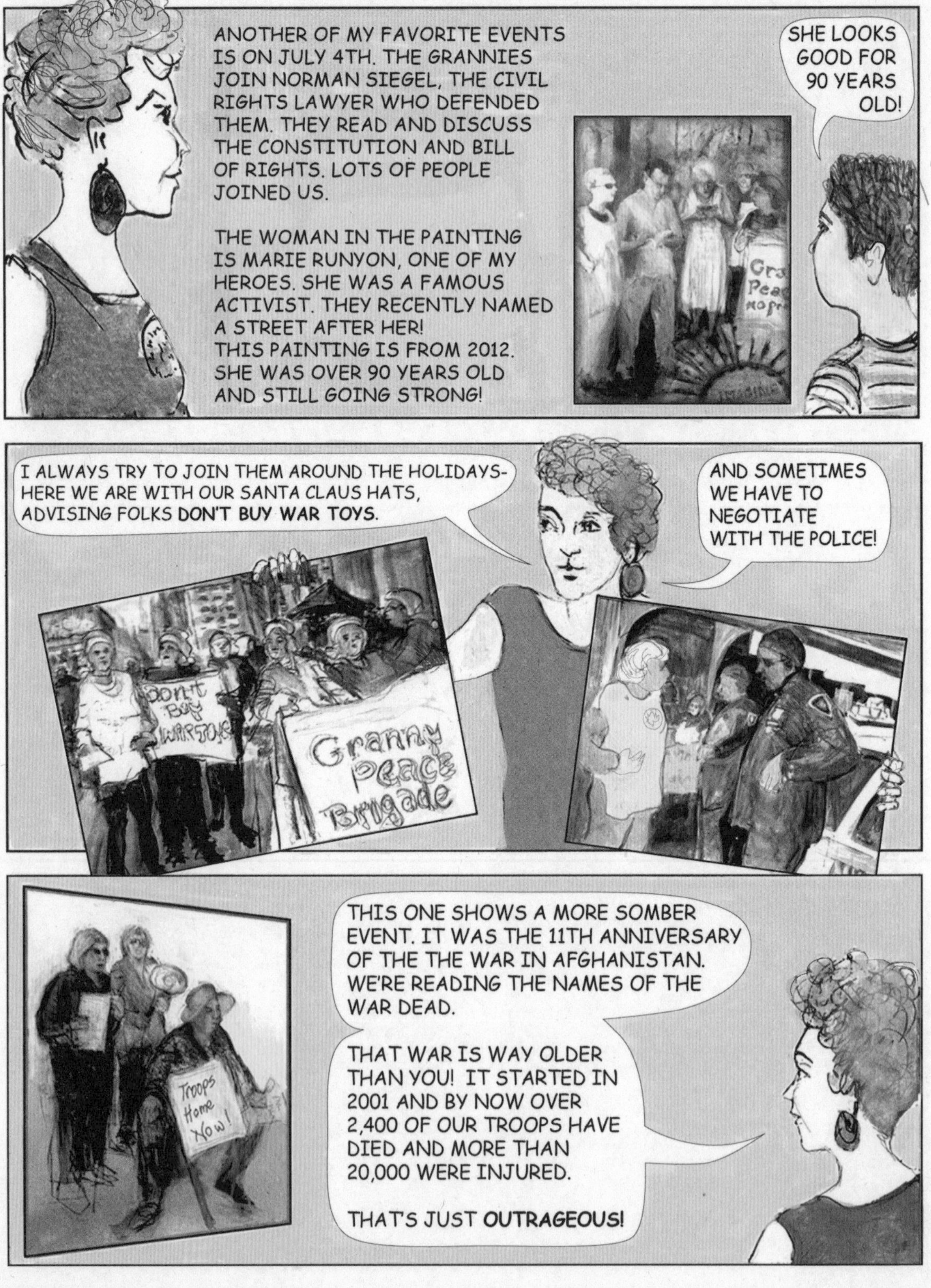
ANOTHER OF MY FAVORITE EVENTS IS ON JULY 4TH. THE GRANNIES JOIN NORMAN SIEGEL, THE CIVIL RIGHTS LAWYER WHO DEFENDED THEM. THEY READ AND DISCUSS THE CONSTITUTION AND BILL OF RIGHTS. LOTS OF PEOPLE JOINED US.
THE WOMAN IN THE PAINTING IS MARIE RUNYON, ONE OF MY HEROES. SHE WAS A FAMOUS ACTIVIST. THEY RECENTLY NAMED A STREET AFTER HER! THIS PAINTING IS FROM 2012. SHE WAS OVER 90 YEARS OLD AND STILL GOING STRONG!
SHE LOOKS GOOD FOR 90 YEARS OLD!
I ALWAYS TRY TO JOIN THEM AROUND THE HOLIDAYS- HERE WE ARE WITH OUR SANTA CLAUS HATS, ADVISING FOLKS **DON'T BUY WAR TOYS**.
AND SOMETIMES WE HAVE TO NEGOTIATE WITH THE POLICE!
Don't Buy WAR TOYS
Granny peace Brigade
THIS ONE SHOWS A MORE SOMBER EVENT. IT WAS THE 11TH ANNIVERSARY OF THE THE WAR IN AFGHANISTAN. WE'RE READING THE NAMES OF THE WAR DEAD.
THAT WAR IS WAY OLDER THAN YOU! IT STARTED IN 2001 AND BY NOW OVER 2,400 OF OUR TROOPS HAVE DIED AND MORE THAN 20,000 WERE INJURED.
THAT'S JUST **OUTRAGEOUS!**
Troops Home Now!

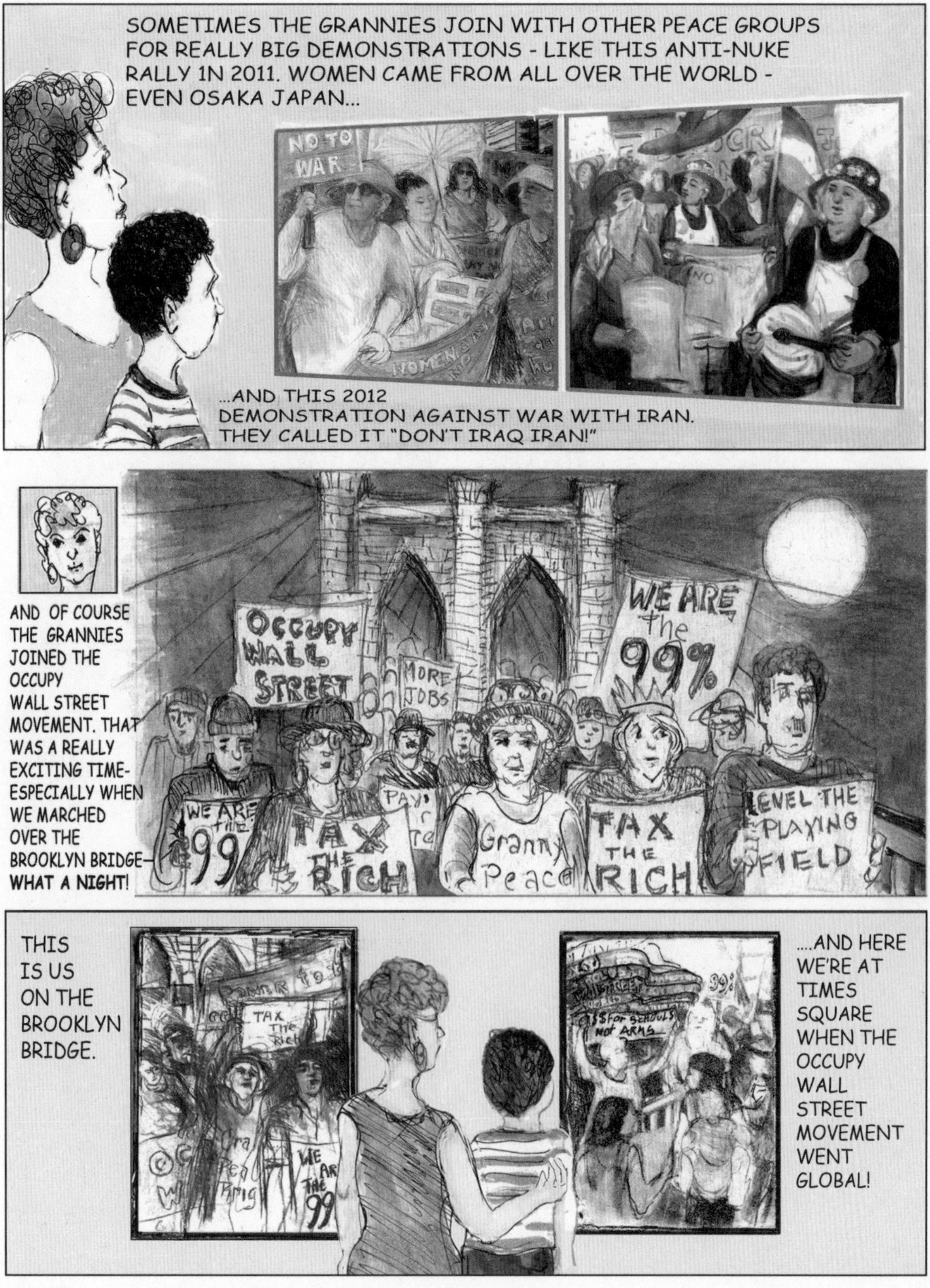
SOMETIMES THE GRANNIES JOIN WITH OTHER PEACE GROUPS FOR REALLY BIG DEMONSTRATIONS - LIKE THIS ANTI-NUKE RALLY 1N 2011. WOMEN CAME FROM ALL OVER THE WORLD - EVEN OSAKA JAPAN...
NO TO WAR
...AND THIS 2012 DEMONSTRATION AGAINST WAR WITH IRAN. THEY CALLED IT "DON'T IRAQ IRAN!"
AND OF COURSE THE GRANNIES JOINED THE OCCUPY WALL STREET MOVEMENT. THAT WAS A REALLY EXCITING TIME- ESPECIALLY WHEN WE MARCHED OVER THE BROOKLYN BRIDGE- WHAT A NIGHT!
OCCUPY WALL STREET
MORE JOBS
WE ARE the 99%
WE ARE THE 99
TAX THE RICH
Granny Peace
TAX THE RICH
LEVEL THE PLAYING FIELD
THIS IS US ON THE BROOKLYN BRIDGE.
TAX THE Rich
WE ARE THE 99
....AND HERE WE'RE AT TIMES SQUARE WHEN THE OCCUPY WALL STREET MOVEMENT WENT GLOBAL!
99%
$$ for SCHOOLS not ARMS

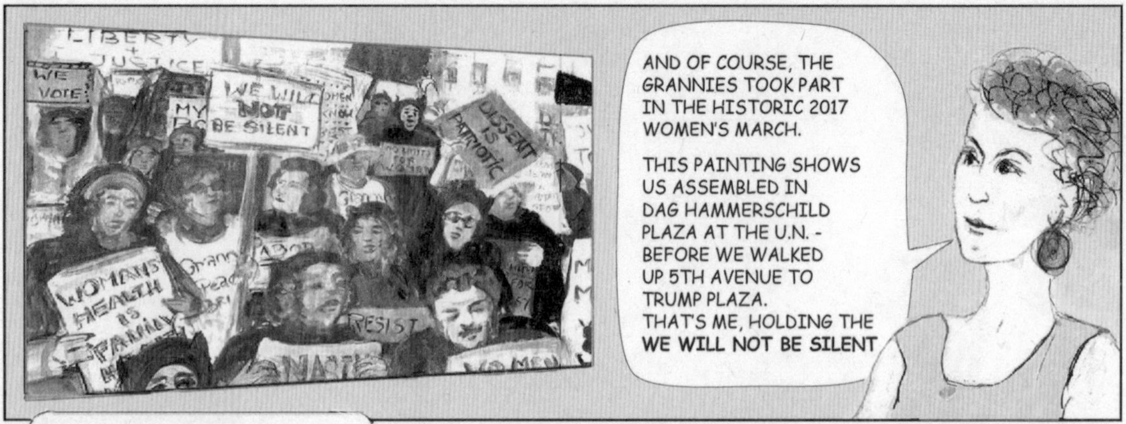
LIBERTY + JUSTICE
WE VOTE!
WE WILL NOT BE SILENT
DISSENT IS PATRIOTIC
WOMANS HEALTH is FAMILY
RESIST
AND OF COURSE, THE GRANNIES TOOK PART IN THE HISTORIC 2017 WOMEN'S MARCH.
THIS PAINTING SHOWS US ASSEMBLED IN DAG HAMMERSCHILD PLAZA AT THE U.N. - BEFORE WE WALKED UP 5TH AVENUE TO TRUMP PLAZA.
THAT'S ME, HOLDING THE **WE WILL NOT BE SILENT**

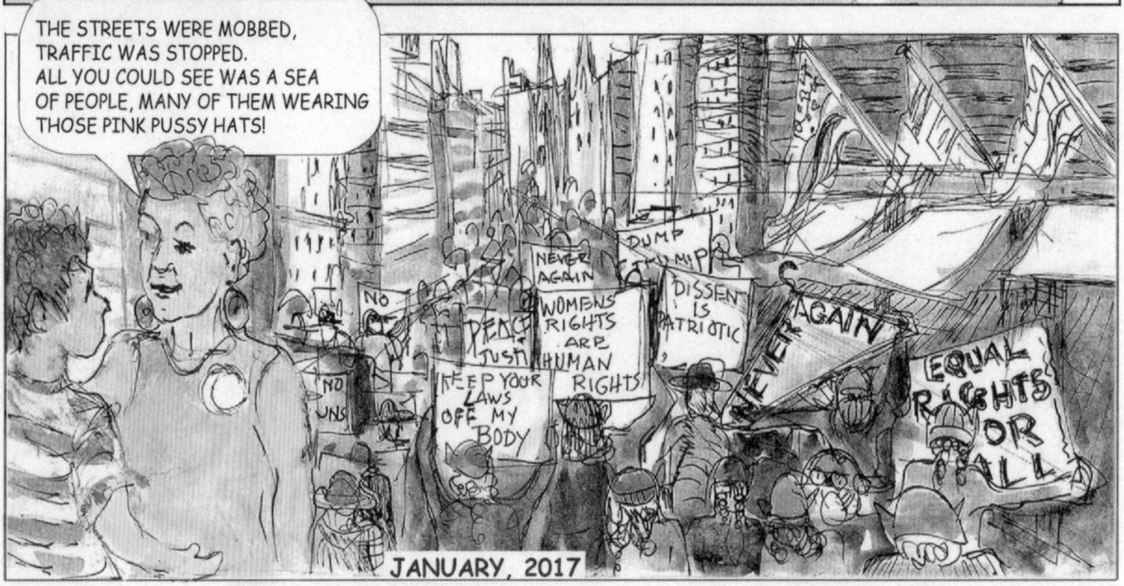
THE STREETS WERE MOBBED, TRAFFIC WAS STOPPED. ALL YOU COULD SEE WAS A SEA OF PEOPLE, MANY OF THEM WEARING THOSE PINK PUSSY HATS!
NEVER AGAIN
DUMP TRUMP
DISSENT IS PATRIOTIC
WOMENS RIGHTS ARE HUMAN RIGHTS
PEACE JUST
KEEP YOUR LAWS OFF MY BODY
NEVER AGAIN
EQUAL RIGHTS FOR ALL
JANUARY, 2017

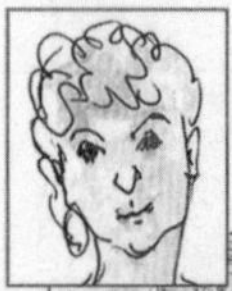

NATURALLY, WE ALSO JOINED THE MARCH TO SAVE OUR LIVES: AGAINST GUN VIOLENCE. IN NEW YORK ALONE THERE WERE MORE THAN 200,000 OF US. IT WAS A MEMORABLE DAY. ONE THAT JUST MIGHT CHANGE OUR GUN LAWS! I KNOW YOU AND YOUR FRIENDS.MARCHED TOO,

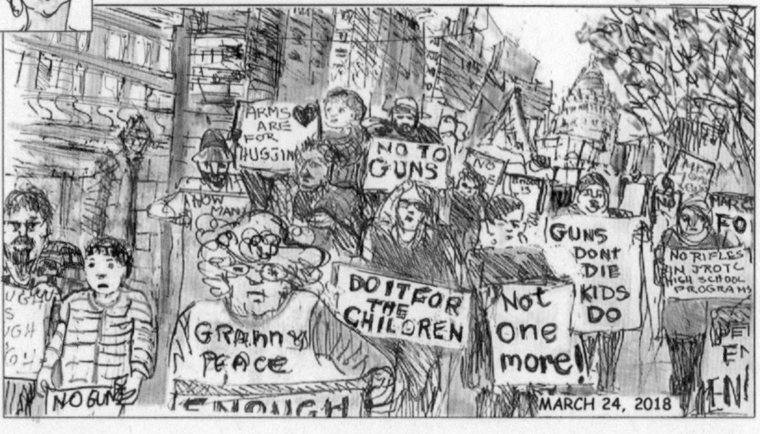
ARMS ARE FOR HUGGING
NO TO GUNS
GUNS DONT DIE KIDS DO
NO RIFLES IN JROTC HIGH SCHOOL PROGRAMS
DO IT FOR THE CHILDREN
Not One more!
GRANNY PEACE
NO GUNS
MARCH 24, 2018

THIS IS A PASTEL I DID OF A LITTLE BOY I SAW WHILE WE WERE MARCHING. SOMEONE SAID THEY THOUGHT HE WAS "CUTE" BUT IT BROKE MY HEART.

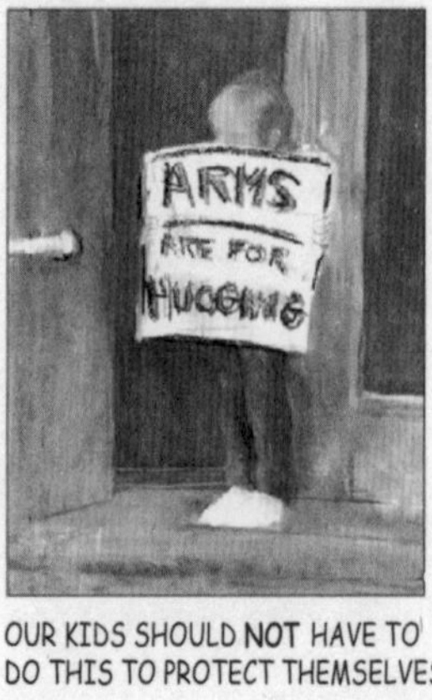
ARMS ARE FOR HUGGING

OUR KIDS SHOULD NOT HAVE TO DO THIS TO PROTECT THEMSELVES!

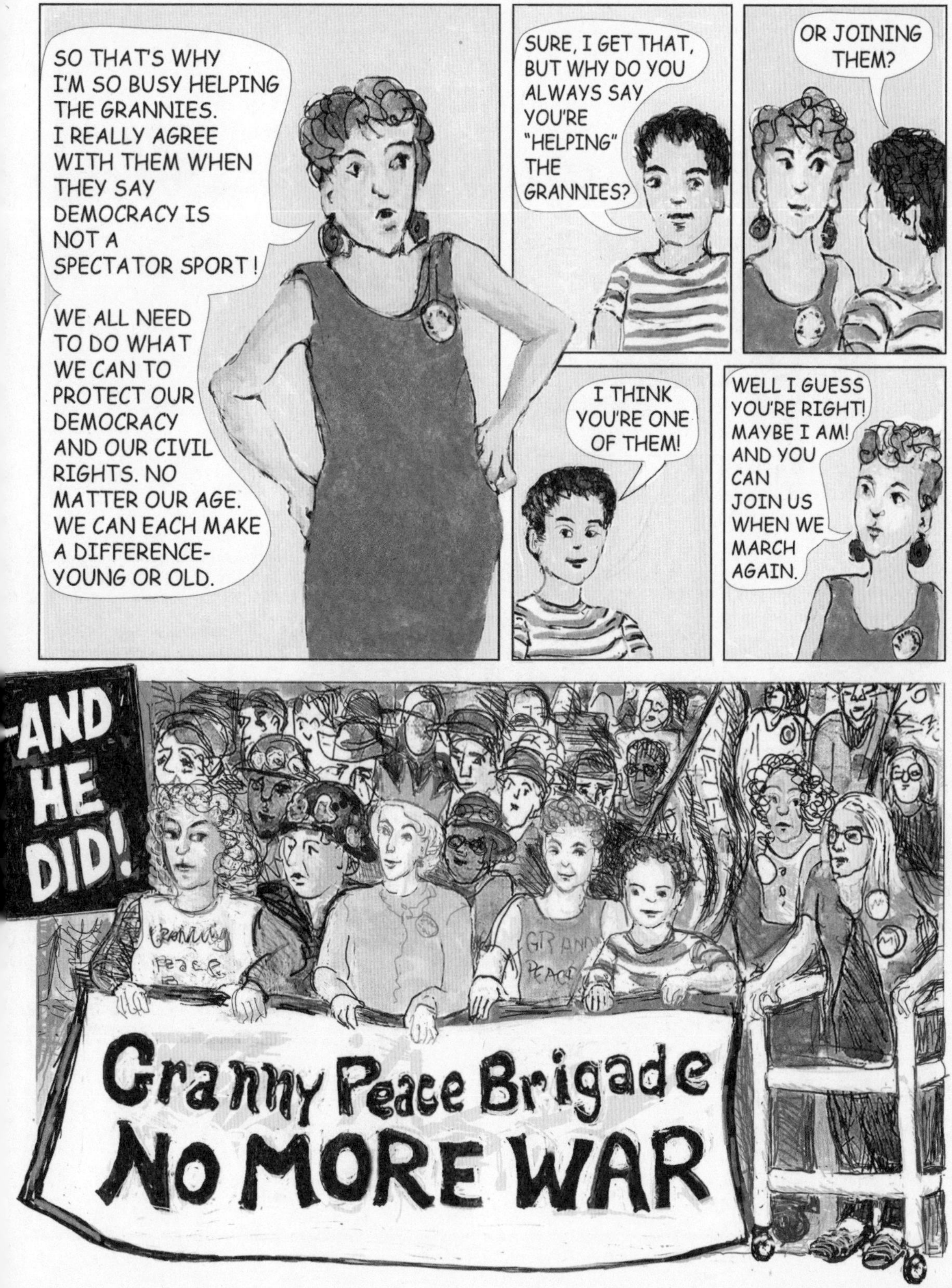
SO THAT'S WHY I'M SO BUSY HELPING THE GRANNIES. I REALLY AGREE WITH THEM WHEN THEY SAY DEMOCRACY IS NOT A SPECTATOR SPORT!
WE ALL NEED TO DO WHAT WE CAN TO PROTECT OUR DEMOCRACY AND OUR CIVIL RIGHTS. NO MATTER OUR AGE. WE CAN EACH MAKE A DIFFERENCE- YOUNG OR OLD.
SURE, I GET THAT, BUT WHY DO YOU ALWAYS SAY YOU'RE "HELPING" THE GRANNIES?
OR JOINING THEM?
I THINK YOU'RE ONE OF THEM!
WELL I GUESS YOU'RE RIGHT! MAYBE I AM! AND YOU CAN JOIN US WHEN WE MARCH AGAIN.
-AND HE DID!
Granny Peace Brigade
NO MORE WAR

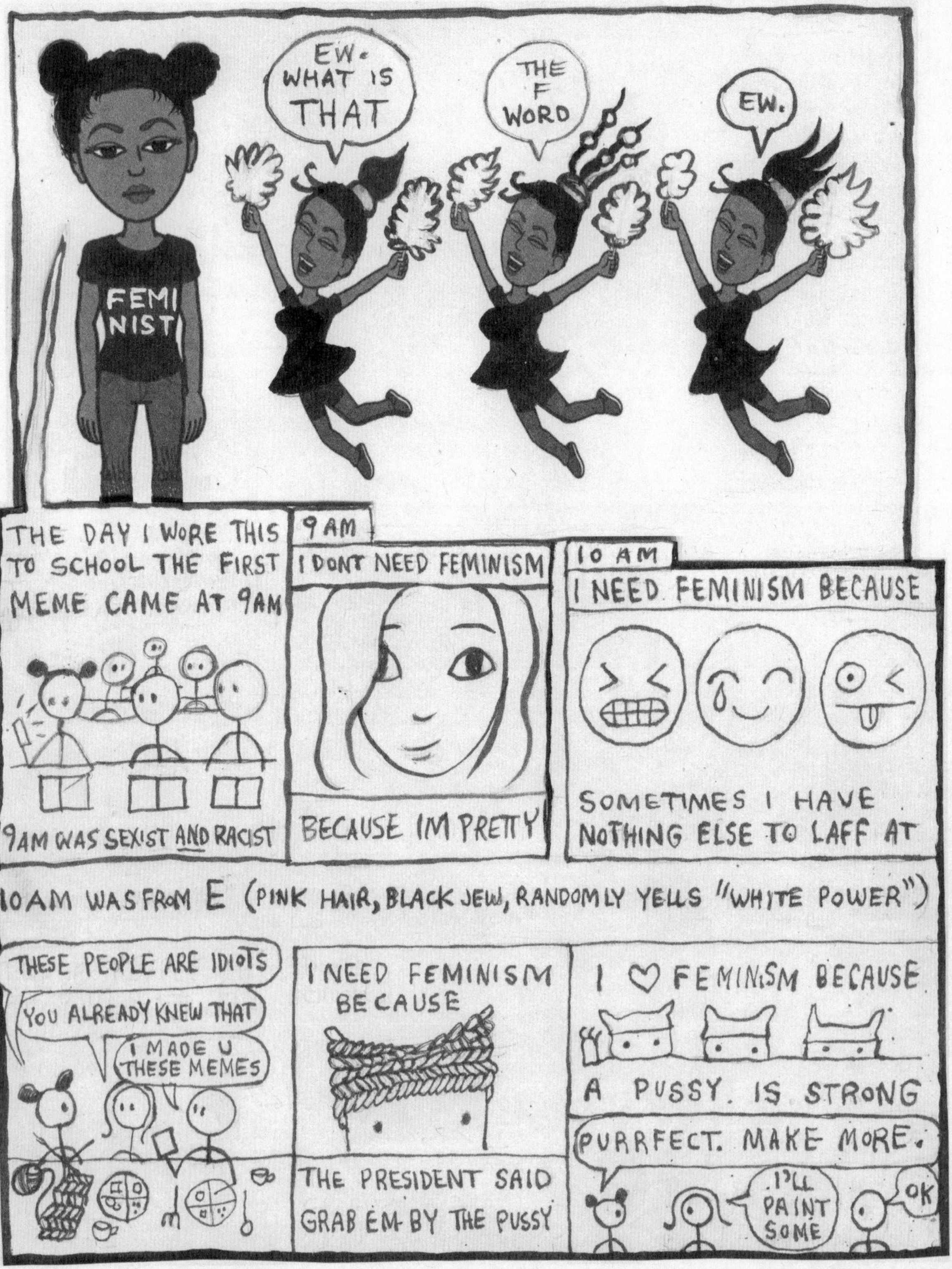
EW. WHAT IS THAT
THE F WORD
EW.
FEMI NIST
THE DAY I WORE THIS TO SCHOOL THE FIRST MEME CAME AT 9AM
9AM WAS SEXIST AND RACIST
9 AM
I DONT NEED FEMINISM
BECAUSE IM PRETTY
10 AM
I NEED FEMINISM BECAUSE
SOMETIMES I HAVE NOTHING ELSE TO LAFF AT
10AM WAS FROM E (PINK HAIR, BLACK JEW, RANDOMLY YELLS "WHITE POWER")
THESE PEOPLE ARE IDIOTS
YOU ALREADY KNEW THAT
I MADE U THESE MEMES
I NEED FEMINISM BECAUSE
THE PRESIDENT SAID GRAB EM BY THE PUSSY
I ♡ FEMINISM BECAUSE
A PUSSY. IS STRONG
PURRFECT. MAKE MORE.
I'LL PAINT SOME
OK

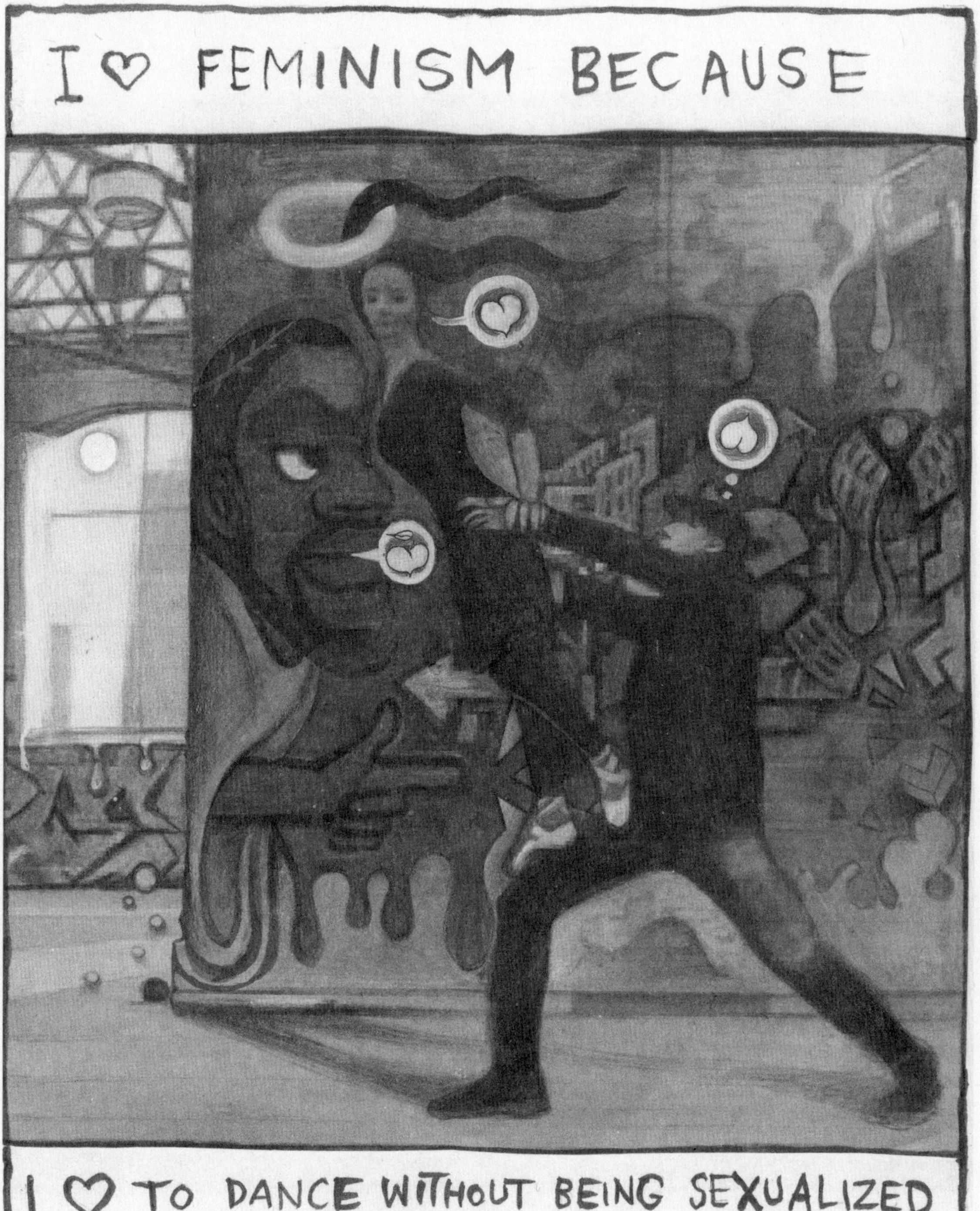
I ♡ FEMINISM BECAUSE
I ♡ TO DANCE WITHOUT BEING SEXUALIZED

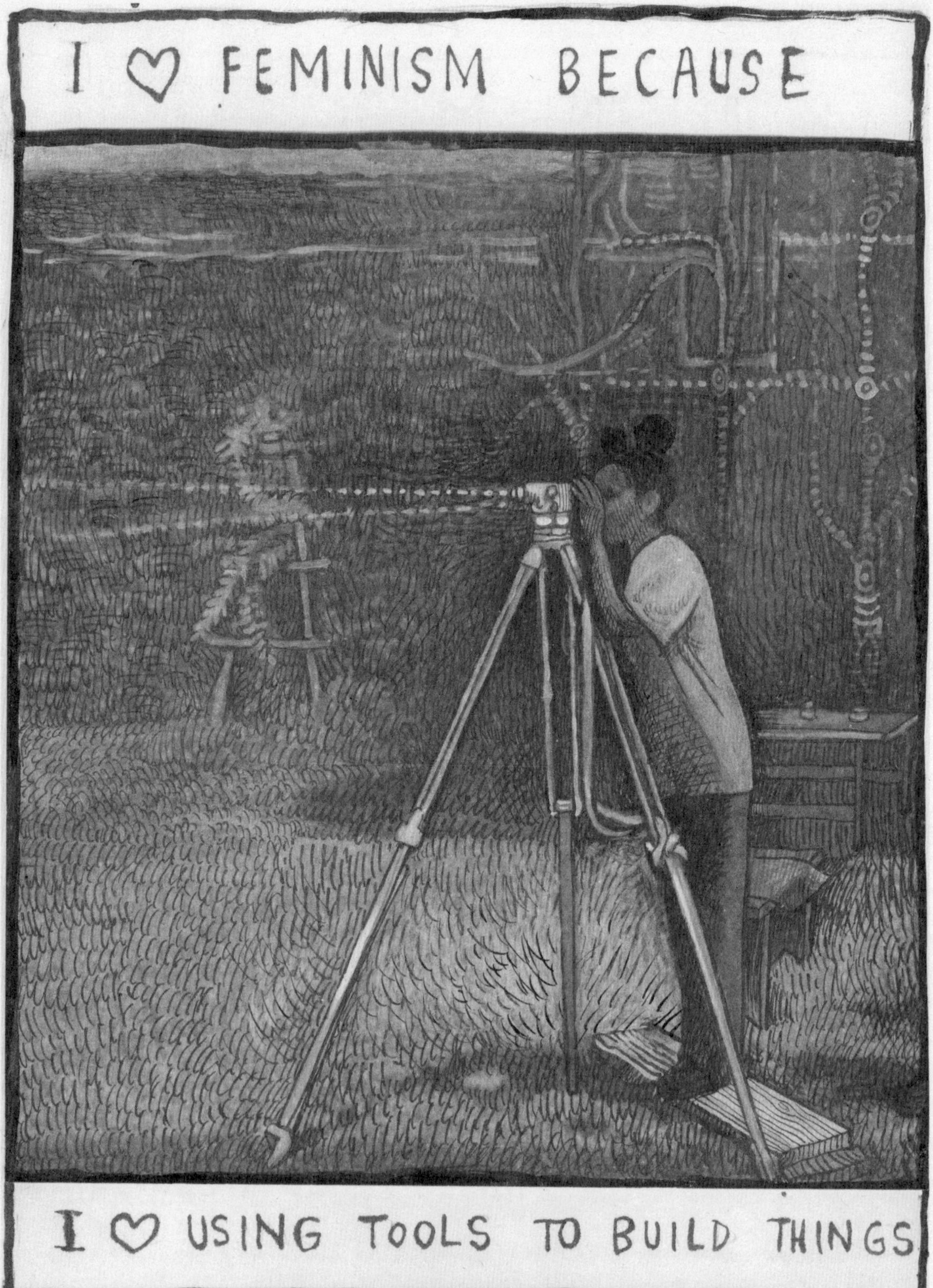
I ♡ FEMINISM BECAUSE
I ♡ USING TOOLS TO BUILD THINGS

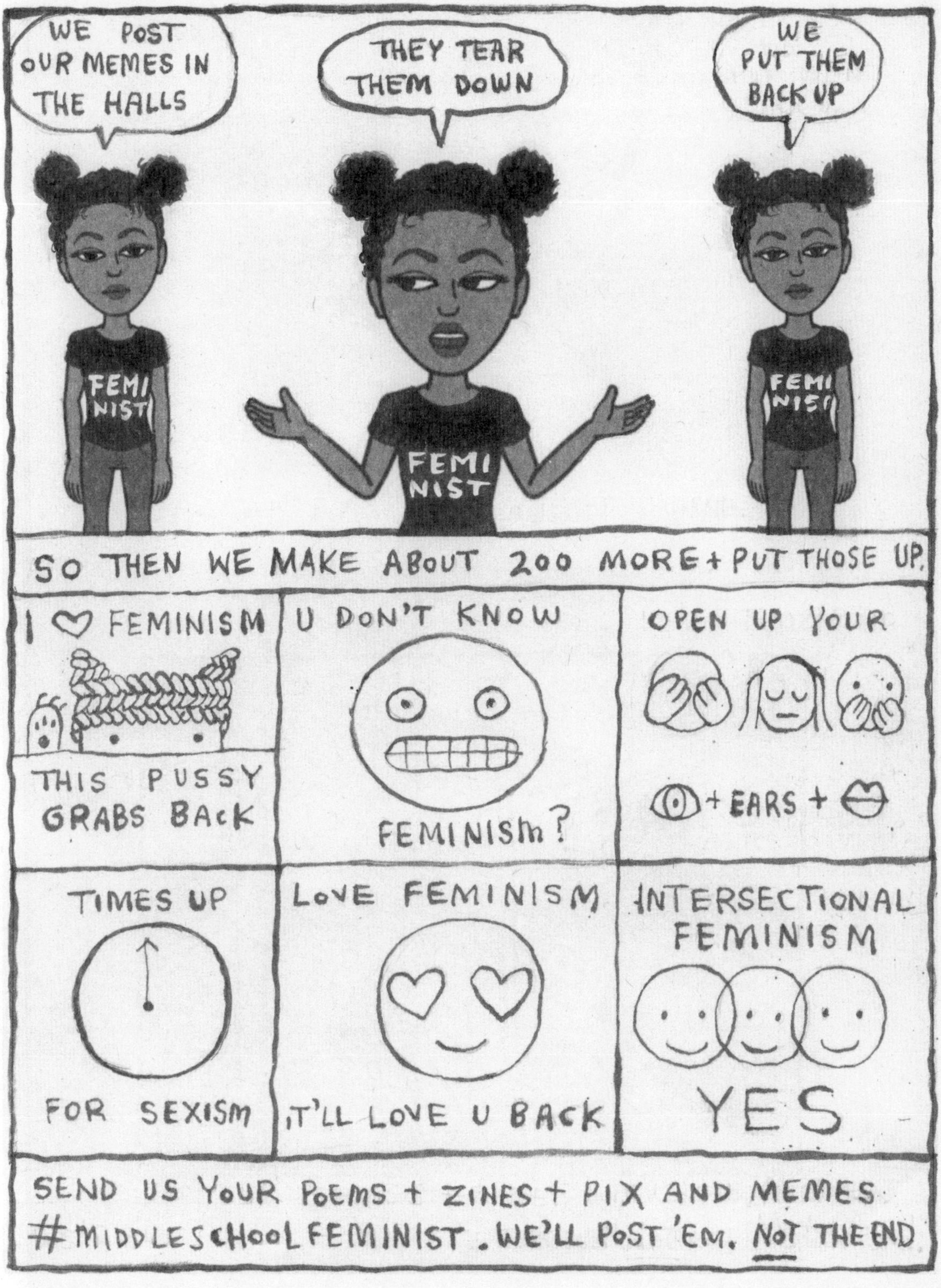
WE POST OUR MEMES IN THE HALLS
THEY TEAR THEM DOWN
WE PUT THEM BACK UP
FEMINIST
FEMINIST
FEMINIST
SO THEN WE MAKE ABOUT 200 MORE + PUT THOSE UP.
I ♡ FEMINISM
THIS PUSSY GRABS BACK
U DON'T KNOW
FEMINISM?
OPEN UP YOUR
+ EARS +
TIMES UP
FOR SEXISM
LOVE FEMINISM
IT'LL LOVE U BACK
INTERSECTIONAL FEMINISM
YES
SEND US YOUR POEMS + ZINES + PIX AND MEMES
#MIDDLESCHOOLFEMINIST. WE'LL POST 'EM. NOT THE END

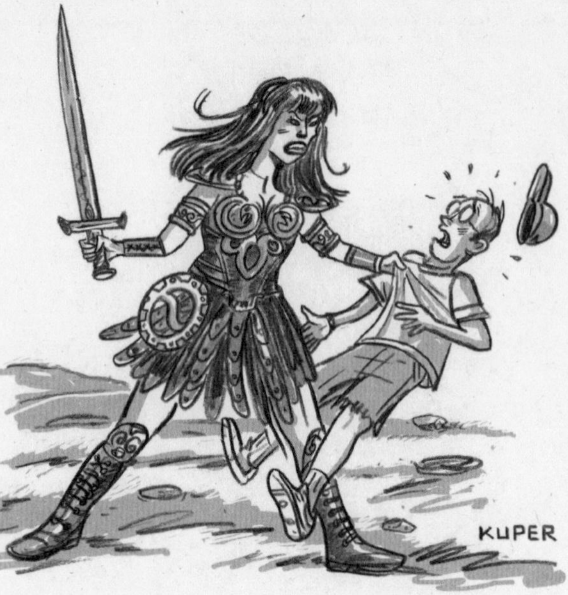
KUPER

"I said I'm a Xena *fan*, not xenophobe!"

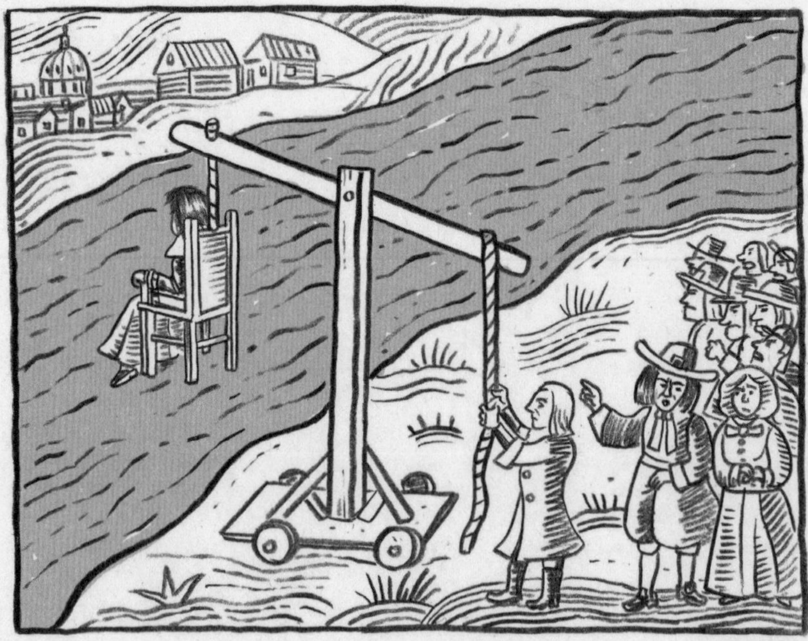
KUPER

"If she floats, she's a witch. If she sinks,
maybe she had a point about women's rights."